GREAT BLACK LEADERS:

ancient and modern

editor
Ivan Van Sertima

Library of Congress Catalog Number:
ISSN: 0270-2495
ISBN: 0-88738-739-X
Printed in the United States of America

CH

CH

GREAT BLACK LEADERS: ANCIENT AND MODERN

Incorporating JOURNAL OF AFRICAN CIVILIZATIONS,
December, 1987 (Vol. 9)

Contents

THE BLACK VALHALLA:
An Introduction

Ivan Van Sertima

When a star dies it does not vanish from the firmament. Its light keeps streaming across the fields of time and space so that centuries later we may be touched by a vision of the fire and brilliancy of its former life. The lives of the truly great are just like that. Death does not diminish them in the firmament of our consciousness, where their words and deeds still twinkle like the lights of long-dead stars.

But we are touched by these lights in different ways in different times and it is not always easy for the observer to distinguish the startling flash of a transitory meteor from the paler, ghostly light of a grander and greater star. We are the eyes of the universe and we often measure the size and significance of what we see through the myopic lenses of our own lives rather than through the high-powered glasses of gods that sweep across the heavens, commanding visions of a more total reality.

Thus it is that any selection of the lights and stars of a nation or a race is inevitably subjective. There were, however, other factors limiting or liberating our choice than the mere subjectivity of individual vision. We tried to be comprehensive, at least in terms of geographical areas and historical periods. We felt we could not exclude the ancient Egyptian (especially in those historical periods when Egypt was dominated by the blacks) we had to be sensitive to the charge of sexist imbalance which has marred so many collections of this sort (we hope future volumes in the series will go beyond Hatsheput, Tiye and Nzingha) we had to ensure that no African figure that had captured the world's imagination (Shaka, for example) or had profoundly affected the modern period (Kwame Nkrumah) were absent from our first volume.

Mandela, in particular, presented problems since he is the only living figure we have dared to include. This breaks the rules we had set down for this collection but we feel that we must do everything in our power to highlight the South African dilemma since it is the gravest question now facing the black world. Also, in keeping with our tradition of challenging old myth with new fact, we have promoted a reexamination of the racial identity of Hannibal Barca of Carthage.

Coming nearer home, we have selected three African-Americans—King, Malcolm X, Frederick Douglass—whom history shows impacted not only on this nation but the world. There are many heroic leaders in the Black Valhalla of the Americas but a distinction had to be drawn in this first volume between those of national and those of global significance. The same holds true of our choices of Toussaint and Garvey in the Caribbean.

Let us enshrine in our hearts the memory of our great dead. For the light of their words and deeds still travels across space and time to touch our souls with the fire and brilliancy of their former lives. . . .

Martin Luther King Jr.

We are fortunate to feature the work of David Lewis, who is considered to have written the best book on King to date. This essay, which was a foreshadowing of his later and larger work, focuses on King's career as a social activist. It analyzes the nature of the innovative tactics he brought to the struggle and the dynamic of the social and political forces that were responsible for his successes and failures. From the Montgomery bus boycott in December of 1955 to his assassination in Memphis on April 4, 1968 we see the gradual unfolding of King's social thought and strategy, the final, radical shift and expansion of his goals, and the source of the growing fears, suspicions and resentments that were to bring thunder down upon his head from every side.

So many of King's detractors underestimate the enormous personal risks he took to mount his non-violent offensives. The phrase "non-violent" gives the impression to those who were not in the thick of the fight, who did not march on the frontlines, that this was some timid, wimpish protest against white authority. It was just the opposite. In Birmingham, for example, there were scenes of shocking brutality "dogs attacking children, police clubbing women, firemen stripping bare backs with hoses, tear gas strangling demonstrators". King himself was stabbed close to the heart in Detroit, his head cracked open by a stone in Illinois, the front of his home in Montgomery shattered by dynamite. Whatever his religious groundings, this was no romantic, playing the game of revolution with mere words. His superb rhetoric, says Lewis, was matched by "his equally superb personal courage".

In spite of one or two stunning defeats—as was the case in Albany, Georgia—King's tactics were effective. White officials who opposed him were eventually cowed or chastised or swept from power. The terror of Birmingham was followed by real advances. Desegregation of the schools, public facilities and commercial institutions, hiring and promotion of Blacks. The Alabama Supreme Court ruled the old city government and the Sheriff out of office while the US Supreme Court declared sit-in demonstrations legal in cities that enforced segregation laws. As Lewis points out "Birmingham fixed the moral stature of King in the national consciousness . . . he became the embodiment of civil rights".

As so often happens, the rebel leader who proves most effective eventually sits down to negotiate with the powers-that-be. He seeks the ear of those who make national law and policy. He sees the possibility through personal contact and influence to bring pressure to bear upon them to fulfill his major demands and objectives. To do this he must walk the tightrope of diplomacy. To wrest a major future concession he must appear at times to offer a minor one. But this is never seen by the powerless, impatient masses as anything short of treachery. This was the irony of the 1963 March on Washington which the White House was persuaded to support but to monitor for fear of violent consequences.

King's initial reluctance to join the March was seen by some leaders and observers of the civil rights movement as "conclusive evidence of his readiness to move only as boldly and rapidly as his various and powerful white allies would condone. Both established spokesmen in the movement as well as young militants alleged that the March on Washington had been co-opted and deradicalized by agents of the White House and the business community— that King had been used".

King's career advanced, however, in spite of this. His historic speech on the steps of the Lincoln memorial vastly increased his national prestige and influence. If he had conceded anything to the White House, President Johnson paid him back by pushing through the Civil Rights Act in 1964 and the Voting Rights Act the year after. But great expectations had been aroused that could not be fulfilled fast enough. Concessions conceived as too little had come too late. Race riots broke out, sweeping across the North.

King did not moderate his assault on American society. He adopted a broader front which cut across race and class and which in effect was more threatening and more radical. Lewis speaks of this change as "a rapid shift leftward . . . grounded in Christian morality and common sense". The logic of his philosophy made his movement towards this position inevitable. He was also becoming increasingly disenchanted with the so-called white liberals. "When Afro-Americans begin to make demands that can lead to full equality," King wrote, "they find that many of their white allies have quietly disappeared".

The war in Vietnam catalyzed everything. It all became so "incandescently clear that no one who had any concern for the integrity and life of America could ignore it". How could a crusader for social justice see 30 billion dollars being squandered on a distant battlefield while millions of Americans were being damned to a slow death in the slums? How could one solve the problem of the Black in isolation when what was required was a whole rethinking of priorities, "a reconstruction of the entire society"?

King had come to the point when he would have to go beyond the demands of his own race in order to achieve social and economic justice for all the victims of the system. These were not mutually exclusive concerns. They were inextricably linked to each other. But this realization of his ultimate mission

and his uncompromising stand against the war alienated many of his potential allies. In his last days, Lewis tells us" the leader who had become the most
hard-headed realist with a plan and a vehicle to alter the course of national
events in a positive, humanitarian direction was widely portrayed as a fuzzy-
minded moralist, disappointing to liberals and held in contempt by Black
Power enthusiasts".

Wendell Beane, a theologian, approaches the phenomenon of King from an
unusual point of view. The dominant tendency, claims Beane, is to view King
and Gandhi in purely secular terms. He attempts instead to deal seriously
with both the mundane and transcendent dimensions of the religious reality
in King's life. He also outlines the ethico-religious problems King had to work
out in order to justify his own strategy of action as a social reformer. He could
not just simply turn the other cheek as Christ did.

"While Christ discourages resistance by saying "Resist not evil" King's civil
rights revolution meant that one could resist evil but only with non-violence.
Can the practice of "universal love" be true to Jesus if it insists upon manifesting itself as a form of nonviolent resistance? For Jesus' ethical spirituality
seems to have presupposed a dynamic multi-dimensional cosmology which
allows for nonviolent non-resistance". To die as Jesus did in a state of pure
love was not to die at all but to move to another spiritual dimension of Reality.
King worked out his own creative, practical interpretation of the universal
love-ethic. He saw Jesus' supreme radical form of nonviolent non-resistance
as being more applicable to one-on-one encounters than to the response of
human beings under institutional forms of tyranny and oppression."

Equally important and coming as a corrective to the tendency to overlook
the "spirituality" of the civil rights movement, Beane underlines the indispensable role that the Black Church played in King's own life and as a bedrock for
the movement's religious hope and strength.

Malcolm X

Not as nationally or internationally known as King but as profoundly
important to the rise of black consciousness in America was Malcolm X. King
had entered the mainstream of the world because the events in which he was
involved thrust him into the international spotlight. His Christian philosophy
and his Gandhi-like strategy of confrontation encouraged the broadest of
human alliances. It alienated him, however, from a significant segment of
those for whose rights he so valiantly fought. They saw him as a great but
distant dreamer, energized by ideals that could only shock into guilt and
compassion for a brief, bright moment the least and most liberal of their
oppressors. Yet those who tolerated or grudgingly admired King, worshipped
every word from Malcolm's mouth. To them he was the shining black prince.
They felt he was nearer to the nerve of the black masses. He spoke the lan-

guage of their need, not with the measured thunder of an organ but with a raw bugle's blast. It was a more direct, authentic and disturbing eloquence.

Unlike King, who was educated in colleges and seminaries, Malcolm's university was the street and the prison. While in prison he underwent a religious conversion. It was not a passive individual transformation. It galvanized him into a disciplined program of reading, study, analysis, public debate. It touched everyone he met in prison. It made him reach out beyond the prison as well, starting a weekly correspondence with the leader of the Nation of Islam, the Honorable Elijah Muhammad. As soon as Malcolm came out of prison in 1952, Muhammad, realising his potential, appointed him National Spokesman for the Nation. He could not have made a better choice.

As Clifton Marsh points out, he was not only an excellent student but a great teacher. He not only preached but refined and updated the theories of Elijah. No one in the movement, including Malcolm's mentor himself, possessed the intellectual clarity and astuteness, the emotional dynamic, the mesmeric mastery of the word, to build the nation as speedily and effectively as Malcolm. And it was not just a question of these personal gifts—a quick intelligence, charisma, eloquence—but an intimate grounding in the life of his people living on the bottomfloor of the world, his ability because of his special experience (pimping, drug-dealing, armed robbery) to enter the bars, the poolrooms, the street corners, to organize his people from the grassroots up.

Thus it was that Malcolm began to serve as Muhammad's Prime Minister throughout the United States. He organized temple after temple in city after city—Detroit, Boston, Philadelphia, New York, Atlanta, Los Angeles. Elijah Muhammad, deeply pleased by his work, gave him the opportunity to make his own decisions. "Elijah said that my guideline should be whatever I felt was wise".

The decade of the sixties, however, brought new national and world problems with a range of new perils and opportunities for the Black, calling therefore for new strategies and approaches.

The sixties internationalized the black struggle. Colonial Africa was in volcanic ferment. The forces of West and East clashed and exploded in Asia in the war of Vietnam. The wave of Black nationalism that flowed over the United States was but a tributary to the larger tide of rebellion and discontent flowing over the world's stage. "That stage was set," as Marsh observes "for Malcolm to emerge from the shadow of Elijah Muhammad and become an international leader." The interdependence of the world, the pivotal position of America, made it clear that one could not successfully fight isolated battles for Black equality and power. Malcolm felt, as did many Black nationalist leaders of the sixties, that the African-American struggle was part of the world struggle. He also felt that "the Nation of Islam should be active in leading the frontline struggle". He could not easily accept Muhammad's insistence that the Muslims not become involved in the 'white man's politics' and spend time instead in self-improvement. He saw this position "as making the Nation of Islam a separate closed community" within the Black world.

Marsh outlines for us the main events of the struggle that followed between the two men—the undermining of Malcolm by the leadership in Chicago, Malcolm's detour from Muhammad's limited doctrine into a discussion of a range of social and economic issues oppressing Black people, the silencing of Malcolm after his forbidden comment on Kennedy's assassination, the excommunication of Muhammad's son, Wallace, for supporting Malcolm, the final break from the Nation on March 8, 1964.

It is at this point that our two biographers—Marsh and Oba T'Shaka—provide us with different interpretations of a significant aspect of Malcolm's ideological development. Malcolm's views on the white man is supposed to have changed fundamentally after his pilgrimage to Mecca. Oba T'Shaka argues that this is not so.

T'Shaka's essay is devoted to a critical examination of all the major works done on Malcolm and to an illumination of the fundamentals of his thinking. Alex Haley in the Autobiography of Malcolm X argues, as does Marsh, that Malcolm after the Hajj began to relate racism to consciousness and behavior rather than to color. T'Shaka argues, however, that while Malcolm was impressed and moved by the warmth and apparent genuineness of white Muslims in Africa, King Faisal and other lightskinned Muslims wanted to use Malcolm's influence to aid in the spread of orthodox Islam and may have adopted a façade of warm and brotherly love. Whether Malcolm perceived this as a façade or not, there was no ground for any fundamental change in his thinking about American whites.

"How could he be expected to change his views towards whites in America," asks T'Shaka "when neither their racist attitudes, behavior or society had changed?" He contends, even more forcefully, that the brotherly feelings displayed by these lightskinned Muslims was not proof that this was the way they thought and practised brotherhood towards their darker-skinned brethren at home. Even the prophet Muhammad had been critical of Arab discrimination against non-Arab, of white against black. T'Shaka reports a statement Malcolm made later in Ghana. "The Muslims of white complexion who had changed my opinions were men who had shown me that the American white man with a genuine brotherhood for a black man was hard to find, no matter how much he grinned." T'Shaka considers Haley's suggestion that Malcolm had come all the way from being a Black nationalist to being an integrationist as facile and unfounded.

T'Shaka's analysis of George Brietman's book The Last Year of Malcolm X: The Evolution of a Revolutionary is particularly illuminating. Brietman's thesis is that Malcolm changed from a separatist who called for Blacks forming a separate nation, to a Black nationalist who remained in favor of maintaining and strengthening the Black community through all-Black organizations. T'Shaka holds that Malcolm never gave up the idea of separatism but saw it as a long-range program. For Brietman, the "return to Africa" which was a physical reality for Garvey had become for Malcolm "a philosophical, cultural and psychological migration". For T'Shaka this may not have been so much a change in ideology as a change in strategy. He admits contradiction in Malcolm's statements on this question but is inclined to see it as an internal conflict created by a complex question rather than as ground for a real and permanent shift in Malcolm's thinking. Malcolm's actual words could lead one to either interpretation. We leave the reader, therefore, to judge.

T'Shaka's real contribution to this subject is not just his critique of those who had gone before him but his attempt to show how powerfully and practically Malcolm sought to connect the African-American to the African past. Malcolm, he claims, was the third African-American in the 20th century to place Pan Africanism on the international political agenda. Malcolm was the first Black leader who was able to move on the African continent and call on Africa to provide political support for the Black movement in the United States. Through his international work, he developed a new respect among African heads of state for the Black struggle in the United States. The growth of a Pan African thrust in the Black movement during the seventies represented, says T'Shaka, the flowering of the seeds Malcolm had planted in the sixties.

Frederick Douglass

Frederick Douglass was a forerunner of both King and Malcolm, prefiguring positions within the broad spectrum of black resistance movements that were later to be espoused by twentieth-century leaders. Like King he was the catalyst for the broadest possible alliance between blacks and whites. America in Douglass's day, of course, was far more polarized, but, because of the extremes of 19th century apartheid, it was easier then to achieve a programmatic unity between blacks, slave or free, and the "liberal" segment of the white majority. Like King also, Douglass for a while embraced the policy of non-violence and attacked his contemporary, Henry Garnet, for calling on free blacks and slaves to revolt.

But though Garnet's stand was too radical for Douglass in 1843, just five years later, his vision no longer modified, perhaps, by his white abolitionist colleagues, he began to insist on the right of the slaves to revolt. As Chinyelu informs us in his biography, "he advocated the right to bear arms and self-defense, much in the same tone as Malcolm X." He was not prepared to turn the other cheek. While Rosa Parks sat down in the bus and refused to give up her seat to white passengers until the police dragged her out, Douglass bluntly told the trolley-car conductor that he would beat him senseless if he tried to eject him because of his color. This was typical of Douglass all through his life. Even when he secured his freedom and a world reputation, had the ear of his people and that of the President, he never flinched from taking a stand that could endanger his name, his family or his life. He sheltered slaves escaping to Canada in his own home, risking violent and bloody confrontation.

Son of a white master and black slave, he suffered whippings and beatings as a field-hand and at the age of 18 tried unsuccessfully to escape. After this attempt some of the slaveholders threatened to shoot him on sight. At 21 he fled to Philadelphia, on to New York, and then to New Bedford, Massachusetts, where his extraordinary ability as an orator attracted the attention of white abolitionists.

No one in the world at that time became such an articulate spokesman for the cause of African-American liberation from bondage. Douglass's influence spread beyond America. he stormed platforms in England and abolitionists there bought him his freedom and amassed monies to help him finance a newspaper, The North Star. Chinyelu dates the recognized leadership of Douglass among his people to the publication of this paper. It was to establish his relationship in particular with the free colored people of the North. Douglass did not only fight for the slaves but also on behalf of free African-Americans who by 1850 numbered nearly half a million. When the slaves were eventually emancipated he took the struggle one step further, so far indeed that his liberal white colleagues blanched at his audacity. He demanded the right of African-Americans to vote. This, they felt, so soon after slavery, was going too far too fast.

The issues of the day were so stark and clear and the voice of Douglass so powerful and persistent that almost the whole black population stood squarely behind him. "There has not been a time" says Chinyelu "since the start of the African slave trade, that the overwhelming majority of African-Americans submitted to the leadership of one person".

But it was not just the victimised black and the liberal white seeking a change in the racial system who unified behind Douglass. He became the spokesman for other causes. Thus women's rights advocates and the opponents of the Mexican-American war rallied around him. For quarter of a century every American President was forced to pay him respect by granting him presidential audiences or appointments—Lincoln, Grant, Hayes, Garfield, Harrison. No other African-American, claims Chinyelu, impacted on the development of the United States as consistently and on as many important topics as Douglass.

Black Roots of Egypt

In a study of leaders, not just men and women of extraordinary talent but of massive historical significance, the ancient Egyptian-Ethiopian world provides us with a galaxy of kings, queens, priests and prime ministers of a brilliancy one must consider dazzling in any age. Some of our readers, who have not followed the controversy in earlier volumes about the Black-ness or African-ness of certain ancient dynasties in the Nile Valley, may well question the appropriateness of our inclusion of Hatshepsut and Tiye, Imhotep and Ramses II. Since time and space does not allow us to go over this thesis, explored again and again in the Journal of African Civilizations, we have decided to insert at the beginning of the Egyptian section the latest essay on the subject—"The Black Roots of Egypt's Glory" by Charles S. Finch, which was published by The Washington Post on October 11, 1987.

Black Rulers of the Golden Age

In this section Legrand Clegg II introduces us to major figures of the Seventeenth and Eighteenth dynasties. The Seventeenth Dynasty began a major war of liberation that ended victoriously in the founding of the Eighteenth, which dynasty "brought Egypt to new heights of technical achievement and military might, marking the first time that any nation expanded its borders to encompass a vast world empire." Not only does Clegg meticulously build up the family tree of the great kings and queens of this "golden age", tracing their African ancestry. His work is accompanied by a series of brilliant photographs, critical in the scrutiny of dynasties where this element is still so vigorously disputed.

Queen Hatshepsut

Great Black women of that period include Queens Hatshepsut and Tiye. In Hatshepsut Danita Redd introduces us to a powerful queen who dominated the times in which she lived. She was a warrior queen, almost masculine in her aggressive assertiveness, overpowering, a born dynast. But she waged no wars abroad. Egypt had just thrown off the Hyksos yoke, and though her father, Thutmose I, smashed his fist against the face of Asia, his armies charging even up to the Euphrates, this great black queen concentrated on building rather than on fighting. She organized commercial expeditions instead of military campaigns. She is remembered to this day for her famous expedition to the land of Punt (Somalia?) And though she trumpeted the war cry "I came as Horus, darting fire against my enemies" it is largely of enemies within her own camp and country that she speaks. She is the most unusual of Egyptian queens.

Diedre Wimby, the Egyptologist, has pointed out, "She created a new science of rulership, the essence of which was the female manifesting male attributes." She confounded those who would deny her the role of supreme sovereign by donning regalia of Pharaoh, even the beard, and referred to herself and insisted on being referred to, as he. It is important to understand this in the context of the Egyptian concept of rulership which retained Ethiopian aspects (the woman being key to the succession of power, for example) but became qualitatively different. Women came to the throne only under particular circumstances, even though they wielded considerable power behind the throne. If the pharaoh died and left no male heir, then the queen would be allowed to rule until such time as a new dynasty could be initiated. Nevertheless the rulership of Egypt was a more balanced situation than would appear on the surface. "The man was the personification of divine authority, the woman the source of his power." That was not enough for Hatshepsut. To establish the absoluteness of her power, which was to last for half a century, she had to redefine the rules that sought to contain her, throw down the gauntlet to a male priesthood envious of her embrace of both male and female roles, the double dimension of her authority.

Queen Tiye

Sometimes it is the quiet subtle force of an unusual woman, a combination, perhaps, of beauty and a majesty of character, that overrides male chauvinistic prejudices and conventions. Such an individual was Queen Tiye, mother of Akhnaton, mother in-law of Nefertiti. Lady of Both Lands, she was born in Nubia but reigned as queen consort and queen mother of Egypt for half a century. In her sensitive portrait of Tiye, Virginia Simon shows us how she quietly wielded power during three critical periods of the 18th dynasty, becoming the stabilizing force of the nation. These are the years when the powers of Amenhotep III (whose bride she became at 13) began to wither with age, when his son Akhnaton, the religious innovator, neglected the defence of the nation when her youngest sons, Smenkare and Tut, were too immature to rule.

She moved into the power vacuum. She became Secretary of State for her sick husband. Kings of Asia bypassed him to deal directly with her. And when the priests insisted that, in the royal sculptures, a queen should be depicted knee-high to a king, Amenhotep, ruled by a love that transcended the idiocies of convention, swept their objections away. He built massive statues in which she sat beside him as an equal. He dug an ornamental lake one mile long and named it after her. Poems and palaces rose to immortalize her beauty and his love. And, following the strongest African custom, strengthened by a Nubian in the royal bed, it was the princesses, not the princes, who enjoyed venerated status. The importance of the female in the royal family was once more stressed. Even fashion was profoundly influenced by Tiye. Her hairstyle, her earrings, her wigs, set the style for female beauty in the royal court.

Imhotep

Imhotep is perhaps the leading intelligence that shines through the mist of the distant past. He is "the world's first universal genius of whom we have any knowledge". He was not just leader of a government, prime minister to Pharoah Djoser of the Third Dynasty. He served also as chief scribe, ritualist, architect. Mastery of any one of these would have marked him as a great man but he was a master in all. He was the leading architect of his time, the man who designed and built the world's first great edifice in stone, the step-pyramid at Saqqara. He was also, and most importantly, the leading physician of the ancient world. "His powers as a physician", Dr. Finch tells us, "made such an impression on succeeding generations both in and out of Egypt that he was eventually deified in his own country and identified with the healing god Asclepios by the Greeks from the 6th century B.C. on."

Finch shows us that the major medical documents that survive from the plundered and partially destroyed libraries of the Egyptian, reveal diagnostic, prognostic and therapeutic methodology unsurpassed in clinical acumen until modern times. Imhotep was the epitome of this science. It shatters the myth of Hippocrates as the Father of Medicine. Only Imhotep, by virtue of his greater antiquity and level of scientific thought, deserves that title.

Fascinating is the story of how this African genius came to be conceived and worshipped, by Africans and Europeans alike, as a god. "He seemed to have achieved a perfect synthesis of mind, intellect, and soul, so much that men thought they saw in him the spark of divinity".

Ramses II

Chiekh Anta Diop, the great Senegalese Egyptologist and historian, hails the nineteenth dynasty of Ramses II as "the highest point of Egyptian history". Rashidi calls it a pivotal phase in African history and outlines the situation that faced the Ramessides as they ascended to power in Egypt. Decades earlier the idealistic reformer, Akhenaton, had divided the country with his religious revolution, his insistence that the Aton be accepted as the supreme and the only God. It pitted the forces of the monarchy against the priesthood of Amon and practically led to a civil war. So serious and prolonged was the political instability it engendered, that what had been won by the military campaigns of the 18th dynasty were practically lost. Egypt became internally weak and the enemy without and within rejoiced. Many Semitic and Indo-European speaking clans, tribes and kingdoms rose up against their African overlords, threatening the very foundations of the empire. It is against this darkening sky that we glimpse the rising star of Ramses II.

We see him at his boldest in the battle of Kadesh, fought in the fifth year of his reign, when his army marched deep into Syria to meet the greatest force Egypt ever faced. This was led by the formidable king of the Hittites. Misinformed by his scouts, Ramses II walked into a trap with a small personal bodyguard. Had he been overpowered, the Egyptian forces, already outnumbered, would have been routed. Pharoah charged the Hittite lines four times until the main division of his army came up to rescue him.

But it is not simply as a warrior king that he is remembered. Ramses II was a builder of incredible colossi. His buildings and statues and temples stagger the imagination. He seemed, with every major work he attempted, to challenge nature itself. Very little of what he built, even after the passage of millenia, have vanished. Perhaps no human beeing has built such gigantic monuments to himself. He carves out a house for his Nubian wife, Nefertari, from a mountain of fine enduring sandstone. He takes the light of the rising sun and sends it flashing through the sanctuary of his greatest of temples at Abu Simbel. He sits on a great cliff like a family of gods, his four forms rising 65 feet high, taller than the Colossus of Memnon.

Rashidi meticulously traces his lineage and introduces us to his whole family—father, grandfather, mother and favored son, wife. He establishes through iconography and the eyewitness accounts of Diop (to which I myself can attest) the African ancestry of this remarkable Pharaoh. But why do we turn all the way back to Egypt for our heroes and heroines? Because, says Rashidi, "Egypt was the heart and soul of Africa. We need only glance at her noble traditions, her dignity, humanity, her regal splendors, to measure our true fall from power. When we examine the Egyptian civilization we note what is perhaps the proudest achievement in the annals of human history. We must learn from Egypt that what Black people did, Black people can do."

African Military Geniuses

Shaka

Shaka is perhaps the most difficult of all African leaders to write about. No one can question his genius. He was a military strategist of the first order. He even devised a new method for facing the enemy in close combat, redesigning the spear and using the shield not only as a defensive but as an offensive weapon. His innovations in African warfare are unparalleled . But Shaka's greatness lay in more than that. As Kunene points out "he transformed society and thinking in the whole of central and southern Africa. In little more than ten years he had imprinted his political and military ideas in the vast region of southern Africa and prepared the regions for later confrontations with the invading whites".

Since almost all historians, black and white, are agreed on the above, why does the study of Shaka pose such a dilemma? It is because he is usually represented as a man of insane and monstrous excesses, so filled with hatred for those who had wounded him in his youth, so driven and possessed by a lust for power that he would kill at the slightest whim. Thus is he seen in most of the histories and plays and novels and films written by non-Africans—as a force of evil, a being of the darkest dimensions.

Mazisi Kunene presents us with a different vision of Shaka. This is not a man who imposed a draconian discipline on his army without just cause nor proceeded on his sweep across southern Africa without a political plan. With African states that he did not incorporate into his grand plan, he maintained the most cordial diplomatic relations. Kunene is no romantic. Like Shaka he is from Southern Africa. He does not seek to present his countryman as an angel but to make us aware of the cultural, social, and political circumstances that made Shaka what he was. He is at pains also to expose the dubious nature of some of the sources that first formed the fiction that Shaka was a brilliant but barbaric beast, let loose with wild irrational ambitions across the southern plains.

We must look at the sources of the Shaka story closely. On the one hand, notes Kunene, we have the white traders and adventurers who visited Shaka at his court, on the other, the African historical and oral sources. The views of the white traders diverge sharply from those expressed by most African historians. First of all, most of the white outsiders did not speak the language and had no access to the intimate thoughts and ideas of the people. They did not fully understand what was happening at the time, the complexities of Shaka's position, the logic behind many of his actions. They were too quick to credit third-hand reports from Shaka's enemies planted by his ambitious brothers. They knew so little about the customs and institutions that governed the life of the Zulu people and could not tell what was just or unjust within the canons of the culture nor within the realm of authority occupied by the Zulu emperor.

The most memorable fictional history of Shaka is the novel of the African Mofolo. Unlike the works of Dlomo, Kunene and Senghor, Mofolo depicts Shaka as a leader of darkness whose power is pitted against the leader of light (the white missionaries). Even in the latest film version, which millions have recently watched on television, Shaka's acute intelligence shines through the distortions. But Mofolo presents him not as a man moved by reason and the pragmatics of his situation but as a man influenced by an evil diviner. This is what is supposed to control his mind. This, of course, is the famous Faust and Mephistopheles fantasy of Europe. Kunene analyzes it as "a typically European middle-ages attitude to intellectuual or physical deviation. Innovation is depicted as the work of the devil. The devil controls the minds of those who have surrendered their lives to him in order to attain some ambitious goal. This is not part of the Zulu world view and never was. Shaka detested anything that suggested diabolical manipulation. His attitude to social action was practical and based entirely on the principle of causation."

But, accepting all this, how does one deal with Shaka's behavior after the death of his mother, Nandi? Surely this could not simply be a fiction of the white traders, however grossly exaggerated. The story of this terrifying episode is told with a hundred variations not only by the Europeans but by the Africans themselves.

Kunene responds to some of the legends of Shaka's atrocities by placing them upon the scale we have used to judge the heroes of other races. Any history, he says, that involves military discipline and military conquests involves excesses. "But it does not mean that these excesses characterise the individual or era. Such excesses would be characteristic of such great heroes as Alexander the Great, Charlemagne, Napoleon, Peter the Great, Gupta, Chin etc. Peter the Great of Russia personally chopped off the heads of thousands of rivals and enemies publicly and before his son to teach him how to rule". Does European and Asian history project these men to us as monsters and villains? Their excesses are counterbalanced by their historical achievements.

It is worth noting by the way that Shaka did not kill his mother, as the latest film version seems to suggest. His killing of the potential heir is something done throughout history by insecure emperors whose powers are threatened by conspiracies within their families. Shaka deeply loved his mother and the anguish he shared with her as a boy and the effect this link and bond was to have upon him for the rest of his life was something that moved me so powerfully that in 1978 I began a very close study of his psychological history, particularly the events of his childhood. It is there that I found the seed that was later to flower not only in his earlier triumphs but in the dementia and disaster that struck him and his kingdom after Nandi died.

The lovelessness of Shaka's early life, as I say, may partly account for the excesses of his later days. They can be explained in the context of that awful personal trauma and, also as Kunene has tried to do, in terms of larger socio-cultural and military imperatives. But they can never fully be explained away, whether we claim exaggeration by Europeans or not, although those claims are certainly valid, considering the express policy of the colonial power to destroy our heroes by promoting the most negative of images. Greatness, however, we must accept, does not always go with goodness, and the noblest of ends—even the making of a nation—can never justify the means. Africans have to come to terms in the end with the terrifying contradictions in Shaka. He was a combination of complex things and we can admire and reject him at one and the same time. We do not have to make a Christ of him, as Senghor does.

Hannibal

There are other great African military leaders such as Sesostris, Tuthmosis III, Ramses the Great, Taharka, who shared the combination of military genius and extraordinary humane qualities one does not expect to find in men who devoted so much of their lives to war. Into this company we can place Hannibal. This is not to belittle Shaka. The circumstances were very dfferent. Hannibal came from a world already made. Shaka had to carve out and remake a world for his people. The cruelties of this Zulu emperor, legendary or real, were not peculiar to the African. "Julius Caesar" Chandler informs us, "executed 40,000 Gauls in a single day to teach them obedience. As common practice, Roman commanders cut off the hands of their prisoners".

Hannibal became the scourge of Rome for fifteen years. His tactical feats have awed the military strategists of many different lands and centuries. He single handedly put his nation on the world's historical map, for without his existence, says Chandler, Carthage would be unknown save to a few erudite scholars.

But who was Hannibal? He has always been placed in a context that has removed him from our consideration of him as an African. He is simply known to us as the great Carthagenian general and we have always been led to assume that Carthage was a white or semitic enclave in North Africa and that its people were very different from that of the indigenous Africans. Wayne Chandler, therefore, first addresses himself to this question. I shall not go over this matter which has been dealt with at length in other journals. Suffice it to say, that the Phoenicians were not homogeneous. Whatever their early beginnings (which Diop calls Africoid) and whatever their close connections, as brothers and allies of the dynastic Egyptians, their racial composition became rather complex in certain periods. At the time of Hannibal, however, there is no question that they had so intermixed with the African people in Carthage that the African element had become the dominant strain, not in the Phoenician city-states of Tyre and Sidon but in Carthage itself. This contention is proven by skeletal remains, by inconography, by many cultural elements found in the historical strata associated with Hannibal. The works of Pittard and Gsell, in particular, establish this.

But the question of Hannibal's identity itself seemed to be one that could only be solved by general deductions and implications. Coins were struck to celebrate the victory of Hannibal's army over the Romans. They show quite clearly Africoid types on one side and the famous elephants that accompanied the troops on the other. But Eurocentric commentators kept insisting that these Africans were merely the elephant riders, not figures indicating the racial composition of the victors. But now Chandler presents us with a coin on which we find an African head on one side and Surus, the favorite elephant of Hannibal, on the other. This was the last elephant to survive the march across the Alps. Hannibal usually mounted this elephant and no other. Why would anyone laboriously carve out the head of an insignificant mahout on the back of this coin which so clearly represents the general's mount? It is hard not to conclude that we have here an image of the Carthagenian general himself.

Hannibal was born in 247 B.C. to Hamilcar Barca who had three sons. Hannibal was the eldest. Trained as a soldier from boyhoood, along with his brothers, he was high-born but not soft-skinned, maturing swiftly into a youth of formidable toughness. The brothers Barca were known as "the lion's brood". Hannibal took command of the Carthagenian army when he was only 25. His father had died from drowning and his father's son-in-law, who had taken command, was murdered by an angry soldier.

Youth posed no problem to his command. Although he was born to the rich and powerful, he hated luxury. He liked living under harsh conditions. He ate sparingly, just enough to sustain his strength. History records that he had only one woman in his life, his wife, and that he treated female captives of war with such exemplary kindness that the Roman historian Justin was forced to remark, in the teeth of his prejudice, "one would not think he was born in Africa".

He was tireless, indefatigable. He never slept until a job was done, working through the day and night if it were necessary. He often slept in his cloak on the bare ground among the common soldiers. He could endure heat and cold with equal ease.

No man was better suited to inspire fighting men. This was no easy task since quite a few of them were mercenaries, not held together by a blind faith and loyalty, not eager to throw away their lives for god and king and country. Lacking a common cause, as Chandler tells us, it was faith in this unusual man above all else that led them to accomplish what is considered even today as the most incredible military feat in history—the march across the icy and treacherous terrain of the Alps with horses and elephants. Hannibal and his men confronted almost immovable frozen boulders in their path, sudden meltings of the ice into avalanches and swamps, drowning both men and animals, ferocious attacks and ambushes from European tribes.

The unflinching resolution of one man, challenging the shocks of nature as though it were a rehearsal against the enemy itself took them on to the gates of Rome. Here Hannibal defeated the greatest force Europe had ever thrown into a single battle. The troops that set out initially under his command were mainly African. The African contingent alone numbered about 12,000 men. To this were added 300 Ligurians, 500 from the Balearic Islands, 450 Libyo-Phoenicians of mixed blood, nearly 2000 Numidians from the Atlantic coast, 21 elephants and 200 horses from the Ilergetees in Spain. Hannibal lost an eye and practically half of this initial force perished in the march.

One cannot summarize in an introduction the dramatic highlights of that march and the ingenious strategies Hannibal employed to hold his men together and to outmaneuver the enemy at every turn. It has all the ingredients of an epic. Hannibal, however, came to a tragic end. He was undercut at home. He had held the Romans at bay for more than a decade but his brother was beheaded by the Romans while trying to bring up reinforcements to him from Africa. His countrymen for whom he had fought so valiantly, growing fearful of continued war with a reviving Rome, left him to perish. On three separate occasions he begged for help from Carthage but received none. He was finally defeated at the battle of Zama and took his own life in the emptiness of his exile. "Thus in many ways," says Chandler, "Carthage sealed her own doom and destroyed the force that could have been her salvation".

Nkrumah

Ghana was the first African country to become independent from colonial rule. It began a trend that was to shake all Africa and, as a consequence, inspire independent movements in the Caribbean and the struggle for civil rights in America. Nkrumah is forgotten by many now or at least his significance in the movement for colonial liberation is not fully appreciated by the generation of the seventies and eighties. This is unfortunate for when the struggle against British colonialism was being waged, no name rang in our heads so loudly, no light shone so brightly as that great star of Ghana—Kwame Nkrumah.

He was born in the little village of Nkroful in 1909. He grew up under the joint influence of the Akan tribe and a Catholic education. He graduated from training college in 1930 and after teaching at Catholic schools for five years travelled to the United States and entered Lincoln University. He got his Bachelor's there and a Master's from the University of Pennsylvania. He also taught at Lincoln and was recognized in 1945 as "the most outstanding professor of the year".

His American sojurn was critical to his later development. His political and organizational work and training began here. Here also he met the illustrious West Indian, C.L.R. James, author of the classic work on Toussaint, The Black Jacobins. From James he claims to have learnt how an underground movement works. Here also he became acquainted with the work of Marcus Garvey which left a very deep impression on his mind and encouraged him to commit himself to the liberation of Africa.

Nkrumah went on to London in 1945 and began organizing his countrymen there. James introduced him to Padmore, a major force in the Pan African movement, and Nkrumah soon became the general secretary of the Working Committee elected to implement the program for African liberation. He also founded the West African National Secretariat. Then a letter came from Ghana inviting him to come home and become general secretary of the United Gold Coast Convention. This was committed to use all legitimate means to bring internal self-government to Ghana.

So Nkrumah returned home and organized the national movement. In six months he had set up more than 500 branches. He knew the political education of his people would be decisive and so he founded several newspapers so that his views could be propagated all over the country. It began to make a difference, such a difference in fact that the British decided he had to be taken out of circulation. He and several of the leaders were arrested and he was exiled to Lawra in the Northern Territories.

The organization split while Nkrumah was detained and soon after his release he launched a new party—the Convention Peoples' Party (the CPP)—in the presence of 60,000 people. It demanded self-government within a year. Nkrumah began a program of "non-violent positive action". The British government had appointed a committee to work on a new constitution for Ghana but when this was published in 1949 the CCP under Nkrumah denounced it as "unacceptable to the country as a whole". 90,000 Ghanaians marched to the

Legislative Assembly to demonstrate their loyalty to the CPP and to repudiate colonial rule. Nkrumah's campaign had begun to take effect and the British Governor had to declare a state of emergency. Nkrumah was arrested again and sentenced to three years in prison for causing unrest in the country.

But the very next year his party won the elections. The government could not be formed without the leader and so the British had to release him. He became leader of the Legislative Assembly and in 1952 he became the first prime minister of Ghana. By 1960 Ghana had become a republic and he became its first President.

Nkrumah aroused great expectations all over the world. It seems, however, he lacked the pragmatism and political adeptness to match his idealism and theoretical brilliance. He was totally committed to a united Africa and the end of neocolonialism but could not keep his finger on the pulse of his own people, preferring to fight the battles of the world at large before facing up to the crises of change in his own backyard. He realised that the economic structure he had inherited was streamlined by the colonisers to exploit the African and he began with foresight and vision to lay down the basis for a new economic system. Yet he could not respond to the growing tide of criticism welling up from his own people, that party members were milking the treasury, that the wealth being diverted from the imperialists was not trickling down to the masses, as he had planned, but into the coffers of corrupt black bureaucrats.

He was a vain man, as are most leaders, and encouraged a personality cult. This in itself need not be a bad thing since it can sometimes give one's program unquestioned authority, vital to a leader in periods of grave transition and doubt and instability. But it opens the door to dictatorship and a leader's preference for sycophants rather than honest and constructive critics. He declared a one-party state, alienating the rank and file. "Nkrumah began to become too distant and isolated from the people and could not discern their genuine concerns".

So blind had he become to his political problems at home that in spite of assassination attempts on his life, increasing strikes in the country and other disturbances, he kept up with his international agenda. He was so oblivious to what was going on around him that he went off to China in 1966, carrying proposals for Ho Chi Minh on how to end the Vietnam war. He became the casualty of another war—a war within his own state. The army overthrew his government while he was in China and brought a swift and lamentable end to a reign that had started with the highest hopes of colonial peoples the world over.

But this was not the end of Nkrumah. So great was the affection in which he was held for what he had done for Africa, that Sekou Toure offered to share the presidency of Guinea with him and he was made general-secretary of the ruling party of that country. During this time also Nkrumah wrote his most important books, to which Professor Cudgoe provides an excellent introduction. Ghana did not forget him. When he died in 1972 his body was brought back to his native land in great state. The tribute of Colonel Acheampong, then Ghana's leader, is a fitting epitaph:

"In his lifetime he waged a relentless war against colonialism and racism, and even after his death his spirit will, no doubt, continue to inspire the valiant fighters against the twin enemies of Africa."

Mandela

Nelson Mandela, sixty-nine years old at the time of writing, has been a political prisoner of South Africa for a quarter of a century. How is it, asks Mary Benson, his biographer, that a man imprisoned for a whole generation, not allowed to be quoted by the South African media, has become "the embodiment of the struggle for liberation in that country and the vital symbol of a new society". Hunt Davis Jr addresses himself to that question in his essay and introduces us to the man and the main events of that struggle.

Mandela was born on July 18, 1918 near Umtata in the Transkei region. His father was a close relative of the chief of the Thembu and when he died Mandela became a ward of the chief. He got a good education, enrolling at Fort Hare University College in 1938, thus becoming one of the few African college students in the country. The 1930's saw African political agitation against government legislation to disenfranchise the few African males who could still vote on the common rolls. Mandela became involved and was suspended from college for his part in a student protest boycott. His guardian pleaded with him to give in to the authorities but he decided to leave home rather than submit.

At 22 he headed for Johannesburg. There he faced the horrors that most blacks had to face in the cities of South Africa—"exclusion from skilled work, overcrowded slums and constant harassment by the police under the pass laws". But he pushed on with his education, gaining a B.A. degree through correspondence from the University of South Africa and studying law at the University of Witwatersrand. His was not just an academic education. As Professor Davis tells us "he became part of a circle of young Africans in the formative stage of becoming the new national leadership".

These young men, "sensing a potential for fundamental changes in the wartime era, better educated than their elders, and impatient with the cautious approach of the existing African leadership" founded the Youth League of the African National Congress. They became, in the words of their manifesto, "the brains-trust and power-station of the spirit of African nationalism". No longer was it a matter of polite petition by mild-mannered leaders but direct and forceful action involving the masses. Mandela became general secretary of the Youth League during its formation in the forties and by 1950 he was its president.

As president of the League, he played a key role in the ANC call for civil disobedience. Working with the Indian Congress and other allies they gave an ultimatum to the government, calling upon it to repeal six "unjust" laws. The South African government, of course, rejected the ultimatum and the ANC with its coalition of allies launched the Defiance Campaign in June, 1952. By the time this campaign was halted in early 1953 nearly 8,500 protestors went to jail for deliberately breaking the "unjust" laws.

Mandela was one of twenty leaders arrested for his part in this. He was sentenced to nine months in prison. The ANC members, recognizing his qualities as a leader, made him president of the Transvaal branch. This made things worse for Mandela. It led to the government banning him from making any public appearances. In the mid-1950's he married Winnie Mandela, who cannot be excluded from this story since she became her husband's co-worker and has in recent years "emerged in her own right as one of the most visible and articulate champions of her people's cause".

Through the fifties the ANC kept up its challenge to the apartheid state and the Government in turn became more represssive in its attempts to stifle African protest. Mandela, though silenced, was at the heart of events. A multiracial coalition was developed under the ANC and it adopted a Freedom Charter in 1955. Mandela called it a revolutionary document because it envisaged changes that "cannot be won without breaking up the economic and political set-up of present South Africa. To win the demands calls for the organization, launching, and development of mass struggles on the widest scale."

The South African government effectively silenced the top strata of the leadership and the second and third levels by the use of banning orders. But Mandela devised a plan, named after him as the M-plan, which "organized at the grassroots level, developing a mass organization from the bottom up". With the head gone, the body could still function.

Then came the most serious of all threats. Faced with the growing militancy of the ANC the government arrested 156 people in December, 1956. The most famous black leaders—Mandela, Luthuli, Tambo, Sisulu—were charged with treason. It was the classic colonial charge—international communist conspiracy to overthrow the state by force. Mandela's skills as an orator and a lawyer made him one of the key spokesmen for the defendants. The ANC won the case but at a great cost. During the long years the case dragged out in the courts they were unable to organize. And then came the unkindest cut of all. "With Mandela and other key leaders distracted by the Treason Trial, a group of dissidents, known as the Africanist faction and opposed to the alliance approach . . . broke away from the ANC to form the Pan-Africanist Congress (PAC).

This changed everything. PAC, under Robert Sobukwe, a highly committed uncompromising leader, provided the vanguard for an anti-pass campaign in 1960. This led to the Sharpeville Massacre. Riots swept through the country.

The government cracked down hard. It outlawed the ANC and the PAC. The ANC still tried one last effort at non-violence but unable to be effective Mandela went undergound "We will have to reconsider our tactics," he said "we are closing a chapter on this question of a non-violent policy".

Mandela remained underground until April 1962 when he was tracked down, tried, and sentenced to five years. At his trial Mandela defended the right of his people to resort to violence since they had exhausted all other legitimate means in their quest for justice. When the Government offered him freedom on the condition that he rejected violence as a political weapon, Mandela refused. This is why he is the spirit of the revolution, this is why after twenty five years he is still the symbol of the struggle. Even though he can no longer speak to us, his voice is still heard all over the world.

Nzingha

John Clarke's essay introduces us to one of the great warrior queens of Africa—Nzingha of Angola. It is an important chapter in the struggle against Portuguese imperialism. In 1623, at the age of forty-one, Nzingha became queen of Ndongo (Angola). Like Hatshepsut, she forbade her subjects to call her queen. She insisted on being called king and marched into battle in the clothing of a man. But according to Clarke, "she possessed both masculine hardness and feminine charm, which she readily used, depending on the need and occasion." She fought the Portuguese all her life, suffering severe setbacks. Her sister was beheaded, her body thrown into a river. Yet this did not break Nzingha's spirit. As Professor Glasgow points out: "Nzingha failed in her mission to expel the Portuguese [but] her historic importance trancends this failure, as she awakened and encouraged the first known stirring of nationalism in West Central Africa."

Marcus Garvey

Leaders of thought and action from the Caribbean have often had as profound an impact on the African-American community as on their own countries. The trade in ideas and influence, however, has been twofold since many West Indian leaders were first politicized in America or at least influenced at a distance by the philosophy and strategy of liberation movements developing in this country. A conception of America as embracing both the islands and the continental land mass is critical to a vision of universal Black brotherhood and the ultimate success of a Pan-African movement. In no historical instance was this bond between the Black branches of the world more dramatically demonstrated than in the life and work of Marcus Garvey.

James Spady provides us with a heavily detailed background to Garvey, down to the friends he met at school, the house where he was born, the places he visited. A brief outline may prove useful to young students and laymen but the plethora of detail is important to scholars specialising in a study of the man in all his minutiae, to those who would like to examine "each cell within the body's growth" as Spady, quoting the poet Mc Farlane, would put it.

Garvey was born in St Ann's Bay, Jamaica, on August 17, 1887. As a very young man he was apprenticed to his godfather who operated a printery. He went on to Kingston in 1906 to continue work as a professional printer and it was not long before he was elected Vice-President of the Kingston Typographical Union. His firm stand on the rights of the workers attracted attention and in 1910 he was elected Assistant Secretary of the National Club, Jamaica's first nationalist political organization. The Club published a newspaper, *Our Own*. It provided Garvey with his first experience in newspaper publishing and campaigning for a political candidate. Garvey soon began to publish a paper of his own, *The Watchman*. Although the latter was short-lived he saw with great clarity then, as later, how crucial to influencing his people, and gaining power to alter their condition, was the effective use of the media.

Garvey was to become a world figure because he saw his mission from early as one not confined to Jamaicans but involving his brothers and countrymen dispersed all over the world. He travelled to Guatemala, Panama, Nicaragua, Bocasdel-Toro, then down to South America (Ecuador, Chili and Peru). It was not a lecture-tour. In all of these places he tried to organize West Indian immigrants. He edited newspapers in some of these places—La Prensa in the city of Colon, La Nacionale in Costa Rica with Simon Aguileria. He was harassed by the authorities and returned home, sick unto death. He placed the plight of West Indians abroad to the governor of Jamaica, seeking protection for them from the British government, but was simply told that his countrymen should come home if they were suffering. Then he went to England, gaining employment along the docks of London, Cardiff and Liverpool. His extensive contacts with African and West Indian seamen during this period, Spady tells us, proved to be "one of the most significant relationships. Many of these same seamen would show up at ports with *Negro World* [Garvey's paper] in their waistbands . . . they got messages into areas sealed off by the official colonial powers."

On August 1, 1914, Garvey launched the U.N.I.A. (Universal Negro Improvement Association). It established a universal confraternity among all branches of the race, aiming at mutual economic assistance, cultural exchange and enrichment, the development of racial pride and love through self-reliance, and worldwide cooperation in commercial and industrial enterprises.

Garvey came over to the U.S. in 1916. His extensive lecture-tour took him through 38 states. He established many important associations and sought the help of influential African-Americans. Some of them, like Du Bois, who was later to attack him with great force, refused to accept an invitation to share his platform. A powerful Jamaican group also denounced him. Garvey looked beyond this jealousy, conservatism and narrow-mindedness. He turned with anger and impatience on his countrymen, calling them "stagnant" and "sleeping" West Indians, who, in spite of their educational advantages, had failed to change things around in their own country and had to flee into exile.

Eventually Garvey decided to lay down roots in Harlem and began to build a mass organization that would embrace Africans all over the world. He developed a coherent and cohesive ideology around "Africa for the Africans: Those at Home and Abroad". It became an organizing instrument for attracting millions. There had never been a mass movement more capable of unifying dispersed Africans into a whole.

The UNIA grew by leaps and bounds. It established many business enterprises. Thousands of blacks were employed by its businesses worldwide. Then Garvey envisioned a shipping business—the Black Star Line—that would take Blacks from the Americas back to Africa. A great many people subscribed to this but it became a spectacular disaster. Garvey and some of his associates were charged with "using the mails to promote the sale of Black Star stock, after they had become aware that the financial condition of the venture was hopeless".

Enemies of the UNIA created a climate in which Garvey's character was assassinated even before the court had found him guilty and jailed him. The movement against him was a formidable coalition of the most influential Black integrationist leaders in America. He was sentenced to five years. He served less than three. President Coolidge commuted the sentence and he was deported from the U.S., on December 2, 1927. He survived the sentence, still a hero to millions.

Toussaint

Readers who have never heard of Toussaint or know of him only vaguely should acquaint themselves with the outlines of his life before reading Wilson Harris' "Open Letter to Toussaint L'Ouverture of the San Domingo Revolution." For more detailed biographical information, they may consult the heavily documented and dramatic study of Toussaint–The Black Jacobins by C.L.R. James.

The final essay in our first preliminary survey of the heroes and heroines in the Black world is by far the most unusual. Here, over the divide of centuries, we have a dialogue between the two most complex and enigmatic sensibilities of the Caribbean, both of them revolutionaries in a sense, one whom we associate with the revolution of the masses in the eighteenth century, the other with the revolution of the mind of man in the twentieth.

Harris is the author of poems, novels and critical essays that have placed him among the most important writers now living. His earnest concern is not with the outer face of social movements and their presiding figures and forms which come and go, rise and fall, in the infinite rehearsal of the human spirit. He is interested in the deposit or essence each generation secretes and how its signal and message may be translated by succeeding generations. He reaches out to communicate with the mind of Toussaint by way of strands that reside in the dialogue of his letters. The ambiguity in some of these letters have mystified even the most astute of his biographers but Harris probes them for a hidden consistency in the apparent contradictions. It is an attempt to understand through the inner drama of his life the psychology or psyche of revolution.

The uprising in Haiti, which found its leading spirit in Toussaint, coincided with great turmoil in Europe, with the initial success of the French revolution followed by the ominous rise of Napoleon. It coincided as well with the expansion of the British Empire and of the prosperity and power of the Southern plantocracy in America. Toussaint strode upon the world stage, intuitively sensitive to the peril and possibility that lay in all these things, in spite of his lack of a formal education. He knew, far more than his black colleagues and white sympathisers, that a true and meaningful independence for Haiti could not be won in virtual isolation. He sensed and feared that the "liberal" lights that flashed in the French revolution were fading fast under the shadow of Napoleon. He was also acutely aware of the impatience of his companions for instant change and the willingness of his lieutenant, Dessalines, and possibly the Frenchman Sonthonax, to simplify matters through a wholesale slaughter of the opposition.

All this weighed upon Toussaint and people who did not know the balancing act, played out in secret on the stage of his mind, could not reconcile the harsh and severe measures he sometimes imposed to hold the black population in check, with the considerable humanity he showed to those who had been their former slave masters.

Toussaint spoke a broken dialect and to the end of his days could hardly speak French. He dictated and dispatched his many letters to members of the Haitian plantocracy, foreign powers, the Directory in Paris etc by the use of many agents and secretaries. James tells us that his dictated thoughts had to be "written and rewritten by secretaries until their devotion and his will had hammered them into adequate shape". They did not come with the facility of men with a liberal education.

Harris takes James up on this point. Perhaps the broken dialect of Toussaint made him struggle through to fragments of a dismembered truth he had begun intuitively to glimpse, a truth which might have been more easily eclipsed by his having at his disposal the facile verbal clarity of a socalled liberal education. "How false is such clarity," asks Harris, "the clarity of politics, how susceptible is it to disinformation, to half-truths if not lies, how consistent it is with expedience and propaganda? How remote it is from what it seeks to translate?" Toussaint, perhaps, came closer to the psyche of revolution than his more literate counterparts—the Tom Paines and the Jeffersons—with their so-called liberal education. What mattered more than this ex-slave's illiteracy was the literacy of his imagination. For the psyche, says Harris, is "a pregnant but half-eclipsed vessel of universal insight in the world's unconscious and the vocabulary of politics is but an inadequate translation of that vessel".

Harris shows how the old flesh creeps back in the wake of revolutions, how a potential for the profoundest change may be defeated by deepseated cultural factors and by habits of restrictive vision. But he insists that, in spite of the failure of mass movements, there is the necessity for a dialogue with the complex, inner sensibility of the past.

Despite the accumulative tragedy, there is hope. "Something is perceived," he says, "that bears on the innermost unshackled spirit of humanity despite every political or economic ghetto that entrenches itself again and again".

Toussaint, alas, suffered from his complex vision which set him apart from others, which made him secretive and aloof. He walked into a trap because he believed in the French revolution and in preserving a link with France. He had hoped he could negotiate sensibly and as a free man with Napoleon. "You knew the risk you ran," says Harris, in a letter to his ghost "when you met the French in a situation that exposed you to seizure. It was a gamble on behalf of cementing a meaningful accord". Toussaint was taken on board a French vessel and transported to France. There he was imprisoned in a cold mountain cell until he died.

In him perished the true promise of the Revolution for though Haiti became independent under Dessalines in 1804 and was the first sovereign state in the Caribbean, "the consequences of such sovereignty links Dessalines with the later Duvaliers in one of the greatest political tragedies of the modern world".

One thing stands out above all else in our survey of these remarkable men and women. That the struggle for a changing world occupies both a tragic and hopeful dimension. That again and again the light of the human spirit shines brightest against the shadow of almost invincible odds and that disaster seems to stalk anyone who challenges things as they are in the hope of transforming them into things as they should be. Disaster strikes the hero in the form of an assassin's bullet, a grievous slander, exile or the prisonhouse, deportation or betrayal or (most tragic of all) the loss of the love of one's people through a misinterpretation of one's role or a misunderstanding of one's actions.

Heroes are usually tragic figures who seldom die quietly in their sleep, yet our memory and vision of them should bring us to a new faith, not deepen our sense of despair. It is often through the crucifixion of these figures that we glimpse something noble and beautiful beyond their suffering and their death. It is this light they spark in our souls against the overwhelming appearance of darkness that rekindles our hope in the possibilities of rebirth in the world.

Acknowledgements

The *Journal of African Civilizations* would like to thank the following organizations and persons for permission to use previously published essays and photographs in this issue *Great Black Leaders: Ancient and Modern.*

1. The University of Illinois Press, for permission to reprint the essay "Martin Luther King Jr. and the Promise of Non-Violent Populism," by David Levering Lewis, which first appeared in *Black Leaders of the Twentieth Century*, edited by John Hope Franklin and August Meier.

2. Robert Parent, for permission to reprint 3 photos of Malcolm X illustrating the Clifton E. Marsh essay.

3. Alice Windom, for permission to reprint the photo of Malcolm X in Accra, Ghana, in May, 1964.

4. Pathfinder Press, for permission to use 4 photos of Nelson Mandela reprinted from "Nelson Mandela: The Struggle is My Life."

5. PanAf Books, London, for permission to use photos of Nkrumah from "Ghana: The Autobiography of Kwame Nkrumah" published in 1957.

6. The *Washington Post*, for permission to reprint "Black Roots of Egypt's Glory: by Charles S. Finch III.

MARTIN LUTHER KING, JR., AND THE PROMISE OF NONVIOLENT POPULISM

By David Levering Lewis

In the late eighteenth and nineteenth centuries ministers had often played important roles as black leaders, both in politics and civic life. But the turn of the century, with the ascendency of Booker T. Washington and later of W. E. B. Du Bois, marked the transition both to greater specialization of function among Negro leaders and the ascendancy of secular national spokesmen in civic and political affairs. (Adam Clayton Powell, Jr., in this as in other ways, was unusual.) In the South churchmen did retain a more influential role, often as intermediaries between blacks and influential whites. Martin Luther King, Jr., therefore, presents a fresh departure—a militant black protest leader with his base in the masses of southern black Baptists who played a critical role on the national stage in the battle for Afro-American freedom. Moreover, he not only symbolized the spread of militant black protest from the North to the South, but he was unique among black leaders in the way in which he became an important spokesman for broader social and economic concerns as well.

King's career was directly connected with the continued escalation of black expectations and the rising tide of Afro-American protest that followed World War II and that flowered in the early 1960s. The tactics of "nonviolent direct action" that he and his followers employed—mass marches, boycotts, sit-ins, filling the jails rather than paying bails or fines—were not new. Pioneering work in these tactics had been carried on by both A. Philip Randolph and the interracial Congress of Racial Equality, founded in 1942, but King crystallized a growing dissatisfaction with the limited changes effected by the strategies of the National Association for the Advancement of Colored People. He captured the imagination of black Americans—and many whites as well—and paved the way for the contemporary ascendancy of militant demonstrations that swept the country in the early 1960s.

The civil rights career of Martin Luther King, Jr., can be divided into two major periods—before Selma and after. The first begins with the December

Reprinted, with permission from *Black Leaders of the Twentieth Century*—University of Illinois Press.

1955 Montgomery bus boycott and ends with the march from Selma to Montgomery, Alabama, in late March 1965. The second begins with the Chicago demonstrations for jobs and housing during 1966 and ends with the assassination of King in Memphis, Tennessee, on April 4, 1968. The first period is characterized by a decade of innovative protest tactics employed to achieve traditional citizenship rights for Afro-Americans. The second—less than three turbulent years—was a time of nontraditional tactics in pursuit of increasingly radical goals for the larger society. The first was partially successful, but its relative success accentuated what yet remained to be done before the poor, the powerless, and the racially disadvantaged could begin to achieve equality of opportunity in America. The second period was marked by relative failure, and its legacy was the vision of political power and economic well-being devolving increasingly upon the poor, the powerless, and the racially disadvantaged. In the first period King and his allies brought about the beginning of the desegregated community. In the second the remote prospect of their "beloved community" vanished at Memphis. The greatness of the decade ending with Selma was in the nobility of the protesters; that of the times after Selma was in the far-reaching implications of the protest.

When Mrs. Rosa Parks, a seamstress at a downtown Montgomery, Alabama, department store, a loyal member of the National Association for the Advancement of Colored People, and a model of personal industry and propriety, defied the city's segregated transportation ordinance by refusing to surrender her bus seat to a white person on the first day of December 1955, she inaugurated an era in the struggle for civil rights. Her deed made King possible. The twenty-five-year-old Atlanta-born pastor of Dexter Avenue Baptist Church, in Montgomery less than a year and not well known in its Afro-American community, found himself at the head of a bus boycott movement before there had been time to weigh the full significance of the honor. Others had been more active and for far longer in the local civil rights activity. Others (the Pullman porter E. D. Nixon was clearly one) might have been more plausible leaders, but the city's Afro-American leadership, divided, contentious, and apprehensive, chose the newcomer to lead the Montgomery Improvement Association (MIA). It happened so quickly, King recalled, "that I did not even have time to think it through." Montgomery's Afro-American citizenry selected, almost by chance, not only the best person to lead their boycott but the person best suited to become the leader of the larger struggle for racial rights. And as the inevitable worked its purpose circumstantially in the choice of leader, the tactics by which the leader's strategy was achieved were similarly determined. If the concept of nonviolent passive resistance was as old as Christianity, with Thoreau and Gandhi as illustrious practitioners, and as recent as philosopher A. J. Muste's Fellowship of Reconciliation (FOR), its adoption by the MIA was more a matter of circumstance than of philosophy. Montgomery's Afro-Americans *had* to be nonviolent and passive in order to resist successfully.

Parks had been arrested December 1, 1955. On December 21, 1956, King, accompanied by several allies, boarded a public bus in front of his house. The MIA had won. Victory had come about through community solidarity (largely inspired by King's superb oratory and equally superb personal courage), despite jeopardized jobs, intimidation by the Ku Klux Klan, and harassment by police—and bombs. One night, as his wife, Coretta, rushed to the read with their infant daughter, the front of the King home was shattered by dynamite. For a brief period, the Reverend King even carried a pistol. Once he was arrested on a trumped-up charge of speeding, and denied bail until his loyal lieutenant, Reverend Ralph David Abernathy, arrived at the head of hundreds of followers. A city ordinance was invoked to prohibit organized taxi transport of bus boycotters. With money raised locally and from steadily rising contributions from national labor, libertarian, and religious organizations, from benefit performances and compassionate individuals the world over, the MIA purchased a fleet of vehicles. The city sought and won an indictment of King, Abernathy, and more than eighty other MIA members for conspiracy to interfere with normal business activity. Conviction by the Montgomery court and appeal to the federal courts followed, and in the interim the city pressed the attack, belatedly seeking a local injunction of the MIA car pool. Then, just as MIA leaders awaited the inevitable adverse decision from the municipal court on November 13, the U.S. Supreme Court decreed Alabama's state and local laws enforcing segregation on buses unconstitutional.

The formula for nonviolent civil rights campaigns was perfected in Montgomery: unsuccessful presentation of elementary grievances; mounting of increasingly provocative peaceful demonstrations; gross acts of violence by white citizens and outrageous misconduct by local law enforcement and judicial bodies, relentlessly reported by the national media; infusion of money and talent from national liberal organizations and increasing participation of nonresident whites (clergy, labor, students) in nonviolent demonstrations; single or multiple atrocities perpetrated by local whites, leading to direct or indirect federal intervention and negotiated settlement with chastened or cowed white officials. King's pulpit rhetoric, electric presence in the community and at the head of singing columns, his internationally reported sojourns in jail, fund-raising prowess in the North, and unyielding enforcement of nonviolent discipline in the South, and his consistent reasonableness at the negotiating table were (more often than not) highly effective.

In retrospect, the combination of King's personal assets and nonviolent tactics have a far more formidable appearance than in reality they often did at the time. In fact, he and his movement were continually menaced by the cruel paradox that unless they triggered savage reactions from their opponents, the nation (white and black) tended to impugn his organization's motives and reproach King for disrupting what was perceived as slow yet orderly racial progress in a given community. There was also a second paradox that tended

over time to undercut the performance of King and his organization: the young Afro-American and white students enrolled in the other two non-violent direct action organizations, the recently formed Student Nonviolent Coordinating Committee (SNCC) and the older Congress of Racial Equality (CORE), were at first uneasy with and then hostile to King's "conservative" role as race leader. Despite the ink spilled over matters of doctrine both by historians and the participants themselves, what increasingly divided the SNCC and CORE "militants" from King and his followers was not so much "genuine" versus "tactical" nonviolent passive resistance, but King's leadership credibility. Thus, this critical pool of leadership and manpower—SNCC, CORE, and their less permanent analogues—was available to King often on a qualified basis and sometimes even a hostile one.

Complications arising from this second paradox were largely avoided for a time. When King left Montgomery permanently for Atlanta at the end of 1959, the doctrine of nonviolent passive resistance and the vehicle to advance it were firmly in place. By then, King had traveled widely (Europe, Ghana, India), written his first book (*Stride Toward Freedom*), lobbied nationally for civil rights, indirectly contributed to the large Afro-American vote that gave candidate John F. Kennedy a slim presidential victory, and presided over the birth of the Atlanta-based Southern Christian Leadership Conference (SCLC). In April 1960 he was present for the founding of what was to become SNCC, at Shaw University in Raleigh, North Carolina. He fully endorsed the spreading student sit-in movement, carefully participated in it when it reached conservatie Atlanta, and had SCLC advance small sums to SNCC for its Freedom Rides throughout the South during spring and summer 1961 (probes into the South by interracial cadres to test compliance with federal regulations governing interstate travel). Even so, many SNCC rank and file were suspicious of King and SCLC, and the uneasiness of many SNCC leaders developed into aversion when their organization split over the debate of whether to escalate the nonviolent, direct action campaign or to shift emphasis, as the new Kennedy Administration and many northern philanthropies urged, to a voter education and registration campaign. SCLC, by encouraging SNCC to adopt the voting rights project and by serving as a conduit for funds from the Field and Taconic foundations, confirmed the worst suspicions of many in SNCC that King and his movement were too moderate. For Attorney General Robert Kennedy, Senator Hubert Humphrey, New York Governor Nelson Rockefeller, and many other concerned politicians, however, the SCLC leader was the best promise for steering Afro-American anger into what they regarded as safe channels.

Albany, Georgia, a rigidly segregated town, was King's first major setback. The initial objectives were modest: integration of interstate bus and rail facilities (the municipal bus company was added later) and formation of a permanent biracial civic committee. But three fundamental elements were amiss in

Albany: (1) SCLC planned poorly; (2) local white opposition was resolute and intelligent; and (3) the federal governmental withheld active support. Each of these elements operated synergistically, so that the conduct of one rapidly determined that of the others. Had Albany been studied carefully rather than plunged into enthusiastically at the end of 1961, King would not have been surprised to find himself at the center of an internecine Afro-Americam struggle of maddening complexity. There were the SNCC operatives who, after spending months overcoming local derision of their clothes, hairstyles, youthfulness, and "crazy ideas," had only recently won the confidence of the NAACP Youth League and the Albany State College students in order to maneuver the solid church people and professionals into opposing the white community. There were the local NAACP dignitaries, middle-aged pillars of the community, who were still as resentful of being shunted aside as they were hostile to SNCC's confrontational policies. There were the Afro-American businessmen, highly successful but also highly vulnerable, who courageously advocated racial progress, but not at any price. There were the local preachers, never more given to homiletics than when action was required, whose outstanding egos made collaborative efforts difficult. There was the strong sense of local pride shared across warring generations and personalities. When SCLC's leader and his lieutenants accepted the December 15th summons from the president of the Albany Movement, extended without prior consultation of the membership, they walked into a situation of intolerable unpredictability.

Planning would have helped in Albany, yet there was little the SCLC could have done to undercut the determination of its white adversaries. The leader of the white business community, James Gray, owner-editor of the Albany *Herald*, was an intransigent racist whose newspaper regularly inflamed white public opinion, contributing to a climate in which the political risks to city officials of meaningful biracial negotiations were prohibitive. Counting on firm support from Senator Herman Talmadge's machine in Atlanta, local white leadership drew up plans to close some public facilities and to "sell" parks, pools, playgrounds, and libraries to a group of businessmen headed by Gray, which was eventually done. When the municipal bus company, reeling from a boycott, offered to desegregate service and hire one Afro-American driver, the white establishment forced it to renege on the informal promise and declare bankruptcy. Unlike white Montgomery, which had never fully recovered from shock and lurched from tactic to tactic, or white Atlanta, which was embarrassed by sit-ins and mass demonstrations, Albany was never shocked or embarrassed. During the eight-month period of active SCLC involvement, with headlines such as "Keep on Fighting for Albany," the *Herald* spoke for businessmen and politicians determined to make their city a symbol of uncompromising racial separatism.

But what made Albany even more formidable was the form taken by its intransigence. In Sheriff Laurie Pritchett, King met a travestied image of himself—a nonviolent segregationist law officer. Off camera and especially in temporary prisons set up outside the city limits to handle the swelling population of demonstrators, there were frequent acts of police brutality. But Sheriff Pritchett was always an efficient, correct—even humane—custodian of order while the news camera rolled. "It's not a matter of whether I'm a segregationist or an integrationist," he told the press. "I'm a duly constituted law enforcement officer, dedicated to the enforcement of the law." As demonstrators marched to Albany's court house to press demands that escalated over the months to end all segregation ordinances and cause adoption of a fair hiring and employment policy for the city and its businesses, Pritchett and his men, after issuing polite orders to disperse, patiently arrested and assembled the demonstrators for transport to jails. "He tried to be decent," no less an authority than Coretta King concedes in her autobiography. "He would allow the protestors to demonstrate up to a point. He would bow his head with them while they prayed. Then, of course, he would arrest them." When violence finally erupted on the night of July 24, 1962, the perpetrators were not, as the nation was learning to expect from the South, red-faced, overweight policemen wielding clubs, they were 2,000 rampaging Afro-American teenagers. King's embarrassment was so great that he adjourned demonstrations and called for a "day of penance." It is highly likely that if Pritchett's nonviolent law enforcement technique had been followed in other southern cities, civil rights advancement would have been greatly retarded. City officials elsewhere would have been able to boast, as one in Albany did to the New York *Herald Tribune*, "We killed them with kindness. Apparently, it was a condition M. L. King and the other outsiders had never encountered before."

King's trump card, played elsewhere with perfect timing and devastating consequences—jail until an agreement to negotiate—failed in Albany. His first arrest, with Abernathy and the Albany Movement president at the head of 250 singing, praying demonstrators on December 17, 1961, was followed by refusal to post bond and a vow he knew the world would notice: "If convicted, I will refuse to pay the fine. I expect to spend Christmas in jail. I hope thousands will join me." But the next day King and Abernathy surprised the world by leaving Pritchett's jail. With the New York *Herald Tribune* calling his performance "one of the most stunning defeats of his career," the Pittsburgh *Courier* deciding that little had been achieved, and much of the Afro-American community dismayed, King eventually offered *Time* magazine an explanation: "We thought the victory had been won. When we got out, we discovered it was all a hoax." The SCLC leader was the victim of a hoax by his own allies. The fractious leadership of the Albany Movement chafed at what it regarded as high-handed behavior by several SCLC officers, resented the almost exclusive attention the media paid King and the SCLC, was suspicious of the use made of the large outside donations flowing mainly to the SCLC,

unconvinced of the wisdom of SCLC's national call to Albany of volunteer demonstrators, and, finally, preferred no settlement at all to one negotiated by King and the SCLC. "There was constant war between us as to strategy," a prominent SNCC leader confessed. SNCC feared King would be too moderate at the negotiating table. Others in the Albany Movement were simply jealous of King's getting the credit.

King's second prison stay occurred on July 10, when, after a five-month delay, he and Abernathy returned to be sentenced for the December 17 infraction, refusing to pay the $178 fine and choosing instead forty-five days at hard labor. Again the media sizzled, donations arrived at SCLC headquarters, northern students and activists (mostly white) headed for Albany, Governor Rockefeller, prominent members of Congress and labor leaders urged President Kennedy to take action, while downtown Albany resounded to the strains of "We Shall Overcome." Three days later, King's jailers released him and Abernathy, explaining that his fine had been paid by an unidentified Afro-American. "Never before have I been thrown out of jail," Abernathy told a puzzled church gathering. On July 17, King, Abernathy, and the Albany Movement president were rearrested for demonstrating, again vowing not to leave their cells. Again, press and television coverage put King at the center of the nation's business. A group of ministers and rabbis conferred with Kennedy about the outrage. Others motored to Albany. Finally, the president found it politically wise to wonder aloud why the people of Albany were unable to negotiate their differences. Meanwhile, the Sunday New York Times (August 5) carried King's morally compelling article, "The Case against Tokenism," which praised the Kennedy administration for its international diplomacy but roundly lambasted its inaction on civil rights. Kennedy's New Frontier was "unfortunately not new enough," he charged. "And the Frontier is set to close to the rear." Five days later King and his fellow offenders were found guilty by the local court and given suspended sentences. King promptly announced his belief (encouraged by the Justice Department and local white leadership) that, if he departed for Atlanta, the city and the Albany Movement would reach an accord.

Instead, race relations deteriorated in Albany. This time, as with his second incarceration, the hoax was engineered by the whites who finally understood, as southern whites elsewhere never did, that to keep King in jail was to guarantee their own defeat. After three abortive attempts to remain imprisoned long enough to humble adversaries through the power of national and international condemnation, King left Albany for good in late August 1962. Had he offered himself for arrest a fourth time, it is very likely that the response of northern opinion and Albany's Afro-American citizenry would have been distinctly lukewarm. Writing in a southern journal, SCLC leader Wyatt Tee Walker conceded that things had gone badly, but he thought that valuable lessons had been learned: "Albany is a milepost in the early stage of the nonviolent revolution. Our nonviolent revolution is not yet full-grown. I do not know if it will ever reach adulthood, but I pray that it will."

Birmingham, Alabama, in the spring of 1963, answered the Reverend Walker's prayers. It was a magnificent triumph for King and his movement, as well as a considerable moment in the evolution of democracy in America. The objectives were to desegregate schools, public facilities, and commercial institutions, initiate hiring and promotion of Afro-American personnel in downtown retail stores, and establish a biracial committee to monitor racial progress. Here the three fundamental elements were propitious: (1) SCLC planned well; (2) local white opposition was divided and part of it ideally intemperate; and (3) the federal government intervened decisively on the side of equity. Much preparation went into the Birmingham venture. In the first week in January 1963, King, Abernathy, and Walker visited Anniston, Gadsden, Talladega, Montgomery, Birmingham, and the rural areas around Selma as part of SCLC's People-to-People tour to stiffen the resolve of Alabama Afro-Americans to place their names on voter rolls (thirty-seven teachers had recently been fired for trying) and to garner needed area support and national publicity for the campaign. Additionally, there was a highly successful Los Angeles fund-raising rally organized by singer Harry Belafonte and a subsequent secret meeting in Belafonte's New York apartment of seventy-five influential friends of civil rights and members of the press (representatives of New York's Mayor Robert Wagner and Governor Rockefeller and members of the business, literary, film, and religious community). King's message was clear. Despite numerous U.S. Supreme Court rulings and federal directives, racial desegregation continued to proceed, if at all, at a snail's pace throughout most of the South. The Kennedy White House and Justice Department demonstrated little inclination to risk a slim electoral margin by angering the white South. To ameliorate the condition of Birmingham's Afro-Americans would constitute a major victory over Jim Crow, the repercussions of which would be felt throughout the South. The mobilization of thousands of Afro-American citizens in the city (using children for the first time) and the brutal white counterreaction would compel the federal government to implement vigorously the decision of the Supreme Court. "We've got to have a crisis to bargain with," the Reverend Walker explained. "To take a moderate approach, hoping to get help from whites, doesn't work. They nail you to the cross." After two false starts (postponed because of mayoral elections in early March and a runoff between "progressive" candidate Albert Boutwell and racist Eugene "Bull" Connor in early April), demonstrations began in Birmingham on April 3.

Birmingham fixed the moral stature of King in the national consciousness. In three documents coming at the beginning, middle and immediate aftermath of the campaign, the SCLC leader became for a time, the embodiment of civil rights. The *Birmingham Manifesto* spelled out the circumstances that had driven the people of that city to active defiance and the moral basis of that defiance: "We act today in full concert with our Hebraic-Christian tradition, the law of morality, and the Constitution of our nation. The absence of justice and progress in Birmingham demands that we make a moral witness to give our community a chance to survive." Pledged to the Ten Commandments of Nonviolence (e.g., 1. MEDITATE daily on teachings and life of Jesus. 8. REFRAIN from violence of fist, tongue, or heart), drilled in nonviolent techniques by members of the Alabama Christian Movement for Human Rights (ACMHR) and SCLC, and fired by King's oratory, Birmingham's Afro-Americans filled Sheriff Connor's cells day after song-filled day.

King's arrest and solitary confinement resulted in the second document, the magisterial "Letter from Birmingham Jail," written in the margins of newspaper and on scraps of paper. Refuting several white southern preachers and rabbis who condemned his conduct as unworthy of a man of God, the imprisoned author wrote that he had come to bring the gospel of freedom to a city of injustice. Like the prophets of the eighth century B.C., like the Apostle Paul, he felt the urge to carry the gospel far beyond his own home. "Like Paul," he wrote of the need to "respond to the Macedonian call for aid." What had Jesus meant, King asked rhetorically, in saying "I have not come to bring peace, but a sword?" King answered that "positive peace" entailed wrathful social dislocation by the just. Citing examples from the lives and principles of Socrates and Gandhi, he justified his and his followers' "lawlessness" by arguing that only just laws need by obeyed, that, to be just, a law made by people had to correspond to God's law, and that any law that degraded people was bad. "Letter" ended on a high civic and religious note: "One day the South will know that when these disinherited children of God sat down at lunch counters, they were in reality standing up for what is best in the American dream and for the most sacred values in our Judeo-Christian heritage."

At first Sheriff Connor, in agreement with Mayor-elect Boutwell, had adopted the restrained tactics of Albany's Chief Pritchett, but when the demonstrations escalated and the incumbent city administration (seizing a technicality in the charter) decided not to leave office for another two years, Connor's police turned violent. The evening television news carried scenes of shocking brutality—dogs attacking children, police clubbing women, firemen stripping backs bare with hoses, tear gas strangling demonstrators and press alike. Burke Marshall, assistant U.S. attorney general in charge of civil rights, arrived to negotiate with 125 white civic leaders at the Birmingham chamber of commerce. Secretary of Treasury Douglas Dillon contacted the chairman of Royal Crown Cola, the president of Birmingham Trust National Bank, and the board chairman of the city's largest real estate mortgage company. Secretary of Defense Robert McNamara used his influence as former director of the Ford Motor Corporation. Eugene Rostow, dean of Yale University Law School, urged Yale graduate and U.S. Steel board chairman Roger Blough to

intercede with the president of his corporation's Birmingham subsidiary. Attorney General Kennedy telephoned city officials. Nearly $300,000 in bail money was quickly raised by the United Automobile Workers (UAW) and the National Maritime Union. On May 15, 1963, what King called a "bold new design for a new South"—the Birmingham Pact (opening up schools, stores, jobs and transportation)—was struck. The Alabama Supreme Court ruled the old city government and Connor out of office, and the U.S. Supreme Court declared sit-in demonstrations legal in cities that enforced segregation ordinances. Segregation began to end in Birmingham.

With the March on Washington at the end of August, King and other civil rights leaders hoped to inaugurate an era of racial integration and social justice on a national scale. The September 22nd bomb killing four little Afro-American girls attending Sunday school in a Birmingham church cruelly underscored a few weeks later how distant was the reality from the dream. Yet the dream of racial equality was probably never more powerfully evoked than it was by King on the steps of the Lincoln Memorial on August 28, 1963. The 250,000-strong crowd on the mall was saluted that hot day by statesmen, celebrities, writers, and actors, and addressed by John Lewis of SNCC (whose speech had been tone down before delivery), Whitney Young, Jr., of the Urban League, Walter Reuther of the UAW, Roy Wilkins of the NAACP, and A. Philip Randolph, who deserved credit for the original idea of the march. But nothing—not even the singing of Odetta or Mahalia Jackson—electrified the interracial crowd as much as King's "I Have A Dream" speech, the third great document of the Birmingham period.

King declared that despite bitter temporary setbacks and frustrations he held fast to a dream, a profoundly American dream that one day the nation would really practice its creed that "all men are created equal"; that the children of slaves and of slaveowners would one day live in brotherhood. He had a dream that one day his four little children would be judged not by their color but by their character. The day would come, he cried in closing, "when all God's children, black and white men, Jews and Gentiles, Protestants and Catholics, will be able to join hands and sing in the words of that old Negro spiritual, 'Free at last! Thank God almighty, we are free at last!" To make the dream come true, the leaders of the March on Washington met with President Kennedy after the speeches and left a forest of specific demands: a comprehensive civil rights law; a Fair Employment Practices Act to bar federal, state, city, and private employers, unions, and contractors from job discrimination; extension of the Federal Fair Labor Standards Act to employment not covered and establishment of a national minimum wage of not less than two dollars an hour; desegregation of all public schools by the end of 1963; a massive federal program to train and place unemployed workers; withholding of federal funds from all institutions guilty of discrimination; greater power to the attorney general to provide injunctive relief for persons denied constitutional rights; a federal order prohibiting housing discrimination in all enterprises using federal funds; and reduction of congressional representation in states disfranchising minority groups.

The White House had originally tried to discourage the March on Washington, warning leaders of the civil rights movement not only of the far-reaching ramifications of possible violence in the nation's capital but of the more likely immediate damage to civil rights legislation pending before Congress. King had been impressed by the merits of the argument, but he had also been impressed by the considerable personal and organization risks involved in open defiance of the Kennedy administration. Neither the Urban League nor the NAACP had endorsed the idea of the march when it had first been presented by Randolph. For a time King restricted his collaboration to formal approval while doing little to assist the march organizers. As plans for the demonstration developed (pushed by Randolph, CORE, and SNCC), it became clear that the Kennedy administration was divided. Apparently, the president and his advisors decided on an all-out effort in June to insure the success of the March on Washington. Stephen Currier, husband of a Mellon heiress, president of the Taconic Foundation, and an official Kennedy advisor, assembled nearly one hundred chairmen of the most powerful corporations at New York's Hotel Carlyle to raise a civil rights war chest. Three days later, Currier, along with King, Randolph, Wilkins, Young, and James Farmer of CORE, attended the crucial White House meeting at which the general objectives of the March on Washington were agreed upon. King now argued that, rather than being ill-timed and counterproductive, the march was the best means of "dramatizing the issues and mobilizing support in parts of the country which don't know the problem at first hand." Vice-President Lyndon Johnson and Attorney General Kennedy concurred.

In light of his historic speech and the vast enhancement of his national prestige and influence, there is irony in King's initial reluctance to be a participant in the March on Washington—a reluctance that was seen by some leaders and careful students of the civil rights movement as conclusive evidence of his readiness to move only as boldly and rapidly as his various and powerful white allies were willing to condone. Both established spokesmen in the movement as well as young militants alleged that the March on Washington had been co-opted and deradicalized by agents of the White House and the business community—that King had been used. The SCLC leader began to be regarded as an accommodationist, a leader walking a slender tightrope between those forces (mainly and significantly white) that supported him financially and politically because King appeared to them as the most "responsible" and "effective" Afro-American leader—and those forces (younger and mainly Afro-American) that believed the speed and scope of racial advancement were threatened by moderation. Increasingly, as a prominent civil rights historian wrote of this general phase, King was a leader who occupied the "vital center." The question was, how long could the center hold?

The year 1964 was the best and worst of times for King, Afro-America, and the country. *Time* magazine chose him as its Man of the Year in January, the first Afro-American selected. President Johnson, taking great pains to reassure the civil rights leadership, pushed hard for passage of the long-stalled civil rights bill. After eighty-three days of Senate debate and a historic two-thirds cloture vote, the legislation passed on June 19 and was signed into law as the Civil Rights Act of 1964 in early July and King and other civil rights leaders present. Yet, less than three weeks later, race riots swept through the North, beginning in Rochester, New York, and spreading to New York City, Chicago, and, by early August, Jersey City, New Jersey. There would now be a steady discharge of northern riots for almost the balance of the decade. Violence of a very different sort increased in the South, where the Mississippi Freedom Summer campaign (largely a SNCC and local NAACP operation) to register Afro-Americans to vote was attracting large numbers of mostly white college-student volunteers from the North. On August 4, the nation was horrified when the bodies of three murdered young SNCC volunteers from the North were exhumed from a Philadelphia, Mississippi, cattle pond in which local whites had hidden them. Four days later, President Johnson signed his billion-dollar poverty program into law. Meanwhile, King, appalled by the compounding violence and deeply worried that Republican Senator Barry Goldwater might win the presidency, joined other civil rights leaders in calling for a moratorium on all civil rights demonstrations until after the elections. Significantly, CORE and SNCC rejected the moratorium. The year ended on a high note for King with a trip to Norway to receive the Nobel Peace Prize, the second Afro-American so honored. Speaking with eloquent modesty on this occasion, King represented himself as merely the "trustee" of a people's struggle, placing his own achievements within the context of collective heroism and the rightness of a cause. He was no longer a southern pastor fighting against regional racism; the Nobel Prize was the outward emblem of a larger sense of mission that had already begun to tug at his thinking.

The watershed in King's career occurred between early March and mid-August 1965. After enactment of the 1964 Civil Rights Act, federal legislation was badly needed to facilitate the right to vote for Afro-Americans in the South. SCLC had targeted Selma, Alabama, for its major voter registration campaign at the end of 1964. The federal government was disposed to help. Selma's white leadership was divided. The young major, Joseph T. Smitherton, was a timid moderate; the chief of police, Wilson Baker, was a disciple of Albany's Pritchett; and the county sheriff, James "Jim" Clark, was an out-of-control racist. But Selma was not to be another Birmingham. It was more like Albany. In Albany the cost of losing had been too high; in Selma, the cost of winning was too high—in both cases, largely due to poor generalship. On Sunday, March 7, as thousands of singing demonstrators marched across Selma's Pettus Bridge on their way to petition the right of ballot of Governor George Wallace in Montgomery, they were savagely repulsed and chased by state troopers and Sheriff Clark's deputies. Some demonstrators retaliated with rocks and bottles. A massacre was probably averted by the determined intervention of Police Chief Baker. King and Abernathy were in Atlanta, ostensibly to preach to their congregations but most probably to avoid a second Selma arrest in order to raise funds for the campaign. They promised to lead a second march to Montgomery. Volunteers came to Selma in all colors, classes, and faiths from every section of the country.

On March 10, SCLC attorneys asked a federal judge to enjoin Selma officials from interfering with the march; instead, Judge Frank M. Johnson, Jr., enjoined both sides from activities. "We've gone too far to turn back now," King told the demonstrators. The next afternoon he exhorted 3,000 people in a Methodist church: "I have got to march. I do not know what lies ahead of us. There may be beatings, jailings, tear gas. But I would rather die on the highways of Alabama than make a butchery of my conscience." But when the demonstrators had crossed the bridge, King knelt in prayer, then rose, and led them back into Selma (even though Alabama state troopers left the highway open). SNCC militants had never favored the Selma-Montgomery march, but they regarded King's turnabout on the bridge as an incredible waste of morale and opportunity. When they heard rumors of a secret pact between SCLC and President Johnson's special emissary, the head of the new Community Relations Service of the Justice Department, to march only a distance beyond the Pettus Bridge, thus not violating the federal injunction, dismay turned to outrage.

Had King violated a federal court injunction (something he had never done) and led his nonviolent resisters down U.S. Highway 80 to Montgomery, they might have been attacked by state troopers (also violating the injunction). Snipers, rumored to have been positioned by the Klan along the highway, might have decimated their ranks before federal officers could act. Although Johnson's Justice Department might have asked for severe penalties against King, student militants believed that the national shock and furor of any or all of these consequences would have ultimately greatly advanced the civil rights struggle. They observed, cynically, the vigorous public reaction of the White House when one of three white clergymen, the Reverend James Reeb, died of a crushed skull two days after being attacked at the conclusion of the Selma march. On March 15, Johnson brought Congress to its feet with his call for voting rights act in a speech ending, stirringly, "And we shall overcome." The federal injunction against the Selma-Montgomery march had already been lifted. On Sunday, March 21, the momentous walk to Montgomery began under protection of federal marshals and military units. It reached the Alabama capital the following Thursday, where, after many of the nation's most famous entertainers and actors had performed, King stirred the great crowd with one of his finest speeches.

But what should have been a triumph only made King and his lieutenants more aware of the partial and fleeting nature of their accomplishments. Passage of the Civil Rights Act of 1964 and the Voting Rights Act of 1965 only caused many whites to wonder whether demonstrations any longer served a positive purpose. Such whites found powerful confirmation of their apprehensions in the explosion of the Los Angeles ghetto, Watts, in August 1965. The nation was also now well into a foreign war that would drain away resources to improve social conditions. There was a growing national sentiment, shared by Afro-American supporters of the NAACP and Urban League, that the times were right for pause and consolidation. Had King and SCLC conceded the wisdom of caution, it is certain that neither could have continued to function. NAACP and Urban League leaders, however egocentric, were organization men, and their organizations depended for survival neither upon charisma nor improvisation. SCLC, by contrast, was an improvisation surviving because of the leader's charisma, rather than because of organizational structure.

Cynics explained away SCLC's decision to fight discrimination in the North as merely expedient. If it is unlikely that this decision was wholly devoid of expediency, it is far more significant that it announced a broader and more sophisticated SCLC awareness of fundamental causes of racism. Moving to Chicago in early 1966, demanding housing, jobs, and genuine public school integration, tangling with the city's hard-nosed mayor, and gradually losing the active support of many white allies, King's foray into the North was far from successful. Many northern white supporters—labor leaders, various liberals, and prelates—called the Chicago activities inflammatory, counterproductive, and at best premature. Many Afro-Americans still loyal to SCLC were disappointed with the August 1966 truce between King and Chicago Mayor Richard Daley known as the Summit Agreement, and catalogue of extremely ambitious, loose concessions hastily conceived a few days before thousands of Afro-Americans were to march into white suburban enclaves. Finally, if young and militant Afro-Americans were now openly contemptuous of King (calling him "De Lawd"), the federal government had clearly begun to distance itself from the civil rights leader. At the White House Conference on Civil Rights (June 1966), Johnson's desire the have the issues important to King ignored was respected by the participating white businessmen and numerous Afro-American notables.

Weighing the significance of these reverses, King concluded that after years of laboring with the idea of "reforming the existing institutions of the society, a little change here, a little change there," it was time for major changes. "I think you've got to have a reconstruction of the entire society, a revolution of values," *Harper's* quoted him as saying. The cities of America must be rebuilt so that the poor could live decently and work productively in them. "Some of the nation's industries must be nationalized," and a guaranteed annual wage enacted. The country's foreign investments must be reviewed. The civil rights leader, whose career had been launched by circumstance and whose success,

until then, had been due largely to pushing at the boundaries of racism rather than to an assault upon its fundamental causes, was no more. Having been "bogged down in the paralysis of analysis" in the past, King in late 1966 was preparing for political and economic activity on a scale and of a nature sufficient to outrage, alienate, and even alarm the federal government, the business community, much of organized labor, and most of the senior Afro-American civil rights leadership. What he had begun to perceive was that both religion and society tended to confine their compassion and indignation to injustice and misery susceptible of attenuation without imperiling fundamental economic relationships. When Afro-Americans began to make demands that could lead to full equality, King wrote, "They found that many of their white allies had quietly disappeared."

What might best be described as the "lunch-counter" phase of the civil rights movement (King himself later called it the "Selma and Voting Rights Act phase") had been a period of straightforward moral choices between minority rights of access to public facilities and commercial establishments and the barbarous defense by jowly sheriffs and howling dogs of the southern way of life. The right of Afro-Americans to travel, eat, and vote like white American citizens was not generally construed as unreasonable outside the Deep South. But once in the North—in Chicago, Cleveland, and Detroit—bearing a list of racial grievances greatly enlarged by demands for jobs, open housing, citizen review of police and real estate boards, and economic boycott of racially unresponsive businesses, King's civil rights movement suddenly developed from a regional drama centered on racial segregation into a crusade exposing socioeconomic imbalances in the national structure itself.

A decade earlier King's ideas on the economic uplift of his race had been vintage Booker T. Washington. To succeed, he wrote in his first book, the Afro-American "must develop habits of thrift and techniques of wise investment. He must not wait for the end of the segregation that lies at the basis of his economic deprivation; he must act now to lift himself up by his own bootstraps." As late as summer 1966, he told a church packed with poor Chicagoans that they had to "face the fact" that most would be "living in the ghetto five, ten years from now." But that was no reason not to "get some things straightened out right away. I'm not going to wait a month to get the roaches out of my house." The prophecy was accurate and the summons to household hygiene and responsibility commendable, but neither quite squared with the recent now-or-never rhetoric and goals of his abortive Chicago campaign. Yet Chicago was the cradle for much of SCLC's new economic thought. In the past the formula for SCLC success depended upon arousing what King called the "moral self-interest of the nation." But SCLC quickly discovered the limits of moral self-interest in the cities of the North. If King and his movement were to find a new lease on life after the Chicago Summit Agreement, new tactics were in order. Racial compassion had to be reinforced by old-fashioned American political quid pro quo.

The political for such a quid pro quo existed in the growing opposition to the Vietnam war and the comprehensive issue of national priorities gone awry. One way to the schools, decent jobs, decent neighborhoods, and heftier federal subsidies was as an active participant in an interracial chorus denouncing the $30,000,000,000 spent for Vietnam while the shame of poverty remained in America. King's first tentative foray into international politics (spring 1965) had raised such a firestorm in the civil rights community that the Nobel Peace laureate had quickly dropped the Vietnam war issue for the time being. When Young had attacked King's antiwar views during the White House Conference on Civil Rights in June 1966, Young correctly stated that the "Negro was more concerned about the rat at night and the job in the morning." Senator Edward Brooke, sole Afro-American in that chamber, and Urban League director Young pleaded, each after a 1968 fact-finding mission to Vietnam, that King and other critics give their government the patriotic benefit of the doubt and leave the war to the experts and the president. King replied that American "integrity" was no longer credible. Civil rights leaders and white advisors also pleaded with him to soften his antiwar statements because of the much feared and reported white backlash sweeping the nation.

Opposition caused him to falter on the war issue, but ultimately King's choice of new direction turned on the central point of his moral conception of his role. Racism and poverty were evils; if it meant embracing controversial positions and allies to eradicate them, conscience left him no other choice. War was wrong; if he lost support because he spoke out against the war in Indochina, conscience left no other choice. "Our loyalties must transcend our race, our tribe, our class, our nation," the Nobel laureate told his Atlanta congregation. "This means we must develop a world perspective." "It should be incandescently clear," he proclaimed in New York City's Riverside Church exactly one year to the day before his death, "that no one who has any concern for the integrity and life of America today can ignore the present war. If America's soul becomes totally poisoned, part of the autopsy must read 'Vietnam.'" This was the time when King told a worried financial advisor, "I don't care if we don't get another five cents in the mail, I'm going to keep on preaching my message." In fact, SCLC revenues increased.

Based on the political parochialism of his black followers, the limited allegiance of white liberals and much of the labor movement, and the certainty of federal animosity, King appeared to make all the wrong decisions in this last stage. It is now clear that another consideration, only guessed at then by a few, should have dissuaded him from his path: the malevolence of J. Edgar Hoover's Federal Bureau of Investigation. King was almost certainly aware, moreover, of rumors that a price had been put on his head by unidentified southern businessmen. Instead, he chose to merge civil rights with the larger, institutionally destabilizing crusade for human rights, to turn his back on the safer course of reducing direct action to another prominent libertarian lobby. The post-Chicago phase was not a complete leap into the unknown, of course;

the militancy of the students and financial resources of the antiwar forces were becoming rapidly stronger. There was an effective presidential peace candidate prospect in Senator Eugene McCarthy, and it was credibly rumored that Senator Robert Kennedy might break with President Johnson over the war. But it was a measure of the moral steadfastness and intellectual growth of King that he was prepared to risk so much for the "reconstruction of the entire society."

A case can be made for residual influences on King of the socialism inherent in theologian Walter Rauschenbusch's Social Gospel, and a weaker case for a vague, moderate Marxism acquired at university and in the milieux of protest. Insofar as Marxism exposed the "weaknesses of traditional capitalism, contributed to the growth of a definite self-consciousness in the masses, and challenged the social conscience of the Christian churches," King wrote in *Stride Toward Freedom*, he found Marxism useful. The promptings of Gandhian principles—*satyagraha*—much refurbished by discourse and travel in India, were of major importance, but largely for the global resonance and millenarian gravity they imparted to King's own civil rights campaigns. In the final analysis, his seemingly rapid shift leftward was grounded in Christian morality and common sense. "Any religion," he emphatically stated in *Stride Toward Freedom*, "that professes to be concerned with the souls of men and is not concerned with the slums that damn them, the economic conditions that strangle them and the social conditions that cripple them is a dry-as-dust religion." In what were virtually his last words on the subject, King warned in *Where Do We Go from Here* of the awesome challenges ahead for him in his post-Chicago phase: "The real cost lies ahead. The stiffening of white resistance is a recognition of that fact. The discount education given to Negroes will in the future have to be purchased at full price if quality education is to be realized. Jobs are harder and costlier to create than voting rolls. The eradication of slums housing millions is complex far beyond integrating buses and lunch counters."

In retrospect the logic of his position now seems to have had the force of inevitability. The battle against racial segregation led to the larger assault on discrimination, leading in turn to the final struggle against economic exploitation. No civil rights victory—not even the most complete ones of Montgomery and Birmingham—could be intrinsically conclusive because of the economic nature of the war for equality of opportunity, with each skirmish and battle clarifying further for King and his followers the ultimate objectives. If the Afro-American was the most visible and most vocal victim of social inequality, his plight was neither unique nor, in the final analysis, totally racial. As some of the most perceptive intellectuals, such as W. E. B. Du Bois and A. Philip Randolph, had discerned, any substantive improvement in the condition of the Afro-American necessarily entailed an at least minimal redistribution of national wealth through government intervention.

"'The poor can stop being poor,'" King quoted approvingly an atypically candid assistant director of the Office of Economic Opportunity, "'if the rich are willing to become even richer at a slower rate.'" In *Where Do We Go from Here*, he criticized the black separatists because they gave "priority to race precisely at a time when the impact of automation and other forces have made the economic question fundamental for blacks and whites alike." Because the struggle for rights was "at bottom a struggle for opportunities," King now moved beyond even the vast scale of his 1963 Bill of Rights for the Disadvantaged to the macroeconomics of "total, direct and immediate abolition of poverty." It could be done; it must be done, he said. There was nothing "except shortsightedness to prevent us from guaranteeing an annual minimum—and livable—income for every American family. There is nothing, except a tragic death wish, to prevent us from reordering our priorities, so that the pursuit of peace will take precedence over the pursuit of war. There is nothing to keep us from remolding a recalcitrant status quo with bruised hands until we have fashioned it into a brotherhood."

The appeal grew stronger of coalition with a new army of whites (as well as browns and reds) who could be as useful to King as the liberal-clerical-labor alliance of the past that was now unraveling. Essentially, these were the white antiwar students, the affluent white liberals far more alarmed about the Vietnam war than extremisms on the campus or in the ghetto, the forgotten Native Americans stirring on reservations, the Hispanic-Americans filling up the Southwest, and the ignored of Appalachia. A coalition such as this (of the disenchanted, disinherited, and *déclassés*) appeared, according to one's perspective, to be the vanguard of a splendid new order, an insignificant or potentially influential force for disorder and sedition, or little more than fodder for prime time televiewing.

In any case King now became the principal architect of this coalition, speaking out against the war his government insisted had to be won, calling for an end to poverty, and a "reconstruction of the entire society, a revolution of values." Participating in the huge Spring Mobilization rally in April 1957 in New York Central Park and the United Nations Plaza, he deplored the burden upon the Afro-American poor imposed by the Asian war, drawing a moving word-picture of indiscriminate American devastation of life and property in Vietnam. Yet he withheld his signature from the Spring Mobilization manifesto because of its charge against the U.S. government of genocide; similarly, he refused to sanction the burning of draft cards. He did approve the manifesto's call for a "Vietnam Summer," a massive, peaceful, solid three-month saturation of antiwar protest and propaganda. To the leadership of the older civil rights organizations, King's position was believed to be personally suicidal and racially calamitous. The NAACP and Urgan League made their disagreement unmistakably clear. There were persistent reports, vigorously denied by the parties, of an acrimonious face-to-face exchange between the Urban League's Young and King. Former ambassador and leading Afro-

American columnist Carl T. Rowan attacked King in *Reader's Digest* for the unwisdom of mixing civil rights with foreign policy. Within the ranks of the SCLC itself were many who agreed that opposing the war would bankrupt the organization and turn President Johnson's Justice Department from an already lukewarm friend into a lethal foe. An unrelated but unmistakably premonitory decision by the U.S. Supreme Court in June 1967 strengthened such arguments: King and eight SCLC associates saw the Court uphold by a five to four margin their April 1963 Birmingham conviction for demonstrating without a valid municipal permit. "Terribly saddened by the ruling," King probably correctly interpreted it as the court's signal to "go slow," for as Barry Mahoney and Alan Westin observe in *The Trial of Martin Luther King*, "many black and white leaders . . . felt that the court's ruling was predestined by the flow of events on the racial front during 1965-67."

When King proclaimed for the first time, on March 25, 1967, at the Chicago coliseum that "we must combine the fervor of the civil rights movement with the peace movement," the outlines of nonviolent populism were clear. During the following months he strove to address a larger, more varied audience than ever before, driving home statistics on poverty, repeating that the numerical majority of those living below the poverty line was white, that the whites of Appalachia were worse off materially (and more powerless) than innercity Afro-Americans. He summoned the politically weak, the economically deprived, the angry young of all races, and the disenchanted liberals to form together a community of action sufficiently powerful to force the enlightened attention of Washington and Wall Street. His rhetoric and statistics promised the bare probability of a biracial front. A basic historic reality common to the white and black poor, however, was that they tended to define their worth and prospects in opposition to each other. In the main, the black and white poor also tended to have conflicting expectations of the federal government. Prospects for collaboration between Afro-Americans and other ethnics were no more promising if for different reasons: reservation Native Americans, enveloped by their culture and traditions, not prone to share their thoughts, wanted considerably less rather than more to do with the U.S. government; Hispanic-Americans, perceived as racially ambivalent and as relentlessly occupying Afro-American urban living space, were growing politically powerful in the Southwest and were demographically projected as *the* American minority. It was difficult to believe that church-going farmers, factory workers, and domestics could successfully join with white college students whose presumptively radical politics were financed by affluent parents. It was already difficult enough maintaining a working relationship with Afro-American students and community people, angry at "whitey," supposedly alienated from The Establishment, and demanding billions in reparations from businesses, the churches, government, and quotas in education and hiring. Moreover, many of these young people gave voice to the crude anti-

Semitism found in black ghettos, further distressing libertarian and philanthropic Jews who were already alarmed by the call for quotas.

This was populist politics at its most venturesome, bringing together the ethnically, economically, culturally, and geographically disparate for long-term objectives. "Our challenge," King wrote in *Look* in 1968, "is to organize the power we already have in our midsts." It was to be a force "powerful enough, dramatic enough, morally appealing enough, so that people of goodwill, the churches, labor, liberals, intellectuals, students, poor people themselves" would begin to "put pressure on congressmen." Meanwhile, plans for the Poor People's Campaign were completed by SCLC's staff in mid-February 1968. Initial cadres were to be drawn from ten cities and five rural districts located in the East, Midwest, South, and Appalachia, From Roxbury (Boston's Afro-American ghetto), Chicago's Lawndale community, Mississippi, and West Virginia, 3,000 volunteers would travel in caravan to a shanty town erected in the capital. From there they would make daily sorties over a three-month period to press their demands at the Senate, House of Representatives, and the departments of Housing and Urban Development, Health, Education and Welfare (now Health and Human Services), and Agriculture. The core of this Poor People's Campaign was SCLC's $12,000,000,000 Economic Bill of Rights (originally proposed by A. Philip Randolph), guaranteeing employment to the able-bodied, viable incomes to all legitimately unemployed, a federal open-housing act, and vigorous enforcement of integrated education. An unfavorable response by Capitol Hill would result in thousands more converging on the capital as well as simultaneous demonstrations of the poor on the West Coast. Essentially it was a strategy substituting Washington for Birmingham, forcing even liberal senators and representatives to play parts as economic Bill Connors and hawkish George Wallaces.

If the logic and grand strategy of the Poor People's Campaign make sense today, this was not the case for most Afro-Americans in 1968. King knew that middle-class Afro-Americans and many of the simple church people would recoil at the prospect of an occupation of Washington. Orations at the Lincoln Memorial and a day of interracial songs and processionals were a different order of protest from saturating the capital with an army of potentially unruly—even riotous—unemployed, underemployed, juvenile militant, and politically unsophisticated for three months, if necessary. Opposition of Johnson to the campaign and the president's reportedly fierce dislike of King could only distress, if not alarm, such civil rights leaders as Wilkins Young, and Farmer, who were fearful of the much reported white backlash sweeping the nation.

King professed to discount the depth and duration of the white backlash. The reality was that King dreaded the backlash and believed that nothing short of luck and quick, decisive, "creative" action could preclude it. But it was not the backlash then being recorded in the polls and reflected by articles in national publications that distressed King. What little truth was contained in NAACP charges that SCLS's Chicago campaign had cost liberal Illinois Senator Paul Douglas his seat undoubtedly troubled the Nobel laureate, as did the desertion of his traditional white allies and sympathizers, who warned that the pace of civil rights had become improvidently rapid. But the SCLC leader saw beyond these concerns to the graver racial and national peril. To slow the pace of racial progress now was, he believed, to make certain that the exhortations of young racial extremists, like H. Rap Brown, Stokely Carmichael, and Floyd McKissick and the Black Panthers, would be translated into reality. "The white liberal must escalate his support for the struggle for racial justice," King pleaded in *Where Do We Go from Here*. "This would be a tragic time to forsake and withdraw from the struggle." But, instead, many white allies succumbed to "radical chic," finding, as did most of the national media, much more to be fascinated by the fiery demands and threats of the rising Black Power movement. "Dr. King's faith was draining," Andrew Young said of this period, speaking to a New York *Times* reporter, "because even people inside the organization were running around the country spouting talk about violence." Meanwhile, derisory articles such as that in the *New York Review of Books* dismissing *Where Do We Go from Here* as warmed-over middle-class reflections and alleging that the author had been "outstripped by his times" made it clear that even professional white liberals had not grasped his message. In July 1967, three months after the publication of the book, race riots engulfed Newark and Detroit—the Detroit riot was one of the worst in American history. King's verdict, quoted in the April 1968 edition of *Look*—"The flash point of Negro rage is close at hand"—seemed beyond dispute.

Disappointed and deserted as 1968 unfolded, King was still absolutely certain that his was not only the more viable politics but the sole politics possessing authentically reformist socioeconomic potential. Black Power—retaliatory violence, inverted racism—was not the path to social revolution but to racial backlash and official repression. In 1964 King had with arresting candor placed the civil disobedience and demonstrations of the civil rights movement in the perspective of public policy: "White Americans must be made to understand the basic motives underlying Negro demonstrations. . . . It is not a threat but a fact of history that if an oppressed people's pent-up emotions are not nonviolently released, they will be violently released. So let the Negro march. Let him make pilgrimages to city hall. Let him go on freedom rides. And above all, make an effort to understand why he must do this. For if his frustrations and despair are allowed to continue piling up, millions of Negroes will seek solace and security in black-nationalist ideologies." In recent years since this lecture, King had repeatedly warned the nation that a rhythm of legal and political and, later, socioeconomic concessions had to be maintained in order to avoid Afro-American violence and permanent alienation. With the rhythm of concessions almost arrested by

1968, he expected the data of the unfinished Kerner Commission on Civil Disorders to fulfill James Baldwin's terrible predictions in *The Fire Next Time*. He expected much worse, for, although he usually left it unsaid, King knew that after the fires were extinguished, the arsonists would pay a fearful price. What he feared most was the backlash that would surely come after the explosion of "black rage" he was racing to head off.

It is a signal irony of recent history that the leader who had become the most hard-headed realist with a plan and a vehicle to alter the course of national events in a positive, humanitarian direction was widely portrayed in his final months as a fuzzy-minded moralist, disappointing to liberals and held in contempt by Black Power enthusiasts. King's new approach—a Popular Front of the racially abused, economically deprived, and politically outraged, cutting across race and class—was prospectively potent. It was also an approach that revealed King at his imaginative best as a leader and demonstrated the pragmatist who calibrates his swing leftward the better to construct a basis for civilized, moderated, genuine social progress.

King went to Memphis on March 28, 1968, to lead a demonstration in support of striking municipal sanitation workers. There was violence. Afro-American teenagers known as the Invaders clashed with police, lightly damaged some commercial property, and one of them was fatally shot by an officer. A deeply disturbed King left the city, promising to return to organize and lead a proper nonviolent march within a few days. Before this fateful return to Memphis, there were astonishing developments that portended great success for the SCLC leader. Johnson announced that he would not seek reelection. With Kennedy already campaigning for the Democratic nomination on a peace and poverty platform satisfactory to King (and McCarthy still a strong contender), the SCLC leader could reasonably anticipate a Democratic national convention much more than ceremoniously interested in what he had to say. The Economic Bill of Rights and a presidency capable and willing to push it through Congress were imminent possibilities. King's assassination produced literally overnight the political climate and consequences he had devoted his feverish final days trying to prevent.

During his twelve years on the national scene King pursued a policy of conciliatory confrontation that depended for success upon the perception by controlling forces in the larger society (namely, labor, religious, business, government) that, however premature, costly, or destabilizing his demands, the probable consequences of hostile or ineffective response would be much graver than the crisis created by such demands. When the immediate scope of objectives was mainly constitutional and regional—desegregation and voting rights in the South—King's allies (willing and reluctant) more often than not came effectively to his assistance. The minimal demands of integrated schools, open public facilities, and access to the ballot were always recognized as legitimate in principle by a majority of Americans. King used the same tactics of conciliatory confrontation when the scope of his objectives was enlarged as he moved northward. The specter of terrible social and economic upheaval was put forward as inevitable, unless swift and profound national advances were achieved in the area of human rights and economic opportunity. This time, however, resistance was far greater; many of King's powerful Establishment supporters came to regard him as a major contributor to rather than the antidote for intolerable socioeconomic disorder. Among many Afro-Americans—leaders and citizens—there was honest confusion about the role King was forging for himself in the final months. They believed that the combination of civil rights with other issues (e.g., the peace movement) would detract from the former. Whether he could have constructed the effective new coalition symbolized by the Poor People's Campaign is far from certain.

Sources

Primary Sources

Coretta Scott King. *My Life with Martin Luther King, Jr.* New York: Holt, Rinehart & Winston, 1969.
Martin Luther King, Jr. "A Comparison of the Conceptions of God in the Thinking of Paul Tillich and Henry Nelson Wieman." Ph.D. diss., Boston University, 1955.
———. *The Measure of Man.* Philadelphia: United Church Press, 1968.
———. *Strength to Love.* New York: Harper & Row, 1963.
———. *Stride Toward Freedom: The Montgomery Story.* New York: Harper Row, 1958.
———. *Trumpet of Conscience.* New York: Harper & Row, 1968.
———. *Where Do We Go from Here: Chaos or Community?* New York: Harper & Row, 1967.
———. *The Wisdom of Martin Luther King in His Own Words*, ed. by Bill Adler. New York: Lancer Books, 1968.
———. *Why We Can't Wait.* New York: Harper & Row, 1964.

Secondary Sources

Lerone Bennett. *What Manner of Man*, 3rd rev. ed. Chicago: Johnson Publishing, 1968.
Jim Bishop. *The Days of Martin Luther King, Jr.* New York: G. P. Putnam's Sons, 1971.
Charles E. Fager. *Selma, 1965.* New York: Charles Scribner's Sons, 1974.
David Garrow. *The FBI and Martin Luther King: From 'Solo' to Memphis.* New York: W. W. Norton, 1981.
———. *Protest at Selma.* New Haven, Conn.: Yale University Press, 1978.
David Levering Lewis. *King: A Biography*, 2nd ed. rev. Urbana: University of Illinois Press, 1978.
August Meier. "On the Role of Martin Luther King" in Meier and Elliott Rudwick, *Along the Color Line: Explorations in the Black Experience*, Urbana: University of Illinois Press, 1976. Reprinted from *New Politics*, 4 (Winter 1965).
William Robert Miller. *Martin Luther King, Jr.: His Life, Martyrdom, and Meaning for the World.* New York: Weybright & Talley, 1968.
Lawrence Reddick. *Crusader without Violence.* New York: Harper & Row, 1959.
Hanes Walton, Jr. *The Political Philosophy of Martin Luther King, Jr.* Westport, Conn.: Greenwood Publishing, 1971.
Alan F. Westin and Barry Mahoney. *The Trial of Martin Luther King.* New York: Thomas Y. Crowell, 1974.
Harris, Wofford. *Of Kennedys and Kings.* New York: Farrar, Straus and Giroux, 1980.

THE ESSENCE OF KING'S TRUE GREATNESS

by Wendell Charles Beane

That irony is a perennial feature of history no serious historian, philosopher, theologian, or political scientist can afford to doubt or deny. And in American history the pinnacle of irony was reached when the "grandchildren" of slaves became in the 50s and 60s the means through which a nation "conceived in liberty and dedicated to the proposition that all men are equal" was at last driven to face the issue of living up to its creed. This ironic remark is not original, having been stated in many books on Black history and, especially, with regard to the significance of Martin Luther King, Jr. The tragedy is that the "American Dilemma" has been so persistent that the remark has recurrently posed a formidable challenge to the United States every time it is uttered or written.

Martin Luther King, Jr. not only stands in a long line of great American Black leaders. He represents the historical culmination and the living dramatization of a spirit rooted in Black African culture and in the American Dream. It is a "spirit of freedom," or the determination *to be free*, which in the almost 400 years of Black experience in American culture was manifested in the lives of his great predecessors, who were also ardent lovers of liberty, such as Pierre Dominique Toussaint L'Ouverture (1743-1803), Nat Turner (1800-1831), Harriett Tubman (1820-1913), Frederick Douglass (1817-1895), Booker T. Washington (1856-1915), Mary McCleod Bethune (1875-1955), Marcus Garvey (1887-1940) W. E. B. Dubois (1868-1963), and many others, perhaps even nameless but heroic Black souls.[1]

Numerous biographers, critical commentators, and journalists have had much to say about this modern leader: his background, character, and meaning not only for American but for all human social history. The aim of this essay, however, is not primarily to rewrite their "histories" or merely to reiterate their laudations or their denigrations, whatever the case may be. The present viewpoint will reflect in larger measure a philosophical-religious interpretation of this great personality, while taking account of extremely important "moments" in his historical and spiritual odyssey.

Martin Luther King, Jr., was born the grandson of a slave into a segregated society in Atlanta, Georgia in 1929. Reared under the compassionate yet firm parental guidance of Martin and Alberta King, he inherited via the Baptist Church tradition a thorough Judeao-Christian orientation. The second in a line of three children, he soon became aware that there was something special about himself, especially when he skipped the ninth grade in high school, entered college at only 15, and graduated from Morehouse College at the age of 19. Subsequent graduate education at Crozier Theological Seminary (June, 1951), and at Boston Theological School (June 5, 1955) gained him a doctorate in Systematic Theology. Married to the former Coretta Scott, in Marion, Alabama (June 18, 1953) King took over the pastorate of the Dexter Avenue Baptist Church, Montgomery, Alabama (1954); later he became co-pastor with his father of the Ebenezer Baptist Church in Atlanta, Georgia (1960). It was in the Black Church that the social, economic, political, but, especially, the *religious* bedrock for future civil disobedience in civil rights campaigns was to be found. A stunningly charismatic preacher and lecturer, King had no national political ambitions, even after he was elected head of the Southern Christian Leadership Conference (1957). He seems, nonetheless, to have been virtually catapulted either by history and/or Providence toward becoming the leader of the grandest civil rights revolution movement in the history of the United States.

King's adventures with ideas were rooted in a keen and innate potential for mastering the discipline of theology which has been defined as "the systematic exposition and the rational justification of the intellectual content of religion."[2] His doctoral dissertation on two of the world's most prominent theologians (Paul Tillich and Henry Nelson Wieman) was, probably, not a mere exercise in intellectual *savoir faire*, but an adventure within his own mind to fathom further how to correlate the practical, pathetic, and, indeed, tragic demands of history, with the vision of an omnipotent, omniscient, omnipresent, omniprovident God who works *in* history. The former two theologians became seminal foci for King's understanding of the inseparable link between correlative love and creative value, the paradox of theological principle and ethical creativity, the dialectic of finite human nature and God as the infinite ground of being. That keen and innate capacity was variously stimulated by other such eminent thinkers as Rauschenbusch, Niebuhr, Carlyle, and others.[3] Six books, numerous articles, speeches, sermons, and addresses mark the ability of a mind who, having been cut off so soon (at 39), probably had the potential for an even greater intellectual evolution and practical contribution for future generations to ponder and appreciate. Some of his greatest remarks on 'contemporary problems and struggles' were succinctly chosen by the editors of *Ebony Magazine* (Special Section): "The Living King" (January, 1986, pp. 62-63).

If a host of Western theological giants could contribute to King's theoretical and, to some extent, his practical understanding of the possibilities, impossibilities, to be sure, even the "impossible possibilities" (Niebuhr) inherent in divergent Christian visions of God in history, it was Mahatma Gandhi whose vision critically galvanized that keen and innate reformative splendour which was to become King's legacy to his own people *and* to the nation as a whole.

Mahatma Gandhi was perceived by King to be the further decisive Providential unfoldment of the Love (Agape) ethic of Jesus of Nazareth. "Agape," King held, "is an overflowing love . . . When you rise and love on this level, you love all men not because you like them . . . but because God loves them."[4] In Gandhi, King found that "the Christian doctrine of love operating through the Gandhian method of nonviolence was one of the most potent weapons available to oppressed people in their struggle for freedom."[5] Ultimately, the historic uniqueness of this idea was that it became a radical and redemptive strategy for the socio-cultural or ethical-political transformation of a racist society in *religious* terms—what King called "The American racial revolution." A striking occurrence of continuity and relatedness with the past with a uniqueness and originality for the present was, therefore, manifested in both Gandhi and King. They were certainly two distinct personalities, but their philosophical roots lay in rich theistic traditions which were sacred to them. They had both experienced the Eternal, under the form of the Hindu avatar, Rama, for the Indian pragmatic sage, and under the form of Jesus of Nazareth, the "Son of God" for the American theological-ethical reformer. Gandhi's "soul-force" or "truth-force" (*satyagraha*) became King's "Love of God" spread abroad in the human heart (I Corinthians 13; Romans 5:5); Gandhi's non-violence or non-injury (*ahimsa*) became King's blessed Beatitudes (Matthew 5), and Gandhi's welfare for all (*sarvodaya*) became King's "Beloved Community."

King's philosophy of nonviolent resistance, which tells us much of his character and convictions, encompassed the following: (1) his awesome felt obligation to challenge the civil rights flaws of the American system of government with a willingness to suffer the penalties for the violation of laws, however unjust (although King, as St. Augustine, held that "an unjust law is no law at all."); (2) his insistence upon the method of nonviolent resistance through demonstrations as a practical unfoldment of *universal love* (*agape*) that, ultimately, seeks to "win over" not denigrate the segregationist enemy;[6] (3) his recognition of the pre-existence of an already morally sensitized conscience among many liberal-minded American Caucasians inside a more massively racist majority, thus allowing for constructive political (-religious) coalitions (e.g., Jews, Catholics, Protestants, Humanists, etc.);[7] (4) his realization that desegregation is not tantamount to *integration*: that the removal of the shackles of American "apartheid" did not mean the presence of the magnetic bond needed to move from where we were toward community instead of more chaos and (5) his Vision of the "Beloved Community," i.e., "the aftermath of nonviolence is the creation of the beloved community,"[8] wherein, via an expanding (-centrifugal) ethical concentrism, the abolition of the wall of separation between all Americans of various ethno-cultural backgrounds means *also* the emergence of a global consciousness of the spiritual unity of all humankind.

King's adventures with ideas meant not only the study of all the pre-emi-

nent theological and ethnical minds whose works continue to challenge the faculties and students of seminaries everywhere. For it is an historical and religious wonder that the usual disillusioning hiatus between theory and practice, tradition and transformation, word and spirit, did not overtake King's visionary dream. His perusal and reflection upon the works of his intellectual predecessors became a type of philosophical initiation, a *rite de passage*, through which a decisive, even comparatively rare, cumulative, mergence of rational thought and emotional faith occurred in his being. The wonder continues to be that the almost inevitable reification that tends to envelop ordinary dreams was to be somehow transcended in King; so that with him (as with Gandhi) there occurred both the complementarity of dream and historical reality and the absorption of the dream into a vision of Divine Reality.

His adventures with the idea of God and Divine creation, therefore, included a God who was both transcendentally and immanently the Supreme Being of the Universe and thus, as he once said, "bigger than all our denominations." Humankind, in the Divine's eyes, though torn between two natures (i.e., self-sacrifice and self-centeredness) is inherently possessed of a dignity, lovability, and value that the affirmation of God's Holiness and transcendence was never meant to depreciate. The Universe (and/or the World as we know it) is governed by God's Eternal Laws, which mark out an arc that, though spread widely over and beyond the evils of men, tends to "bend toward justice." "Dreaming" thus meant, primarily, dreaming the Dream of God and, only derivatively, the Dream of Man. But dreaming there must be, for it is the stuff of dreams that provides the vital impetus for the American "Negro" to accept the responsibility for himself, and to demand the abolition of the disparity in American life between a National Anthem's glorification of a "land of the free . . . [a] home of the brave" and the lack of even the opportunity and the wherewithal to buy a hamburger in any public restaurant of one's own country.

It is out of this same spirit that the Montgomery Bus Boycott was born. It was the event which marked the movement of masses of Blacks toward concerted action in behalf of civil rights in the South, as well as other places across the country. The name of Rosa Parks, who refused to surrender her seat to a White man (1955), means something far beyond her arrest for breaking the city of Alabama's segregation code. She symbolizes a larger refusal of the human spirit to tolerate any longer the blight of racism and second class citizenship. And this, in a land whose very name has become a synonym for "Freedom."

Still, the response of some leaders in state and national power to the first manifestation of this generation of "the American racial revolution" was in large measure one of humanistic naivete. On the on hand, there was the criticism that the Boycott was ill-timed; on the other, as in the Reconstruction Era, 'the good White people of the South' were supposedly, themselves, engineering changes to transform the fate of "Negroes" in their midst. However, just as the South had mastered the art of segregation, it would now, at best, turn itself toward mastering the art of "Gradualism." But the success of the Montgomery Boycott was to bury the dominant trend of Black inferiority and the mystique of White superiority. For Blacks, unity had not only been found in strength, but strength had been found in the unity of 'the souls of Black folk.' Subsequent decades would witness the rising momentum of that event's impact when non-White human beings in other continents began to chant "We Shall Overcome" in their own languages and for their own purposes of liberation from 'man's inhumanity to man.' For the practical unfoldment of their adventures with ideas had to be shaped by their own indigenous needs. So the spirit of King lingers on, signaling a glorious communion of protest and power for all believers in nonviolent, sacrificial love as a method of social change.

King's adventures with ideas, moreover, encompassed, implicitly, the idea of "Black Power"—a sloganization of the "Dream" as more militantly understood by competitive civil rights factions.[9] But, for him, "Black Power" unrooted in his God's Divine Power, could only lead to the power that finally corrupts all political movements—even political-*religious* movements! Hence, if the essence of "Black Power" did not symbolize the Power and the Presence of God's Divine Reality, then the ethico-spiritual principles of Jesus of Nazareth would be critically compromised. It would, ultimately, lead to the illusion of "Black Supremacy," which King insisted would be no better than "White Supremacy." For, then, violence would occur and recur; and the Blacks of the United States do not have the military power to take on the entire White power structure and its formidable arsenal of destructive weapons without massively tragic and irreparable losses to the Black Community. King contended that "even the extremist leaders who preach revolution are invariably unwilling to lead what they know would certainly end in bloody, chaotic and total defeat." Moreover, the times we live in are such that, as we ponder the absence of a larger "Beloved Community" in the United States in relation to the chaos of values in the world at large, "the choice today is no longer between violence and nonviolence. It is either nonviolence or nonexistence."[10]

It seems, nonetheless, that with every great thinker or reformer there is an earlier and a *later* turn of thought that yet remains undergirded by a dominant trend of philosophy. Thus in a later phase of his decisive mergence of rational thought and emotional faith, King rejected the tactics of the militant Black Radicals, such as Malcolm X, Stokely Carmichael, Floyd McKissick: although he appreciated their non-advocacy of "aggressive violence" as such.[11] King, himself, seems to have experienced a kind of philosophical revaluation of *the wider dimensions of the nonredeemed nature of the American society.* Noticed by several more recent biographers and something to be seriously pondered by future interpreters, King, finally, said of his country:

> America is deeply racist and its democracy is flawed both economically and socially . . . the black revolution is more than a struggle for the rights of Negroes. It is forcing America to face all its interrelated flaws—racism, poverty, militarism, and materialism. It is exposing evils that are rooted deeply in the whole structure of our society. It reveals systemic rather than superficial flaws and suggests that radical reconstruction of society itself is the real issue to be faced.[12]

This statement by the greatest Black leader of human rights in American history illustrates both his greatness *and* his dilemma as a political-religious reformer. For the utterance reflects not only a change in his former more limited horizon of concern; it gives rise to a question for which the lack of a practical—not a theoretical—answer would outlive King himself. In a sense history itself had long ago posed the question but refused to give humankind an answer: how can an individual or a people, or a nation, secure or guarantee a nonviolent solution to a widespread human predicament (even in the single society) for which an ultimate solution would appear to require as a precondition the transformation of the entire fabric of that society? It is an old dilemma, which restated, means that one cannot change completely the nature of even a part of a whole which needs changing unless the whole is first changed. In fact the apparently rectified distortions of democracy have sometimes been known after an initial transformation to reconfigurate negatively under the influence of the dominant milieu of a society not yet radically changed. Hence the various historical recourses to enlightened despotism, anarchy, or dialectical materialism. Though suspected of Communist connections by J. Edgar Hoover of the F. B. I., King had full and critical knowledge of the limitations and distortions of non-Democratic ideologies, especially Communism. In fact, he said, "Civil rights is an eternal moral issue which may determine the destiny of our civilization in the ideological struggle with Communism."[13] Of course, any revolutionary political action which commits itself to a form of *communalism*, (Acts 4; 32-35) though nonviolent and in harmony with Christianity, is bound to attract Communist-prone individuals and to be ideationally (but not ideologically) associated with Communism *per se*. Thus King had to endure suspicions, slanders, and sufferings of which many Whites and Blacks are not fully aware.

In King's view the impact of the aforementioned dilemma of democracy would seem to be assuaged by the strategic maxim that a thousand mile journey begins with a single step. However, situations did exist where there were not always any guaranteed, supportive, legal preconditions, no local collective spirit for the protection of even nonviolent demonstrators. That is, morally debased places where not only did it seem that non-violent resistance "invited" violent counter-resistance, but where violent resistance to nonviolence seemed to reduce the practical political aims of nonviolence to moral absurdity. The experience of radical leader, Robert F. Williams is a case in point. Monroe, North Carolina, Williams felt (*Negroes With Guns*, Chicago, IL., Third World Press, 1973), was totally beyond redemption in terms of the White power structure and the general milieu. He tells us of terrible things suffered by Blacks in unconscionable situations. In a particular case, he names, for example, Dr. Albert Perry as having been falsely charged and unjustly imprisoned. Williams, to be sure, was another advocate of violent self-defense. And the views of Williams and Truman Nelson (in the above work) are not easily discounted given the overall context of Black victimization. King, in his criticism of Williams' tactics of violent self-defense, however, called the subsequent release of "a Negro doctor" (Dr. Perry?) through a method of *nonviolent resistance* "a striking example of collective community action . . . a significant victory without use of arms or threats of violence."[14] In other situations (e.g., Philadelphia, Mississippi, 1968), police forces acted only after nonviolent protestors had already been viciously brutalized. Nonetheless, in another (e.g., the Chicago Civil Rights Housing Campaign, 1966) the threat of the reduction of the nonviolent strategy to moral absurdity was followed by signs of hope, coupled with a cautious optimism and a sombre realism. King was able to wrest from the "Daley Political Machine" some semblance of a fair housing commitment. Just then, however, King could only add to his "victory rally" remarks, "Morally, we ought to have what we say in the slogan, Freedom Now. But it all doesn't come now. That's a sad fact of life you have to live with."[15]

While the Founder of King's religion seems the least resistant by saying "Resist not evil" (Matthew 5:39), King's civil rights revolution meant that one could resist evil but only with nonviolence. The crux of the matter has continued to be whether universal love (*Agape*) itself can be true to Christianity's Founder if it insists, because of the exigencies of history, upon manifesting itself as a form of nonviolent *resistance*. For Jesus of Nazareth's ethical spirituality seems to have presupposed a dynamic multidimensional cosmology which allows for a legitimate description of his method as one of "nonviolent nonresistance." To die in a state of forebearing love was not to die at all but to move to another, spiritual dimension of Reality. King, himself, however, had worked out his own creative, practical interpretation of the *agape* ethic. First, he saw three forms of response to evil in history: (1) pure nonviolence, (2) violent self defense, and (3) violent advancement (-"agressive violence"). Second, he understood Jesus' supreme, radical form of nonviolent nonresistance as being more applicable to one-on-one interpersonal relations than to the response of human beings under institutional forms of tyranny and oppression.[16] Creativity *and* humility, to be sure, are reflected in King's attitude, for he once said, "None of us can pretend he knows all the answers."

The sociopolitical legacy of King for America is nonetheless well-established, notwithstanding the controversy over his methods and what seems to have been his *own* form of personal "situation ethics."[17]

In keeping with his later more prophetic revaluation of his own society and the world, King would eventually go on, practically, to draw out the radical implications of America's involvement in the Vietnam War. He thus embraced an anti-Vietnam War position on the basis that there was a vital moral link between that movement and the civil rights revolution. This far more intimidating commitment was to bring him into inevitable political disfavor with those Federal officials (including President Lyndon Johnson), who had positively considered the uniquely fomenting power of his role in the grandest multi-ethnic demonstration for civil liberties in American history—the March on Washington (August 28, 1963). By that time, despite the momentous and glorious "I Have a Dream" speech, which made many wonder whether the power of the prophets of Biblical times had indeed passed, he had ceased to inspire the powers that be. For limited gradual change they tolerated, but prophetic criticism of long-held foreign-policy presuppositions and strategic initiatives considered inseparably linked to national security and economic objectives could not be endured.

No less than the religious reformer whose name he bore (Martin Luther—1483-1546), King felt irresistibly drawn into an ever-widening vision of renovative responsibility and spiritual adventure. Moreover, his words reflected a level of prophetic challenge that was either to make his most ardent supporters even more certain of his "higher" calling, or to cause others to begin to doubt the soundness of his mind, if not the loyalty that he held toward his own country. He had, indeed, said in a decisive anti-Vietnam War speech in Los Angeles (1967) that "we must demonstrate, teach, and preach until *the very foundations of our nation are shaken*."[18] It was this kind of language, reminiscent of Biblically prophetic proclamations, that precipitated the ever-widening, tragic rift between King and the nation's political leadership. For the import of King's words and actions was not that the traditional ratiocinations of the Just War alone but, in our Nuclear Age, *war itself* was being called into question by the Source of King's charisma.

But the cumulative, relentless verbal abuse that this Black leader was to suffer as a result of the position he had taken is nothing short of shocking. In a sense, it had an impact, perhaps even more devastating than the other kinds of verbal and legal abuse he had suffered from various sources and in sundry situations theretofore. There was, for example, the earlier, literally heart-close stabbing by a woman of his own race in Detroit; and there was the hate-laden brick that struck him in the back of the head while demonstrating in Marquette Park in Illinois (Chicago's white-hate was almost enough to make King rethink his optimism about the redemptive possibilities of human nature). King, nonetheless, never abandoned the conviction that "the image of God is never totally gone" in man. But now, regarding his anti-Vietnam War stand, the criticism came from both White *and* Black persons of prominence. These included some who had already been involved with King earlier in the civil rights campaigns. One has only to read this very specific period as portrayed admirably by Stephen Oates (*Let the Trumpet Sound*, pp. 431-443, 449) to catch a larger glimpse of how a nation can terribly hurt one of its best souls. We are told that King "was so distraught and hurt . . . he sat down and cried."

The odyssey of a great life of leadership, loyalty, and love came to an end in Memphis, Tennessee (April 4, 1968), when a sniper's bullet slew him[19] as if, finally, to dramatize the ever-ambiguous presence of War and Peace in human nature and the human community. Though death itself he did not generally fear, both he and his beloved Coretta had recurrently experienced the foreboding of assassination. Triumphantly, he told a congregation in his final sermon (in Mason Temple, Memphis, Tennessee, April 3, 1968), that though longevity was a thing to be naturally desired, "I'm not concerned about that now. I just want to do God's will. And He's allowed me to go up to the mountain. And I've looked over. And I've seen the Promised Land . . ."[20]

In the words of Frederick L. Downing, in his *To See the Promised Land* (1986), "how is one to understand Martin Luther King, Jr.? Was he a philosopher, a slain civil rights leader, or at a fundamental level, a minister with a broad and philosophical understanding?" Downing's analysis of King's most farreaching significance is extremely important for two specific reasons. First, the author includes but, finally, bypasses the usual attempts to view King as merely an outstanding sociopolitical reformer. And, second, the author understands studies in psychology and religion to be relevant to such a complex character as King's; the former understands King in terms of J. W. Fowler's highly perceptive characterization of a certain religious personality-type, i.e., the individual who has developed a "Universalizing faith."[21] Downing, however, asks more questions than he answers about the spirit in King that, *overall*, transcended the ambiguities humbly acknowledged by King himself and, certainly detected by scrupulous inquiries into his psycho-social background. Downing, however ambiguously, provides the reader with intimations for an understanding of the essence of King's greatness when he poses the question of whether in these times King could actually have been "a prophetic figure," somehow embodying "a divine word . . . an utterance . . . one 'octave too high,'" the "incarnation of a divine pathos?"[22]

The crucial import of Downing's questions is that the dominant tendency is to view King (and Gandhi, too)[23] in merely secular terms. It is as though King's reception of the Nobel Prize for peace at Oslo University (1964) or the legal establishment of January 15, his birthday, as a National Holiday, were the sum total of his significance as a great Black man of achievement. Indeed his undoubted charisma, too, has usually been considered largely in socio-political terms. For such persons, King is one of those "Great Men" of history (Carlyle), without *really* asking why. Fewer persons, then, seem to have taken seriously enough either the occasional yet, ultimately, significant intimations of King's *transcendent religious experience,* or, indeed, *the amazing ethico-religious consistency of his practice of the Agape ethic* in the midst of the slings and arrows of outrageous fortune throughout the Civil Rights Movement.

However, there are at least two specific moments in King's later life that are crucial to a more essential understanding of his greatness.[24] On one occasion, after a time of personal defeat and public misunderstanding, he eventually reappeared publicly and revealed himself to have a qualitatively distinctive mark of *presence* that implies a meaning that takes us back beyond the "public image" and reminds us of the religious significance of the word *charisma.* The incident took place at a press interview during which King was said by both his beloved wife, Coretta, and friends to have been *more than the leader that they had known theretofore.* Ralph Abernathy said, "I saw a quality in Martin I hadn't seen before—a kind of lion quality." Subsequently asked by a newsman, aware of King's depressing experience with a press interview the night before, as to how it was that he seemed so different and to whom had he been talking, King merely said, "No, I haven't talked with anyone. I have only talked with God."[25]

These apparently simple remarks both by King and others (who were, privately, *quite familiar* with him) intimate that one should hesitate to evaluate the dynamism and magnetism of such a personality with more emphasis upon the traumas of transition inherent in the psychological-maturation process, or upon the often valid claim that human beings are sometimes made "great" or "greater" by the power of momentous historical events. For when one considers how long and difficult it is for human beings to rise to para-neurotic states of equanimity *and* magnanimity of the kind and quality shown by King, the psycho-sociogenetic and even the delimiting dogmas of human spiritual potential of diverse traditional theologies may not do his overall personality interpretive justice. It must be emphasized, however, that King was *not* in a transcendent state of consciousness at all times.

The key, therefore, to the essential greatness of King lies in a divine-human dialectic unusually experienced and dramatically symbolized by two of his most renowned public testimonies. For he said both "I have a dream" *and* "I've been to the mountaintop"![26] The ordinary (exoteric) and the extraordinary (esoteric), the mundane and the transcendent dimensions of the religious Reality are, respectively, given in the foregoing proclamations by King. Moreover, it is the endurance and the *prevalence* of an extraordinary spiritual Presence in him, vividly symbolized by King's "mountaintop experience" (-an encounter with the Holy and Divine Providence) which underlay, permeated, and encompassed his "Dream" of social reform. Paradoxically, while the exoteric "Dream" symbolizes the hunger-for-concretion of an ethical ideal yet pointing to a limited sphere of sociopolitical transformation (-"civil rights"), the same "Dream" had its source and gathered its momentum in King and through King's possession of a higher level of spiritual consciousness (cf. Downing's/Heschel's "one octave too high"), a consciousness far surpassing even the level of consciousness manifested by millions of run-of-the-mill "Christians" whose love does not usually excel all other loves, such as the love of race, class, political party, or religious denomination.

This conclusion is thus an *affirmation* of the statements that Downing preferred to present in *interrogative* form. Yet the present perspective is intended to acknowledge, even more, to break out of the molds of the psychology of religion (though they, undoubtedly, help us to gain a more complete picture of him). For within such molds there is no real accounting for the reality of the Gandhis and the Kings of history. And just how many Kings (and Gandhis) have we detected in human history? King's life, notwithstanding the ambiguities in his personal life and in his tactical nonviolent resistance, has implications for the entire human species; that is, if he could by the magnificent manifestation of a love-ethic (*agape*) rise so far above the threshold that separates bogging animality from liberating spirituality, then, perhaps, the other members of our species really do stand a chance of rising toward that same level of spiritual consciousness, or Universal Love.

Still there are in every civilization individuals who, tragically, measure the greatness of human beings in terms of black/white (or dualistic) criteria whether racial, religious, or other. Such persons are also prone to measure *spiritual* greatness with the same inflexible criteria of conformity; so that human imperfection *per se* is uncritically equated with "sinfulness." And the prospect of *degrees* of spiritual transformation and/or perfection is lost to the temptation to look for violations of social mores or taboos in order to embarrass, defame, and to defeat even a soul whose greatness is yet "in the making." For *greatness and fallibility are never mutually exclusive in human beings.*

This characterization of King is not, therefore, made in ignorance of the controversial distinction between King-the-Man and King-the-Myth. It is, rather, an attempt to affirm the ever-mysterious fusion of these two aspects of him. With due respect to the positive contributions to our understanding of *myth* by such existentialist thinkers as Jean Paul Sartre, Albert Camus, and others, there is a blind spot in all humanistic interpretations of King. Humanistic scholars are not necessarily, however, derogatory in their attitudes. But under the influence of such notions as "euhemerism" and "apotheosis," they are often unreceptive to what the mythical dimension itself may symbolize about the being and character of such an extraordinary man as King was. In his case, there are serious grounds—already indicated—to consider that what many commentators see as merely mythical magnification, is really a Cosmic Presence in King, a veritable transhuman force, transcending the typical denominational religious consciousness as well as the categories of humanistic theories of mind. This does not mean that the latter are not integral to a holistic outlook regarding the interpretation of King's life. It is, nonetheless, true that King represents a rather rare instance in human evolution of the "historicization of myth" (-myth *becoming* historical reality) more than the "mythicization of history." In the former case it is the universal claim of all Christian churches (in a rewording) that in Jesus of Nazareth we have the largest and longest glimpse of the Greatest Reality of the Universe, no matter What (Who) It Is. It is time, then, to understand King within such a perspective, for it goes to the heart of his own living testimony and further grounds him in the history of religious experience, though in a highly distinctive way.

It should not surprise us therefore, that Wyatt Walker could candidly remark of King, "I'm not a mystic. But I am absolutely convinced that God is doing something with Martin Luther King that He is not doing with anyone else in this country."[27] And Lerone Bennett, Jr. (*What Manner of Man*, 1964) could say, "There is in King a deep strain of mysticism ... He gives the impression of a man driven by some overpowering force." Kelly Miller Smith's designation of King as "a martyred prophet of God who was killed for doing what prophets do"[28] cuts closest to the core of the meaning of the "force" in King. In a more philosophical-religious perspective, then, King's "Larger Consciousness" gives humankind a greater than usual glimpse of the Mystery of, in, and behind Jesus of Nazareth. It is not incidental that Eric Erikson, himself, speaking of Gandhi as *homo-religiosus* re-sensed "the affinity of that Galilean and the skinny Indian leader enshrined in Delhi. There is a word for what they seem to have had in common: *presence*—as pervasive a presence as only a silence has when you listen."[29] In the light of King, one need not fear any hermeneutical indiscretion in positing a Palestinian-Indian-American continuum of Spirit in Jesus, Gandhi, and King. One would do well to ponder, at any rate, what America and the world will do about War and Peace—and Love—in view of this very recent reconfirmation of a Caring Presence in the universe.

Notwithstanding this interpretation of King, James Melvin Washington (*A Testament of Hope*) is right to call our attention to the fact that there is a tendency in King biographies to overlook the "spirituality" of the civil rights movement, especially the indispensable role that the Black Church played in King's own life and as a bed-rock for the movements' religious hope and strength. Historian of religions, Charles H. Long, adds that "The fact that black churches have been the locus of the civil rights struggle is not incidental ... The location of this struggle in the church enabled the civil rights movement to take on the resources of black cultural life *in the form of organization, music, and artistic expression, and in the gathering of limited economic resources.*"[30] King, himself, could affirm this truth by saying, "I am grateful to God that, through the influence of the Negro church, the way of nonviolence became an integral part of our struggle.[31]

In an historical-theological sense, therefore, these affirmations confirm the spiritual continuity of the civil rights movement with the original ethical monotheism and communalism envisioned by both the Founder of Christianity and the earliest Christian Church. To the extent that one accepts the inevitable, and indeed, the desirable, transformations that history thrusts upon any great vision of Reality or sociology of Humankind, one can also recognize that the *new shape of Agape* as itself a transformative sociopolitical agent heralds only a metamorphosis of method and not a metamorphosis of meaning. Thus, Paul Tillich, whose theological-ethical perspective King thoroughly understood, asserted that "Love [-Agape] alone can transform itself according to the concrete demands of every individual and social situation without losing its eternity and dignity and unconditional validity. Love can adapt itself to every phase of a changing world."[32]

From Montgomery to Memphis the unconditional validity of *Agape* was manifested in the life of Martin Luther King, Jr., in the hearts of countless "congregations" of demonstrators, and through the hands of numerous contributors to the economic viability of the Civil Rights Movement. Moreover, the earlier mentioned continuity between the Movement and the vision of the Primitive Church invites our reflection upon another significant aspect of the Palestinian-Indian-American continuum. It is the fact that there is also a vital link between the "Dream" of King and the hope for America which the Dreamer had in his heart. For, despite the terrors of American history, the effects of which, for many Blacks, are still not past healing, it is to the very best that is in the deepest heart of America that he sought to appeal. To that extent, although he lived a vision that is rooted in Eternity and yet seeking more fully to break into time, King's contribution to America has been so great that America's fulfillment of its own national greatness depends much on how it responds to this great Black leader. As Coretta Scott King has put the matter,

> "By reaching into and beyond ourselves and tapping the transcendent ethic of love, we shall overcome these evils ['poverty, racism, and war']. Love, truth, and the courage to do what is right should be our own guideposts on this lifelong journey."[33]

Notes

1. Of course, these personages reflected varying degrees and types of militancy. They are listed all together here because of their common strides toward freedom for all Blacks in an ethically contrdictory civilization. For further general reading, see Henry J. Young, *Major Black Religious Leaders, 1755-1940*, Nashville: Abingdon, 1977; *Major Black Religious Leaders Since 1940*, Nashville: Abingdon, 1979; G. S. Wilmore and J. H. Cone ed., *Black Theology: A Documentary History*, New York: Orbis Books, 1979.

2. Albert Knudson, *The Doctrine of God*, New York: Abingdon-Cokesbury Press, 1930, p. 1.

3. Cf. K. L. Smith and I. G. Zepp, Jr., *Search for the Beloved Community: The Thinking of Martin Luther King, Jr.*, Judson Press, 1974.

4. *The Trumpet of Conscience*. New York: Harper and Row, Publishers, 1967, p. 73.

5. James Melvin Washington, ed., *A Testament of Hope: The Essential Writings of Martin Luther King, Jr.*, San Francisco: Harper and Row, Publishers, 1986, p. 38.

6. Cf. *Stride Toward Freedom*, New York: Harper and Row, 1958, pp. 66-71.

7. Cf. Washington, *op. cit.*, p. 17.

8. Cf. *Stride Toward Freedom*, pp. 102ff., 189-224.

9. Cf. Stephen B. Oates, *Let the Trumpet Sound: The Life of Martin Luther King, Jr.*, New York: Harper and Row, Publishers, 1982, pp. 400-405.

10. Washington, *op. cit.*, p. 39.

11. *Where Do We Go From Here: Chaos or Community?*, New York: Harper and Row, Publishers, 1967, p. 54f.

12. David J. Garrow, *The FBI and Martin Luther King, Jr., From "Solo" to Memphis*, New York, W. W. Norton and Company, 1981, p. 214.

13. Washington, *op. cit.*, p. 33.

14. *Ibid.*, p. 14.

15. Oates, *op. cit.*, pp. 402, 415-416.

16. Washington, *op. cit.*, pp. 32, 38.

17. See Washington, *op. cit.*, p. xxii; Garrow, *op. cit.*, esp. Chapter 3; Oates, *op. cit.*, pp. 312-318, esp. 332-334; cf. Frederick L. Downing, *To See the Promised Land: The Faith Pilgrimage of Martin Luther King, Jr.*, Mercer University Press, 1986, Chapter 11.

18. Oates, *op. cit.*, p. 431.

19. See the account in Oates, *op. cit.*, pp. 487-493.

20. *Ibid.*, p. 486.

21. Cf. Downing, *op. cit.*, pp. 283f; 287-293.

22. *Ibid.*, p. 286.

23. See J. Lelyveld, "In the Mahatma's Centenary Year—India Finds Gandhi Inspiring and Irrevelant," *The New York Times Magazine* (May 25, 1969); cf. D. M. Datta, *The Philosophy of Mahatma Gandhi*, 1953, pp. 24, 36-37.

24. Portions of the following narrative appear in my article, "The Nature and Meaning of Modern Religious Experience." *World Faiths Insight*, New Series 6 (Jan., 1983), pp. 16, 17-19.

25. Coretta Scott King, *My Life With Martin Luther King, Jr.*, New York: Holt, Rinehart and Winston, 1969, p. 311.

26. Cf. Washington, *op. cit.*, pp. 217-220; 279-286.

27. Oates, *op. cit.*, p. 436.

28. Downing, *op. cit.*, p. 9. One has merely to read King's "Letter From Birmingham Jail," (*Why We Can't Wait*, New York: Harper and Row, Publishers, 1964, Chapter 5) to understand in part the truth of Smith's remark. The present writer believes that the "Letter" ought to be added to the Christian canon.

29. Eric H. Erikson, *Gandhi's Truth*, New York, Norton, 1969, p. 20 (italics added).

30. Charles H. Long, *Significations: Signs, Symbols, and Images in the Interpretation of Religion*, Philadelphia: Fortress Press, 1986, pp. 152, 153 (italics added).

31. Washington, *op. cit.*, p. xiii.

32. Paul Tillich, *The Protestant Era*, Chicago: University of Chicago Press, 1963, pp. 154-155.

33. Coretta Scott King, *The Words of Martin Luther King, Jr.*, New York: Newmarket Press, 1983.

MALCOLM X—FROM DETROIT RED TO MECCA: THE EVOLUTION OF A BLACK LEADER'S VISION FROM SEPARATION TO THIRD WORLD LIBERATION

By Clifton E. Marsh

Malcolm X Shabazz was the most charismatic leader of his era. The era of Civil Rights and Black power endured over a decade and the ideologies of the various social movement organizations dramatically changed the lives of an entire generation of people. Malcolm X Shabazz's personal odyssey takes him from the socio-economic bowels of Black America as Detroit Red to the power-centers of Arab and African heads of state as Malcolm X Shabazz. He was an organizer, theoritician, a pragmatic spiritualist and a devoted family man.

Malcolm X Shabazz's organizing ability was recognized by the Honorable Elijah Muhammad, who personally wrote to him, a defiant "Satan" as Malcolm was known, while incarcerated. Malcolm's release from prison in 1952 was the catalyst for the Nation of Islam to remain at the forefront of Black radical politics in America. Malcolm helped to organize temples in Detroit and all over the East Coast. Eventually Elijah Muhammad appointed him National Spokesman of the Lost and Found Nation of Islam.

His national spokesman role enabled young Malcolm to propagate the Honorable Elijah Muhammad's theories on Yacub, nationalism and economic development. Eventually Malcolm X's travel, reading/study and analysis had him revising, updating and adding to the nationalist theories devised by his mentor the Honorable Elijah Muhammad. Just like any excellent student the mark of greatness is to refine, challenge and eventually add to the knowledge of one's teacher. Malcolm proved to be an excellent student and a great teacher. He eventually became the Dean of a Third World Internationalist School of Thought that incorporated and extended the ideas of Garvey, Blyden, Noble Drew Ali and the Honorable Elijah Muhammad himself.

Eventually a world-traveled Malcolm X began to stop introducing each idea with "the Honorable Elijah Muhammad teaches us." Malcolm broke the ideological tie that bound him to the will of Elijah Muhammad and the policies of the nation of Islam. Malcolm began to address the needs of Blacks outside the "Lost Found Nation." He began to discuss the Vietnam War, apartheid and the struggles of oppressed peoples all over the world.

Malcolm X addressing the Militant Labor Forum, New York City, May 29, 1964. Photo by Robert Parent.

Malcolm X Shabazz's spiritual pragmatism was fueled by the unorthodox ideas of his mentor, the Honorable Elijah Muhammad. For Elijah Muhammad knew that hungry people cannot digest radical ideas. A powerless people who have no African dignity or self esteem cannot know themselves and therefore will not know Allah or God. The worldly Malcolm X Shabazz knew that Muslims in America must unite with the world community and the Yacub-inspired nationalism of Elijah Muhammad was too restrictive to encompass a world Islamic Community.

Finally there is Malcolm the man, the husband, the father and provider. Malcolm X is often ridiculed, scorned and rebuked for the fierce political public persona he was forced to display. For those who berate the 50% female-headed households and irresponsible men who turn their backs on family, their children and women, Malcolm was the ultimate role model. Malcolm was a loving, sensual and "sweet" husband to his wife Betty. Betty often boasted how Malcolm wrote her love poems, sent her flowers "just because" and called her long distance while on speaking engagements to say, "I love you."

Malcolm had six daughters and he was a caring, understanding, loving, teaching parent for his girls. Malcolm never "complained" that he just had girls, nor did he engage in any sexist fantasies about more boy children.

Malcolm or any man was paid the supreme compliment by his wife Betty, "I haven't had a romantic experience like that since, but I'm delighted that I had it once."

Malcolm X Shabazz's personal odyssey from inmate to world figure and loving family man is a journey too wide, too deep and too uncertain for most of us to travel. It represents a personal and social struggle to redefine American/World politics and redefine what it means to be male and human. For those of us who were fortunate to observe Malcolm's struggle we are in awe of his endurance, will to win, love for his family/people, and absolute passion for life and loving. What more could you ask of a revolutionary?

Malcolm Little was born May 19, 1925, in Omaha, Nebraska. His father, the Reverend Earl Little, was tall (six feet four inches) and "very very dark." Malcolm's mother, Louise, was born in Grenada, which was then a British colony in the Caribbean. The Little family consisted of eight children. Earl supported them as a free-lance Baptist minister. He also was an organizer of Marcus Garvey's Universal Negro Improvement Association. Young Malcolm often accompanied his father to UNIA meetings and was impressed as the Garveyites exclaimed, "Africa for Africans and Ethiopia Awake." Reverend Little raised the ire of the local white community because of his attempts to organize black people in Omaha. Their home was burned to the ground one evening by the Klu Klux Klan while he was away.

Shortly after Malcolm's birth, the Littles moved to Milwaukee and even-

tually to Lansing, Michigan. When Malcolm was six years old his father was murdered, "Laid across some tracks for a street car to run over him." Louise Little raised her eight children during the Depression. Eventually, the strain of poverty and the dehumanizing welfare system rendered Mrs. Little helpless. She suffered a nervous breakdown. Mrs. Little remained in the hospital for twenty six years. The children were supported in state institutions, boarding homes, or lived with relatives.

During his elementary school years, Malcolm Little was an exceptional student. He was the only black person in his class at Mason Junior High School and was elected class president in the seventh grade. Malcolm participated in basketball and, urged on by the success of his brother Philbert, boxed as a bantamweight. Malcolm's height and rawboned frame enabled him to deceive the officials into believing he was 16 years old—even though he was just 13 at that time. His boxing career ended when he was knocked out twice by the "same white boy."

During a Careers Day at Mason Junior High, Malcolm was reprimanded by his counselor for aspiring to become a lawyer. The school counselor suggested carpentry as a realistic occupation for a "nigger."

From that moment on, Malcolm became alienated from school, Lansing, and white America. He began corresponding with his older sister Ella in Boston, requesting to live with her. Ella gained official custody of Malcolm, transferring him from Michigan to Massachusetts.

The move from Lansing to Boston was the beginning of Malcolm's street education which catapulted him into a life of crime. Between the ages of 15 and 21, Malcolm spent his life in the ghettos of Boston and Harlem engaged in part-time "legal" employment—drugs, gambling, and hustling.

Malcolm's first job was shining shoes in the Roseland State Ballroom where he unscuffed the toes of great musicians like Duke Ellington, Count Basie, Lionel Hampton, and Lester Young. While employed at Roseland, Malcolm began to smoke marijuana, play numbers, wear zoot suits, "conk" his red hair, and dance a frantic Lindy Hop. Malcolm left Roseland and was employed by the railroad as the fourth cook on the Yankee Clipper train, which traveled between Boston and New York City. Malcolm's first visit to Harlem narcotized him.

In 1942, at the age of 17, he quit his railroad job and became a waiter in Small's Paradise Bar. Malcolm was eventually fired and barred from Small's for procuring a prostitute for a serviceman while in the restaurant. When Malcolm was dismissed from Small's he turned to crime for full-time employment and acquired the name "Detroit Red." Initially he sold reefers (marijuana cigarettes), but within six months Malcolm began to engage in armed robbery. Armed with a .32, .38 or .45 pistol and snorting cocaine for courage, "Detroit Red" prowled the streets looking for victims.

Prison and the Conversion of Malcolm X

Malcolm was almost 21 before he was arrested and sentenced for a term of up to ten years on a burglary charge..In February of 1946 Malcolm Little was sent to Charlestown State Prison and in 1948 he was transferred to the Norfolk Prison Colony. He served a total of six years in prison.

Malcolm Little underwent a religious conversion in prison, with encouraging words from his family to "face east and pray to Allah." Malcolm began to investigate the Nation of Islam and correspond with Elijah Muhammad. Malcolm spent most of his time studying, researching, and developing his penmanship. He took correspondence courses in English and Latin and developed his vocabulary by memorizing a dictionary. Malcolm developed his political consciousness by reading volumes of African and African-American history and Oriental philosophy. He eventually led prison debates and discussion groups which enhanced his public speaking.

Malcolm Little was released on parole at the age of 27 after six years in prison. When he was released in August of 1952, he was a "Black Muslim," although he had not acquired his X. By writing Elijah Muhammad weekly and being counseled by his brothers, Wilfred and Philbert, "Detroit Red" became a devoted follower of Elijah Muhammad.

Minister Malcolm X

Malcolm moved to Detroit after his parole to live with his brother Wilfred. There he received his X in temple #1, the original temple organized by Wali Fard Muhammad. The Detroit Temple was located in a storefront at 1470 Frederick Street.

It was the practice each month for the Detroit Temple to motorcade caravan-style to Chicago to hear sermons by Elijah Muhammad. The Sunday before Labor Day in 1952, a two-car caravan transported Malcolm X and several ministers to Chicago. During this period Malcolm was employed by the Garwood Furniture Company and later as an assembler with the Ford Motor Company. Every evening after work Malcolm walked the ghetto looking for new recruits in bars, pool rooms, and on street corners.

Malcolm's aggressive tactics tripled the membership and in a few months he lead a caravan of twenty-five automobiles to Chicago to hear Elijah Muhammad speak. Needless to say, Elijah Muhammad was very pleased by the increased membership generated by the converted ex-convict, Malcolm X. During the summer of 1953, Malcolm X was appointed Assistant Minister of Temple #1 and became a full-time minister for the Nation of Islam.

Malcolm X began to serve as Elijah Muhammad's Prime Minister throughout the United States, going from city to city preaching, recruiting, and establishing new Temples. In the 1950's there was a period of expansion which produced most of the one hundred Temples in the United States. From

Detroit, Malcolm X was sent to Boston to organize Temple #11. In March 1954 Malcolm moved from Boston to Philadelphia and in three months Temple #12 was opened in the City of Brotherly Love. From Philadelphia, Malcolm X moved to New York City and became minister of Temple #7.

Malcolm X returned to New York, where a few short years before his colleagues had been West Indian Archie, Sammy the Pimp, and Cadillac Drake. Clean-shaven and walking tall in suit and tall, his former friends in crime exclaimed in disbelief, "Red my man! This can't be you!"

From the storefront of Temple #7 Malcolm roamed the boroughs of New York recruiting on street corners, in Christian churches, and in other nationalist groups. On weekdays he traveled by bus and train to preach in other parts of the country. Many times he preached in private homes until the membership became large enough to rent a Temple.

In 1955 Malcolm organized Temple #15 in Atlanta, Georgia. To reward and assist the young minister, the Nation of Islam supplied him with a new 1956 Chevrolet. Malcolm X put 30,000 miles on the automobile in five months. In 1957 Elijah Muhammad sent Malcolm X West where he organized the Los Angeles Temple. By 1957 the Nation of Islam began to attract educated people with skills. A more remarkable metamorphosis appeared among the ministers of the Nation of Islam.

Imam Wallace D. Muhammad explained how Malcolm persuaded the youth to follow Elijah Muhammad: "Malcolm's new thinking, courage and youth attracted most of the young people into following the Honorable Elijah Muhammad and I was one of them."[1]

Through Malcolm's training and recruitment of top ministers, he was indirectly shaping the destiny of the organization.

During this period, Elijah Muhammad's very ambitious three-year economic plan began to bear fruit. Numerous small-business service enterprises began to emerge under the aegis of the Nation of Islam. Bakeries, restaurants, dress shops, barbershops, grocery stores and cleaning establishments. The businesses derived most of their income from members of the organization and from residents of the black community patronizing the Muslim enterprises.

Malcolm X, Devoted Husband and Father

On January 14, 1958, Malcolm X married Sister Betty X, a tall brown-skinned beauty and former student at Tuskegee Institute in Alabama. Betty and Malcolm's marriage was the beginning of a beautiful love affair and the caring for 6 daughters.

The personal side of Malcolm the man is always neglected and ignored. Malcolm X was a non-smoking, non-drinking, non-drug consuming, non-sexist husband and a great role model for his 6 girls.

He had the ability to communicate to thousands on stage and communicate

in an intimate setting in his home. His wife Betty Shabazz says, "he was open to me and confided in me. Intimacy and communication between husband and wife were very important to him and he thought if people weren't ready for that, they shouldn't get married."[2] Malcolm encouraged Betty to pursue her career and express her own ideas.

Betty remembers a cultured, refined Malcolm who was well read and a lover of music. Malcolm often took Betty to concerts to hear Max Roach, Abbey Lincoln, Aminata Maseka and Duke Ellington. Malcolm also took Betty to operas: La Traviata and La Boheme were just two they enjoyed together.

Can you imagine Betty holding hands with her man, Malcolm X, at a Miles Davis Concert? Can you imagine Malcolm X taking moon light walks or gazing at the stars as lovers often do? Can you imagine Malcolm X writing love poems to his first lady? Well imagine it, because he was a sensitive poet. Betty remembers, "Malcolm was a poet, he expressed himself well verbally, and he often read to me. Sometimes it was a poem he'd written down. Oftentimes he'd give a verse off the top of his head to suit the particular occasion."[3] When Malcolm was away from his family on one of his frequent speaking engagements he often called Betty 3 or 4 times a week and sometimes twice a day.

Malcolm was a lover in the purest sense. He knew that relationships glow under the sunshine of love and perish when neglected. Malcolm thought everyday was Valentine's day, Betty recalls, "he said that loving was a whole year's activity, that it was 24 hours a day, seven days a week. I received gifts from him throughout the year, not just on birthdays and anniversaries. He gave me books, good jewelry, trips that we could take together, or that I could go on alone if I wanted to. Whenever he went away, he invariably brought back a personal gift for me, something that clearly said, "I love you."[4]

Malcolm X, National Spokesman

In 1959, the media played an important role in providing the Nation of Islam and Malcolm X with national and international recognition. Newsman Mike Wallace, with the help of a black writer, Louis Loma, persuaded the Nation of Islam to participate in a television documentary entitled, "The Hate that Hate Produced," which brought the organization into homes of millions of television viewers. Also, Malcolm began to speak before a wider audience by appearing on college campuses, and radio and television talk shows. The organization received coverage in *Life, Look, Newsweek, Time* and *Reader's Digest*.

Because Elijah Muhammad was confined to Phoenix, Arizona, in 1959 for his bronchial condition, he was unable to regulate the decision-making and administrative duties of the Nation of Islam. He carried on the work through his family members and loyal ministers and eventually appointed Malcolm X

National Spokesman. Elijah gave Malcolm the opportunity to make his own decisions in governing the affairs of the Nation of Islam. Malcolm stated, "He said that my guideline should be whatever I felt was wise—whatever was in the general good interest of our Nation of Islam."[5]

Malcolm was still a devoted and obedient follower of Elijah Muhammad, echoing his doctrine wherever he spoke. Beginning each response with 'The Honorable Elijah Muhammad teaches us,' he would espouse the virtues of separation for the black man in America as the only solution.

Malcolm X believed that the American economic and political system was unequal and unjust and that to integrate into such a system would do nothing for the masses of poor and working class blacks. Only through separation (not segregation, which results in white control of the black community) would true equality be created.

Malcolm also felt that Christianity assisted in the subordination of blacks and insisted "Christianity is the white man's religion." The Bible in ". . . white man's hands and his interpretations of it, have been the greatest single ideological weapon for enslaving millions of non-white human beings."[6]

On matters of race, Malcolm still parroted the doctrine initiated by Wali Fard and carried on by Elijah Muhammad. Malcolm still believed that "Our enemy is the white man!" and he equated the "enemy" with the devil. "Oh yes, that devil is our enemy," he would preach. Late in 1959, however, he broadened the concept from a classification based purely on race and color to one based on actions and behavior. Malcolm explained, "We are not speaking of any individual white man. We are speaking of the collective white man's historical record. The white man's collective cruelties, evils and deeds, that have seen him act like a devil toward the non-white man."[7]

Malcolm: Prince of the Black Revolution

Entering the 1960's the stage was set for Malcolm to emerge from the shadow of Elijah Muhammad and become an international leader. The rise of black nationalism in the 1960's in the United States came during the escalation of the Vietnam War and liberation struggles in Colonial Africa. The nationalist leaders perceived the African-American struggle as part of the world struggle against colonialism, racism, and capitalist expansionism. The Nation of Islam was one of the oldest and most powerful black nationalist organizations in the United States. Malcolm X became the "Prince of the Black Revolution."

With the mood of nationalism sweeping Black America, Malcolm felt the Nation of Islam should be active in leading a frontline struggle. Elijah Muhammad advocated that Muslims should not become involved in the "white man's politics" and insisted that members invest their time on self-improvement. Malcolm perceived the self-improvement position as making

the Nation of Islam a separate, closed community within the black community.

Wallace D. Muhammad, Heir to the Throne

In April 1960 Elijah Muhammad's son Wallace was sentenced to prison for three years for failure to report for hospital work as a conscientious objector. For the next three years, Elijah Muhammad spent over $20,000 in legal fees appealing the decision. On November 4, 1961, Wallace entered prison. Even before he entered prison Wallace had doubts about his father's version of Islam. Wallace also questioned his father's interpretation of Wali Fard as Allah. Wallace had seen many of Fard's writings in which he referred to himself as the messenger of Allah.

The same year that Wallace went to prison, Malcolm began to encounter jealousy and hostility within the hierarchy of the Nation of Islam. Rumors were spread that "Malcolm is trying to take over the Nation." He was accused of taking credit for Elijah Muhammad's teaching and building a financial empire.

By 1962, Malcolm noticed he appeared less and less in the organization's newspaper, *Muhammad Speaks*. Eventually, he received no coverage at all in *Muhammad Speaks*. In addition, the Chicago headquarters began to discourage him from holding rallies and public speaking engagements.

In January 10, 1963, Wallace D. Muhammad was paroled from Sandstone Correctional Institution. While in prison, Wallace meditated, discussed and wrote about Islam, and made comparisons with his father's version of the religion. Wallace consulted several relatives and organization members (including Malcolm X) to clarify his doubts about his father's teachings. Wallace regularly attended Nation of Islam functions and taught classes at the University of Islam. Wallace stirred up much controversy concerning his father's activities both nationally and in Chicago.

When it appeared Malcolm was becoming more powerful and influential than Elijah Muhammad, the leadership in Chicago began to sever Malcolm's powers within the organization. Malcolm was being forced out of the leadership circle and eventually the organization. Malcolm was aggressive, eager, and articulate and was often moving faster than Elijah Muhammad wished, as well as moving in political directions that Elijah Muhammad did not approve. Malcolm was gaining more and more prominence within the organization. Domestically and abroad, he became better known than any black leader in the United States, including Elijah Muhammad.

Malcolm X's ideological growth began to ripen by 1963. He started to question more and more the Nation of Islam's doctrine, political activities (or lack of them), and religious beliefs. Malcolm began to detour from Elijah Muhammad's doctrine and addressed social and economic issues oppressing black people domestically and internationally. He began to speak out against the United States government for its involvement in the Vietnam War and the lack of commitment toward solving domestic problems.

Silenced, No Mosque Duties

On November 22, 1963, President John F. Kennedy was assassinated. After-wards, Elijah Muhammad issued a directive to all Muslim ministers to refrain from commenting on his death. In a speaking engagement in New York's Manhattan Center during a question and answer period, Malcolm X was asked his opinion of the assassination. He replied, "I saw it as a case of chickens coming home to roost."

Malcolm X was silenced for ninety days by Elijah Muhammad for making these remarks. For a month after the silencing many conferences were held between Malcolm, Elijah Muhammad, and national leaders. The differences between Malcolm and the Nation of Islam became more pronounced. Elijah Muhammad removed Malcolm as a minister of Temple #7 in New York in January 1964. The same month, Muhammad excommunicated his son Wallace for working closely with Malcolm. Wallace explained the excommunication, "I was charged with trying to influence Malcolm's theological thinking and with giving him personal private knowledge of the Honorable Elijah Muhammad's living."[9] Wallace protested the excommunication to no avail. He wanted to face his accusers, but Muhammad declared, "Malcolm X is not facing his accusers either."

Cassius Clay

The following month, a young Louisville heavyweight was training in Miami, Florida, to fight Sonny Liston for the Heavyweight Championship of the World. The young challenger, Cassius Clay, invited Malcolm X and his family to his training camp to honor Malcolm and Betty on their sixth wedding anniversary. Malcolm had known Cassius as early as 1962 when Cassius and his brother Rudolph came to Detroit to hear Elijah Muhammad speak. They consequently became close friends.

Young Clay won a gold medal in the 1960 Rome Olympics. When he returned home to Kentucky, he and his friend Ronnie King were refused service in a restaurant because they were black. After leaving the restaurant, Clay and King were attacked by a white motorcycle gang, which Clay and King fought off. Discouraged and angry, Clay heaved his gold medal into the Ohio River as a silent protest. Clay became interested in the Nation of Islam shortly afterward. Cassius even spoke before a Nation of Islam rally in January 1964 while training for the Sonny Liston fight.

Prior to the fight with Sonny Liston on February 25, 1964, no one gave

Talking to reporters at Kennedy International Airport upon his return from Africa, November 24, 1964. In the background are Malcolm's wife and children. Photo by Robert Parent.

Cassius Clay a chance to fight. In Clay's dressing room Malcolm X gave Young Clay a pep talk. Then Malcolm and the young contender faced east and prayed to Allah.

Malcolm X left Cassius Clay's dressing room and took a seat among 8,000 fans at Miami's Convention Hall. The "Louisville Lip" shocked the sports world and won by a technical knockout in the seventh round. The bleeding and exhausted Sonny Liston was unable to leave his stool to answer the bell for the seventh round. After the fight, Clay announced he had joined the Nation of Islam.

Soon after the fight, newspapers carried pictures with Malcolm X introducing Cassius Clay to numerous African diplomats in the United Nations. Malcolm and Clay rode through Harlem and other parts of the country with Malcolm as the champion's friend and religious advisor. On March 6, 1964, Elijah Muhammad bestowed on Clay the name Muhammad Ali. Malcolm predicted that Muhammad Ali would "develop into a major world figure."

The Organization of Afro American Unity

On March 8, 1964 Malcolm announced he was leaving the Nation of Islam to establish his own organization based upon Orthodox Islamic principles called the Muslim Mosque Inc. with an associate political body, the Organization of Afro-American Unity. Malcolm's organization consisted of approximately 50 former Nation of Islam members. The headquarters for his organization was the Hotel Theresa on 125th Street and Seventh Avenue in Harlem. The organization of Afro-American unity was "a non-religious and non-sectarian group organized to unite Afro-Americans for a constructive program toward the attainment of human rights."[10] Malcolm was willing to work with white people and requested their financial support. He urged whites to confront racism in their own communities to create a brotherhood of all races. However, Malcolm did not permit whites to join the OAAU. He was convinced there could be no black and white coalitions before black solidarity was achieved. Ultimately, black and white organizations would have solidarity, but only after African Americans had been organized.

Malcolm X, in Mecca and the Hajj

In April 1964, Malcolm X made the pilgrimage, known as the Hajj, to the Holy City of Mecca. During his pilgrimage, Malcolm began to alter his perspective on the Nation of Islam's doctrine and Islam practiced by Muslims throughout the world. Malcolm was embarrassed because, as a Muslim minister, he did not know the prayer ritual, nor did he practice the "Pillars of Islam" and other Islamic principles. He was impressed with the spirit of brotherhood, lack of color-consciousness and non-racist attitudes among Muslims. He met with Islamic scholars and read volumes of literature on religion.

The following month, Malcolm X went on an 18-week trip through Africa and had private audiences with several African Heads of State. In Egypt Malcolm was the guest of King Faisal and also talked to Tamal Abdel Nasser of Egypt, President Julius K. Nyerere of Tanzania, President Nnamai Asikiwe of Nigeria, Dr. Kwame Nkrumah of Ghana and the President of Uganda. Malcolm's travels convinced him that Islam, as taught by Elijah Muhammad, was out of synch with 800 million Muslims worldwide. The Hajj resulted in his conversion to Orthodox Islam.

El Hajj Malik El-Shabazz

Malcolm changed his name to El Hajj Malik El-Shabazz after he accepted Orthodox Islam.

Betty Shabazz, Malcolm X's wife, described her husband's change, "He went to Mecca as a Black Muslim and there he became only a Muslim. He felt all men were human beings; we must judge a man on his deeds."[11] Malcolm Shabazz felt the Muslim world's religious community and the societies built upon Islamic principles had eliminated racism. He began to separate whiteness as a color from attitudes and actions. Malcolm truly believed color and race were irrelevant in the Muslim world.

Malcolm Shabazz' changed attitude toward white people was based upon his international travels and observing other social systems and economic means of production. By virtue of his observations he believed that capitalism and racism are related be reinforcing racial inequality for private gain. It was not white people per se who were inherently evil, but the United States' political, economic, and social system which was demonic. Malcolm said, "most countries that were colonial powers were capitalist countries," and the last bulwark of capitalism today is America. It's impossible for a white person to believe in capitalism without racism."[12] In Ghana, Malcolm talked to Dr. Kwame Nkrumah about Pan-Africanism. Malcolm wanted to internationalize the plight of African-Americans. He was convinced of the inherent limitations of moral pressure and an "Americanized" struggle. Perceiving the race question as a domestic problem, leaders were limited to resolutions within the confines of the United States, where blacks sought support from the same officials, organizations, and institutions that were oppressing them. Malcolm linked the African-American struggle with cultural and philosophical ties in Africa. Malcolm explained his Pan-African perspective as follows. "The positive image that is developing of Africans is also developing in the minds of Black Americans. Consequently they develop a more positive image of themselves. So you can't separate the African revolution from the mood of the Black man in America."[13]

Malcolm perceived the plight of the Africa American as similar to that of blacks in South Africa. The crosscultural likeness of oppression qualified the United States' "race problem" as a denial of human rights and not merely a civil rights violation. Malcolm Shabazz wanted to present the cause of African Americans before the United Nations.

> One of the first steps we are going to become involved in as an organization of Afro-American Unity will be to bring the negro problem before the United Nations. We feel that the problem of the black man in this country is beyond the ability of Uncle Sam to solve. We must internationalize the problem and take advantage of the United Nations Declaration of human rights, and on that ground bring it before the world body wherein we can indict Uncle Sam for the continued criminal injustices that our people experience in this government.[14]

He went purely beyond a Pan-African perspective to include the Third World. He often spoke of Latin-American "brothers" and 800 million Chinese "brothers" supporting such a United nations resolution. Minister Malcolm Shabazz did not live long enough to work toward these ideals.

The Assassination

On February 21, 1965, at 2:00 p.m., Malcolm Shabazz arrived at the Audubon Ballroom in New York City to speak to approximately 500 people. He greeted the audience with "Al-salaam alaikum" ("Peace be unto you"). "Wa-alaikum salaam" ("And unto you be peace"), answered the crowd. Then, in approximately the eighth row from the stage a fight started. "Hold it! hold it! Don't get excited," Malcolm pleaded. Three men in the front row stood and pointed guns at him and fired. The bullets hit him in the head and chest with such force that he was pushed over the chairs behind him. Sixteen gunshot pellets and revolver slugs dotted his shirt with blood. Malcolm laid on the stage, his mouth wide open and his teeth bared. His wife, Betty Shabazz, pushed her way through the crowd of people surrounding his body, fell to her knees, grabbed his chest and cried, "They killed him." He was rushed to the Vanderbilt Clinic one block away and at 3:00 p.m., Minister El-Hajj Malik El Shabazz was pronounced dead.

The autopsy performed by Dr. Milton Helper, Chief Medical Examiner, revealed that Shabazz died from shotgun wounds in the heart, inflicted by a sawed-off shotgun, and he had wounds from .45 and .38 caliber pistols. Assistant Chief Inspector Joseph Cule, in charge of Manhattan North Detectives, described the killing as a "well-planned conspiracy." Following Shabazz' assassination, three men were arrested and accused of his murder: Talmadge Hayer, age 22; Thomas 15X Johnson, age 30; and Norman 3X Butler, age 26.

The three men charged with the murder of Minister El-Hajj Malik El-Shabazz were former Muslims, which created suspicion that the Nation of Islam had him killed. Imam Wallace D. Muhammad felt the former Muslims were used: "I don't believe that the Nation of Islam planned the assassination of Malcolm X. I believe outsiders assassinated Malcolm X and members were used."[15]

Talmadge Hayer admitted he purchased the guns (12 gauge shot gun, a .45 pistol, and a Luger) "hot" from the street underworld. Hayer and his colleagues investigated the Audubon Ballroom on two occasions before the night Malcolm was killed. They attended one of Malcolm's rallies to see if they would be searched. He halted all searching of people who attended his OAAU rallies because it reminded him too much of Elijah Muhammad and the Nation of Islam. He dismissed the search by saying, "If I can't be safe with my own kind, where can I be?" Hayer attended a dance on February 20, 1965, to observe the exits for escape routes. The signal for the murder to begin was when Malcolm greeted the audience with "Al-salaam alaikum." Initially Hayer refused to say who his co-assassins were. The police, equipped with eyewitness descriptions of the assailants, arrested Johnson and Butler because they matched the descriptions. There was such circumstantial evidence as their "strong man image" in New York's Fruit of Islam. Also, both men were out on bail for attempting to kill Benjamin Brown, who had defected from the Nation of Islam and founded a rival organization in the Bronx. Neither Johnson nor Butler confessed to killing Malcolm X; Hayer is the only confessed assassin and he implicated the other two. The three men were sentenced to life in prison. They were sent to Sing Sing and later shipped upstate to Dannemora and maintained in solitary confinement. For most of the 15 years of their incarceration, they had been separated from each other—Hayer at Napanoch, Johnson at Dannemora, and Butler at Sing Sing.

In the autumn of 1977, Talmage Hayer confessed to Nuriddin Faiz, a Muslim prison chaplain, that he had lied and Butler and Johnson were innocent. Hayer named four men who were still active Muslims living in New Jersey. Faiz contacted Defense Attorney William Kunstler, who agreed to take the case for Johnson and Butler. Hayer supplied the names, addresses, detailed descriptions, and occupations of the four who, he now claimed, assisted him. Kunstler attempted to have the case reopened based upon Hayer's sworn testimony.

In 1978, Kunstler was refused a new trial by Judge Harold Rathway, who ruled Hayer's new testimony did not constitute enough evidence for another trial. The District Attorney's office of New York also resisted Attorney Kunstler's legal pleas.

Kunstler petitioned the House of Representatives in the spring of 1979 via the Congressional Black Caucus. The Black Caucus was discussing the virtues and merits of Kunstler's petitions. It was Attorney Kunstler's view that the Federal Bureau of Investigation and the New York City police played a supporting role in Malcolm's death. The FBI had Malcolm and other leaders in the Nation of Islam under surveillance for years as an "internal security risk" and also infiltrated the organization with paid informants.

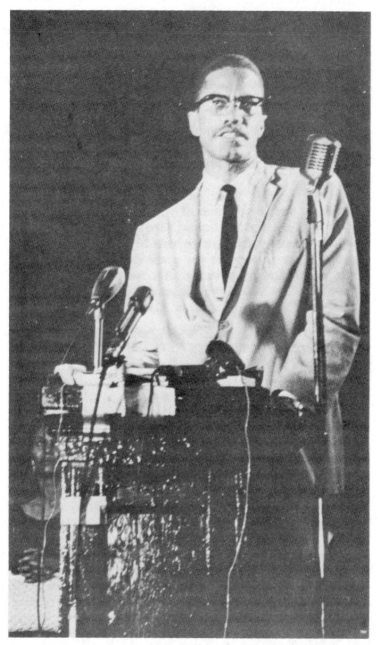

The founding meeting of the Organization of Afro-American Unity, June 28, 1964.
Photo by Robert Parent.

Hayer may have told the truth. Whoever killed Malcolm X, whether they were Muslims or agents of the state, as others have suggested, there are many riddles which remain unsolved. Why weren't there searches at the door? Had Malcolm become so unrealistic that he thought his "own kind" wouldn't attempt to kill him? Why did he refuse police protection? Why weren't the armed guards on stage? Why didn't Malcolm arm himself? How could three members of the Nation of Islam as well-known as Hayer, Johnson, and Butler were to Malcolm and his organization, slip into the room without being noticed? Many of these questions will go unanswered and we can only guess why Malcolm and his colleagues made such tragic mistakes.

There could have been inside help within Malcolm's organization to set him up which enabled the assassination to occur so smoothly. Many of the mistakes Malcolm made concerning his own personal security may relate to the drastic changes he had undergone during the year. Malcolm was fresh from the Hajj in Africa where he experienced genuine love and forgot that he may have been loved all over the world except in the United States. He had allowed himself the luxury of false consciousness concerning his security. Also, since he accepted Orthodox Islam, he might have assumed "Allah will protect me" and neglected to protect himself. It is ironic that El-Hajj Malik El-Shabazz made these fundamental errors because "Detroit Red" would have never allowed himself to be put in such a situation. Another ironic twist of Malcolm's murder is the fact that both he and his convicted assassins eventually moved away from Elijah Muhammad's doctrine and embraced Orthodox Islam. His assassins underwent a religious conversion in prison and now Talmage Hayer is called Majahid Abdul Halim, Norman Butler is Muhammad Abdul-Aziz, and Thomas 15X has changed his name to Khalil Islam.

Conclusion

We cannot say with any certainty where Malcolm was headed ideologically. His assassination brought an abrupt halt to the process of redefining his perspective. It would be foolish to predict his direction and use it to support a specific ideology. It would be just as foolish not to use his life as a lesson, his leadership as an example, and his original approach to human rights to instruct others on their own development. He made enormous contributions to Pan-Africanism, as an advocate of human rights and toward efforts to acquire equality for people of African descent living in the United States. Malcolm X Shabazz was a leading spokesman in the struggle for human rights. His influence and charisma transcended the Nation of Islam and the domicile of the United States.

By the time Malcolm X met his death via an assassin's bullet, he had become an international leader. Malcolm X Shabazz was the chief spokesman and traveling representative of Elijah Muhammad for 12 years. Malcolm's dynamic personality and articulate speaking was instrumental in recruiting, organizing temples, and providing exposure domestically and internationally for the Nation of Islam.

Malcolm adopted three names during his life; each represented an evolutionary stage in his ideological development and life-style. "Pulled from the mud" by a religious conversion in prison, Malcolm Little, or "Detroit Red," as he was known, was a pimp, racketeer, and dope pusher. After his acceptance of the Nation of Islam's doctrine, Malcolm X became a black nationalist devoted to the separatist teaching of Elijah Muhammad. When he defected from the "Black Muslims" and accepted Orthodox Islam, Malcolm then adopted the name El Hajj Malik El-Shabazz. Where he came from and what he did in his lifetime makes a remarkable biography.

Notes

1. Marsh, Clifton E., *From Black Muslims to Muslims, The Transition From Separatism to Islam*, Metuchen, New Jersey; Scarecrow Press, 1984, p. 115.

2. Betty Shabazz, Ph.D., "Remembering Malcolm X," *Essence*, February 1987, p. 61.

3. Ibid, p. 61.

4. Ibid, p. 61.

5. Malcolm X, Alex, Haley *The Autobiography of Malcolm X*, New York; Grove Press, 1964; New York; Balluture Books, 1973 p, 265.

6. Ibid, P. 241-242.

7. Ibid, p. 266.

8. Ibid, p. 313.

9. Marsh, Clifton E. *From Black Muslims to Muslims*, p. 112.

10. Malcolm X, Autobiography, p. 416.

11. Pittsburgh Courier, March 6, 1965, p. 4.

12. George Breitman, *The Last Year of Malcolm X*, New York: Pathfinder Press, 1967, p. 33.

13. Breitman, George Ed., *By Any Means Necessary*, New York: Pathfinder Press, 1972, p. 161.

14. Ibid, p. 57.

15. Marsh, Clifton, E., *From Black Muslims to Muslims*, p. 119.

THE LEGACY OF MALCOLM X

By Oba T'Shaka

To understand the political legacy of Malcolm X, one must understand that Malcolm was part of an African warrior tradition in the Americas. The fighting spirit that beat in him was the same that beat in the hero-warriors of Segu, the hearts of the Haitian rebels, the brave Maroons who founded the state of Palmares in Brazil, the guerillas of Surinam who fought back their Dutch slavemasters for more than a hundred years. This warrior tradition was based on a fearless attitude, a contempt for pain and a high moral code of honor. Although Malcolm did not lead a group of armed soldiers against the whites he set a fearless example and taught a fearless image. His message was a battle-cry to the faint-hearted, to those who had lost the will to wage the war after facing odds that seemed insuperable. Malcolm would never accept the invincibility of such odds:

> "Never let anybody tell you and me the odds are against us—I don't even want to hear that. Those who think the odds are against you, forget it. The odds are not against you. The odds are against you only when you're scared. The only things that make odds against you is a scared mind. When you get all of that fright off of you, there's no such thing as odds against you. Because when a man knows that when he starts playing with you, he's got to kill you, that man is not going to play with you . . ."[1]

Malcolm taught us to remove fear from our hearts and follow the example of our ancestors. He constantly taught us about Toussaint, Nat Turner, Denmark Vesey, and Marcus Garvey because he wanted us to model ourselves after them. Malcolm courageously called for self-defense in the early sixties when the civil rights movement was following a policy of turn-the-other-cheek. It took courage for Malcolm to speak the truth no matter what the price. This fearless dedication to the truth was his greatest strength. True to the African warrior tradition, Malcolm challenged us to 'change our attitude-patterns,' our thought-patterns and our behavior-patterns, from fearful negro ones to fearless African ones. Yes, to know Malcolm is to know the meaning of courage and Black manhood. This is the soul of Malcolm's meaning to us. He, in the way of the warriors of Surinam, was teaching the future generations the spirit of "the fighting ancestors" through living a fearless life and teaching fearless thoughts. His message taught us to stop being afraid. He called on us to think and act as men and women with a great past and a great future.

Malcolm X in Ghana. Courtesy of Alice Windom.

In 1966 I began writing a book entitled *The Political Legacy of Malcolm X*,[2] because I wanted to pass on Malcolm's legacy of warriorhood to future generations of African people, For me, as well as for many other Africans and freedom-loving people, Malcolm X, El Hajj Malik El-Shabazz, was a symbol of courage and brilliance. As a member of the Congress of Racial Equality, I was one of those young Blacks who took an uncompromising approach to the Black liberation struggle. As I became exposed to racism and began to study African and African-American history, the teachings of Malcolm X began to have special meaning to me. Malcolm had predicted that Black nationalism would rear up its head inside the civil rights movement. By his teachings he helped to transform a wing of the civil rights movement, into a movement for Black Power and Black Nationalism. I was a part of that nationalist transformation and, for me as well as many other Blacks, Malcolm was the symbol of Black Pride, Black Power, Black Creativity, and Black Manhood.

I wanted to record the legacy of a major hero of the Black liberation movement. My political philosophy was close to Malcolm's. As a Black nationalist and Pan Africanist, I saw the need to build an independent Black movement that was led, organized and financed by Black people. I also agreed with Malcolm's call for an internationalization of the Black liberation movement. While I shared and continue to share an ideological kinship with Malcolm, this and my near worship of him posed real problems when it came to writing a serious book on his political legacy. Because he was my hero, I had trouble seeing Malcolm as a great historical figure who was also human. In the beginning I found it extremely difficult to gain a balanced perspective of Malcolm, one which explored strengths and weaknesses. It was also hard for me to distinguish my beliefs from his, since my political outlook was so close to his, and I was heavily influenced by Malcolm's political thoughts.

Fortunately for me, the first draft of the *Political Legacy of Malcolm X*, complete in 1968, did not see the light of day. Every major publisher turned it down. Accordingly, over a number of years I was able to develop a political outlook of my own. I also began to stand back and look at Malcolm as a hero who could not only teach us through his brilliance but who could also teach us through his mistakes.

My second reason for writing the *Political Legacy of Malcolm X*, was that I believe that African people have the responsibility to write our historical record so that our history will be viewed through our own eyes. When our history is truthfully told, it serves as a source of wisdom and inspiration for our people. When our history is told through the eyes and words of others, the perspective changes and the historical figures or events become distorted. This is true even when the white historian has good intentions, because the white historian brings an Euro-centric view that makes it impossible for them to see history through the eyes of the African. The African historian who retains his Euro-centric perspective has the same problem.

So whether we are talking about well-intentioned or not so well intentioned whites or European-oriented Blacks, these so-called experts on Malcolm have attempted to present him in their image. It could not be otherwise, whether intended or not. The white historians could not abandon their caste position of boss. To paraphrase Malcolm X, 'when you say white in the West, you mean boss.' The white authorities on Malcolm presume to know better than we what Malcolm stood for. In their writings they seek to be the ideological bosses, telling us what Malcolm really meant, when his words speak for themselves. What is especially tragic is that too many Blacks have been conditioned to accept the white definition of Black reality as the truthful definition. Too many Blacks have accepted the white view of Malcolm as the correct one. This is certainly because psychological colonialism rests on 'seeing the world through the colonizer's eyes.' Blacks who accept the white distortions of Malcolm are only acting out their role as worshippers of white values and white skins. For them, imprisoned in self hatred and fear of white, Malcolm was a symbol to be feared. Better to accept a watered-down version of him than to have to face the awesome responsibility of African manhood and African womanhood.

The book *The Death and Life of Malcolm X*, by Peter Goldman, rests squarely on the Euro-centric viewpoint. Goldman states in his foreword that:

> "This is a white book about Malcolm X. That makes it an anomaly by the politics and aesthetics of color in our time; one ought accordingly to say it before anything else, so that those who believe a white writer incapable of dealing honestly or compassionately with a Black hero can tune out immediately. Obviously I disagree with this proposition, but a lot of Black people do believe it is so. . . ."[3]

It's interesting that Goldman has the nerve to tell us that his book on Malcolm is a "white book," even though its subject is one of the Blackest-minded men of the twentieth century. One cannot help but ask how can a "white" viewpoint, with all that such a viewpoint entails, "honestly" deal with a figure who posed such a serious psychological threat to the white west. One would think that at the very least, a white writer trying to be fair would do everything possible to overturn his Eurocentric bias and orientation. Rather than attempt to commit philosophical suicide, Goldman takes the attitude of the boss and tells us that if we accept the popular Black view that a white cannot deal honestly with a Black subject then we should "tune out." By this it would seem that he is suggesting that mainly whites, and the few Blacks who accept him on good faith, should read his book.

It's too bad that we can't take his advice. Tragically, major publishing houses such as Harper and Row have a way of getting their message over. So, inasmuch as many Blacks may agree with the proposition that whites cannot accurately and honestly portray Black history, we can test this assumption by examining Goldman's book.

Goldman interviewed many of Malcolm's associates as well as Establishment figures who interacted with Malcolm. Goldman's thesis is summarized in his own words:

> "It does not diminish him at all to say that none of these were his particular gifts for leadership—that he had no interest in fund-raising, and too little time and concentration for the hard labor of organizing or writing a program.... He was not a saint, really, neither was he a strategist or a seminal thinker or even a major leader, if one defines leadership in the narrow sense of having a large and organized following under one's proximate control. Malcolm was something more important than any of these things. He was a prophet ... Malcolm would have traded the poems and the eulogies for commitments when they counted for him—when his ministry and even his life depended on them. He didn't get them then, but that is the way with prophets, too; they live in the scriptures and their heirs."[4]

Goldman tells us that defining Malcolm as a prophet he does not diminish him. Yet it seems to be the proverbial fate of prophets to cry in the wilderness and to be heard only when the prophet reaches the promised land. To Goldman, Malcolm's legacy was that of a prophet that preached and used semantics and a reading of Black history "full of exaggerations and chauvinisms,"[5] to decolonize the Black mind. Certainly the liberation of the Black mind was at the heart of Malcolm's work. But this mission is seriously diminished by charges of historical "exaggerations and chauvinisms." Malcolm's genius as a student of history was his ability to apply history to the conditions Blacks face today. He encouraged us to study the past so we could have confidence in our ability to achieve greatness in the present and future. He showed how whites distort our past to keep our minds on the plantation by focusing mainly on slavery while ignoring the great civilization of Egypt (Kemet) Ghana, Mali and Songhay.

To a white writer, who glories in his white orientation, this would appear chauvinistic because it challenged the Euro-centric historical view. Of course Goldman found no contradiction between his white orientation which he views as being honest and sympathetic and Malcolm's Afro-centric perspective, which Goldman calls "chauvinistic."

The worst thing about Goldman's "prophet" thesis is that it makes Malcolm trivial by denying his other significant strengths. Malcolm was an organizer who developed the Nation of Islam from a small sect to a large organization which was the best disciplined Black organization in our history. His careful organizing work in the Nation of Islam enabled the organization to grow from a small group to an institution with 75 million dollars in assets. His skills extended to organizing the propaganda arm of the Nation, *Muhammad Speaks*. Malcolm's thoughts were seminal enough to have dominated the political thinking of a generation of Black youth. While it is true that his following outside of the Nation was small, we can only guess what that following would have been had he had more time to organize.

The most popular book on Malcolm written by a Black author, (Alex Haley) has perpetuated the myth that Malcolm made fundamental changes at the end of his life.

The central thesis of the *Autobiography of Malcolm X*, was that Malcolm underwent three transformations in his life, that of Malcolm Little, Malcolm X, and El-Hajj Malik-Shabazz. Certainly there can be little question that Malcolm experienced changes in his life. The three distinct changes mentioned above are useful in showing a development in Malcolm the man. The problem with the theory that Malcolm made fundamental changes has to do with the nature of the changes described in Haley's autobiography.

The myth that Malcolm underwent fundamental changes centers around the impact of the Hajj (pilgrimage) to Mecca on Malcolm's thought. According to the *Autobiography*, Malcolm was extremely impressed by the hospitality, warmth, and attention he received from influential white-skinned Muslims in Saudi Arabia. He was particularly moved by their seemingly unselfish intentions.

This led him to begin a reappraisal of the "white man." According to Malcolm: "In America, "white man" meant specific attitudes and actions toward the Black man, and toward all non-white men. But in the Muslim world, I had seen that men with white complexions were more genuinely brotherly than anyone else had ever been."[6]

Malcolm was also impressed by the brotherhood displayed by Mulsims of all colors on the Hajj. In writing about the experience of the Hajj, Malcolm described how he ate, drank and slept with white Muslims who displayed a brotherly attitude toward him. According to Malcolm, "We were truly all the same (brothers) because their belief in one God had removed the 'white' from their minds, the 'white' from their behaviour, and the 'white' from their attitude."[7]

On his second trip to Africa, Malcolm had another insight into the cause of racism. Malcolm came to see "that the white man is not inherently evil, but America's racist society influences him to act in evil ways. The society has produced and nourishes a psychology which brings out the lowest, most base part of human beings."[8]

Now what did this re-evaluation of whites mean? First, Malcolm's reappraisal of whites had a lot to do with the way he was treated by influential white-skinned Muslims, who displayed warmth and hospitality. Malcolm could see no ulterior motives behind their hospitable treatment. Yet, when he met Prince Faisal, the Prince spent his time criticizing the "Black Muslims," under the leadership of Elijah Muhammad, for teaching "the wrong Islam."[9]

When Malcolm assured the Prince that he took the Hajj to gain the correct understanding of Islam, the Prince encouraged the spreading of the correct information on Islam.

It is very likely that Faisal and other influential Muslims viewed Malcolm as an influential figure who could aid in the spread of the correct information about orthodox Islam, in America. Malcolm did in fact receive the endorsement of orthodox Islamic leaders for his Muslim Mosque Inc.

As far as brotherly feelings shown by Muslims on the Hajj, this was not a basis for concluding that Islamic societies were societies based on brotherhood. Neither was the brotherly treatment on the Hajj proof that these lightskinned Muslims thought and practiced brotherhood back at home. The prophet Muhammad himself had been critical of Arab Muslims who thought that they were better than non-Arab Muslims. The prophet Muhammad taught that: "An Arab is not more privileged than non-Arabs, nor white than Black. Spiritual excellence and true piety are the only distinctions amongst humans recognized by God."[10]

While this was good spiritual teaching, the fact that the prophet had to preach against ideas of Arab superiority indicated that those ideas existed among Muslims of his day. Not only did racism exist during Muhammad's time, but in the nation where the holy city of Mecca exists, Saudi Arabia. Blacks, the original inhabitants, are on the bottom of that society. Clearly, feelings of brotherhood generated by the religious experiences of the Hajj were not necessarily the same as brotherhood away from the Hajj.

While Malcolm was caught up in the spirit of the Hajj, and the good feelings generated by the hospitality he received in Saudi Arabia, he had no trouble distinguishing between the attitudes expressed by Muslims on the Hajj and the attitudes of whites in America.

In Ghana, Malcolm considered the difference between white-skinned Muslims in the Holy Land, and the attitudes of whites in America. As Malcolm observed:

> "And I knew that my reacting as I did presented no conflict with the convictions of brotherhood which I had gained in the Holy Land. The Muslims of "white" complexions who had changed my opinions were men who had showed me that American white men with a genuine brotherhood for a black man was hard to find, no matter how much he grinned."[11]

So a careful reading of Malcolm's own words reveal that he did not change his views towards whites in America because he knew that the society had not changed. As Malcolm had observed the American society created a racist mentality.

> "Despite the fact that I saw that Islam was a religion of brotherhood, I also had to face reality, and when I got back into this American society, I'm not

in a society that practices brotherhood. I'm in a society that might preach
it on Sunday, but they don't practice it on any other day. America is a
society where there is no brotherhood. This society is controlled primarily
by racists and segregationists, who are in Washington, D.C. in positions of
power."[12]

How could Malcolm be expected to change his views towards whites in
America, when neither their racist attitudes, behaviour, nor society had
changed? So whether we agree with Malcolm's conclusions about brotherhood
in Islam, it is clear that he was not prepared to embrace American whites as
bearers of brotherhood and sisterhood. Malcolm was a long way from embracing integration.

The *Autobiography of Malcolm X*, was not only deficient because it suggested that Malcolm changed from a Black nationalist to an integrationist,
but it also failed to convey a clear and profound understanding of the "fundamental thinking of Malcolm X."[13] In the *Autobiography*, Haley states that he
nearly gave up on writing the autobiography because Malcolm would only
talk about the Nation of Islam and the messenger. Haley wanted to write
about Malcolm's life. Certainly the strength of the *Autobiography* is the very
human account of Malcolm's life that Haley captures from Malcolm's words.
But a book about a major political figure is not only important because of the
hardships and achievements of that person. It should provide an opportunity
to examine in depth the political thoughts of this creative political thinker.
Unfortunately, the *Autobiography* fails to achieve this objective. Still, it does
succeed in exploring the personality of Malcolm and his personal history. It is
a well-written book and should be read by all who want to understand Malcolm X the man.

Of all the books about Malcolm X, the book that has most seriously distorted the Political Legacy of Malcolm X, is the *The Last Year of Malcolm X:
The Evolution Of A Revolutionary* by George Breitman. Breitman is a member of the Socialist Workers Party, and he has edited a number of books
containing the speeches of Malcolm X. *The Last Year Of Malcolm X* is Breitman's attempt to interpret Malcolm's political development.

In developing his analysis of Malcolm's political thrust, Breitman makes a
distinction between separatism and Black Nationalism. According to Breitman, separatism has a number of different tendencies, including Blacks withdrawing from the U.S. and forming a nation in Africa, or some part of the
United States.[14] Some who use the term "separation," according to Breitman,
are simply expressing their opposition to assimilation, and favor preserving
the Black community.[15] One who wants to preserve the Black community
would be called a believer in "separation," not a "separatist." A separatist,
according to Breitman's definition, favors forming a separate Black nation.
Another category that falls under Breitman's label of "separation" includes

Blacks who favor all-Black organizations. Breitman points out that advocates of all-Black organizations can be either advocates of integration or separation.

After defining separatism and separation Breitman puts forward the following definition of Black nationalism:

> "It is a tendency for Black people in the United States to unite as a group, as a people, into a movement of their own to fight for freedom, justice and equality. Animated by the desire of an oppressed minority to decide its own destiny, this tendency holds that Black people must control their own movement and the political, economic and social institutions of the Black community. Its characteristic attributes include racial pride, group consciousness, hatred of white supremacy, a striving for independence from white control, and identification with Black and non-white oppressed groups in other parts of the world."[16]

Breitman then makes the observation that one "can also be a Black nationalist without being a separatist."[17] Breitman's thesis is that Malcolm changed from a separatist who called for Blacks forming a separate nation, to a Black nationalist who "remained in favor of maintaining and strengthening the Negro community, and he was and remained in favor of all-Black organizations in the struggle for freedom."[18]

In analyzing Breitman's theoretical framework and thesis, the distinction between separatist and nationalist has some validity, but it is not definitive enough. It is correct to say that Black nationalism contains advocates for a separate nation-state and advocates of Black pride and Black power who have not advocated national independence. The problem with this formulation is that it excludes some other very important aspects of Black nationalism for nation-state and non-nation-state advocates. First, most advocates of Black nationalism, whether they favored forming a separate Black nation or not, have argued that Blacks in America are a "Nation within a Nation." This component of Black nationalism speaks to the existence of a national identity among Black people and sees national identity as the glue that binds Black people together culturally, economically, religiously, politically and internationally. It is interesting that Breitman chooses to ignore this very important aspect of Black nationalism.

The "nation within a nation" thesis has been used in different ways. Some advocates of a "nation within a nation," have called for armed self defense; others have defined this to mean that we are a "cultural nation," and others have argued for a plan of economic development. Most Blacks who have called for a separate Black state have argued that Blacks in America are a "nation within a nation."

What is particularly important about Breitman's separatist, Black nationalist distinction is that Malcolm did not make such a distinction in his speeches. When Malcolm was asked about the relation between Black nationalism and separatism at a March 19, 1964 Socialist Workers Party meeting, Malcolm said:

> "A pamphlet, Freedom Now, is on sale in the back"—good plug—"and it contains the statement 'All separatists are nationalists but not all nationalists are separatists.' "I don't know anything about that. . . ."[19]

Before discussing the rest of Malcolm's statement, it's important to note his direct response to the assertion that "all separatists are nationalists but not all nationalists are separatists." He said "I don't know about that." This response indicated that Malcolm had not made a distinction between nationalists who were separatists and nationalists who were not. This was a distinction made by the Socialist Workers party. Malcolm then went on to respond to the question, "Can one be a Black nationalist even though not interested in a separate, independent Black nation? Similarly, is every integrationist necessarily an assimilationist?" Malcolm's response was:

> "Well, as I said earlier, the Black people I know don't want to be integrationists, nor do they want to be separationists—they want to be human beings. Some of them choose integration, thinking that this method will bring them respect as a human being, and others choose separation, thinking that that method or tactic will bring them respect as a human being. But they've had so much trouble attaining their objectives that they've gotten their methods mixed up with their objectives, and now instead of calling themselves human beings, they're calling themselves integrationists and separationists, and they don't have either one—now. So I don't know about the integrationists and the assimilationists and the separationists, but I do not know about the segregationists—that's the Americans."[20]

Breitman interprets this answer to mean that Malcolm "showed a lack of interest in discussing separatism altogether." Actually, Malcolm showed no interest in answering the specific question posed by the Socialist Workers Party. He never did answer whether "All separatists are nationalists but not all nationalists are separatists." Instead he stressed what the two positions (integration and separation) had in common, the fact that the advocates of both positions are human beings. This answer was consistent with Malcolm's attempt to forge closer links with the Civil Rights movement, by among other things stressing what advocates of separation and integration had in common. At other times he would place emphasis on the fact that both advocates of integration and separation wanted freedom. By stressing the common conditions and objectives that tied Black people together, Malcolm was trying to make his own position more acceptable.

To provide further support for the argument that Malcolm was moving away from a separatist position, Breitman cites Malcolm's March 12, 1964 press statement where he announced his break with the Nation of Islam. In

that statement Malcolm stated that "separation, back to Africa [is] still a long-range program, and while it is yet to materialize, 22 million of our people who are still in America need better food, clothing, housing, education and jobs right now . . ."[21] Because Malcolm treated the return to Africa program as a long range program, Breitman argues that Malcolm was placing separation to Africa in the background. If Malcolm wanted to place the return to Africa program in the background, why did he commit himself to it in such clear terms? Logically, it's correct to regard political separation as a long term program since it represents an ultimate objective that could not be achieved overnight. In addition, once out of the Nation of Islam, Malcolm was able to pay attention to the immediate needs of Black people. From the March 12th statement on, Malcolm would place emphasis on the need to struggle for "better food, clothing, housing, education and jobs . . ." Malcolm had been critical of the Nation for not joining the Civil Rights movement in its struggle for these same basic necessities. Malcolm's March 12 statement, and his statement to follow, would simply emphasize that he was going to pursue a balanced approach between the long-range struggle for land, and the short-range struggle for food, clothing, housing, education and jobs.

Breitman cites Malcolm's May 21, 1964 statement to show that Malcolm had abandoned separatism completely. At this conference Malcolm X stated that, after speaking to African leaders, he was convinced that "If Black men become involved in a philosophical, cultural and psychological migration back to Africa, they will benefit greatly in this country."[22]

Yet on July 5, 1964, at this second Organization of Afro-American Unity meeting, Malcolm said:

> "Brother, if all of us wanted to go back to Africa you wouldn't be satisfied to go back all by yourself, I know that. Your desire would be to see all of us go back if I am judging you correctly.
>
> Then how would you create a situation, number one, that would make all of us Black minded enough to want to go back, or make this man so fed up with us he'd want to send us there? How would you go about getting 22 million people to go to a place they think is rotten, insect-infested jungle? How would you go about getting them to go back when they cringe when you use the word African or Africa? What strategy would you use? Or else you'd end up going back by yourself?
>
> Don't know that you've got some Nationalists right here that aren't ready to go back. They'll talk that talk, but when it comes to taking some concrete action, that's just talk. Well, let's face reality. Our people have to be brought up to the point where we have sufficient understanding of the assets that are due us if we do go back. And as long as you can't get 22 million people to that level or to that point, then while you are trying to point them in that direction, you have to at the same time have some kind of program which will enable them to take maximum advantage of every opportunity that exists here.

I want to go back to Africa. But what can I do while I'm waiting to go? Go hungry? Live in a rat infested slum? Send my children to a school where their brains are being crippled? No, if we are going to go, but time is going to pass between now and our going, then we have to have a long range program and short range program. One that is designed to turn us in that direction, to take maximum advantage of every opportunity under this roof where we are right now."[23]

At a later period, November 23, 1964, during a meeting sponsored by *Presence Afraciane*, in Paris, we get another glimpse of Malcolm's thinking on the subject.

Question: "Is there a (Black) movement in the United States that wishes to form an African state with the Africans?"

Malcolm: "Yes, they are important. There are an increasing number of Afro-Americans who want to migrate back to Africa. Now if it were to take place tomorrow you would probably have a limited number. So in my opinion if you wanted to solve the problem, you would have to make the problem more digestible to a greater number of Afro-Americans. The idea is good, but those who propagated the idea in the past put it to the public in the wrong way, and because of this didn't get the desired results. The one who made the greatest impact was the honorable Marcus Garvey. And the United States government put him in prison and charged him with fraud."[24]

When these statements are compared, we get a different interpretation that Breitman wants us to reach by treating the "philosophical, cultural . . . psychological migration" as though it represented all of Malcolm's thinking on the subject of Afrikan return. If the 'philosophical, cultural, psychological' migration home was Malcolm's final position on so-called separatism, then we could easily reach the conclusion that Malcolm no longer favored a physical return of Blacks to Afrika.

On the contrary, however, the July 5, 1964 and November 23, 1964 statements say "I want to go back to Africa . . ." and "The idea (migration to Africa) is good. . . ." Both of these statements, made after the May 21st statement, indicate support for a so-called separatist position. The July 5th and November 23rd statements raise the question of how would one go about making the question of a return to Africa "digestable" to Afro-Americans who have a negative image of Africa.

Could the idea of a "philosophical, cultural and psychological migration back to Afrika" have been Malcolm's way of making the idea of a physical migration "digestable"? Or is it possible that Malcolm had not reached a clear idea of how to move on this question? Could the different ideas reflect an inner struggle that Malcolm did not resolve before his death?

It is quite likely that progressive African leaders (Nkrumah, Toure, Nyerere) voiced support for African-Americans using their political leverage on behalf of Afrika, while African-Americans fought for their rights in the U.S. This is the standard position advocated by most African heads of state. If Malcolm heard this kind of advice and it is very likely that he did, then he may have had cause to re-evaluate his ideas about an African return.

Yet, to conclude as Breitman does, that Malcolm abandoned separatism is too simple. His statements at the very least indicate that the idea of a physical return still had a strong hold on him, and on many of his followers. It is understandable how the question of a philosophical versus a physical return could be a difficult question for Malcolm to resolve. As the son of Garveyite, and a former follower of the Nation of Islam's position on land, Malcolm would feel at home with the African land position which had been a central part of his message for years. As a student of African and African-American history, Malcolm knew that the idea of a physical return was a dominant trend in the 19th and early 20th century Black nationalist history. As the Civil Rights movement changed from an integrationist to a Black nationalist movement, there was a strong possibility that the movement would shift to an African land orientation. These considerations must have weighed heavily on Malcolm's mind.

However, if we are to be honest, the best we can say is that Malcolm's contradictory statements on the land question would indicate that he may have been torn between a "philosophical return" versus a physical return. This may not satisfy ideologues who want a clear cut answer, or who want to shape Malcolm into their own image. Malcolm's seeming ambivalence on this question should not be surprising, because the question of the long range direction of the Black liberation struggle is one of the most complex questions on the world's political agenda. Malcolm could hardly be expected to answer this question in less than one year.

Breitman's real motives come to light when he concludes by saying:

> "What he was questioning about Black nationalism was not its essence but its pure-and-simple form. He was questioning this because *it was alienating people who were true revolutionaries—in this case, white revolutionaries*. A pure and simple Black nationalist wouldn't care what effect he had on whites, revolutionary or not. Malcolm cared because he intended to work with white revolutionaries; he knew their collaboration was needed if society was to be transformed. Malcolm was beginning to think about the need to replace capitalism with socialism if racism was to be eliminated. He was not sure if it could be done, and he was not sure how it could be done, but he was beginning to believe that that was the road to be travelled."[25]

In the above excerpt, Breitman reveals his true motives. His intention is to create the false impression that Black nationalism that does not seek to move the masses toward socialism is pure and simple. Put another way, to be a revolutionary one must inevitably be a socialist, and further, Malcolm was beginning to embrace socialism even though he was not sure how a socialist transformation could occur in America.

Placing Breitman's argument into a historical perspective, Dessalines, Turner, Vesey and Garvey, to name only a few, would be considered "pure and simple" Black nationalists because they had either not heard of socialism, or had not embraced it. Dessalines, according to Breitman's thesis, would be considered a "pure and simple" Black nationalist, even though he enacted a land program that called for the equitable distribution of the land to all Blacks in Haiti. The "pure and simple" argument ignores the revolutionary aspect of nationalism. When nationalism seeks to overturn colonialism and to establish systems of economic and political power where the wealth and political power is placed in the hands of the people, that form of nationalism is revolutionary. It is not pure and simple, nor is it reactionary. Where nationalism seeks to advance the interests of an elite group, economically and politically, then it can only succeed at the expense of the people's stomachs, and political power. This type of nationalism is reactionary. To lump the two types of nationalism together (reactionary and revolutionary) is to deny the essence of the Political Legacy of Malcolm X.

Above everything else, Malcolm was a revolutionary nationalist who was committed to fundamental change. This commitment grew from Malcolm's study of history; it grew from his love of himself and his people; it grew from his efforts to broaden his views politically, and spiritually, and it was rooted in his personality.

Nowhere in any of his statements did Malcolm say that he had embraced a socialist analysis. He certainly criticized capitalism; he looked with favor upon the African socialist initiatives taken by progressive heads of states in Afrika. But he did not take a socialist position. In fact Malcolm acknowledged that he hadn't read Marx.

As for Breitman's assertion that Malcolm was moving away from Black separatism because it "was alienating people who were true revolutionaries— in this case white revolutionaries—," it has to be said that this assertion is really Breitman's way of saying that Black political activists are only acceptable to whites when they adopt the definition of revolution endorsed by white revolutionaries. For white so-called revolutionaries to assert that Black separatism alienates them is to say that they do not respect the right of African-Americans to self-determination.

Yet they respect the right of American revolutionaries to separate from Britain during the American revolution. So white separatism in the name of freedom is broad and revolutionary, but Black separatism in the name of freedom is "pure and simple" as well as alienating to white revolutionaries.

Further, this charge of alienation is really a cover for dismissing a whole trend of African-American history (Black Nationalism or Black Separatism) with the racist label of "pure" and "simple," or simply narrow. This is not very different from the response of the Algerian ambassador to Malcolm's control-of-the-Black-community definition of Black nationalism. The Algerian ambassador observed that this definition of Black nationalism alienates Africans such as himself, who are white.

As Maulana Karenga notes, the fact that an Algerian revolutionary would consider himself "white" is an indication that he bought into the racist-identification with the white colonizer.[26] Malcolm's definition of Black nationalism as being the Black people's struggle to control the economy, politics, education, etc., of the Black community, is no more alienating than the Algerian struggle to wrest control of Algeria from France. French alienation from the Algerian revolution occurred because the Algerian revolution was fought to transfer power from France to Algeria. The Black struggle for liberation in America only alienates those who are not committed to total freedom for Blacks and other people of color "by any means necessary." True white revolutionaries will not attempt to determine the political direction of the Black liberation movement, with concepts of 'alienation.' Instead they will commit themselves to a round the clock effort to organize their white brothers and sisters for what they call revolution.

Ultimately, the definition of our heroes, and our history is part of the struggle we must carry out to make history. For the image we have of our great heroes, and our past history, shapes the philosophies, strategies and tactics that we choose to achieve liberation. When our heroes and history is seen through our own eyes, we gain a sense of our own power and capacity for change. *The Political Legacy of Malcolm X*, places Malcolm within the African-American historical context.[27]

Malcolm can be compared to the great Black classical (jazz) musicians. To understand a Coltrane, we must understand the cultural, musical legacy he drew upon. Coltrane drew on the legacy of the Blues, the spirituals, Bebop, and hardbop.[28] His music places our people at the center, with his saxophone sounding like the preacher, Billie Holiday or a soulful rapper.[29] Coltrane's music built on this great African-American musical legacy, and he can only be understood when we understand the cultural roots that he sprang from.

Malcolm sprang from the rich cultural and historical roots of Afro-America. To understand Malcolm's poetic, fiery, creative delivery is to understand the African-American oral tradition. Malcolm was a rapping man, whose words carried you the way Coltrane's saxaphone did, to new dimensions of thought.

Malcolm's cultural base was dual. African-Americans come out of a historical tradition where the spiritual and the secular are not separated. The Nat Turners were spiritual men whose belief in God inspired them to overthrow their masters. Malcolm was a spiritual man, whose religion inspired him to struggle for full liberation.

Malcolm was a student of African and African-American history. To understand Malcolm we have to understand Paul cuffe, Nat Turner, David Walker, Henry Highland Garnett, Edward Wilmont Blyden, Martin R. Delany, Harriet Tubman, Bishop Henry McNeal Turner, Marcus Garvey, W. E. B. Dubois, Earl Little, Ella Baker, Fannie Lou Hammer, and the Honorable Elijah Muhammad, to name just a few. Malcolm built on the foundation developed by Africans who came before him. He also found himself faced with a new political movement, the Black movement of the sixties, that required him to improvise some new notes for the Black political score.

Malcolm pursued a balanced approach to Black liberation. He called for a spiritual, cultural, political, economic and international approach to Black liberation. The core of this balanced approach was Malcolm's struggle to connect us to our African past, and to give us thereby a sense of our identit and purpose in life. To quote Malcolm:

> "When you deal with the past, you're dealing with history, you're dealing actually with the origin of a thing. When you know the origin, you know the cause. . . . It's impossible for you and me to have a balanced mind in this society without going into the past, because in this particular society, as we function and fit into it right now, we're such an underdog, we're trampled upon, we're looked upon as almost nothing. Now if we don't go into the past and find out how we got this way, we will think that we were always this way. And if you think that you were always in the condition that you're in right now, it's impossible for you to have too much confidence in yourself, you become worthless, almost nothing. But when you go back into the past and find out where you once were, then you will know that you once had attained a higher level, had made great achievements, contributions to society, civilization, science, and so forth. And you know that if you once did it you can do it again; you automatically get the incentive, the inspiration and the energy necessary to duplicate what our forefathers did . . ."[30]

Our past greatness revealed our potential and served to inspire us to achieve future greatness. For Malcolm, study of the ancient past was not simply an intellectual exercise, it was a way to overhaul our attitudes, thoughts and behaviour patterns. Malcolm knew from personal experience that deep study and internalization of the past could instill life and a sense of direction into a people.

In reconditioning our thought patterns, Malcolm encouraged us to see things from an international perspective. He wanted us to see how international events in the areas of Asia, Africa, Latin America and the Caribbean affected our struggle. Malcolm was the third African-American in the 20th century to place Pan Africanism on the international political agenda. Garvey and Dubois had linked the struggle of Blacks in America with the struggle for African liberation on the African continent. Malcolm was the first African-

American leader who was able to move on the African continent and call on Africa to provide political support for the Black movement in the United States. Malcolm's efforts to criticize the United States government for violating Black people's human rights made it clear that the struggle for Black liberation was part and parcel of the worldwide struggle for liberation. Through his international work, Malcolm developed a new respect among African heads of state for the Black struggle in the United States. Malcolm helped to build a bridge of mutual support between Africans throughout the world and Africans in the United States. The growth of a Pan African thrust in the Black movement during the seventies represented the flowering of the seeds planted by Malcolm in the sixties.

Through his international work, Malcolm began to adapt lessons from the African continent to the Black liberation movement in the United States. One of the important organizational lessons adapted by Malcolm from the African to the American scene was the United Front concept. Malcolm observed the operation of the Organization of African Unity through first hand meetings with African heads of state. He came to appreciate the importance of having an organization that could bring together different leaders and groups under one umbrella. The Organization of Afro-American Unity, Malcolm's organization, was patterned after the Organization of African Unity, an organization that contains African states and African liberation movements. Through the OAAU, Malcolm attempted to introduce the concept of the Black United Front approach into the Black Liberation struggle. Unfortunately, Malcolm was unable to get the idea off the ground. Yet, the younger generation of Blacks in America had learned an important lesson from Malcolm. Stokely Carmichael, now known as Kwame Toure, popularized the idea of the Black United Front during the middle and late sixties. In 1980 the National Black United Front was formed in Brooklyn, New York. The National Black United Front grew out of Malcolm's vision of Black Unity as a prerequisite for Black liberation.

Perhaps the most important legacy of Malcolm was least understood. During his last year, Malcolm attempted to form a working relationship with the Civil Rights movement. On March 9, 1964, in an interview with the New York Times, Malcolm discussed his future plans:

> "I am prepared to cooperate in local Civil Rights actions in the South and elsewhere and shall do so because every campaign for specific objectives can only heighten the political consciousness of Blacks and intensify their identification against white society."[31]

Malcolm would later say that he was joining the Civil Rights movement to raise it to a human rights movement. This was an attempt by Malcolm to correct an error of the Nation of Islam, which had isolated itself from the Civil Rights movement. Malcolm wanted to get close to the movement and help radicalize it.

But Malcolm was attempting to do more than simply influence the younger members of the Civil Rights movement. Malcolm could see that the movement was changing gears from Civil Rights to Black Nationalism. Malcolm was attempting to consolidate the movement, taking the best out of the Civil Rights movement, while injecting more radical ideas, tactics and strategies. After his break with the Nation of islam, Malcolm called for using the ballot to decide "who went to the white house and who went to the dog house," and to elect Blacks who represented the interest of the Black community. This represented an appreciation of the electoral thrust of the Civil Rights movement and the electoral power of northern Black communities. Malcolm also endorsed rent strikes, and other forms of Black mass action that were not demeaning.

Malcolm came to appreciate what many nationalists still fail to understand, that in America reform is a basic part of revolutionary nationalist politics. This is simply because the people respond to struggles for jobs, economic development, housing, and a better education. These kinds of struggles are reformist because they do not threaten to overturn the system itself. Their reformist character poses special problems for the nationalist organizer. If the struggle for jobs, better housing and quality education are treated as ends rather than means to an end, such struggles can lead to cooptation by the capitalist system. Those who gain the benefits of the struggle could easily adopt the attitude that they had reached the promised land of freedom. If on the other hand, the struggle for better housing, quality education, and more jobs is viewed as one of the means to the ultimate goal of national power, then reformist tactics serve as a way to nationalize the minds of the people. Like it or not, this is part of the American dynamic. The majority of Black people will not adopt nationalism through reading a book, the majority of Black people will adopt it because the struggle for better jobs, better schools and better housing teaches them that the American system is incapable of providing these basic requirements without a fundamental alteration in the system as a whole. Malcolm was beginning to work out a synthesis between the strategy of nationalism and the tactics of reform in order to develop a flexible many-sided mass struggle for human rights and liberation.

My book *The Art of Organizing*, which has just been published, demonstrates how this synthesis between reform and nationalism can be made.

Benny Stewart, former chairman of the San Francisco State Black Student Union and leader of the San Francisco State strike, understood that the San Francisco State strike was only successful because it drew from the two wings of struggle, reform and Black nationalism.

> "When we look at King we see that he was a spark. King brought out the contradiction. King came up with a methodology or technique with a minimum of casualties. However, Malcolm was the Spirit. From Malcolm we learned to demand what we wanted, to take no jive, and go get it."[32]

Toward the end, Malcolm came to appreciate a basic law of Black political struggle. Just as day precedes night, and life precedes death, on the political level, a King is a precondition for a Malcolm; nonviolence is the precondition for self defense; Civil Rights is the precondition for human rights, and reform is the precondition for revolutionary Black nationalism. Malcolm inspired us to have the courage to kill the fear in our hearts. His insights inspire us to go within ourselves to shape a vision of African-American nationalism that grows out of our history, and which inspires us to create a towering legacy of power, self respect and liberation for the generations to come.

Notes

1. Malcolm X, Edited by George Breitman, *By Any Means Necessary*: Speeches, Interviews and A Letter By Malcolm X, New York: Pathfinder Press Inc., 1970, pg. 154.

2. Oba T'Shaka, *The Political Legacy Of Malcolm X*, Chicago, Third World Press, 1983.

3. Peter Goldman, *The Death And Life Of Malcolm X*, New York, Evanston, San Francisco, London, Harper and Row Publishers, 1974, pg. xi.

4. Ibid., pgs. 430-432.

5. Ibid., pg. 437.

6. Malcolm X with the assistance of Alex Haley, *The Autobiography of Malcolm X*, New York, Grove Press, 1964, pg. 338-339.

7. Ibid., pg. 345-346.

8. Ibid., pg. 377.

9. Ibid., pg. 353.

10. "Islam And The World," Iran: 1975, pg. 180.

11. Malcolm X with the assistance of Alex Haley, *The Autobiography Of Malcolm X*, New York, Grove Press, 1964, pg. 358.

12. Oba T'Shaka, *The Political Legacy Of Malcolm X*, Chicago, Third World Press, 1983, pg. 213.

13. Asa G. Hilliard, Book Review on the Political Legacy of Malcolm X, San Francisco, 1984.

14. George Breitman, *The Last Year Of Malcolm X: The Evolution Of A Revolutionary*, New York, Merit Publishers, 1967 pg. 53.

15. Ibid., pg. 53-54.

16. Ibid., pg. 55-56.

17. Ibid., pg. 56.

18. Ibid., pg. 54.

19. Ibid., pg. 62-63.

20. Ibid., pg. 62-63.

21. Ibid., pg. 54.

22. Ibid., pg. 63.

23. Oba T'Shaka, *The Political Legacy of Malcolm X*, Chicago, 1983, pg. 125-126.

24. Ibid., pg. 131-132.

25. George Breitman, *The Last Year of Malcolm X: The Evolution Of A Revolutionary*, New York, Merit Publishers, 1967, pg. 68.

26. M. Ron Karenga, "The Social Political Philosophy of Malcolm X," *The Western Journal of Black Studies*, 1979, pg. 254.

27. Oba T'Shaka, *The Political Legacy Of Malcolm X*, Chicago, Third World Press, 1983, pg, 167-208.

28. Leroi Jones, *Blues People*, New York, 1968, pg. 223-224.

29. Ibid., pg. 227.

30. Malcolm X, *Malcolm X On Afro-American History*, New York, Pathfinder Press, 1979, pg. 4.

31. Oba T'Shaka, ibid., 1983, pg. 57.

32. Oba T'Shaka Editor Publisher, "The San Francisco State Strike: A Study Of The First Black Studies Strike In The United States," San Francisco, *S.F. State Journal Of Black Studies*, 1982, pg. 16.

THE POLITICAL LEGACY OF
MALCOLM X
By Oba T'Shaka

"Professor Oba T'Shaka has written a book, *The Political Legacy of Malcolm X*, a book which dwarfs all other writings on Malcolm X. *The Autobiography of Malcolm X* was written or edited by Alex Haley, the famous author of *Roots*. And yet one can read this Autobiography and remain uninformed about the fundamental thinking of Malcolm X. The three books, the *Autobiography of Malcolm X*, *Malcolm X Speaks*, and *By Any Means Necessary* are the most popular books on Malcolm X today. A careful reading of T'Shaka's *Political Legacy of Malcolm X* will show that he has eclipsed these writers, one of whom has an international reputation. By this book Professor T'Shaka has established himself as a foremost authority, if not the foremost authority on the thought of Malcolm X."

> Dr. Asa G. Hilliard III
> Fuller E. Callaway
> Professor of Urban Education
> Georgia State University

"I am fascinated by this book *The Political Legacy of Malcolm X*. The book is written in a style that is very simple, I admire that in a writer. This kind of book can be read by adults and older children. It is the kind of book that all of us can read. I highly recommend this book."

> Lu Palmers Notebook
> WVON radio Chicago

"For Oba T'Shaka;s good work in the organization and uplift of Afrikan and Afrikan-American people he achieved both national and international eminence. I regard Oba T'Shaka as one of the key social philosophers in the Afro American race today. A reading of his manuscript on the life and death of Malcolm X would have been instructive to me. Its careful, even meticulous scholarship is reminiscent of W.E.B. DuBois' *The Philadelphia Negro*.

> Dr. Nathan Hare
> Clinical Psychologist
> Sociologist and publisher of the
> "Black Male Female Relationships Journal,"
> as well as lecturer at
> San Francisco State University.

To order a copy please send $11.95 plus $1.00 postage to: Oba T'Shaka, 4717 Wall Ave. Richmond, California 94804

Pathfinder

FREDERICK DOUGLASS: FORERUNNER OF AFRICAN-AMERICAN LEADERS

By Mamadi Moses Chinyelu

It is difficult to define "leadership" of a people when there are no sovereign political or national boundaries to consider. A people with a history such as that of African-Americans (i.e., the history that begins with the African slave trade in the 15th century) must allow for a broader definition of "leadership." This broder definition must consider that for years the dominant culture has chosen who should lead the African-American, rather than the leaders being chosen by African-Americans themselves. This is a means of protecting the interests of the dominant culture. Also, the dominant culture tries to destroy the African-American leadership which it considers poses the greatest threat to its well-being.

Although African-Americans have never elected anyone to represent their separate nation, there are those who have emerged to lead large segments of that nation with the consent and endorsement of the people. The various segments of the African-American nation have simultaneously had their leaders but, other than Frederick Douglass, there has not been a time, since the start of the African slave trade, that the overwhelming majority of African-Americans have submitted to the leadership of one person. Perhaps this is due to the issues being less complex in his day but, nevertheless, Douglass stands alone as the leader who led and influenced the largest percentage of the African-American populace at any time in history.

Frederick Douglass, born a slave on the Eastern Shore of Maryland, escaped to freedom in 1838 and became a spokesman for the cause of abolishing slavery in 1841. His reign over the African-American populace began when he started publishing *The North Star,* an anti-slavery journal. This began in December, 1847 and ended with his death in February, 1895.

> "The recognized leadership of Frederick Douglass among colored people of the country may be dated from the publication of the North Star. Prior to that time he was regarded as an Abolition orator and a conspicuous example of the possibilities of the Negro race. He had no yet established his relationship with the free colored people of the North."[1]

During the slavery period, Douglass' leadership was two-fold. He was the best known, most visible and most articulate spokesman and activist engaged in liberating African-Americans from their bondage. At the same time, he agitated on behalf of *free* African-Americans (of whom in 1850 there were 230,000 in the Slave-States and 200,000 in the Free-States) for equal protection under the law and the right to vote.[2] Following the emancipation of the slaves, Douglass devoted his career to gaining full citizenship for all African-Americans.

"Though slavery was abolished, the wrongs of my people were not ended. Though they were not slaves they were not yet quite free . . . I, therefore, soon found that the negro had still a cause, and that he needed my voice and pen with others to plead for it . . . I felt that the work of the [American Anti-Slavery] Society was not done, that it had not fulfilled its mission, which was not merely to emancipate, but to elevate the enslaved class . . . the freedman should have the ballot."[3]

Frederick Douglass was the great forerunner of African-American leaders. He saw the need for industrial schools and self-reliance three years before the birth of his protégé Booker T. Washington, whose career was devoted to developing a viable African-American economy as the course for attaining full citizenship. Douglass wrote in 1853 that his people had need "of an Industrial College in which shall be taught several important branches of the mechanic arts . . . live in houses; We must construct bridges as well as pass over them, before we can properly live or be respected by our fellow men."[4]

In 1854, long before W.E.B. DuBois made the pronouncement, Douglass, as commencement speaker at Western Reserve College, foresaw that America's most critical problem was the problem of the "colorline.":

> "The relation subsisting between the white and black people of this country is the vital question of the age."[5]

As for non-violence, Douglass was a champion of that strategy a century before its best known apostle, Martin Luther King. Douglass opposed his contemporary, Henry Highland Garnet, in 1843 at the National Negro Convention in Buffalo, who called for both free African-Americans and slaves to militantly resist slavery: "Douglass, at this time a peace advocate and a moral suasionist, led the successful opposition to the convention's adoption of Garnet's message which failed to pass by one vote. The address, he contended, was too radical."[6]

But Douglass was not long an advocate of nonviolence. He addressed a Boston audience on "The Slaves' Right to Revolt" in 1848. As a freeman, he advocated the right to bear arms and to engage in self-defense, much in the same tone as Malcolm X would later, when threatened with ejection from a Philadelphia trolley car because of his color, Douglass said to the conductor of

Figure #1:
Frederick Douglass, as he appeared in his later years, with all of the regal bearing of a
    monarch.

the trolley car "I will do no such thing and, if you try to remove me by force, you do so at your own peril."[7] The cries for disinvestment in South Africa by present-day anti-apartheid activists remind us of Douglass who, while traveling in Scotland in 1846, urged the Free Church of Scotland to return the "blood-stained money" received from their slaveholding countrymen in the United States. Even Marcus Garvey, who advocated developing a world-wide African economy, held Douglass in high esteem. A biography of Douglass was included in the history section of Garvey's *Universal Black Men Catechism,* which was taught to his adherents.

Douglass also set a precedent for African-American leaders conferring with presidents at the White House. He was granted an audience with Abraham Lincoln in July, 1863. He also attended the inaugural ball for Lincoln's second election in 1865. Likewise, he took the lead in receiving presidential appointments: President Grant appointed him to the Santo Domingo Commission in 1871; Douglass, in 1877, became the U.S. Marshal for the District of Columbia under President Rutherford B. Hayes; President James A. Garfield appointed Douglass Recorder of Deeds for the District of Columbia in 1881; President Benjamin Harrison appointed him Minister-resident and Consul-general of Haiti in 1889.

Frederick Douglass' leadership on behalf of African-Americans made him an international figure. By late 1845, he was well known throughout Europe. Between October, 1845 and December, 1846, he made no fewer than 51 speeches, at 24 different locations throughout England, Ireland, Scotland and Wales. But more than his speaking engagements, Douglass' fame was due largely to the publishing of his *Narrative of the Life of Frederick Douglass: An American Slave* in 1845. By 1850, 30,000 copies had been distributed throughout America and the British Isles, as well as a French edition.[8] "Douglass's reputation had preceded him to Bristol, England. Mayor John K. Haberfield noted that the *Narrative* had been extensively read in this city."[9]

Not only was Douglass popular because of the cause that he represented, but also because of his more-than six-foot frame, which gave him the appearance of strength, his bushy head of hair, which gave him a look of ferocity, and his ability to articulate the issues, which underscored his intelligence. Such a bearing possessed by Douglass could be applied to any cause. Indeed, representatives of other causes did look to Douglass for support, most notably women's rights advocates and the opponents of the Mexican-American War. And Douglass was heard on these issues:

> "Let the press, the pulpit, the church, the people at large, unite at once; and let petitions flood the halls of Congress by the million, asking for the instant recall of our forces from Mexico."[10]

> "All that distinguishes man as an intelligent and accountable being, is equally true of woman, and if that government only is just which govern

by the free consent of the governed, there can be no reason in the world for denying to woman the exercise of the elective franchise, or a hand in making and administering the laws of the land."[11]

Perhaps the most celebrated instance of Douglass' constituency extending beyond African-Americans is when, in 1866, he was elected a delegate from Rochester, N.Y., his place of residence, to the National Loyalist's Convention, convened in Philadelphia. The purpose of the convention was to establish policy for reconstructing the South, following the Civil War. "It was unprecedented for a city of over sixty thousand white citizens and only about two hundred colored residents, to elect a colored man to represent them in a national political convention, and the announcement of it gave a shock to the country of no inconsiderable violence."[12]

While Douglass' focus was on the condition of his people in the United States, his scope was far and wide. He was ever in search of another cause on another front that would lend support to the abolition cause in America. Such was the case in 1848 when he congratulated the French people for replacing the king with a republic.

"I say, if anything can put our republic to blush, it is that glorious consistency with which the Provisional Government of France has made and set in operation measures which must bring about the entire overthow of Slavery in all dominions."[13]

No sense of success or level of acceptance from the dominant culture swayed Douglass from opposing, with all the might of his faculties, the barbarity of slavery, in any form. Six years after the American Civil War had ended and slavery was forever abolished, he scourged the ruling class of the West Indies for exploiting East Indians and Chinese for cheap labor, in what was commonly called the "Coolie trade." Douglass wrote in his newspaper, "This Coolie trade—the cheap labor trade, as now called and carried on—is marked by all the horrible and infernal characteristics of the slave trade."[14]

By no means was Douglass the only African-American spokesman for his people during his career. It was not the lack of contemporaries that enabled him to be the most distinguished and effective anti-slavery activist of his day. Many men and women in the race came to prominence and it is doubtful that the end of slavery would have been realized at the hour that it was without the commitment of these freedom fighters. Included in these ranks are pan-Africanists Alexander Crummell and Henry Highland Garnet. Garnett was active with the African Civilization Society, which sought to destroy the American cotton economy by developing the African cotton economy, as a means of destroying slavery.[15] It was Garnet who called for the slaves to rebel, a measure which failed to be officially adopted by the convention in 1843. "Even so, the Negro mood underwent a sharp shift toward more militant

Figure #2:
Cedar Hill, Douglass' last place of residence in Washington, D.C., which open to the public for tours, under the auspices of the National Park Service.

action against slavery. In fact, a similar National Negro Convention held in 1847 in Troy unanimously approved a similar speech given at the convention by Garnet."[16]

According to historian Benjamin Quarles, Robert Purvis served five terms, from 1845 to 1850, as president of the Pennsylvania Anti-Slavery Society and Charles Lenox Remond served in the same capacity for about the same length of time with the Essex Anti-Slavery Society.[17] In his book, *Black Abolitionists,* Quarles lists a number of others who distinguished themselves in the fight to end slavery, including J. McCune Smith, Robert Douglass, Jr., Martin Delany, Sarah Parker Remond, William H. Day, William L. Douglass, William G. Allen, Henry "Box" Brown (who escaped from slavery when mailed in a box from Richmond to Philadelphia), William and Ellen Craft and William Wells Brown, who wrote more than a dozen books, including *Clotel; Or, the President's Daughter: A Narrative of Slave Life in the United States,* which is about the daughter that Thomas Jefferson had for his slave mistress. For years this was considered to be the first novel written by an African-American.[18] [19]

Whereas, these leaders at times held differences with Douglass and others within their ranks, they closed ranks when it came to their common cause. "The leading colored men of the period who, in various ways, were helping the cause of emancipation, rallied around him" said Booker T. Washington "and lived and labored in intimate association with him."[20]

But it would be a gross misrepresentation of history and reality to say that Douglass was in perfect accord with his fellow abolitionists, both African-Americans and Caucasians. To the contrary. Besides taking issue with Garnet's call for a slave rebellion (a position that Douglass later altered as demonstrated by his speech, "The Slaves' Right to Revolt") the most grievous charge that Douglass endured from his African-American contemporaries concerned the closing of Freedman's Bank. Douglass said he was the victim of "malicious and envious assaults" from those who believed the bank could be saved. he was attacked by these envious and malicious elements when he recommended to the Senate Finance Committee that the bank be closed because it had no reserve. In disgust, Douglass wrote that he had been "accused of bringing the Freedman's Bank into ruin, and squandering in senseless loans on bad security the hardly-earned moneys of my race." Douglass said in his defense that all of the loans made by the bank were made prior to his becoming its president, four months before its closing.[21]

He was also at variance with a segment of the African-American population that sought to migrate from the South to the North and to Kansas and Nebraska. Douglass argued that the African-American would be better off economically in the South since the farm industry needed their labor. Another argument against the exodus centered on his belief that the former master-class viewed the exodus, caused by the abuse of the recently freed slaves, as evidence that the South, even after the Civil War, still was not obligated to abide by the Constitution.[22]

Figure #3:
Douglass was an avid researcher and writer, as he is seen doing here at his Cedar Hill
   residence.

Another difference of policy between Douglass and his African-American contemporaries, was the advice he received not to publish in his *Narrative* that he was an escaped slave. "Some of my colored friends in New Bedford thought very badly of my wisdom in thus exposing and degrading myself."[23]

Although Douglass' career as a spokesman for the anti-slavery cause began when he came into association with William Lloyd Garrison and other white abolitionists of the Massachusetts Anti-Slavery Society, one could hardly argue that he was merely a creation of his white colleagues. The record shows that Douglass' life, whether he officially earned his living as an agent for an anti-slavery society or not, was as strong an argument for abolishing slavery as could be articulated. It is precisely for that reason that he was so effective and why he was recruited to be an agent. He had experienced and endured slavery as a victim, escaped from slavery, educated himself and sought refinement in other ways. What his new found colleagues were advocating in the safety of their New England communities, Douglass did in the belly of the beast of a Southern plantation. In hearing Douglass speak for the first time, Garrison said his "perception of the enormous outrage" caused by slavery "on the god-like nature of its victims" gained in clarity.[24] "It was at once deeply impressed upon my mind," wrote Garrison, "that, if Mr. Douglass could be persuaded to consecrate his time and talents to the promotion of the anti-slavery enterprise, a powerful impetus would be given to it, and a stunning blow at the same time inflicted on northern prejudice against a colored complexion."[25]

By the time Douglass had been put on the payroll as an anti-slavery spokesman, he had been out of slavery himself for a mere three years and still subject to recapture as set forth by the Fugitive Slave Law of 1793. It was only natural for him, having yet the occasion to consider the variety of arguments confronting the question of abolition, to embrace the policy of his new colleagues. But as Douglass became more acculturated in the society of freedom, so too his awareness of all the issues at hand began to increase. Thus it is not surprising that his position—being an escaped slave, unlike his white friends—would modify with time. For example, Douglass came into conflict with the Garrisonian position that the Constitution was a pro-slavery document. Douglass called the Constitution a "warrant for the abolition of slavery in every State of the Union."[26]

> "My first opinions were naturally derived and honestly entertained. Brought directly, when I escaped from slavery, into contact with abolitionists who regarded the Constitution as a slaveholding instrument, and finding their views supported by the united and entire history of every department of government, it is not strange that I assumed the Constitution to be just what these friends made it seem to be. I was bound not only by their superior knowledge to take their opinions in respect to this subject, as the true ones, but also because I had no means of showing their unsoundness."[27]

Garrison and company, much to Douglass' surprise, were also opposed to Douglass publishing *The North Star*. For that reason, Douglass moved his residence from New England to Rochester, N.Y., where he lived for 25 years, so that his new publishing enterprise would not encroach upon the circulation of Garrison's newspaper, the *Liberator*, which was published in Boston.[28]

After the war had ended and the slaves had been emancipated, Douglass was at odds with his white abolitionist friends over the questions as to whether the former slaves should have the right to vote. "The demand for the ballot was such a vast advance upon the former objects proclaimed by the friends of the colored race, that it startled and struck men as preposterous and wholly inadmissable. Anti-slavery men themselves were not united as to the wisdom of such a demand. Mr. Garrison himself, though foremost for the abolition of slavery, was not yet quite ready to join this advanced movement."[29]

On another important issue of the day, Douglass and his former longstanding ally Charles Summer, the Massachusetts Senator, took different positions when President Grant, who Douglass supported, tried to annex Santo Domingo. According to Douglass, Summer saw the move as a means to "extinguish a colored nation" while to Douglass it meant "the alliance of a weak and defenseless people."[30]

A less critical difference held by Douglass and his friends occurred when he allowed his "freedom" to be purchased by his friends in England. "Some of my uncompromising anti-slavery friends in this country failed to see the wisdom of this commercial transaction, and were not pleased that I consented to it, even by my silence. They thought it a violation of anti-slavery principles, conceding the right of property in man . . ."[31]

Along with Douglass' three autobiographies, there are several good biographies, chronologies and analyses of Douglass' life but a brief sketch of the highlights of his life would be appropriate here.

Frederick Douglass was born on Maryland's Eastern Shore, in Talbot County, in February, 1818. Born a slave, by virtue of his mother's slave status, Douglass' father is said to have been a white man and very possibly his master. The pain that young Douglass endured as a slave child were not physical as much as they were emotional, by his own account. As an infant he suckled at his grandmother's breast and, when older but still too young to work in the field, played in the big-house yard with other children his age.

For Douglass, slavery's cruelty took the form of not enjoying his mother's presence more than a few times and never again seeing her after he became about seven years old.

"To me it has ever been a grief" he wrote "that I knew my mother so little, and have so few of her words treasured in my remembrance."[32]

One fond memory that Douglass had of his mother was that she was said to be the only "colored" person on the plantation—he didn't distinguish be-

Figure #4:
In his Cedar Hill sitting room, Douglass' portrait can be seen reflected in the mirror
above the fireplace.

tween free or slave—who could read. Douglass didn't know where or whom his mother learned to read but because of it he credited her with "an earnest love of knowledge."[33] This fact, Douglass was not aware of until much later in life but he became one of the first slaves on the plantation to read also.

Douglass' sojourn into book-learning began in Baltimore, where he was sent at age eight to work for his master's brother as an aid to the Baltimore man's son, who was Douglass' junior by a few years.

Because of a dispute between Douglass' master and the brother in Baltimore, Douglass had to return to the Easter Shore plantation where he was born and, for the first time, he worked as a field hand. During this time, Douglass suffered whippings and beatings from cruel masters which fired his desire to one day escape to freedom. Such a plot by Douglass was foiled in April, 1836. Because the other slaveholders in the county threatened to shoot him on sight, Douglass' master sent him back to Baltimore. Two years later, Douglass escaped to Philadelphia and on to New York where he was joined by Anna Murray, a young free African-American, who he married. The couple were advised to relocate to New Bedford, Massachusetts, where Douglass could get work in his trade as a caulker in the ship-building industry.

Within three years of escape, after working a series of odd jobs for a living, Douglass came to the attention of white abolitionists after he was invited to speak at a rally. So impressed were these anti-slavery proponents that Douglass was hired as an agent with the Anti-Slavery Society. In this capacity, Douglass travelled extensively and spoke often. For example, between 1855 and 1863, he had speaking engagements in no fewer than nine months per year. Actually, of that nine year period, he spoke as few as nine months in only one year, 1860. For the remaining years, he had speaking engagements 10 months for each of five years, 11 months for each of two years and in 1957, he had speaking engagements in every month. And those months were quite demanding as well. During January, 1855, he spoke 19 days and in August of that same year, he had speaking engagements 20 days. That nine-year period took him to 14 states and three countries.[34]

The early education that Douglass the self-made man received served him well as a spokesman for the anti-slavery cause for within a mere seven years after his escape from slavery, in 1845, he wrote and published a narrative of his life. The widely read account of his experiences as a slave gained noteriety for him. With this sudden fame as an escaped slave, Douglass was advised by his abolitionist friends to seek refuge in England. His time there was well spent. During a 21-month stay in Europe, Douglass made anti-slavery speeches in England, Ireland, Scotland and Wales. He told his listeners:

> "To tear off the mask from this abominable system, to expose it to the light of heaven, aye, to the heat of the sun, that it may burn and wither it out of existence, is my object in coming to this country."[35]

Figure #5:
Douglass is seen working in his Cedar Hill library.

It was during this visit to Europe that Douglass' friends approached him about allowing them to raise funds to purchase his freedom from his former master. The transaction was completed.

If allowing his "freedom" to be purchased seemed reactionary and counterproductive in abolishing slavery, Douglass' allowing those same European friends to raise money for him to start publishing an anti-slavery newspaper more than made up for any weakness in the anti-slavery ideology. Douglass was able to begin publishing *The North Star* on December 3, 1847. While Douglass' English friends were very supportive of such a venture, his white American abolitionist friends were equally opposed to his starting a publication. Douglass defended this newspaper in particular and the African-American press in general, when he wrote in *The North Star* in an editorial titled "Colored Newspaper," on January 8, 1848:

> "They are sometimes objected to, on the ground that they serve to keep up an odious and wicked distinction between white and colored persons, and are a barrier to the very equality which we are wont to advocate . . . we must do what white men do. It must be no longer white lawyer, and black woodsawyer, white editor, and black street cleaner: it must be no longer white intelligent, and black, ignorant."[36]

Douglass published his newspaper from Rochester. N.Y. Because this thriving city was close to Canada, Douglass' home was an important station on the underground railroad. "On one occasion," he revealed "I had eleven fugitives at the same time under my roof, and it was necessary for them to remain with me, until I could collect sufficient money to get them on to Canada."[37]

Douglass' most notorious underground railroad experience, beyond his own escape, was the aid he gave to three fugitive slaves, who, being pursued by slave catchers under the authority of the Fugitive Slave Law of 1850, killed one slave catcher, wounded another "and drove away the officers" in Christiana, Pennsylvania. Douglass succeeded in getting the three Freedom-seeking African-Americans to Canada but it was not done without danger. "The work of getting these men into Canada was a delicate one. They were not only fugitives from slavery but charged with murder, and officers were in pursuit of them . . . I could not look upon them as murderers. To me, they were heroic defenders of the just rights of man against mansteaters and murderers. So I fed them, and sheltered them in my house. Had they been pursued then and there, my home would have been stained with blood, for these men who had already tasted blood were well armed and prepared to sell their lives at any expense to the lives and limbs of their probable assailants."[38]

Frederick Douglass' life was not only filled with dramatic incidents but also with noteworthy achievements. No other African-American and few Americans of any race, have influenced the development of the United States as consistently and on as many important topics as Douglass has. It must be noted that he did all that he did as a private citizen, whereas the only persons who can seriously challenge him on this claim served in elected positions. Only Washington and Jefferson have decidedly done more for the nation. And if Lincoln saved the Union, then, through agitation and wise counsel, Douglass saved Lincoln.

Having worked in one capacity or another all of his life to end slavery ("When I ran away from slavery, it was for myself; when I advocated emancipation, it was for my people," Douglass said.[39]), by the time he was 43-years-old, at which time the Civil War had commenced, he was sufficiently prepared for what would be his finest hour.

Douglass and Lincoln viewed the war from different vantage points. Saving the Union was Lincoln's sole objective. "If I could save the Union without freeing the slaves, I would do it. What I do about slavery and the colored race, I do because I believe it helps to save the Union . . ."[40]

Not surprisingly, Douglass saw the war as the long awaited means by which the dreaded slavery could be abolished. And he said as much: "From the first, I for one, saw in this war the end of slavery; and truth requires me to say that my interest in the success of the North was largely due to this belief . . . The mission of the war was the liberation of the slaves as well as the salvation of the Unin."[41]

As he told African-American men in an editorial in his newspaper, *Douglass Monthly*, in April, 1863, the end of slavery and salvation of the Union were not mutually exclusive:

> "You should enlist because the war for the Union, whether men call it or not, is a war for Emancipation. The salvation of the country, by the inexorable relation of cause and effect, can be secured only by the complete abolition of Slavery."[42]

Although Douglass had never met Lincoln, he supported the Illinois lawyer over the other two candidates in the 1860 election because "Abraham Lincoln proposed his grand historic doctrine of the power and duty of the National Government to prevent the spread of and perpetuity of slavery. Into this contest I threw myself . . ."[43]

In spite of this support, Douglass found reason to take very strong issue with Lincoln early in his presidential administration. Lincoln's plan for returning African-Americans to Africa was one such issue:

> "The President of the United States seems to possess an ever increasing passion for making himself appear silly and ridiculous . . . Our garrulous and joking President has favored the country and the world with two speeches . . . In this address Mr. Lincoln assumes the language and arguments of an itinerant Colonization lecturer, showing all his inconsistancies, his pride of race and blood, his contempt for negroes and his canting hypocrisy . . . The argument of Mr. Lincoln is that the difference between

the white and black races renders it impossible for them to live together in the same country without detriment to both."[44]

In the same editorial, Douglass declared that Lincoln was no friend of the African-American or to the anti-slavery cause:

"Mr. Lincoln is quite a genuine representative of American prejudice and Negro hatred and far more concerned for the preservation of slavery, and the favor of the Border Slave States, than for any sentiment of magnanimity or principle of justice and humanity."[45]

Because Douglass viewed the war as a means of abolishing slavery, he encouraged the North to enlist African-Americans for the war effort. Initially, the Lincoln administration rejected the idea. Furthermore, the Lincoln administration said the war should not be construed by the slaves as an opportunity to revolt. Lincoln's first Commander-in-Chief of the Army, Gen. George McClellan, warned the slaves that "'if any attempt was made by them to gain their freedom, it would be suppressed by an iron hand.' In many places Union soldiers were detailed to guard plantations of Southern slaveowners."[46]

Lincoln's policy began to change in regard to using African-American troops after his army took heavy losses at the battles of Bull Run, Ball's Bluff, Big Bethel and Fredericksburg. These occurences, along with the fact that the Confederacy was employing slave labor in various capacities to aid their rebellious effort, were enough for Lincoln to change his policy.[47] The president soon gave the Massachusetts governor authority to recruit two regiments of African-American troops, the 54th and 55th regiments. Douglass became a recruiting agent, with two of his sons being the first to enlist from the state of New York.[48]

Douglass' activity on behalf of the slaves had touched a Lincoln nerve enough that in 1863 and 1864, Lincoln would have two meetings with him in the White House, the first at Douglass' request and the second at Lincoln's request. In July, 1863, Douglass told Lincoln that African-American troops should get pay equal to that of white troops, as well as promotions for courageous acts. He also wanted the president to retaliate if the South continued to treat captured African-American troops as revolting chattel rather than prisoners of war.[49]

Nearly thirteen months after their first meeting, Lincoln sought Douglass' assistance on a sensitive matter. At the time there was much agitation calling for Lincoln to issue peace terms to the South. Although Lincoln emancipated the slaves in the rebellious states in January, 1863, the president knew that most of the slaves were still within the enemy lines. Lincoln also knew that to offer peace terms at that time, the slaves would probably remain in that status. He wanted Douglass to recruit men who could go into the South and inform the slaves that they had been freed, causing the former slaves to depart from their captivity.[50] Douglass recalled that his friend John Brown had devised a similar plan before his famous raid on Harper's Ferry army arsenal in 1859.

Douglass won the war to end slavery but in doing so he first won several battles such as the slaves being emancipated and African-Americans, both free and former slaves, being enlisted in the Union army. Before the war was over, 186,017 African-American enlisted in the Union army as soldiers, with another 92,576 serving in other capacities.[51]

When it was time to speak, Douglass was heard, whatever the issue, if it lent to the destruction of slavery. He dealt a mortal wound to America's slaveholding Christians when he told the world:

> "While America is printing tracts and Bibles; sending missionaries abroad to convert the heathen; expending her money in various ways for promotion of the Gospel in foreign lands—the slave not only lies forgotten, uncared for, but is trampled under foot by the very churches of the land."[52]

He exposed the Fugitive Slave Law of 1850 and showed how it reduced to mere spiritless words on paper, the Constitution, which guaranteed everyone equal protection under the law and due process except the African-American. "A black man" he said, in a speech in Pittsburg, "may be carried away without any reference to a jury. It is only necessary to claim him, and that some villian should swear to his identity. There is more protection there for a horse, for a donkey, or anything, rather than a colored man . . ."[53] He viewed the Supreme Court's decision in the Dred Scot case (which ruled that African-Americans "are deemed to have no rights which white men are bound to respect") as reason to press on for the abolishment of slavery rather than reason to weaken.

If Douglass had given a nod of approval to the colonization idea, it may have become the official policy of the government and many African-Americans would have been repatriated to Africa in the 19th century. But as stated before, Douglass opposed this policy: "I believe that simultaneously with the landing of the pilgrims, there landed slaves on the shores of this continent . . . We came when it was a wilderness, and were the pioneers of civilization on this continent."[54]

Douglass is credited with performing a significant role in the reelection of Abraham Lincoln in 1864: "On November 6, Wendell Phillips congratulated Frederick Douglass: 'For the first time in history, the slave has chosen a President of the United States.'"[55] He also contributed much to U.S. Grant's election to the presidency in 1868.[56] Douglass also put his considerable weight behind the passage of the Fourteenth and Fifteenth Amendments to the Constitution, the first extending citizenship to the African-American and the latter extending the vote to African-American men.

Figure #6:
A portrait of a young Frederick Douglass thought to have been painted by Elisha Hammond about 1844, six years after his escape from slavery. The portrait is in the collection of the National Portrait Gallery, in Washington, D.C.

However, it was not glory and recognition for all of his achievements that Douglass sought. If so, he would have taken the advice of his friends and relocated to a Southern community where he could easily have been elected to the Senate or House of Representatives. He would also have accepted President Andrew Johnson's appointment to head the Freedman's Bureau but, knowing that Johnson's sympathies were with the former slave masters, Douglass did not care to put himself in a position where he could not criticize Johnson's policies. Douglass would have been replacing Gen. O.O. Howard, whom Johnson had fired but who was regarded as a friend of the African-American.

Frederick Douglass, indeed, lived a full life; he started it as a slave and ended it as a power broker; at the beginning he was ignorant but through the course of it he enlightened others. As a telling symbol of his life's completeness, Douglass, in the company of his second wife, made his third trip abroad, about 1886—not to lecture on behalf of a cause or as a refugee from American slavery but as a tourist. Included in this vacation was a visit to Africa, where Douglass climbed to the top of one of Egypt's pyramids.[57] He had risen from the lowest status of man, where his humanity was denied, to stand upon one of the wonders of the world, the most remarkable monument to African genius and humanity.

When Douglass died in 1895, he was appropriately eulogized by those he encountered at home and abroad:

> "Modern history affords no parallel to the career of Douglass. A slave, lashed and scarred, without a name, merely one amongst a herd of animals, beasts of burden, on the estate of the lordly planter ... Riches, honor and power failed to spoil him."[58]

Frederick Douglass must be remembered as the champion who gave his franchiseless people, a nation unto themselves, citizenship in their newly adopted country. In doing so, he built the mountain upon which all other African-American leaders since have stood.

Notes

1. Booker T. Washington, *Frederick Douglass*, p. 139, 1906
2. Ibid., p. 140
3. Frederick Douglass, *Life and Times*, pp. 384-386
4. Ibid., pp. 293-294
5. John W. Blassingame, ed., *The Frederick Douglass Papers, Vol. 2*, 1982
6. Waldo E. Martin, Jr., *The Mind of Frederick Douglass*, p. 57, 1984
7. Douglass, *Life and Times*, op. cit., p. 466
8. Benjamin Quarles, ed., *Narrative of the Life of Frederick Douglass*, pp. xiii-xv, 1967
9. Blassingame, ed., *The Frederick Douglass Papers, Vol. 1*, p. 341, 1979

10. Philip S. Foner, ed., *The Life and Writings of Frederick Douglass*, Vol. 1, pp. 295-296, 1950
11. Philip S. Foner, ed., *Frederick Douglass on Woman's Rights*, p. 51, 1976
12. Douglass, *Life and Times*, op. cit., p. 395
13. Blassingame, ed. *The Frederick Douglass Papers, Vol. 2*, p. 116, 1952
14. Foner, ed., *The Life and Writings, Vol. 4*, p. 263, 1955
15. Foner, ed., *The Life and Writings, Vol. 2*, op. cit., p. 445
16. Rayford W. Logan and Michael R. Winston, eds., *Dictionary of American Negro Biography*, p. 253, 1982
17. Benjamin Quarles, *Black Abolitionists*, p. 56, 1969
18. Ibid., p. 134
19. Logan, and Winston, eds., *Dictionary of American Negro Biography*, op. cit., p. 72
20. Washington, *Frederick Douglass*, op. cit., p. 140
21. Douglass, *Life and Times*, op. cit., pp. 413-414
22. Ibid., pp. 437-444
23. Ibid., p. 218
24. Douglass, *Narrative of the Life of Frederick Douglass*, p. vi, 1968
25. Ibid., p. vii
26. Douglass, *Life and Times*, op. cit., p. 267
27. Ibid., pp. 266-267
28. Ibid., pp. 264-265
29. Ibid., p. 387
30. Ibid., p. 416
31. Ibid., p. 259
32. Ibid., p. 23
33. Ibid., p. 23
34. Blassingame, *The Frederick Douglass Papers*, Vol. 3, pp. xxi-xxxvi
35. Carter G. Woodson, *Negro Orators and Their Orations*, p. 170, 1925
36. Foner, *The Life and Writings, Vol. 1*, op. cit., p. 291
37. Douglass, *Life and Times*, op. cit., 272
38. Ibid., p. 288
39. Foner, *The Life and Writings, Vol. 4*, op. cit., p. 452
40. Washington, *Frederick Douglass*, op. cit., pp. 218-219
41. Douglass, *Life and Times*, op. cit., pp. 340-341
42. Foner, *The Life and Writings, Vol. 3* op. cit., p. 343
43. Douglass, *Life and Times*, op. cit., p. 332
44. Foner, *The Life and Writings, Vol. 3*, op. cit., pp. 266-267
45. Ibid., p. 268
46. Washington, *Frederick Douglass*, op. cit., 217-218
47. Douglass, *Life and Times*, op. cit., p. 342
48. Ibid., p. 346
49. Quarles, *Frederick Douglass*, op. cit., p. 211
50. Ibid., pp. 216-217
51. Washington, *Frederick Douglass*, op. cit., pp. 223-224
52. Woodson, *Negro Orators and Their Orations*, op. cit., p. 166
53. Foner, *The Life and Writings, Vol. 2*, op. cit., p. 207
54. Ibid., Vol. 5, pp. 203-204
55. Graham, *There Was Once A Slave*, p. 216, 1947
56. Quarles, *Frederick Douglass*, op. cit., p. 241
57. Douglass, *Life and Times*, p. 586, 1892
58. Helen Pitts Douglass, *In Memoriam: Frederick Douglass*, p. 312, 1971

Bibliography

Blassingame, John W., ed., *The Frederick Douglass Papers, Vol. 1-Vol. 3*, New Haven, Conn., Yale University Press, 1979-1985

Chestnutt, Charles W., *Frederick Douglass*, Boston, Small, Maynard and Co., 1899

Douglass, Frederick, *Life and Times of Frederick Douglass*, Boston, DeWolf, Fiske & Co. 1892

————, *My Bondage and My Freedom*, New York, Arno Pess, 1968

————, *Narrative of the Life of Frederick Douglass*, New York, Signet, 1968

————, *The North Star*, Rochester, N.Y., Jan. 7, 1848, Moorland-Spingarn Research Center, Howard University, Washington, D.C.

Douglass, Helen Pitts, ed., *In Memoriam: Frederick Douglass*, Freeport, N.Y., Books for Libraries Press, 1971

Foner, Philip S., ed., *Frederick Douglass on Women's Rights*, Westport, Conn., Greenwood Press, 1976

————, ed., *The Life and Writings of Frederick Douglass, Vol. 1-Vol.5*, New York, International Publishers, 1950-1975

Franklin, John Hope, *From Slavery to Freedom*, New York, Alfred A. Knopf, 1967

————, *The Emancipation Proclamation*, Garden City, N.Y., Doubleday and Co., 1963

Graham, Shirley, *There Was Once A Slave: The Heroic Story of Frederick Douglass*, New York, Julian Messner, 1947

Huggins, Nathan I., *Slave and Citizen: The Life of Frederick Douglass*, Boston, Little, Brown, 1980

Logan, Rayford W. and Winston, Michael R., eds., *Dictionary of American Negro Biography*, New York, W.W. Norton & Co., 1982

Martin, Waldo E., *The Mind of Frederick Douglass*, Chapel Hill, N.C., University of North Carolina Press, 1984

Pyne, Charlynn Spencer, ed., *Frederick Douglass: A Resource Guide for Young People*, Washington, D.C., Howard Unniversity, Moorland-Spingarn Research Center, Oct., 1982

Quarles, Benjamin, *Black Abolitionists*, London, Oxford University Press, 1969

————, *Frederick Douglass*, Washington, D.C., The Associated Publishers, 1948

————, introduction, *Narrative of the Life of Frederick Douglass*, Cambridge, Mass., The Belknap Press of Harvard University Press. 1967

Washington, Booker T., *Frederick Douglass*, New York, Argosy-Antiquarian Ltd., 1906

Woodson, Carter G., ed., *Negro Orators and Their Orations*, Washington, D.C., The Associated Publishers, 1925

THE BLACK ROOTS OF EGYPT'S GLORY

By Charles S. Finch III

"Unfitted by ages of tropical life for any effective intrusion among the White Race, the negro and negroid people remained without any influence on the development of civilization."

Those words in 1926 by James Henry Breasted, dean of American Egyptologists, echoed the dominant sentiment of the time: that black Africa had no share in the creation of any of the first civilizations of man. This message was so powerful and so tenacious that as recently as May 31, Dr. Edward Bleiberg, assistant director of the Institute of Egyptian Art and Archaeology at Memphis State University, stated categorically in the Memphis Commercial Appeal that "Egyptians were considered Caucasians."

This, then, is the crux of a controversy that has flared up repeatedly throughout the 155-year existence of Egyptology. The argument continues today, but in the face of ever-increasing evidence that civilization—like the human race itself—began in Africa, the once-prevailing view is clearly doomed.

The controversy was opened in 1791 by France's Count Volney, scholar, world-traveler, confidant of Benjamin Franklin and an aristocrat of pronounced republican sympathies. In Egypt, he had seen age-old monuments and temples lying half-buried in the sand and had pondered the meaning of civilization, its rise and its fall—reflections that he gave free rein in his "Ruins of Empires." How is it, he mused, that "a people, now forgotten, discovered, while others were yet barbarians, the elements of the arts and the sciences. A race of men now rejected from society for their *sable skin and frizzled hair* [emphasis in original], founded on the study of the laws of nature, those civil and religious systems which still govern the universe."

On this point the count had not the slightest doubt: the Greeks had unanimously proclaimed Egypt's African origins and the stony evidence of the sphinx—whose features were clearly etched in the African mold—confirmed it. Was it not one of the crueler ironies of history that the very people who had given the world civilization were now a race of slaves and outcasts?

Reprinted from the *Washington Post*, with kind permission.

In 1799, Napoleon's engineers on his Egyptian campaign discovered the Rosetta Stone. Immediately, it caused a sensation in the learned circles of Europe, for on it were inscriptions in three languages: Egyptian hieroglyphics, Demotic (a cursive form of hieroglyphics) and Greek. It was evident the three panels represented the same inscription in three languages, so it was possible to proceed with a decipherment of the hieroglyphs and the Demotic by reference to the Greek. In 1822, the genius of Jean-Francois Champollion finally solved the decipherment riddle. With this, the age of Egyptology proper began. A door to the past was opened that many had thought permanently closed.

Astonishment and Vexation

A veritable explosion of interest in things Egyptian occurred. Champollion and others in France, Germany, and England began translating important Egyptian documents. English and German expeditions mounted large-scale digs and collections of Egyptian artifacts, which soon filled museums and private collections all over Europe. Unfolding before the eyes of an astounded world was a material splendor quite beyond the most admiring descriptions of the ancient Greeks.

The re-opening of this door to the past, however, contained some disquieting implications. The newly-translated inscriptions and documents revealed an intellectual culture that had attained a startlingly advanced level of development. The prototypes of mathematics, medicine, astronomy, metallurgy, philosophy, religion and the arts were, by degrees, coming to light among the vast ruins of this intriguing civilization. For a people accustomed to believing for 15 centuries that all learning, all science, and all art had begun with the Greeks, the evidence of Egypt required a radical restructuring of thinking.

This posed vexing problems indeed. The profound success of modern Europe was built upon the system of colonization and African slavery, and Europe, led by her learned men, had persuaded herself not only that the enslavement of Africans was an historical necessity but that it would benefit Africans themselves by passing to them the light of civilization. Volney's ideas were suddenly downright subversive. Cherished Greece, not the father but the child? Not the master but the pupil? Of an African race? It just wouldn't do.

As the 19th century wore on, German scholars began applying their meticulous methods of research to the study of ancient Egyptian language. Finding many similarities in words and syntax between Egyptian and the Semitic languages, the Germans unhesitatingly proclaimed Egyptian to belong to this group. A a result, their leading Egyptologists—Eber, Erman and Brugsch— concluded that the impetus for Egyptian civilization itself came from a western Asiatic or Semitic source. Like others, they saw in the human figures on the Egyptian monuments—many colored a reddish-brown—evidence of a non-African "Mediterranean race." Anthropologically speaking, no such race ever existed, but that did not trouble them overmuch and the term has remained in vogue to this day.

By the early 20th century, paleonatomists had examined many ancient Egyptian skeletons and, using their own craniometric criteria for racial classification, had proceeded to categorize the Egyptian skull samples. Thompson and MacIver classified 24 percent of pre-dynastic skulls and 25 percent of dynastic skulls in their sample as Negroid. The eminent Arthur Keith challenged their parameters because using them to classify a modern English sample of skulls would place fully 30 percent in the Negroid category! Nothing daunted, Falkenburger, using his own parameters, classified pre-dynastic skulls as 36 percent Negroid, 33 percent Mediterranean, 11 percent Cro-Magnoids and 20 percent "mixed."

After Count Volney, there continued to be a few dissenting voices "crying in the wilderness" of learned opinion, and now and then even one of the recognized members of the Egyptological confraternity swam against the tide. The most conspicuous was the prolific E.A.W. Budge. Unusual for an Egyptologist, he had conducted extensive research among the peoples of the Sudan and Ethiopia—encountering cultural practices, religious ideas and languages which showed clear and identifiable linkages to ancient Egypt. It became clear to Budge that everything about ancient Egypt could be understood only by reference to Africa; there was nothing fundamentlally Asiatic about Egyptian culture. In 1920, in his massive and erudite "Egyptian Hieroglyphic Dictionary," Budge, reversing a 100-year trend and his own earlier opinion, classified Egyptian as an African rather than a Semitic language.

The true reversal of the tide, however, came from outside the circles of European scholarship. From the 20th century's second decade on a few obscure black scholars in America began to challenge the de-Africanizing impulse in Egyptian historiography. Among these were the journalist J.A. Rogers, William Leo Hansberry, Willis N. Huggins, John G. Jackson and no less than W.E.B. DuBois. But the man who did more than any other to restore Egypt to her place in African history was from the other side of the Atlantic.

Out of the South

The late Cheikh Anta Diop was a Senegalese scholar who first went to Paris in 1946 to become a physicist. He remained there 15 years, studying physics under Frederick Joliot-Curie, Madame Curie's son-in-law and ultimately translating parts of Einstein's Theory of Relativity into his native Wolof. Diop also mastered studies of African history, Egyptology, linguistics, anthropology, economics and sociology as he armed himself for the task of setting the historical record straight. He developed an investigative method that was comparative, eclectic and Afro-centric. Ultimately his arguments in favor of an African or "Negro" origin of Egyptian civilization won widespread interational support by virtue of his erudition and brilliance and the logical force of his ideas, and with him appears a whole new school of African historiography. The following elucidation of evidence owes much to the work of Cheikh Anta Diop, who died las year.

The first line of evidence in favor of an African origin of Egyptian civilization comes from the Egyptians themselves. They called their land "Kamit," i.e., "the Black Land," and their own name for themselves was "Kamiu," which translates literally as "the Blacks." Their word for the African lands to the south of the was "Khenti"—"Khentiu" denoting the Sudanic peoples who lived there—and this is also their word for "first foremost, beginning, origin, chief."

Furthermore, the Egyptian word for "east" is the same as their word for "left" and their word for "west" the same as their word for "right." This makes sense only if the Egyptians oriented themselves southward and looked in that direction for the land of their origins. No people coming from north of Egypt would have oriented themselves in this way—particularly since Egypt's location in the northern hemisphere lends itself more naturally to a northward orientation. Further evidence is found in the Egyptians' anthropomorphic representations of the passage of the sun across the heavens, in which the boat of the sun begins its morning or eastern ascent on the ledft side of the sky-goddess Nut—who thus is in a southern heaven despite Egypt's northern hemisphere location.

Moreover, whenever Egyptian inscriptions refer to Egyptian origins, the land of Punt—present-day Somalia and northern Kenya—is pointed to as the ancestral homeland. One word for inner Africa, "yau," is the same as their word for "old," making inner Africa "the old country" of immigration. Inner Africa also was Ta-Neter, "the Land of the Gods." Everything about the interior of Africa evoked in the Egyptians a sense of awe, reverence and nostalgia.

Additional evidence of Egypt's origins comes from the genealogy of Noah in Genesis. Noah's three sons are Ham, Shem and Japeth, the ancestors of the three main branches of humankind known to the biblical writers. Ham is indubitably the ancestor of the black race; his name comes from the Egyptian "kam" meaning "black." His sons are Misraim (Egypt), Cush (Ethiopia), Canaan (Palestine) and Phut (Punt or East Africa). Though allegorical on one level, the Old Testament writers were accurately reflecting known ethnic relationships of antiquity by placing the Egyptians in the black or African branch of humanity.

Finally, unequivocal statements on the subject come from the Greek writers of antiquity. Herodotus—an eyewitness—makes the most definitive statement when he compares the Egyptians, by virtue of their black skin and woolly hair, to the Colchians and Ethiopians. There are nearly a dozen other surviving references in Greek literature to the race and color of the Egyptians, from writers as diverse as Aeschylus, Aristotle and Strabo, and they unanimously confirm the remarks of Herodotus. The fact that the Egyptians were black and African was so completely self-evident to the ancient Greeks that it was a commonplace seldom worthy of special notice.

Cheikh Anta Diop was the first to challenge the older description of ancient Egyptians as a "dark red" or "Mediterranean" race. As Diop pointed out, many peoples throughout Africa have a reddish-brown complexion—including the modern-day Masai of Kenya. Diop was also the firsts to propose a systematic study of the melanin content of Egyptian mummy skin. His own investigations had shown that mummies contained concentrations of that dark pigment entirely comparable to that of sub-Saharan Africans. As for Falkenburger's craniometric studies, Diop demonstrated that many skulls from sub-Saharan Africa meet the "Mediterranean" criteria of Falkenburg's schema—in effect invalidating the whole premise.

The last issue that Diop disposed of, in collaboration with his Congolese linguist colleague, Theophile Obenga. was that of language. At a landmark symposium in Cairo in 1973, Diop and Obenga showed beyond all doubt what Budge had affirmed nearly 50 years earlier: that Egyptian was fundamentally an African language. The Semitic elements in the language come from late borrowings and, as the noted linguist Joseph Greenberg has attested, from the Semitic languages' own origins in the northeast African group. The Cairo symposium marked the beginning of the end for scholarship that sought to deny Egypt's African origin.

An African Renaissance

The Diopian thesis broke like a tidal wave upon the bulwarks of conventional Egyptology. It occasioned two kinds of responses: (1) absolute silence or (2) shrill rebuttal, and this pattern continues to the present. But in 1980 Bruce Williams, of the University of Chicago's Oriental Institute, discovered artifacts—originally recovered in 1962 prior to the opening of the Aswan Dam—from a pharaonic kingship in Nubia (northeast Africa) 300 years before the first Egyptian dynasty. With that discovery, the Afrophobic Egyptology born of the 19th century has become a scholarship in retreat.

For Diop and those who have followed him, the study of Egypt's place in African history is fundamental to the African renaissance he envisaged, much the ways the rediscovery of the values of Greek civilization gave impetus to the European Renaissance of four centuries ago. It demands a wholesale reassessment of African and world history. Already the imaginative scholarship of Ivan Van Sertima of Rutgers University has brought forth important evidence of an Egyptian presence in pre-Columbian America in 800 B.C. and perhaps even earlier. Heretofore unsuspected connections between ancient Africa and other civilizations are emerging. Our vision of the past, which informs our present and guides our future, is undergoing a radical revision. The consedquences of this can be expected to have a profound impact on succeeding generations.

BLACK RULERS OF THE GOLDEN AGE

By Legrand H. Clegg II

*When Asia overwhelmed Egypt, Egypt sought refuge in
Ethiopia [Nubia] as a child returns to its mother, and
Ethiopia then for centuries dominated Egypt and suc-
cessfully invaded Asia.*
    —W.E.B. DuBois, *The World And Africa: An In-
    quiry into the Part Which Africa Has Played in
    World History*, New York: International Publish-
    ers, 1961, p. 117.

Over the past quarter of a century during which Americans and Europeans
have gradually lost their total monopoly on the study and interpretation of world
history (and such allied fields as anthropology, archaeology and paleontology),
there have emerged two distinct positions on the racial identity of the ancient
Egyptian people. One view, which was introduced by Nineteenth Century
Egyptologists and has dominated Western scientific thinking ever since, is that
"the people who lived in Ancient Egypt were 'white,' even though their pig-
mentation was dark, or even black, as early as the predynastic period. Negroes
made their appearance only from the XVIIIth Dynasty onwards."[1] Little evidence has ever been presented in support of this position, but it has survived
largely, if not entirely, on the strength of the reputation, power and influence of
the scientists and scholars who espouse it. The opposing view, which holds that
"ancient Egypt was peopled, 'from its neolithic infancy to the end of the native
dynasties,' by Black Africans,"[2] appears to have been the only opinion on the
subject from the time of the ancient Hebrews[3] and Greeks[4] until the birth of the
science of Egyptology in Europe over a century ago.

During the 20th Century the latter view has been resurrected in the writings of
such African-American scholars as W.E.B. DuBois, William L. Hansberry, J.A.
Rogers, Carter G. Woodson, Chancellor Williams, Yosef Ben Jochanan and
John Henrike Clark and a number of African scholars, including Cheikh Anta
Diop and I. Obenga. One of the major periods in Egyptian history that these
scholars have considered in support of their opinion is that of the Seventeenth and
Eighteenth Dynasties (Egypt's "Golden Age") which is the focus of this paper.

Undoubtedly because of their defensive position in the face of the awesome
might of Western scholarship, the advocates of a Black Egypt have been most
meticulous in proving their case as they seek to change prevailing opinion. Chief
among these scholars is Diop, probably the world's greatest living historian and
certainly the foremost contemporary authority on African History and culture. He
relies on anthropology, iconography, melanin dosage tests, osteological mea-

surements, blood groupings, the testimony of classical writers, self-descriptive Egyptian hieroglyphs, divine epithets, Bibical eyewitnesses, linguistics and various cultural data in support of his opinion regarding the ethnicity of the ancient Egyptians.[5]

We enter this controversy as proud disciples of Dr. Diop and the other distinguished scholars who have relied on evidence rather than passion in their pursuit of the truth with respect to the racial identity of the ancient Egyptians. While we understand why the advocates of a Black Egypt have persisted in pressing for the overall acceptance of their position by the moguls of Western academia, we are disinclined to follow this course. It is clear to us that Western authority, as a whole, has conspired to suppress, distort or ignore African history with the intent of perpetuating white historical supremacy; and that this deeply entrenched practice will not give way to the truth simply because the truth is right, just or supported by solid evidence. Therefore, this paper is not intended as another debate with Western scholars over whether the ancient Egyptians as a general rule were blacks. In our opinion, this issue has been settled in the affirmative.

Nevertheless, all points of view should be periodically updated and refined in order to maintain their scientific accuracy. Hence, in further support of our opinion that the ancient Egyptians were essentially a Black people, we hereby propose that a new, comprehensive ethnic examination be undertaken of the general Egyptian population during the Old, Middle and New Kingdoms, the First and Second Intermediate Periods, the Nubian Renaissance (Twenty-Fifth Dynasty) and the period of decline. We also recommend that a similar analysis be made of every possible ruler of each dynasty from the time of Menes in the First Dynasty to the conquest of Egypt by Alexander of Macedonia. This will probably require years of research and it is made difficult by the paucity of available evidence; yet the task must be undertaken if we intend for our work to supplant the lies and inaccuracies of prevailing opinion in African history.

In keeping with the above proposal, our specific intent in this brief paper is to undertake a scientific evaluation of the racial characteristics of the rulers of Egypt's Seventeenth and Eighteenth Dynasties. We have chosen this period because of its significance in African history and world affairs. The Seventeenth Dynasty began a major war of liberation which ended victoriously in the founding of the Eighteenth. This succeeding royal family brought Egypt to new heights of technical achievement and military might, and marked the first time that any nation expanded its borders to encompass a vast world empire. We believe that our scrutiny of the familial ties of the rulers of these two great dynasties will establish a concrete and verifiable genetic continuum that may well remove the ethnicity of these royal families from the realm of speculation.

Background

But in order to lay the foundation for our case here, we must look beyond both the Seventeenth and Eighteenth Dynasties into the Twelfth Dynasty of the Middle Kingdom (circa. 2000-1780 B.C.) at which time Egypt had lapsed into confusion, contention and internal strife that ultimately led to what is called the Second Intermediate Period (i.e., the Thirteenth through the early Seventeenth Dynasties, c. 1786-1567 B.C.). Manetho, an Egyptian priest (ca. 300 B.C.), wrote an historical treatise on Egypt which includes this period, but it has perished. Fortunately, however, Jewish historian Flavius Josephus quotes a portion of Manetho's account of the Hyksos invasion which was the most significant event of the Second Intermediate Period and which transformed Egyptian History. "[A] blast of God smote us," Manetho states, "and unexpectedly from the regions of the East, invaders of obscure race marched in confidence of victory against our land. By main force they easily seized it without striking a blow; and having overpowered the rulers of the land they then burned our cities ruthlessly, razed to the ground the temples of the gods, and treated all the natives with a cruel hostility, massacring some and leading into slavery the wives and children of others... Finally, they appointed as king one of their number whose name was Salitis.''[6]

Manetho designated these invaders as "Hyksos," which he interprets to mean "king-shepherds" in the Egyptian language.[7] Today the word Hyksos is more generally interpreted as "rulers of foreign lands."[8]

These invaders were largely Semitic foreigners driven from Western Asia into Africa by instability and famine. They appear to have established themselves in Lower Egypt and may have extended their influence, if not their actual rule, over much of the remainder of the country.[9]

Although Manetho holds that the Hyksos dominated Egypt for 511 years, [10] modern scholars generally believe that they ruled for no more than about two centuries.[11] During this period their cultural impact was most unremarkable. "The Hyksos left no literary evidence of their occupation of Egypt. Indeed, they left practically no large monuments at all. What we know about them has been painfully gleaned from a host of scarabs.... cylinder seals, and few other isolated objects...''[12]

The Hyksos are of particular significance to us here, however, because they appear to have expelled the native African royal family from Egypt and to have driven its members far to the south. How far southward this family was driven and what ultimately became of its members and their descendants are critical issues.

A number of scholars believe that during the Hyksos period (i.e. the Fifteenth through the Seventeenth Dynasties), "the members of the [Egyptian] royal family retired to Kush [i.e. Nubia] where they lived as guests and wards of the Kushites for many years."[13] In other words, the native rulers were expelled from Egypt entirely and then "sought refuge in Ethiopia [Nubia] as a child returns to its mother''[14] until Egypt could be liberated from foreign domination.

Other authorities hold, however, that Hyksos domination was not nearly so pervasive as had been reported. Diop, for example, insists that the Hyksos "oc-

cupied only the eastern region of the Delta, with Avaris as their capital'' and that
''the Black dynasty'' remained strong in upper Egypt.[15]

What appears to be relatively certain is that during the period of Hyksos occupation the peoples of Upper Egypt and Nubia (the country immediately south of
Egypt) grew close together in the apparent recognition of a common enemy—the
Semitic invaders. From this Black interdependence appears to have come much
''cross-breeding,'' cultural interchange, trading and the forging of strong political alliances. Redford has commented on the special relationship between Egypt
and Nubia at this time:

> During the Seventeenth Dynasty a good deal of contact took place between
> the peoples of Nubia and the Egyptians of the incipient Theban kingdom.
> Egyptian freebooters and adventurers drifted south out of Upper Egypt into
> the wilds of the transcataract region to hire themselves as soldiers to the king
> of Kush [Nubia] while an opposite movement brought Nubian mercenaries
> of Medja extraction into the service of the Seventeenth Dynasty. In numbers
> the latter migration far outweighed the reverse movement of Egyptians. At
> numerous sites in Upper Egypt as far north as Asyut the Medja have left be-
> hind the remains of their settlements and their shallow pan-graves. So large
> was the body of Medja mercenaries present in Egypt at this time that they
> formed a whole contingent of the army Kamose led north against the Hyk-
> sos.
>
> It is inconceivable that so sizeable a settlement of Nubians inside the narrow
> confines of the 'head of the south' should have left the culture of the tiny
> Theban state unaffected. Although the extent of the influence will probably
> never be known correctly, not a few of the distinctive features of New King-
> dom society and religion may have appeared through contact with Nubia.[16]

This prolonged contact between the Egyptians and Nubians also resulted in
considerable intermingling between the two royal houses. So much so that scholars do not know whether the actual founders of the Seventeenth Dynasty were
pure Nubians or Egyptian nationals of Nubian lineage.[17] The emphasis here on
the Nubian origin of the Seventeenth and Eighteenth Dynasties should not be
taken to suggest that the Nubians and Egyptians were of separate racial stocks.
Both appear to have been Black people—the Egyptians having become hybrid-
ized by Asian immigrants, while the Nubians retained the physical characteristics
of the old Egyptian (i.e., African) stock. Therefore, when scholars speak of
Egyptians with ''Nubian features'' or ''Nubian admixture,'' they are referring to
Egyptians of ''unmixed'' African type. The ''purity'' of Nubian ancestry provides a strong case for unmistakable Black lineage, while references to Egyptian
roots alone—at this time in history—leaves some room for ethnic speculation.[18]

Historian William Hansberry quotes British Egyptologist Flinders Petrie as
stating that ''the Kushite [Nubian] characteristics of so many members of the
18th Dynasty stemmed from the fact that many of their ancestors had 'mingled
their blood with the natives' of Nubia during the period of Hyksos domination.''[19] Redford adds that ''[i]t is not unlikely, in view of the heavy influx of

Nubians into Upper Egypt, that the family of the Seventeenth Dynasty could boast of a large admixture of Nubian blood."[20]

The Seventeenth Dynasty

Is there solid evidence on which to base Petrie and Redford's opinions as to the Black roots of the 17th and 18th Dynasties? In search of such evidence, one must focus attention on each of the rulers of this period. As has been noted, the Second Intermediate Period was a time of great confusion. So much so that few details have survived concerning events that transpired during the Thirteenth, Fourteenth, Fifteenth, Sixteenth and early Seventeenth dynasties—all of which fell between 1786 and the late 1500's B.C. Scholars are generally agreed, however, that about 1600 B.C., around the time of the late Seventeenth Dynasty, there arose a family in Upper Egypt that would be strong enough to expel the Hyksos and ultimately consolidate Egypt. Two commoners, Senakhtenre Tao and his wife Tetisheri, became rulers of Upper Egypt at this time. No one is certain how they achieved this power, but James Harris and Kent Weeks note that "[Senakhtenre] Tao may have been related to an earlier king of the Seventeenth Dynasty, Antef V, or he may have usurped the throne. In any case it is clear that he and his wife founded the most powerful line of rulers Egypt was ever to know. Their descendants reigned for three hundred years."[21]

While no mummy has been brought to light that can be identified as that of Senakhtenre Tao, Tetisheri's mummy has been found; unfortunately, however, nothing has been said about its racial characteristics. This royal couple, nevertheless, were the direct forebears of each of the other rulers of the Seventeenth Dynasty; and it has particularly been noted that "Tetisheri's role as mother of the line was strengthened because both males and females of the next several generations could trace their ancestry directly to her."[22] It may be reasoned, then, that evidence of the racial type of the descendants of Senakhtenre Tao and Tetisheri will shed light on the ethnic category into which these founding parents should be placed.

Senakhtenre Tao was succeeded by his son Seqenenre Tao who married his full-blooded sister Ahhotep I. This royal couple began the great war of liberation against the Hyksos people. As a matter of fact it is believed that Seqenenre Tao died in battle[23] and, following his death and the death of his son Kamose,[24] Ahhotep I "rallied the Upper Egyptian soliders to continue to fight the enemy and rid the land of them in order to clear the way for this native dynasty to rule over a united Egypt."[25]

The mummy of Seqenenre Tao has been found and a number of authorities have commented on it. "From the Berber type of [Seqenenre]," writes Petrie, "it seems probable that the [Seventeenth] dynasty had come from Ethiopia... and the earlier part of it... of which we have no names, may have dwelt in Nubia, and only harassed the Hyksos from thence."[26] Hansberry has commented on the "obvious Kushite [Nubian] traits" of the remains of "Seqenenra III" [Seqenenre].[27] And Harris and Weeks have taken special notice of this pharaoh's mummy:

> Of particular interest and importance are the physical features revealed by [Seqenenre] Tao's mummy . . . His entire lower facial complex, in fact, is so different from other pharaohs (it is closest to that of his son Ahmose) that he could be fitted more easily into the series of Nubian and Old Kingdom Giza skulls than into that of later Egyptian kings. . . . Various scholars in the past have proposed a Nubian—that is, non-Egyptian—origin for Seqenenre and his family, and his facial features suggest this might indeed be true. If it is true, the history of *the family that reputedly drove the Hyksos from Egypt, and the history of the Seventeenth Dynasty, stand in need of considerable re-examination.*[28]

The mummy of Seqenenre Tao's wife Ahhotep I has been found, but, as in the case of her mother's remains, no direct mention has been made of Ahhotep I's racial characteristics. This, too, can be inferred, however, from the description given the mummies of two of the children of Seqenenre Tao and Ahhotep I. The royal couple had at least six children, of whom three survived childhood; and it was these offspring, according to most scholars, who succeeded in driving the Hyksos from the Nile Valley.[29] Kamose, the eldest surviving son, followed his father into battle and died shortly thereafter. "How he died is not known, since his mummy was in extremely poor condition when found; it crumbled to dust in the excavator's hand."[30]

Ahmose I, the youngest son of Seqenenre and Ahhotep, continued the war of liberation and finally drove the hated Hyksos out of Egypt. According to Petrie:

> The history of the war of independence then seems to have been, that perhaps for twenty or thirty years before 1600 B.C. the *Nubian princes of Thebes* had been pushing their way northward against the decaying power of the Hyksos. Active warfare was going on at about 1600 B.C.; and a sudden outburst of energy, under the active young leader Aahmes [Ahmose I], concluded the expulsion of the foreigners, and the capture of their stronghold, within a few years, ending in 1582 B.C.[31]

Harris and Weeks have noted similarities between the remains of Ahmose I and those of his father Seqenenre: "Ahmose [I] and Seqenenre Tao shared many general physical features that were strikingly different from those of later Egyptian rulers. . . . [O]ne wonders if both were not genetically influenced by peoples of the south [Nubia]."[32]

The only surviving daughter of Sequenenre Tao and Ahhotep was Ahmose-Nefertari, whom Petrie has described as "the most venerated figure of Egyptian history."[33] While we shall give considerable attention to this queen at a later point in our paper, it is important at this time to consider some observations that have been made regarding her mummy. British anatomist Grafton Elliot Smith was one of the first scientists to examine the great queen's remains. He reported in part that "Nofritari [Ahmose-Nefertari] had very little hair on her head and the vertex was quite bald. Elaborate pains had been taken to hide this deficiency. Twenty strings, composed of twisted human hair, were placed across the top of her head . . . *The appearance of these plaits is not unlike that of the modern Nubian women's hair."*[34] Hansberry has noted that "the queen's teeth were large and healthy, her nose rather short and broad, her mouth wide, her lips full, and her jaws—particularly her upper jaw—tended toward marked prognathism."[35]

The foregoing observations regarding Ahmose-Nefertari's mummy are critical because of her direct familial ties to her predecessors, particularly in the female line. Harris and Weeks have noted the similarity in the physical types of the three queens who stand at the head of this extended family:

> Her head [the head of Tetisheri], broken from the badly damaged body, was one of the first studied. X-rays showed the same prominent dentition, the same type of malocclusion, and the same shape of the skull as the women found in the royal caches of the next four generations. The moderate wear on her teeth and even an impacted third molar, which lay at a very disfunctional angle in the jaw, were the same sort of problems found among her descendants. A comparison of this mummy, now confidently called Tetisheri, with those of her daughter Ahhotep and her granddaughter Ahmose-Nefertiry [Nefertari] showed how well she fit this family group.[36]

It would appear logical to conclude that the physical similarities of the three queens do not end with the observations recorded by Harris and Weeks. In other words, one can infer from their published reports that the mummies of Ahmose-Nefertari's female predecessors bear the same marked Nubian physical features that Hansberry noted in the mummy of Ahmose-Nefertari. As a matter of fact, Harris and Weeks clearly imply this in their references to the possible Nubian origin of this entire family—including patriarch Senakhtenre Tao and his male descendants—on the basis of the mummified remains of the family members whom the two scientists have examined.[37]

While the Nubian origin of the Seventeenth Dynasty is strongly suggested by the remains of the rulers of that period, there is additional evidence that may be even more persuasive. First, the female rulers of the dynasty wielded great power vis-à-vis their husbands and children.[38] This has been a strong characteristic of royal houses in Nubia from ancient through modern times, but it was rather unusual in ancient Egypt.[39] Secondly, there is evidence in the Seventeenth Dynasty of personal names compounded with *I 'h, k3* and *Ghwty.* "These theophorous names," writes Redford, "presuppose a strong attachment to a lunar cult, and there is no reason to believe that it was a Hermopolitan or a Theban one. The moon cult flourished in Nubia, too, and personal names of the Second Intermediate Period compounded with lunar elements are found in Nubia."[40] Redford further notes that "the early Eighteenth Dynasty image of the royal family as carrying on the traditions of the Twelfth Dynasty finds no explanation if the Seventeenth Dynasty was of Theban origin—the connexions of the Twelfth Dynasty were all with the Faiyum area. But if the [Senakhtenre] Ta'o's were in whole or in part of Nubian origin, an explanation could easily be found in the strong impression left by the Amenemhet's and Senwosret's [rulers of the Twelfth Dynasty] in Nubia, where the forts they had built continued to be used during the Hyksos period, and where their deified persons were already ranked alongside the local pantheon."[41]

On the basis of the foregoing evidence it seems probable that the uninterrupted Seventeenth Dynasty, which appears to have been founded by Senakhtenre Tao and his wife Tetisheri, was of Nubian origin—and it is almost certain that each member of this royal family was black. This conclusion is critical to any discussion of the ethnicity of the Eighteenth dynasty—Egypt's new kingdom; because, as Redford points out, "the royal family of the two dynasties is the same: Ahmose [I], the king who in Manetho's list stands at the head of the Eighteenth is a full-blooded scion of the Seventeenth."[42]

The Eighteenth Dynasty

While Ahmose I may indeed have founded the Eighteenth Dynasty, it was his wife-sister, Queen Ahmose-Nefertari, whom the Egyptian people deified as the great ancestress of this family line. We have noted on the basis of their mummies that this royal couple were most probably of Nubian lineage. In the case of Ahmose-Nefertari, this assumption would appear to be reinforced by the fact that in most pictorial representations she is depicted as a woman with black skin. She is so represented in the tomb at Deir el-Medineh and on walls in ruins at Nibnutiru, Unnofir and Sheikj Abd el-Qurnah. A statue in the Turin museum portrays her with Black skin, a wide mouth, full lips, a rather thick nose and more or less prognathous jaws. She is depicted in a similar manner in a bust molded in relief on her mummy case discovered at Dier-el-Bahari.[43]

A number of Egyptologists and historians have taken note of Ahmose-Nefertari's black complexion. "At the Eighteenth Dynasty," writes Samuel Birch, "the negress mounts the throne."[44] Rawlinson observes that Ahmose-Nefertari "is represented on the monuments with pleasing features, but a complexion of ebon (sic) blackness."[45] Osburn speaks of the queen as being "an Ethiop (sic) in complexion and descent."[46] DuBois has stated that "this queen with a black skin has . . . been regarded as a Negress;"[47] and Maspero has noted that Ahmose-Nefertari is generally "painted black."[48]

Ironically, some scholars hold that the fact that Ahmose-Nefertari is generally depicted with black skin is not necessarily conclusive evidence that she was indeed Black. Egyptologist Jules Taylor, for example, has noted that frequently Black Egyptians "are not represented black, but brown, red or yellow . . . ;" while the color black is often used to depict "individuals regardless of their own personal coloration, in ritualistic black guise."[49]

**Plate 1. Queen Ahmose-Nefertari (chief
queen of King Ahmose I).**

The foregoing is of particular significance in the present case when we note
that Ahmose-Nefertari appears to have been the fullblooded sister of Ahmose I;[50]
yet she is always painted black, but he is depicted in the traditional reddish-
brown of the Egyptian male. Historian Lester Brooks has offered some very interesting insight into this whole question:

> [Ahmose-Nefertari] is often shown in pictures of the court with a dark, al-
> most black skin. This is highly unusual, for Egyptian tradition always as-
> signed a fair skin to females, whatever their actual color, and a reddish-
> brown skin to males. One explanation for the unusual treatment of
> [Ahmose-Nefertari] by artists is, of course, that because she was so highly
> regarded, they painted her in her 'true colors', faithful to her real skin tone.
> Another is that as she became more and more venerated she was assigned di-
> vine status and was shown as one of the gods of the Underworld, represented
> in blueblack colors.[51]

Whatever one believes about the significance of the pictorial representations of Ahmose-Nefertari, when all of the evidence is taken as a whole it is apparent that both she and her husband-brother, co-founders of the Eighteenth Dynasty, were Blacks. And, as we shall see, the evidence also suggests that they were succeeded by rulers of the same racial stock.

Ahmose I, whose name, according to Rawlinson, signifies "child of the moon,"[52] ruled from 1570-1546 B.C. His Chief Queen, Ahmose-Nefertari, bore for him at least four sons—of whom all but one predeceased their father—and two daughters. The surviving son, Amehotep I (1546-1526), continued the reorganization begun by his father following the expulsion of the Hyksos.

The "badly battered" mummy of Amenhotep I was found in the Deir el-Bahri cache where it had been placed by priests of the Twenty-First Dynasty.[53] Unfortunately, nothing has been said about the mummy's racial characteristics, but it would stand to reason that Amenhotep I inherited the African features of his parents.

A painting of Amenhotep I and his mother was found by an early Prussian Expedition on the wall of a tomb at Gournon, "the burial place of Thebes."[54] It is now in the Berlin Museum. Noting the pharaohs's racial characteristics as depicted by the ancient Egyptian artist, Osburn states that "he [Amenhotep I] has himself a noble countenance, but his complexion has the sickly, pallid tint which denotes a mulatto."[55] This is a curious observation since there is no evidence whatsoever that either of the pharaoh's parents was Caucasian.

While Amenhotep I probably had several children by one or more of his sister-wives, none of them survived. The pharaoh was therefore forced to designate his brother-in-law, Thutmosis, to succeed him.

The ascension of Thutmosis I (1526-1512) to the throne represents the first break in the royal family line since the Seventeenth Dynasty co-founders Senakhtenre Tao and Tetisheri. But even here the Black genetic continuum appears to remain intact. While Thutmosis' origin is unknown, his mummy has been examined and has been described by Hansberry as presenting "a noticably Negroid or Kushite cast."[56] The remains of the great pharaoh's two wives, Ahmose and Mutnofret, have not been found, but their parentage leaves little doubt as to their ethnic origin. Both were daughters of Ahmose I and Ahmose-Nefertari and sisters of Amenhotep I.

Thutmosis I also had a number of children, but only two are of significance here: Hatshepsut, the daughter of Thutmosis and his Chief Queen Ahmose; and Thutmosis II, the son of Thutmosis I and his lesser wife Mutnofret.

When the elder pharaoh, a great militarist who revived Egypt's glory, died, his sickly son, Thutmosis, ascended the throne and ruled as Thutmosis II (1512-1504). Here, again, we have a pharaoh whose mummy has been described as "noticably Negroid" and whose ancestry is clearly black.[57] His wife and half-sister, the famous Queen Hatshepsut (1503-1482), who succeeded him to the throne and ultimately ruled as pharaoh, bore for Thutmosis II at least two daughters, Neferure and Meryetre-Hatshepsut.

Plate 2. Queen Hatshepsut.

Although Hatsheput's mummy has not been found, it is clear that she is the granddaughter of Ahmose and Ahmose-Nefertari and the daughter of Thutmose I and Mutnofret. From this one can readily infer that she, too, in Hansberry's words, "was neither a blond nor a brunette but rather a person who was in all liklihood either dark-brown or black."[58]

Thutmosis III was the son of Thutmosis II and his lesser wife Isis. Scholars believe that, upon his father's death, little Thutmosis ascended the throne with his step-mother/aunt, Hatshepsut, serving as co-regent. However, "during the second year of her stepson's reign she took over all authority from the young ruler and was crowned King of Upper and Lower Egypt."[59]

Following Hatshepsut's death, Thutmosis III finally achieved independent power. This pharaoh, who earned the reputation of being Egypt's "greatest and most powerful ruler," reigned from 1504-1450 B.C. His roots also appear to have been black. According to Diop, Isis, the mother of Thutmosis III, was from the Sudan.[60] DuBois has stated that the pharaoh's "granite head in the British Museum has distinct Negro features."[61] And Maspero has commented on the great king's mummy: "His [Thutmosis III] statues, though not representing him as a type of manly beauty, yet give him refined, intelligent features, but a comparison with the mummy shows that the artists have idealized their model. The forehead is abnormally low, the eyes deeply sunk, the jaw heavy, the lips thick, and the cheekbones extremely prominent; the whole recalling the physiognomy of Thutmose II [Thutmosis II], though with a greater show of energy. Thutmose

Plate 3. Temple of Queen Hatshepsut at Luxor.

III [Thutmosis III] is a fellah of the old stock, squat, thickset, vulgar in character and expression, but not lacking in firmness and vigour."[62]

Thutmosis III was succeeded to the throne by Amenhotep II, a son borne for him by his half-sister Meryetre-Hatshepsut, the daughter of Queen Hatshepsut. Amenhotep II's uneventful reign extended over a period of about twenty-five years. From his mummy it has been noted that this pharaoh was "taller than both his father and his son [Thutmosis IV];"[63] but nothing has been said regarding the king's racial characteristics. However, both of the pharaoh's parents appear to have been black or "Negroid" and the same may be confidently said of him. The surviving statues of Amenhotep II seem to confirm this hypothesis.[64]

Amenhotep II's chief queen, about whose origin little is known, was Tia. She bore Thutmosis IV, who succeeded his father to the throne. This pharaoh ruled from 1425-1417 B.C. His emaciated mummy has also been found and Harris and Weeks have noted its strong "resemblance to Amenhotep II, a fact that helps confirm the known order of royal succession."[65] Just as in the case of his father, nothing has been said regarding the racial characteristics of the mummy of Thutmosis IV. As the grandson of Thutmosis III and his Chief Queen Meryetre-

Plate 4. Queen Tiye (chief queen of
Amenhotep III).

Plate 5. King Akhenaton (son of
Amenhotep III and Queen Tiye).

Hatshepsut, however, it may be inferred that Thutmosis IV inherited considerable African genetic material.

The final rulers of the Eighteenth Dynasty were the descendants of Thutmosis
IV. At this time a new infusion of Nubian "blood" appears to have entered the
royal family through Mutemwiya[66]—the wife of Thutmosis IV; and through
Yuya and Thuya, the parents of Queen Tiye and the pharaoh Ay.[67]

Amenhotep III, "the magnificent" (1417-1379 B.C.), was the son and successor of Thutmose IV and Mutemwiya. This king married the beautiful Queen
Tiye and, according to early scholars, she bore for her husband the successive
rulers of Egypt—Amenhotep IV (Akhenaton), Smenkhare and Tutankhamun.[68]

A number of scholars have described Amenhotep III as Black. "The features"
of this monarch, writes British Egyptologist John Wilkinson, "cannot fail to
strike everyone who examines the portraits of the Egyptian kings [as] having
more in common with the Negro than those of any other pharaoh."[69] Massey
notes that the sculptures of Amenhotep III "show the Aethopic [Nubian]
type."[70] DuBois adds that the king "inherited his mother's Negroid features."[71]
And Rogers concludes that "[t]he Eighteenth Dynasty was of almost unmixed
Negro strain; in fact, its two principal representatives, Amenophis III
[Amenhotep III] and his son, Akhenaton, seem to have had no 'white' blood."[72]

Much the same has been written of this great pharaoh's chief queen, Tiye.
Desroches-Noblecourt has noted, for example, that during this period "the Nubians played a part about which too little has been said. They enjoyed exceptional

privileges at the court of Malkata. It was ruled by a queen almost certainly of their own race, as some portraits of Tiye, such as the little ebony head now in the Berlin Museum show her to have been.''[73] Tiye's ''sourthern looks are even more pronounced on a pendant (the *Menat* counterpoise) . . . and another similar portrait found at Tell El Amarna. Finally there is little room left for doubt when one studies the small sardonyx tablet, now in the Metropolitan Museum, which depicts the queen as a female sphinx. The face clearly betrays her origins; it was recently compared with another image of her still to be seen at Sedeinga in Northern Sudan in the ruins of the temple, dedicated to Tiye. Even the wigs of the royal ladies at Malkata as well as Tell el Amarna were inspired by the short neat coiffures of the Nubians.''[74]

Rogers has described Tiye as a ''full-blooded African;''[75] anthropologist Ivan Van Sertima refers to the queen as ''the Negroid mother of Tutankhamen;''[76] historian Alexander Von Wuthenau states that Tiye was of ''pure black stock.''[77] But it is probably Brooks who has provided the most graphic portrayal of this great queen; ''Any Sunday morning you may see her modern counterpart proudly entering America's Negro churches across the land.''[78]

The mummy of Amenhotep III has been found, but nothing has been recorded regarding his racial characteristics. In 1978, a team of scientists reported that a ''royal'' mummy, whose identity had been in dispute for over seventy years, was thought to be the remains of Queen Tiye. Regrettably, this team has also failed to publish any information regarding the racial characteristics of this mummy.[79] At least one authority contends that the mummys of Tiye's alleged parents, Yuya and Thuya, have Nubian traits,[80] while another strongly disagrees.[81] It would appear that, whatever one's opinion may be with regard to existent mummys, whose identities may justifiably be questioned,[82] the iconographic evidence with respect to the racial characteristics of Amenhotep III and his chief queen Tiye are most persuasive, and serve to strengthen our position that the Eighteenth Dynasty was essentially Black and largely of Nubian origin.

Amenhotep IV, who later changed his name to Akhenaton (1379-1362), succeeded his father to the throne. This great reformer of Egyptian art, literature and religion inherited his parent's African racial features. Egyptologists Cyril Aldred and A.T. Sandison note that Akhenaton's ''face is shown to be elongated with a prominent prognathous or progeniac jaw, large full lips, a coarse nose, large ears, and oblique eyes.''[83] Another Egyptologists, Edward Wente, speaks of Akhenaton's ''elongated skull, protruding jaw [and] thick lips;''[84] while Osburn observes that the pharaoh's ''dusky complexion, high cheekbones, projecting jaws and thick lips, call forcibly to mind the features of the true Negro;''[85] and Rogers adds that Akhenaton's ''skull. . . is what some scientists call that of a typical Negro. The jaw is exceedingly prognathous. His lips, as seen in profile, are so thick that they seem swollen.''[86]

The skull to which Wente and Rogers refer is apparently that associated with the mummy once thought to be Akhenaton's, but which is now identified as that

Plate 6. King Tutankhamun (ebony statue).

Plate 7. King Tutankhamun and Queen Ankhesenamon.

of his immediate successor, Smenkhare (1364-1361).[87] This ruler, whom traditional scholars believe to have also been the son of Amenhotep III and Tiye, inherited the racial characteristics of his parents. Harris and Weeks have noted that his "skeleton and broken skull . . . reveal a man who resembles the Thutmosid line,"[88] which, as we have seen, was decidedly "Negroid." Moreover, the paintings and sculptures of Smenkhare clearly depict his African features.[89]

Upon Smenkhare's death, his younger brother Tutankhamun (1361-1352 B.C.) ascended the throne. Events of the life and death of this king are so widely known that we need not recount them here. If we accept the traditional view, that King Tutankhamun was the son of Amenhotep III and Queen Tiye, his ethnic affinity is obvious and requires no further elaboration. Even if we adhere to the theory that Tutankhamun was the son of Akhenaton by one of his lesser wives,[90] it is still most probable that the boy-king was Black. As a matter of fact, given Tutankhamun's immediate and distant ancestors, his surviving mummy and the valuable relics that depict his facial features, one cannot escape the conclusion that Von Wuthenau has reached: "The features of this Egyptian king, whose mother was of pure black stock, are almost as Negroid as the ones of his captured Nubian enemies."[91]

The great royal wives of the successors of Amenhotep III also played prominent roles during the reigns of their consorts. However, no mummies of these queens were found. Nevertheless, a persuasive case can be made for the opinion that they too were either Black or "Negroid." Nefertiti, Chief Queen of Akhe-

Plate 8. Queen Nefertiti (chief queen of Akhenaton).

Plate 9. Daughters of Akhenaton and Nefertiti .

naton, appears to have been the granddaughter of Yuya and Thuya and the daughter of their son Ay.[92] We have mentioned the possible Nubian affinities of Yuya and Thuya. One Egyptologist, William Osburn, claims to have observed, or at least to have knowledge of, the physical characteristics of the mummy of Nefertiti's father. Speaking of the pharaoh's tomb, Osburn says, "The Negro countenance of the King was the most remarkable thing in it."[93] Unfortunately, nothing is known about the mother of Nefertiti.

Most paintings and sculptures of Nefertiti depict her as having decidedly African features—often with the same elongated skull, protruding jaw and thick lips that characterize her husband Akhenaton.[94] All of the couple's daughters, including Meryet-Amon, who was the Chief Queen of Smenkhare, and Ankhesenamun, the Chief Queen of Tutankhamun (and later, following his death, the wife of King Ay) also appear to have had African physical features. Proof of this is found in full detail in the large collection of photographs published in Cyril Aldred's *Akhenaton* and *Nefertiti*.[95]

The final rulers of Egypt's Eighteenth Dynasty were Ay (1352-1348 B.C.) and Horemhab (1348-1320 B.C.). Ay was an old man upon ascending the throne and his reign lasted only four years. Horemhab, who had once served as a general under Akhenaton and Tutankhamun, returned Egypt to its traditional and formerly stable ways. While we have mentioned Ay's mummy and his ancestry, little is known of Horemhab's family except for the fact that he married Mutnodjme, the sister of Nefertiti. Nevertheless, it must be pointed out that the published depictions of Horemhab suggest that he too falls within the ethnic spectrum of his predecessors of the distinguished Eighteenth Dynasty.[96]

Conclusion

The evidence presented in this paper tends to indicate that the Seventeenth and Eighteenth Dynasties of ancient Egypt were of Nubian origin and that each of the rulers of these extended families was either Black, "Negroid" or of Black ancestry. We believe it most probable that any newly discovered evidence will support our general premise and will probably also shed more light on the Black (and perhaps Nubian) origin of the first several dynasties, the Middle Kingdom and, of course, the Twenty-fifth Dynasty or renaissance period.

We therefore urge objective scientists to take a new, hard look at Egypt from an African perspective and to discover a whole new universe which the arrogant giants of Western scholarship have grown too blind to see.

Notes

1. Symposium on "The Peopling of Ancient Egypt And The Deciphering of the Meroitic Script" by the International Scientific Committee For The Drafting of a General History of Africa (United Nations Educational Scientific And Cultural Organization), Cairo, January 28 through February 3, 1974. Transcript of symposium distributed in limited numbers: SHC - 73/CONF. 812/4, Paris, June 28, 1974, page 3.

2. Ibid. We are well aware that the new anthropological party line is that "there is no such thing as 'race,'" and that it is now unscientific to delimit mankind on the basis of "race." We do not accept this point of view for the following reasons: First, three major subspecies of the human family, i.e., the Africoid ("Negroid"), Caucasoid and Mongoloid are readily distinguishable and can be scientifically defined without the absurd assumption that racial "purity" is widespread in either category. Secondly, it appears that the abandonment of the study of "race" by modern science is not so much an attempt to stress the unity of the human species as it is to focus away from the inevitable conclusions that such study has forced upon the academic community. Eighteenth century scientists embarked on the study of human subspecies in order to prove the superiority of the white race and it is no accident that, as their modern disciples come to the startling realization that the human family was born in Africa, that the first homo sapiens were probably Black and that Caucasians probably sprang from prehistoric Black people as a genetic mutation to albinism, these scientists are eager to suppress this information. Finally, as long as the world is dominated by White people, as long as those White scientists—who now claim that there is no validity to the study of race—continue to practice racism socially and academically; and, most important, as long as the Black race bears the universal badge of inferiority forced on it by scientists who have distorted or suppressed Black history, we shall not only include race as an integral part of our historical writings, but we shall prominently focus on it whenever and wherever the truth can be told until sincere men of science return the Black race to its former position of respect and reverence on the earth.

As for the Black or "Negro" race, we accept the definition of Cheikh Anta Diop: "Anticipating the agreement of all logical winds, I call *Negro* a human being whose skin is black, especially when he has frizzy hair." Cheikh Anta Diop, *The African Origin of Civilization: Myth Or Reality?* New York, Lawrence Hill & Co., 1974, p. 136. We also agree with DuBois' position that "[t]here was and is wide mingling of the blood of all races in Africa, but this is consistent with the general thesis that Africa is predominantly the land of Negroes and Negroid peoples, just as Europe is a land of Caucasoids and Asia of Mongoloids. We may give up entirely, if we wish, the whole attempt to delimit races, but we cannot if we are sane, divide the world into whites, yellows and blacks, and then call blacks white." W.E.B. DuBois, *The World And Africa: An Inquiry Into The Part Which Africa Has Played In World History,* New York, International Publishers, 1961, p.119.

Finally, we are aware that there is an intermediate view (between the two extremes presented in the text) regarding the racial type of the ancient Egyptians—i.e., the Egyptians were neither Black nor White, but a mixed type. We have omitted this position from our discussion mainly because it is generally presented as nothing more than a variation of the first point of view, i.e., the Egyptians were "mixed Caucasoids."

3. Diop, *The African Origin of Civilization,* pp. 5-9.

4. Ibid., pp. 1-5.

5. Cheikh Anta Diop, "Origin Of the Ancient Egyptians," *General History of Africa,* Ed. G. Mokhtar, UNESCO 1981 Vol. 11, pp. 27-55.

6. *Manetho,* Edited by T.E. Page et al., with an English translation by W.G. Waddell, Cambridge, Harvard University Press, MCMXL, pp. 79-81.

7. Ibid., p. 85.

8. George Steindorff and Keith C. Seele, *When Egypt Ruled The East,* Chicago, the University of Chicago Press, 1942, p. 24. This appears to be the more correct translation of the Egyptian *heku shoswet.*

9. Ibid., p. 26.

10. Manetho, pp. 85-87.

11. Steindorff and Seele, *When Egypt Ruled The East,* pp. 30 & 274.

12. Ibid.

13. William L. Hansberry, "Africa's Golden Past," *Ebony,* November, 1964, p. 37. The names Nubia and Kush (and sometimes Ethiopia) are often used interchangeably to describe the region south of the Nile's First Cataract and sometimes known as Wawat, a land rich in gold. To the east of Nubia, extending along the Red Sea in what today is the coast of Sudan, Ethiopia and Somalia, was the land which the ancients referred to as Punt. The word Ethiopia, which is Greek for "land of burnt faces," was also once used to designate all of Africa.

14. W.E.B. DuBois, *The World and Africa,* p. 117. DuBois was one of the earliest modern scholars to resurrect the ancient view that Egypt was originally a colony of Ethiopia. Also see W.M. Flinders Petrie, *A History of Egypt During the XVIIth and XVIIIth Dynasties,* London, Muthen and Co., Ltd., 1896, p. 4.

15. Cheikh Anta Diop, *The African Origin of Civilization,* p. 209.

16. Donald B. Redford, *History and Chronology of the Eighteenth Dynasty of Egypt,* University of Toronto Press, 1967, p. 67. Kamose, who is mentioned in this quotation, was the third ruler of the Seventeenth Dynasty.

18. Chancellor Williams, *The Destruction of Black Civilization: Great Issues of A Race From 4500 B.C. to 2000 A.D.,* Chicago, Third World Press, 1974, pp. 62-124. Also see Ivan Van Sertima, *They Came Before Columbus,* New York, Random House, 1976, p. 111. We shall not here indulge in the silly argument over whether the ancient Nubians were actually Black people anymore than present-day scholars feel compelled to defend the foregone conclusion that the Greeks and Romans were white Europeans. For a discussion on the racial identity of the ancient Nubians, one may consult *They Came Before Columbus,* pp. 123-138.

19. Hansberry, "Africa's Golden Past," p. 38.

20. Redford, *History and Chronology of the Eighteenth Dynasty of Egypt,* p. 68.

21. James E. Harris and Kent R. Weeks, *X-Raying The Pharaohs,* New York, Charles Scribner's Sons, 1973, p. 120.

22. Ibid.

23. Steindorff and Seele, *When Egypt Ruled The East,* p. 29.

24. Ibid., p. 31.

25. Barbara S. Lesko, *The Remarkable Women of Ancient Egypt,* Berkeley, Scribe Publications, 1978, p. 4.

26. Petrie, *A History of Egypt During The XVIIth And XVIIIth Dynasties,* p. 17. Petrie's reference

to Seqenenre as being of the "Berber type" should not be cause for confusion. He apparently believed the Berbers, Ethiopians and Nubians to have been Black people and, on page 337, he specifically refers to Seqenenre as Black.

27. Hansberry, "Africa's Golden Past," p. 37. Professor Hansberry refers to a Seqenenre III. At one time it was believed that three pharaohs of the Seventeenth Dynasty bore the name Seqenenre. Scholars are generally now agreed that there was only one Seqenenre and his father bore a similar but different name, Senakhtenre.

28. Harris and Weeks, *X-Raying The Pharaohs,* pp. 123-124. Emphasis added. We would take the two scientists' position a step further and say that the history of the Eighteenth Dynasty is also in need of reexamination.

29. Ibid., p. 125.

30. Ibid.

31. Petrie, A History of Egypt During the XVIIth And XVIIIth Dynasties, p. 23. Emphasis added.

32. Harris and Weeks, *X-Raying The Pharaohs,* p. 127.

33. Petrie, *A History of Egypt During the XVIIth And XVIIIth Dynasties,* p. 41.

34. Grafton Elliot Smith, "The Royal Mummies," *Catalogue General Des Antiquités du Egyptiennes du Musée du Caire,* nos. 61051-61100, Cairo, Service des Antiquites de l'Egypte, 1912, p. 13. Emphasis added.

35. Hansberry, "Africa's Golden Past," p. 37.

36. Harris and Weeks, *X-Raying The Pharaohs,* p. 121.

37. Ibid., pp. 123, 127 & 135.

38. Lestor Brooks, *Great Civilizations of Ancient Africa,* New York, Four Winds Press, 1971, p. 49. Also See Redford, *History And Chronology of the Eighteenth Dynasty of Egypt.* pp. 65-69.

39. Brooks, Great Civilizations of Ancient Africa, p. 49. Also see Redford, *History And Chronology of the Eighteenth Dynasty of Egypt,* pp. 65-69.

40. Ibid., pp. 68-69.

41. Ibid., p. 69.

42. Ibid., p. 28. According to this author, Manetho placed Ahmose at the head of a new dynasty "only because he put an end to Hyksos rule in Egypt and inaugurated a period of independence."

43. Hansberry, "Africa's Golden Past," p. 37.

44. Samuel Birch, *Ancient Egypt From The Monuments, Egypt From The Earliest Times to B.C. 300,* New York, Scribner, Armstrong & Co., 1875, p. 83.

45. George Rawlinson, *History of Ancient Egypt,* New York, American Publishers Corp., 1880, Vol. II, p. 114.

46. William Osburn, *The Monumental History of Egypt,* London, Trubner & Co., 1854, p. 175.

47. DuBois, *The World And Africa,* pp. 126-127. DuBois also refers to the now outmoded view to which many early scholars subscribed, i.e., that, because of her color, Ahmose-Nefertari was not Egyptian by birth, but the daughter of a Nubian monarch with whom Ahmose I had entered an alliance for assistance in expelling the Hyksos rulers. The young princess, according to this view, was married to Ahmose I in order to strengthen the Egypto-Nubian alliance.

48. Gaston Maspero, *The Struggle Of The Nations,* New York, D. Appleton & Co., 1877, pp. 98-99.

49. Jules Taylor, "The Black Image In Egyptian Art," *Journal Of African Civilizations,* April, 1979, Vol. I, p. 27. It should be noted that, while many Egyptologists might object to any consideration of iconographic material to verify the racial characteristics of the ancient Egyptians, J. Vercoutter and N. Blanc have stated that "[t]he incongraphic material available . . . has extremely significant characteristics from the XVIII Dynasty onwards." Symposium on "The Peopling of Ancient Egypt And The Deciphering Of The Meroetic Script," p. 3.

50. For an opposing view, i.e., Ahmose-Nefertari may have been the half-sister of Ahmose I, see Petrie, *A History of Egypt During The XVIIth And XVIIIth Dynasties,* pp. 9 & 337; and Harris and Weeks, *X-Raying The Pharaohs,* p. 128.

51. Brooks, *Great Civilizations of Ancient Africa,* p. 50.

52. Rawlinson, *History of Ancient Egypt*, Vol. II, p. 112. This in itself, according to Redford, strongly suggests that Ahmose I was of Nubian origin. *History And Chronology of The Eighteenth Dynasty*, pp. 68-69.

53. Harris and Weeks, *X-Raying The Pharaohs*, p. 129.

54. Osburn, *The Monumental History of Egypt*, p. 175.

55. Ibid.

56. Hansberry, "Africa's Golden Past," p. 38.

57. Ibid.

58. Ibid.

59. Harris and Weeks, *X-Raying The Pharaohs*, p. 134.

60. Diop, *The African Origin of Civilization*, p. 12.

61. DuBois, *The World And Africa*, p. 128.

62. Gaston Maspero, *The Struggle Of The Nations, Egypt, Syria And Assyria*, London, Society for Promoting Christian Knowledge, 1910, p. 289.

63. Harris and Weeks, *X-Raying The Pharaohs*, p. 138.

64. Cyril Aldred, *New Kingdom Art in Ancient Egypt*, London, Alex Tiranti, Ltd., 1951, figs. 49, 50 &51.

65. Harris and Weeks, *X-Raying The Pharaohs*, p. 139.

66. Rawlinson states, "Born, as it would seem, of an Ethiopian mother, Mutemua [Mutemwiya], Amenophis [Amenhotep III] had a somewhat foreign physiognomy." *History of Ancient Egypt*, Vol. 2, p. 261. Also see Gerald Massey, A Book of The Beginnings, Secaucus, New Jersey, University Press, Inc., 1974, Vol. II, p. 405.

67. Christiane Desroches-Noblecourt, *Life And Death of A Pharaoh*, New York, Graphic Society, 1963, p. 116.

68. Ibid., pp. 120-121. Many scholars no longer accept this view. Wente, for example, and a number of others, now hold that both Smenkhare and Tutankhamun were sons of Akhenaton by minor wives.

69. John G. Wilkinson, *The Ancient Egyptians*, London, 1878, Vol. I, p. 42.

70. Massey, *A Book Of The Beginnings*, Vol. II, p. 405.

71. DuBois, *The World And Africa*, p. 129.

72. J.A. Rogers, *Sex And Race, Negro-Caucasian Mixing In All Ages and All Lands*, New York, published by the author, 1944, Vol. 1, p. 54.

73. Desroches-Noblecourt, *Life And Death of A Pharaoh*, p. 121. Also see Grafton E. Smith, *Tomb of Queen Tiyi*, London, Constable & Co., 1910.

74. Ibid.

75. J.A. Rogers, *World's Great Men of Color*, New York, Collier Books, 1972, Vol. II, p. 63.

76. Van Sertima, *They Came Before Columbus*, p. 29.

77. Alexander Von Wuthenau, *Unexpected Faces in Ancient America*, 1500 B.C.–A.D. 1500, New York, Crown Publishers, 1975, p. 136.

78. Brooks, *Great Civilizations of Ancient Africa*, p. 58.

79. James E. Harris et al., "Mummy of the 'Elder Lady' in the tomb of Amenhotep: Egyptian Museum Catalog Number 61070," *Science*, June 9, 1978, vol. 200, p. 1149.

80. Desroches-Noblecourt, *Life And Death of A Pharaoh*, p. 116.

81. Barbara Mertz, *Red Land, Black Land*, New York, Dodd, Mead & Co., 1966, 1978, pp. 11-17.

82. The mummified remains of the kings and queens of the New Kingdom of Egypt (c.1575 B.C. to 1070 B.C.) were first examined by the French Egyptologist Gaston Maspero in 1889 and the English anatomist Grafton E. Smith in 1912. The mummies had been deposited in two hiding places at Thebes. In 1881 the first cache was discovered in the reused tomb of Queen Inhapy at Deir el-Bahari. The second find, reportedly made in 1898, was in the tomb of King Amenhotep II of the middle Eighteenth Dynasty. "From these two caches were recovered the mummies of most of the kings of

the New Kingdom and a number of the queens. The mummies had been hidden in these two tombs about 3000 years ago after robbers had plundered the original tombs of the kings and queens in the Twentieth Dynasty. During the Twenty-First Dynasty, the mummies were collected and restored or rewrapped, since for the most part they had been badly damaged by tomb robbers looking for treasures placed on the mummies beneath the wrappings

"In a number of cases no identification whatsoever was found on the wrappings or coffins of these mummies. This should not be completely surprising since the grave robbing had occurred over a long period of time, and the royal mummies, after having been badly damaged at the hands of the grave robbers, had been moved from place to place for safety. The priests of the Twenty-First Dynasty were rewrapping mummies some of which were even then as old as 500 years." Harris, "Mummy of the 'Elder Lady'...," vol. 200, p. 1149.

Certain scientists have raised questions concerning the integrity of the white Egyptologists who exhumed the ancient mummies and thereafter indentified them. In this vein, Dr. Diop has written:

> It is customary to mention the straight hair of certain carefully chosen mummies, the only ones found in museums, to affirm that they represent a prototype of the white race, notwithstanding their prognathism. These mummies are displayed conspicuously in an attempt to prove the whiteness of the Egyptians. The very coarseness of their hair precludes acceptance of that contention. When such hair exists on the head of a mummy, it merely indicates the Dravidian type, in reality, whereas the prognathism and black skin—pigmented, not blackened by tar or any other product—excludes any idea of a white race. The meticulous selection process to which they have been subjected ruled out any possibility of their being a prototype. In fact, Herodotus told us, after seeing them, that the Egyptians had wooly hair ... [One] may well wonder why mummies with such characteristics are not exhibited. Those that should be most numerous are currently the least discoverable, and when we are lucky enough to stumble upon one, we are assured that it represents a foreign type. *The African Origin of Civilization,* p. 165.

83. Cyril Aldred and A.T. Sandison, "The Pharaoh Akhenaton, A Problem in Egyptology and Pathology," *Bulletin of the History of Medicine,* XXXVI (1962), p. 305. We should point out here that Aldred, Sandison and a number of others have speculated that Akhenaton's "grotesque," "appalling" and "frankly hideous" facial features as rendered by Egyptian artists are a "distortion of the human form," or on the other hand, may be an accurate depiction of a pharaoh who suffered some physical malady. Most scholars explain away the king's apparent "Negroid" features in this manner. We reject this in its entirety because we do not believe that science must resort to conjecture in order to explain Akhenaton's features. He was a black African who chose to be depicted "true to form" rather than to be represented in the traditional nondescript Egyptian fashion. It is highly possible that other pharaohs had physical characteristics similar to those of Akhenaton but chose, for whatever reasons, not to be portrayed as they actually appeared. Even if we accept the far-fetched theory that Akhenaton was truly "deformed," this still need not carry him out of the Black race. Is it not possible for him to have been a Black man with "exaggerated" facial characteristics?

84. Edward F. Wente, "Tutankhamun And His World," p. 23.

85. Osburn, *Monumental History of Egypt,* Vol II, p. 329.

86. Rogers, *World's Great Men of Color,* vol. I, p. 63.

87. Harris and Weeks, *X-Raying The Pharaohs,* p. 146.

88. Ibid., pp. 146-147.

89. Cyril Aldred, *Akhenaton And Nefertiti,* New York, Brooklyn Musuem in association with Viking Press, 1973, pp. 98 & 101.

90. Edward F. Wente, "Tutankhamun And His World," p. 26.

91. Von Wuthenau, *Unexpected Faces in Ancient America,* p. 136.

92. Harris and Weeks, *X-Raying The Pharaohs,* p. 189.

93. Osburn, *Monumental History of Egypt,* vol. II, p. 341.

94. Cyril Aldred, *Akhenaton and Nefertiti.* We are aware that a number of scholars believe that the art of this period was stylized and therefore the representation of the ruling family with "exaggerated

Negroid'' features was a distortion of its actual appearance. Here, as in our reference to Akhenaton, we find it quite possible to believe that the artists were simply depicting Black people in an accurate manner. But, even if we assume that the artwork was stylized, is it not possible for Black people to have stylized art? Does stylized Greek art mean that the people generally depicted were not White Europeans?

95. Ibid.

96. Cyril Aldred, *New Kingdom Art in Ancient Egypt*, fig. 174. Also see Maspero, *Struggle of Nations*, p. 348.

HATSHEPSUT

By Danita R. Redd

Hatshepsut, a great Black leader of Africa's Golden Age, has been called "the first great woman in history." In addition, she is the only woman known to have actually ruled Kemet (Egypt) as the "Living Horus" (pharoah). She was both brilliant and beautiful. She was a lover of peace and prayed for it frequently. She was not completely a pacifist however, and became a fierce warrior when Kemet was threatened by enemies. Her own eyewitness accounts of battle engagements have survived to reveal this little known aspect of Hatshepsut's life. She possessed a great curiosity about foreign peoples and distant lands. She was loved, admired and respected by both the masses and elites of ancient Kemet. Hatshepsut was also a profoundly religious person, and commissioned stupendous and awe-inspiring construction projects in honor of the gods. Most importantly, Hatshepsut well understood her family history, a history marked by illustrious deeds and proud traditions. Indeed, it was the knowledge of her family history, which stretched back through Kemet's Seventeenth Dynasty, that served as the basis of Hatshepsut's own character development.

Hatshepsut's African Heritage

Although Hatshepsut's mummified remains have never been found, her undeniable African heritage can be ascertained from X-ray measurements on the mummies of the male rulers: Ahmose I, Amenhotpe I, Thutmose I, Thutmose II, and Thutmose III. Measurements for living stature were applied to the Trotter-Gleser Negro equations for femur, tibia, and humerus, and yielded high levels of correspondence. Also, measurements were compared to equations for Caucasians with living stature not matching.[1]

Blackness of the family line can also be seen in its matrilineal nature and matriarchal streak, both of which are dominant features in African societies. Inheritance, including power of the throne, was matrilineal. Also consanguinity, a feature not common in African societies, was prominent in the Kemetic royal family and, to a smaller extent, in its nobility. Thus, the "Royal Daughter" (princess) would marry her whole or half brother and, by doing so, ensure the purity of the solar (divine) blood line. Consanguinity was not condoned for the entire Kemetic population, but it was acceptable for the

Hatshepsut, Kemet's Great Black Leader!

royal family because they were believed to be descendants of gods (bearers of solar blood). The gods Asr and Aset, who were siblings and spouses, had created a union that the Kemetic people believed was the holiest bond possible between a man and woman. Kemetic love poetry informs us that spouses would refer to each other as "brother" or "sister" in deference to this belief. The matriarchal streak can be seen when we consider the fact that the royal women of the Seventeenth and Eighteenth Dynasties consistently held prominent positions. Some of Kemet's most celebrated women lived during these dynasties and blazed the trail for Hatshepsut's energetic leadership.

Hatshepsut's Seventeenth Dynasty Ancestors

Kemet was in a disorganized state of affairs during the Fourteenth Dynastic period. This disorganized state made it simple for Hyksos raiders to invade Kemet.[2] When the Hyksos invaded Kemet, they burrowed through it like mice in wheat and succeeded in vandalizing sacred monuments, brutalizing people, and destroying farm lands. The Hyksos set up military garrisons and forced the Kemetic people to accept one African puppet king after another.

The Hyksos built few monuments on which to record their history, so only a few facts are known about them. Egyptologists purport that the Hyksos introduced horse-drawn chariots which aided in their ability to subdue and dominate. The Hyksos were overthrown during the Seventeenth Dynasty by revolutionaries led by the Kemetic royal family. "Great Royal Wife" (queen) Tetisheri was one of the first revolutionaries to formulate plans against the Hyksos from the Kemetic base in Waset (Thebes or its sub-section Luxor). She is chiefly known to us through royal records made generations after her death. A commoner by birth, she was the daughter of the Honorable Cenna and Lady Neferu. The noted Egyptologist Winlock wrote of Tetisheri:

> Tetisheri must be looked upon . . . as in every way a predecessor of that remarkable line of XVIIIth dynasty queens whose rights and prerogatives were so high that they were virtual rulers of the country. Presumably . . . the family strain was purest and through them that the inheritance passed. Most of them survived their husbands, and in widowhood held enhanced influence. . . . Tetisheri is not only the earliest of this line whose name has survived—she must have actually headed it, for she was by birth a commoner. . . . Lowly as her origin may have been, however, she was the (ancestor) of a line of women famous in Egyptian history: Ahhotep, Ahmose-Nefretiri, Ahhotep II, Ahmose and finally Hatshepsut with whose ambitions the female line of the royal family reached its climax and suffered its eclipse.[3]

The royal spouse of Tetisheri has not been ascertained, but he is thought to have been Senakhtenre Ta'o I. Actually Tetisheri gained her greatest prominence, not as "Great Royal Wife," but as "Great Royal Mother" (dowager queen). After her husband's death, Tetisheri served as prime advisor to her son, Sekenenre Ta'o II. As Ta'o II's advisor, she would have been one of the first individuals to learn the contents of a document sent from the Hyksos capital by King Apophis. This document which caused the royal family to spearhead the revolt, was an insulting message about noise coming from the Waset Hippopotami pool which was hundreds of miles from Avaris. Ta'o II relayed the message to the Kemetic people:

> King Apophis . . . bids me to say to you . . . get rid of the hippopotamus pool in the east end of your city. I cannot sleep for them. . . . The indignant Sekenenre curbed his temper. He did not punish the messenger as another king might, or command his death. He ordered that the man be 'treated with courtesy' . . . given good things, with meat and cakes and sent back to the Hyksos ruler 'with the pacifying words' all that you have told me to do, I shall do. Then the papyrus read 'then one and all remained silent for quite a while.' . . .[4]

The papyrus account is torn at this point but Ta'o II's battered mummy serves as testiment to the battle which occurred sometime shortly after the message was received. When exhumed, his mummy revealed he was killed while in his thirties by a battle-axe. His skull has five deep wounds and his body was hastily mummified, probably near the site of the battlefield.

Ta'o II was survived by Tetisheri and his "Great Royal Wife" Ahhotpe I. Ahhotpe's titulary included "Divine Wife of Amun," "Royal Mother," and "Great Royal Wife who is joined to the beatiful White Crown." Ahhotpe and Tetisheri, at this point, had to maintain the revolution since the men had perished on the battlefield. The insurgent Ahhotpe I lived to advise her sons when they took up the revolt. Kamose, who ascended first, was a mighty warrior who died on the battlefield during his third regnal year. His brother, Ahmose I, then ascended (c. 1580 B.C.) and he succeeded in expelling the Hyksos.

Hatshepsut's Eighteenth Dynasty Predecessors

Ahmose I, "Glorious Liberator," "Unifier of Kemet," "Great Conqueror," and "Final Conqueror" ended the period of great humiliation" (Hyksos domination). A resolute military commander, his battle cry had been "never again!"

> . . . the terror he inspired in entire armies, so that when he approached across a battlefield, mace in hand and wearing on his forehead the flaming uraeus, the cobra crown, entire phalanxes of the armed enemy fell prone in the dust, immobilized with fear.[5]

Ahmose was married to his sister, Ahmose-Nefretiri. She was so well loved

Ahmose-Nefretiri was said to be the most brilliant "Great Royal Wife" in the history of Kemet. She was Hatshepsut's great-grandmother.

Ahmose-Nefretiri depicted side-by-side with her son Amenhotpe I.

and gained so much status that she was deified and worshipped for hundreds of years. After Tetisheri's death, Ahmose and and Ahmose-Nefretiri, concerned about her afterlife, dedicated a pyramid chapel to her. Tetisheri's chapel demonstrated that love, concern, and esteem for her was magnanimous.

Ahmose-Nefretiri had gained even greater esteem. Her titulary included "Royal Daughter," "Royal Sister," "Great Royal Wife," "Royal Mother," "Divine Wife of Amun," "Divine Mother," "Lady of the Two Lands," and "Great Ruler who is joined to the Beautiful White Crown." Her personality, which was dominated by both a rebellious character and independent spirit, compelled her to become the most brilliant "Royal Wife" in Kemet's history. During the twenty-five years Ahmose-Nefretiri co-ruled with Ahmose, she was highly respected by not only Kamet's masses but also by its elite and foreign dignitaries. It was not unusual for individuals seeking audience with Ahmose to first confer with Ahmose-Nefretiri.

Ahmose was one of the first absolute rulers to portray his "Great Royal Wife" as his equal in awesome figures, side-by-side with his. In previous dynasties the "Great Royal Wife" was either depicted as a small doll-like figure or not at all. Ahmose-Nefretiri was illustrated with black or dark-blue skin. The people of Kemet believed that black or dark-blue skin was a divine attribute.

Ahmose-Nefretiri survived her husband and lived to advise their children Amenhotpe I and Aahotpe II. Obviously, Ahmose-Nefretiri wielded immense power as "Great Royal Mother" because she was represented side-by-side with her son, Amenhotpe. The "Great Royal Wife," Ahhotpe II, was frequently illustrated behind them.

Amenhotpe maintained a military power which ensured peace and prosperity for Kemet. He helped establish Waset as Kemet's richest city. He was a soldier and builder of sensational temples and colossal monuments. He raised spectacular structures in Upper Kemet, Waset, and Western Waset. His shrine at Lpetesut (Karnak) has the inscription, "Amenhotpe I, the 'Living Horus' Zeser-Ka-Re, son of the sun, living forever."[6]

There is not substantial material available about the "Great Royal Wife Aahotpe II. But, without question, historians know that she held the same titulary as her mother and that she was filially devoted to her daughter (and successor), Ahmose. Ahmose was married to the Amenhotpe's son, borne by a lesser wife of non-royal blood, Senseneb.

Thutmose I ascended the throne about 1504 B.C. His name meant "he who is born of the moon god." Born during his father's second regnal year, Thutmose I received the finest tutelage for leadership until he reached his midthirties, at which time his father died. Thutmose served as a soldier for many years and gained recognition as a great commander and military genius. His grueling life as a soldier shaped him for leadership. He brought the whole of

Senseneb, Hatshepsut's paternal-grandmother.

Thutmose I had been a courageous and intelligent man. As Hatshepsut's father, he
instilled her with his leadership qualities.

Ahmose was a filially devoted mother to Hatshepsut.

the territory, as far south as the Third Cataract, under his influence. After expanding Kemet's borders, Thutmose ruled in relatively peaceful conditions. He commissioned an extensive building campaign which focused largely on the sacred Amun Temple complex at Lpetesut. In its day the Amun Temple building was not only the largest at Lpetesut, but one of the largest buildings in the world.

Amun had been the leading diety of Waset. Considered to be king of the gods, he was the father in a trinity comprised of Mut (wife) and Khons (son). In the northern cities the leading trinity had been Asr, Aset, and Hor (Horus). The people of Kemet would appeal to the gods for questions of conduct and morality. Whether a person was a ruler, priest, or commoner, they knew that one day, after they had died, they would stand before the gods for judgment and have their hearts weighed on the scales of justice. The Kemetic people believed that the essence of their morality was expressed when they said, "control your hand, restrain your heart, and seal your lips." Every member of the pantheon had an associated priesthood and Amun's priesthood was the most influential and the richest. Thutmose, distinguished and shrewd, relied heavily on the Amun priesthood for advice and political backing as would his successors.

Ahmose also had the full support of the Amun priesthood. Always depicted with a smile, her portraits reveal that she had been a pleasant, serene woman. She upheld the titles she inherited from her female predecessors but, demonstrating a lack of interest in power, she yielded her rights of rulership to Thutmose I. Together they had four children, two girls (Neferukheb and Makare) and two boys (Madjimose and Amunmose).

The Woman Who Ruled As "Living Horus"

The alchemy of the union of Ahmose and Thutmose would be realized in Makare, their only child who reached adulthood. Through Makare, Ahmose proved her true greatness by being a filially devoted mother. From her father, Makare received valuable tutelage. Recognized as an especially gifted child, Thutmose I must have been instrumental in developing her qualities for leadership. From both of her parents, Makare would have learned the deeds of her eminent ancestors, especially her great female forebears whom she came to honor and revere. It is even probable that her decision to break tradition and secure ultimate rulership of Kemet came from the knowledge that her female ancestors were wielders of awesome power.

Thutmose I had associated Makare with the rule of Kemet and, as the designated heir to the throne, she would have learned how to walk gracefully in a stately manner, how to greet individuals, how to develop and maintain friendships, and how to hold conversation. Royal women were taught science, mathematics, linguistics, the liberal arts, and elocution. Moral codes would

The god Amun was the leading deity of Waset. His priesthood was the most influential in Waset.

The divine spouses, Amun and Mut.

have been dominant in her lessons. Many of her tutors would have been of the Amun priesthood. As did all people of Kemet, she would have learned her family history. For Makare that would have included her ancestors' victory over the Hyksos.

Thutmose had other children by lesser wives and concubines, including a son by Mutnefert. She had the titles of "Royal Daughter," "Royal wife," and "Royal Mother" but her origins are uncertain. She may have been Thutmose I's half-royal sister and plausibly they shared paternal parentage. Her statue in the Cairo Museum has the inscription, "the good god, Lord of Both Lands Akheperure (Thutmose II) made by him, his monument of his mother, 'Royal Wife,' 'Royal Mother' Mutnefert Makheru."[7]

Thutmose II was married to Makare and it may have been shortly before their marriage that she received the crown name Hatshepsut which meant "chieftain of noble women." Hatshepsut clearly delineated herself as dominant spouse and records do not indicate that Thutmose II felt resentment at having to take on a secondary role. His mummy indicated that he had been an overweight, sickly man. Even though Hatshepsut had been the real power behind the throne, she was still officially considered the "Great Royal Wife." Possibly, Thutmose II was selected because it was known that he would allow Hatshepsut to employ power. Hatshepsut had to have demonstrated great leadership qualities in order to secure this position because Thutmose II, by right of his marriage to her, had sole power to govern. Hatshepsut had to have had the cooperation of most members of the Amun priesthood, thus proving they too had considered her a great leader.

Hatshepsut and Thutmose II had two daughters, Nefrure and Merytra-Hatshepset. The eldest, Nefrure, received special tutelage. For thirteen years, 1492 B.C.-1479 B.C., Hatshepsut and Thutmose II ruled jointly. This was a short period of time compared to the twenty-one years she ruled after his death.[8] During their coregency they engaged in several titanic building projects and commissioned extensive additions to the Amun Temple complex at Lpetesut.

Thutmose II fathered a son with his concubine Aset, who would come to be known as Thutmose "The Great." Thutmose II died when he was about thirty years of age but before he died, he named his young son (about twelve years old) as his successor. The Kemetic records noted his death:

> The King (Thothmes II) ascended to the Heavens and joined the company of the gods; his son (Thothmes III) took his place. . . . His sister, the divine woman Hatshepsut, adjusted the affairs of the two kingdoms according to her own mind. Egypt, bowing the head before her, cultivated the excellent seed divine, sprung from the god. She was the cable which drew the North, the stake to which was moored the South; she was the perfect tiller-rope of the North, the Mistress who issues commands, whose wise plans bring peace upon the Two Lands. . . .[9]

Makare (Hatshepsut) wearing the white crown of Kemet. She claimed that her father associated her with the throne during the latter years of his reign.

Aset, mother of Thutmose III. She may have been one of the individuals responsible for gaining support for Thutmose III from the faction of the Amun priesthood which opposed Hatshepsut.

Now ruling as "Great Royal Mother," Hatshepsut was virtual sole head of state because Thutmose III, even though he was being groomed, was too young to wield power. During this period, Hatshepsut clearly delineated herself as a great Black leader and developed her advisory board which consisted largely of Amun priests. These men helped her secure ultimate, governmental control and were led by the noteworthy Senmut.

A commoner by birth, Senmut rose to a position of eminence that was unusual but not unprecedented (Imhotep had achieved a much more exalted position in earlier history). The rarity of Senmut's position has influenced modern historians to speculate that Senmut was Hatshepsut's lover but there is no evidence to prove this true. He was a multi-faceted genius who achieved the titles of "Chief Steward of Amun," "Chief Steward of the 'Living Horus'" and "Overseer of the Royal Residence," "Overseer of the Fields, the Gardens, the Herds, the Serfs, the Peasant Farmers, and the Granaries of Amun Weavers," "Heriditary Prince and Count," Sealbearer of the 'Living Horus' of Lower Kemet," "Sole Companion," "Chief Prophet of Montu in Hermonthes," "Spokesman of the Shrine of Geb," "Headman in the House of the White Crown," "Controller of the Broad Hall in the House of the Official," and the list continues.[10] Senmut had boasted that he had over eighty titles. He was a genius, a man with an extraordinary range of talents.

The embodiment of Senmut's remarkable talents was in Zoser-zosru (Deir el-Bahari), The mortuary temple, dedicated to Amun, was considered to be the Holy of the Holies and the most splendid of all. At Hatshepsut's command, Senmut designed and supervised its building on a site sacred to Hathor in Western Waset. It sits at the end of a long valley, built into high cliffs. The design has a clean, uncluttered look and appears to compliment the landscape. Like a line between heaven and earth with its series of courtyards (each smaller than the first), colonnades decorated with reliefs, shrines, inscriptions, and painted reliefs, Zoser-zosru recorded much of Hatshepsut's history. Centuries later, the Greeks would adopt its architectural style for their structures.

Other men had important but less prominent roles as advisors to Hatshepsut. Ineni, "Chief of the Royal Works" was an architect who began his service to the royal family under Thutmose I. He excavated Thutmose I's tomb which was the first one dug in the Valley of the Kings. He also excavated Hatshepsut's tomb which is the deepest of all tombs at that location. His relationship with Hatshepsut may have been pleasant and he may have been one of her childhood tutors. In his tomb, Ineni inscribed:

> Her majesty pleased me, she loved me, she recognized my worth at the court, she presented me with things, she magnified me, she lifted my house with silver and gold, with all beautiful stuffs of the royal house. ...[11]

Hapuseneb, architect and Vizier of Upper Kemet, was in charge of the Amun priesthood. Nihisi was guardian of the royal seal, chief treasurer, and

Senmut, the multi-faceted genius depicted in double portraiture.

Senmut with the cow-eared goddess Hathor. He completed one personal tomb and
began another one. His unfinished, second tomb was discovered under Zoser-zosru.

chancellor. Another architect, Puemre, was inspector of monuments. The Viceroy of Ethiopia, Ibebny, was in charge of the Nubian gold-mines. Senmen, Semut's brother, was a high priest in the Amun sect. There was Ahmose Panekhbit an old soldier and treasurer; Dejehuty who would later distinguish himself under service to Thutmose III; Yamunefru of Nefrusi; User-Amun, Vizier; and Sebner a treasurer. Thuty, head treasurer, was in charge of the royal fortune. These men were essential to Hatshepsut's ability to rule as a great Black leader.

To effect total control, with the help of her advisors, Hatshepsut usurped the throne and accountrements (kilt, crown, uraeus, gold braided beard) of "Living Horus." These events may have occurred during Thutmose III's second regnal year. Hatshepsut then became known as "Living Horus of the North and South," "Ka-Ma-Ra," "Son of the Sun," "Khnum-Amun-Hatshepsut," "The Horus of Gold," "Bestower of years," "God of Rising," "Conqueror of all Lands"; "Lady of Both Lands"; "Vivifier of hearts"; "Chief Spouse of Amun," and "The Mighty One." She took all titles associated with supreme rulership, except one, the "Mighty Bull of Maat," which implied male fertility.

Hatshepsut shrewdly concocted one of the most amazing historical stories by announcing she was the male incarnate of Amun. She said Amun, in the guise of Thutmose I, blessed the astonished, but elated Ahmose with his seed (immaculate conception). Ahmose was depicted giving birth to a male child (Hatshepsut). Hatshepsut, dressed in boyish garb, was then illustrated standing between Amun and Khons, undergoing the ritual of purification. As they poured water over her head, Amun and Khons, in unison, recited "thou are pure, together with thy Ka . . . the great dignity of the 'Living Horus' of Upper and Lower Kemet."[12] Amun and Khons promised Hatshepsut a brilliant future and presented her to the pantheon. Conceivably the people should have found Hatshepsut's change of gender confusing, but, in actuality, it was overwhelmingly accepted. In contrast to the majority of commoners and those of the Amun priesthood, there was a small political faction that opposed Hatshepsut's policies and her usurpation of the throne.

In a cavern above Zoser-zosru, there exists graffiti which has been identified as a satirical commentary on Hatshepsut's adoption of male gender. A cartoon sketch of a woman, identified by several Egyptologists as Hatshepsut, is poised in a compromising sexual position with an unidentified male figure. The Egyptologist Wente believes the sketch, along with accompanying hieratic script, poked fun at Hatshepsut's inability to accrue the title "Mighty Bull of Maat."[13] This sketch also illustrated the governmental strife that existed between Hatshepsut's political faction and a smaller political faction which desired imperialistic leadership. Hatshepsut directed her leadership efforts to maintaining domestic peace. She was highly successful at this, but, unfortunately, she did encounter a major opposition from the Shemau.

Hatshepsut, dressed in boyish garb, is presented by Amun as his divine son and "Living Horus."

**Hatshepsut oppressed the Shemau when they refused to perform their public duty.
When they fled Kemet, she sent the royal army after them in hot pursuit.**

A sub-group of the Amu, an African term for Semitic-speaking people from Palestine who had settled in Avaris, the Shemaus presented Hatshepsut with a very serious administrative problem. They refused to perform their assigned obligation of laboring for public building projects. The Shemau, who felt that Hatshepsut would never gain total rulership, ignored her demands to perform their assigned duty. When she became "Living Horus," Hatshepsut sought to punish the Shemau by oppressing them until they fled Kemet with the royal army in hot pursuit. Regretfully, it seemed that she had made an error in judgement when the royal army was drowned in a flood which aided the Shemau's escape into Sinai. Hatshepsut, who always made excellent use of her ability to make public announcements, refused to concede defeat and informed the Kemetic people that the Shemau, not royal army, had drowned in the flood which may have occurred south of Lake Menzaleh.[14] Egyptologist Hans Goedicke has theorized that during Hatshepsut's reign the volcano on Thera erupted and caused a tidal wave which rolled across the Mediterranean and drowned the Kemetic army.[15] This highly unusual incident (if it did indeed occur), intriguingly comparable to the biblical story in Exodus, may have been a propaganda tool used to oust the powerful Hatshepsut from the throne at the end of her reign.

Hatshepsut received her largest opposition from a faction of the Amun priesthood which was expansionistic. This faction was headed by Thutmose III after he reached adulthood and distinguished himself as a determined soldier. His political faction desired to add more wealth to their fully stocked coffers and discourage invasion from foreign raiders. On the other hand, Hatshepsut loved peace and had a spiritual nature. She may have very well served as a role model for Amenhotpe IV who would, in a later generation, lead Kemet's government to total disarray because of his pacifist tendencies.[16] Hatshepsut had been described as a pacifist by modern Egyptologists, but actually this is not accurate because she was a warrior.[17] In the same mode as other great African warrior queens, such as the Kentakes of a later era, Hatshepsut rode into battle. Even though there were not any major wars during her reign, there was a Nubian revolt. Im Zoser-zosru, Senmut's tomb, and Djehuty's stela there are inscriptions attesting to Hatshepsut's accomplishments as a warrior.[18] One ancient scribe recounted Hatshepsut's military accomplishment:

> I followed the good god. The ('Living Horus') . . . of Upper and Lower Egypt (Makare) may she live! I saw when he overthrew the Nubian Bowmen, and when their chiefs were brought to him as living captives. I saw when he razed Nubia, I being in his Majesty's following . . .[19]

This account, denoting Hashepsut with masculine pronouns, was just one method used to exalt her position as "Living Horus." She also exalted herself

Thutmose "The Great" had been a mighty warrior.

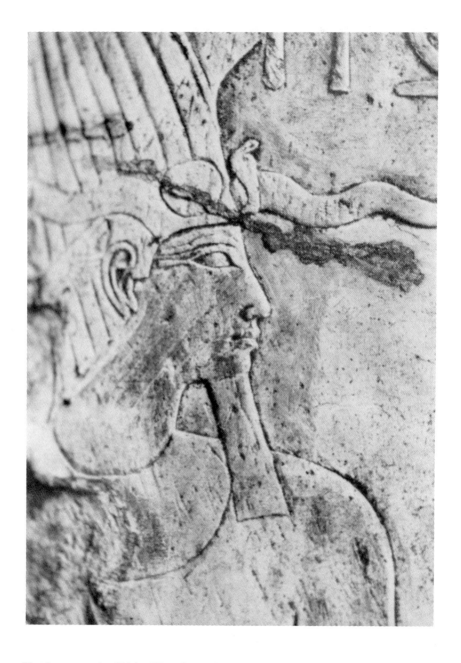

Hatshepsut as the "Living Horus" wearing the sacred Atef crown.

during her celebrated "*myrid* of years." Senmut led an expedition to Aswan which "entered the mountain" (a term explaining the process of cutting obelisks) and brought to Waset the magnificent obelisks which graced the Lpetesut Amun Temple complex. The people of Kemet celebrated when the obelisks were raised:

> With joy of heart, the whole land is in rejoicing . . . they give praise, they celebrate the "Living Horus." Lord of the two Lands . . . Star of the Two Lands . . . (Hatshepsut). . . .
>
> Himself (Hatshepsut) took the lead . . . priests and officials joining in processional, offering the gifts that had brought to Amun. . . . They rejoiced in their hearts when they saw the monument she had established for her father (Amun).[20]

Thuty measured a mixture of electrum (gold and silver) to coat the pillars. Hatshepsut then apologized to Amun:

> Concerning the two great obelisks which my Majesty has covered with electrum for my father Amun, that my name may live forever in this temple, throughout the centuries; they are hewn from a single stone which is hard granite, with no joints. . . . I did it in my fidelity to Amun, as "Living Horus" to every god. It was my wish to have them cast in gold. I have at least placed a surface upon them.[21]

At the tip of one obelisk, Hatshepsut had inscribed that she was "Living Horus" and had solar blood which designated her as the sun's male heir.[22] Hatshepsut had to ensure that her designated heir would rule Kemet after her death or descent from the throne. Even though Thutmose III had been selected as "Living Horus," Hatshepsut seemed to have had designated Nefrure as her successor and Senmut shaped the young girl into a strong personality. Nefrure's shaping was never realized because she died before reaching adulthood. Thutmose III was then married to the less ambitious Merytra-Hatshepset.

Towards the end of her fifteenth regnal year, Hatshepsut sent an expedition to the holy land of Pwenet (Punt). The major text of this expedition, inscribed on the walls of Zoser-zosru, stated that the journey took two years. Known as "God's Land, the Land of Incense, and Hathor's Land" Pwenet, which may have been located in the region of Somalia, was highly valued because of its incense and myrrh. Senmut, expedition leader, carried in five kebenits (ships), varied offerings of Kemet.

Limners (reliefs) of Pwenet, clearly delineating it as an African land, indicated ebony, sycamore, myrrh, and palm trees; long and short horned cattle; domed grass huts which sat on stilts over marsh land; and people who looked like the people of Kemet since they had African facial features and were slender in size.[23] The exception to the small-boned size was Ati, queen of

Pwenet, who was steato-pygiac (common to women of African descent). Parihu, the prince of Pwenet, was depicted with gold rings on his right thigh and a boomerang in one of his hands. The assembled men and women wore kilts and both sexes were naked waist up. The men wore beards braided in the same style as gold "Living Horus" beard.[24]

The people of Pwenet questioned members of the expedition. They asked, "How have you reached this country unknown to men? Have you ascended from the pathway of the sky?"[25] Senmut, dominant in this scene, replied, "All good things are brought by order of Her Majesty to Hathor, Lady of Pwenet."[26] Senmut then exhibited an axe, sheathed dagger, tools, leg bangles, necklaces, rings, and strings of beads which were gifts for the people of Pwenet. A statue of Hatshepsut was displayed to which everyone paid homage. Afterwards they ate a feast of beer, wine, fruits, and vegetables. Following are scenes focused on loading the kebenits with fragrant woods, fresh myrrh trees, ebony,ivory, gold, cinnamon wood, khesyt wood, eye cosmetics, apes, monkeys, dogs, leopard and panther skins, jewelry, cattle, a live cheetah and seven males of Pwenet with their wives and children.[27] The fleet of kebenits returned to Kemet where Hatshepsut is shown looking out for them. While the explorers had been away, Hatshepsut reopened the Sinai mines which furnished gold and turquoise.[28] The ships landed and Senmut is shown congratulating Hatshepsut for sponsoring a successful journey. Then Senmut and Senmen are illustrated sitting at Hatshepsut's feet while the people of Pwenet and dignitaries from other places are shown knelling at her cartouches.[29] Hatshepsut made the announcement that Pwenet had been transferred to Kemet and then, with the gathering, prayed for peace.[30]

At this point, Hatshepsut felt she had accomplished Amun's divine order by conveying Pwenet to Kemet. Items from Pwenet were incorporated into the Zoser-zosru building project. Reliefs of Hatshepsut assisting in the weighing of gold and scooping of myrrh resin, expressed her complete joy:

> She exhaled the odors of the divine dew, her fragrance reached as far as Pwenet, it mingled with the odors of Pwenet, her skin was like kneaded gold, and her face shone like stars in a festal hall. . . .[31]

In her report to Amun, Hatshepsut proclaimed:

> I will cause you to know that which is commanded me, I have harkened to my father (Amun) . . . commanding me to establish for him a Pwenet in his name in Kemet, to plant the trees of God's-land beside his temple, in his garden . . .

> I was not neglected of that which he needed . . . he hath desired me as his favorite, I known all that he loveth . . . I have made for him a Pwenet in his garden, just as he commanded me. . . .[32]

The Pwenet excursion concluded at the end of Hatshepsut's seventeenth

Senmut holding his special ward, Nefrure.

Ati, the queen of Pwenet (Punt).

These myrrh trees were incorporated into the Zoser-zosru building project.

regnal year. Records do not mention Senmut after the Pwenet expedition. He may have died or it is even possible that he permanently left Waset. Hatshepsut was nearing the end of her reign. She had been depicted as supreme ruler while Thutmose III was depicted, full-size, a step or two behind her.[33] This evidence indicated that she was in power at the conclusion of the Pwenet endeavor. Her advisors either worked on government monuments, the most notable being Zoser-zosru, or their personal tombs. Hatshepsut's tombs and smaller chapels were constructed. The Sinai mines were reopened. Kemet was prosperous and Waset its richest city. The appeased people of Kemet had abundant work, shelter and food.

The Destruction of Hatshepsut

Thutmose III and his faction of Amun priests however, were not appeased! It is possible that they had Hatshepsut killed or banished from rulership, but there is no solid evidence to prove this. Towards the end of Hatshepsut's reign, Thutmose III's position became more prominent as evidenced by a stela dated to the twentieth year of Hatshepsut's reign which depicted them standing parallel.[34] Obviously, this indicated Thutmose III's rise in status to Hatshep-

Hatshepsut and Thutmose III. At the end of her seventeenth regnal year, Hatshepsut was depicted a few steps ahead of Thutmose III.

sut's equal.[35] She may have had to yield domination as a bid for domestic peace. Indications of disorder at the end of Hatshepsut's reign lend substance to the theory that she was murdered or permanently left Kemet after accumulating thirty-three years of rulership (twenty-one years as absolute ruler, c. 1479-1458).[36] Unquestionably, within five years after Hatshepsut's death or disappearance, mass destruction of her portraits, statues, and records began. This can be determined because many of her shattered statues were so freshly painted that they could not have weathered for more than five years before being buried under rubble.[37] Hatshepsut's name was removed from all documents that listed the absolute rulers of Kemet ("Living Horus"). The most widespread destruction occurred at the beautiful Zoser-zosru.

The walk-way to Zoser-zosru had been lined with sandstone sphinxes of Hatshepsut. The sphinx was usually reserved for the male "Living Horus" but since she had taken over the role, Hatshepsut had felt justified in portraying herself as such. Inside the temple there had been a multitude of statues (over one hundred of Hatshepsut), wall portraits, and shrines to various gods. Her Zoser-zosru portraits characterized her to have been a feminine, graceful woman despite the fact that she often dressed as the male "Living Horus." Scribes write that she was intelligent, lovely to look upon, graceful in her movements, and fragrant as a flower.

In Zoser-zosru, Hatshepsut's statues, along with the symbols associated with male rulership (i.e., uraeus and gold-braided beard) were tossed and shattered in a rock quarry near the temple. Her name was erased in the names of Thutmose I, II, or III now cover these spaces, but outlines of Hatshepsut's figure or cartouches are distinguishable. Destruction also occurred at Lpetesut and her Valley of the King's tomb was never used. Even more disquieting, the tombs of Hatshepsut's closest advisors were entered and the inscriptions mutilated.

Senmut's tomb and sarcophagus were never used. Effacings occurred in his tomb and, from two cubed styled statues of him holding Nefrure, his name was chiseled. With sincere love, he had inscribed in his tomb prayers for Hatshepsut. One prayer said, "for the life, prosperity, and health of Hatshepsut, by her Steward Senmut."[38] The tombs of Senmen, Thuty, and Hapuseneb were also vandalized.

What had befallen for Thutmose "The Great" to seek eradication of her form and memory on such a scale? The people of Kemet had viewed the obliteration of a name as a form of spiritual murder because an inscribed name was believed to hold a person's essence. There had been two strong political factions during Hatshepsut's paramount rule. Her faction emphasized internal order and had abandoned military campaigns needed to discourage Asiatic aggressors. Thutmose III led the political faction which had imperialistic goals necessary for repressing the morale of foreign militia and adding wealth to already ample coffers. Apparently, Thutmose III attempted

This sculpture of Hatshepsut was tossed into a quarry near Zoser-zosru. Note the broken beard and uraeus.

Hatshepsut as the sphinx. At one time, the walkway to Zoser-zosru was lined with
sphinx sculptures of Hatshepsut.

to erase Hatshepsut's memory, but may not have done so out of hatred as
commonly believed. His executive order may have been purely a political
move (backed by his faction of the Amun priesthood) to eradicate what they
considered a heresy. They did not destroy inscriptions and illustrations of
Hatshepsut's coregency with Thutmose II, when she served as "Great Royal
Wife" since this had followd tradition. As a means to usurp Hatshepsut,
Thutmose III and his faction may have tried to show that she had committed a
breach of religious law by reigning as the male "Living Horus." Hatshepsut
was not the first woman to have unqualified rule over Kemet, but she was
unique by claiming to be the male off-spring of a god when everyone knew she
was a woman. Diedre Wimby suggests that Hatshepsut simply expressed the
harmony of her *ying* and *yang* but Hatshepsut's opponents proclaimed that
she used her expression of masculinity as a means to beguile the people of
Kemet.[39] Undeniably, Hatshepsut had been a great leader, but her policies
were out of step with the times. Hatshepsut's true greatness can be ascribed to
her ability to secure the position of "Living Horus."

Also, it seems that Hatshepsut intended to exalt Nefrure as her successor. If
Nefrure had lived to adulthood, she might have exerted enough influence over
Thutmose III to make him amenable to Hatshepsut's policies. Hatshepsut

breached protocol by exalting Nefrure since Thutmose III had been designated as "Living Horus."[40]

Conclusions

Hatshepsut was an absolute ruler whose character developed from familial
role models dating back five generations before her birth. Family history was
important to the people of Kemet and Hatshepsut's family history would have
been known to her, important to her, and instrumental in her personality
development. Also, she displayed characteristics of both her parents. Thutmose I had been militaristic and shrewd, while Ahmose, who had no love of
power, had been a gentle, serene woman. Hatshepsut typified both parents by
being a brilliant, strong Black leader in one aspect and a woman who loved
peace and domestic order in another. She was depicted both as a lion overcoming the enemy and as a woman praying for peace.

Peace ended with Hatshepsut's death or disappearance. For two long generations after her death Kemet was constantly in a state of war. But, for many
generations after her reign, memories of Hatshepsut persisted. She was remembered in prayers and prayers were said to her. She had become a god in
the eyes of many and stories were passed down, generation after generation,
which told of her godly deeds, brave nature, beauty, and ingenuity. Hatshepsut
could see her shadow lengthening over time when she wrote:

> My command stands firm like the mountains, and the sun's disk shines
> and spreads rays over the titulary of my august person, and my falcons rise
> high above the kindly banners to all eternity.[41]

Notes

1. Robins, G., and C.C.D. Shute, "The Physical Proportions and Living Stature of New Kingdom
Pharaohs," *Journal of Human Evolution* 12 (1983): 455-465.

2. Manetho wrote that the name Hyksos meant "shepherd kings." A modern interpretation of the
name is "rulers of foreign lands." The Hyksos were thought to have been a predominantly Semitic
racial group. Current evidence reveals that they were largely Semitic but were also a cultural group
with several racial elements. The Fifteenth and Sixteenth Dynastic periods in Kemet were dominated by Hyksos kings who ruled from Northern Kemet (Avaris). It is possible that the Hyksos built
monuments which were later torn down after they were expelled from Kemet.

3. Winlock, H.E., "On Queen Tetisheri, Grandmother of Ahmose I," *Ancient Egypt* (1921): 16.

4. Wells, Evelyn, *Hatshepsut* (Garden City: Doubleday & Company, 1969), p. 30.

5. Ibid., 31.

6. Ibid., 40.

7. Buttles, Janet R., *The Queens of Egypt* (1908).

8. Egyptologists have found it difficult to ascertain exact dates for Hatshepsut's reign as "Living
Horus." It has been set as anywhere from thirteen to twenty-one years. The most common belief is
that she ruled for twenty-one years as absolute ruler.

9. Wells, Evelyn, *Hatshepsut* (Garden City: Doubleday & Company, 1969), p. 183.

Close-up on Hatshepsut as the sphinx. Her deeds were godly and her nature was brave. She restored the monuments that had been vandalized by the Hyksos.

10. Ibid., 170-171.
11. Ibid., 227-228.
12. Ibid., 79.
13. Wente, Edward F., "Some Graffiti From the Reign of Hatshepsut," *Journal of Near Eastern Studies.* 43 (1984): 47-54.
14. Shanks, Hershel, "The Exodus of the Crossing of the Red Sea According to Hans Goedicke," *Biblical Archaeology Review* 7 (1981): 42-50.
15. Ibid.
16. Also, during Amenhotpe IV's reign Kemetic art reached its apex.
17. Redford, Donald B., *History and Chronology of the Eighteenth Dynasty of Egypt* (Toronto: University of Toronto Press,, 1967), p. 57.
18. Ibid.
19. Ibid.
20. Wells, Evelyn, *Hatshepsut* (Garden City: Doubleday & Company, 1969), pp. 202-203.
21. Ibid., 207
22. Ibid., 209
23. Ibid., 241
According to some Egyptologists, the Pwenet (Punt) expedition occurred between Hatshepsut's fifteenth and seventeenth regnal years. According to Murnane, the onset of Hatshepsut's Pwenet expedition occurred during her ninth regnal year.
24. Ibid.
25. Ibid., 241-242.
26. Ibid., 242.
27. Ibid., 243.
28. Ibid., 238-239.
29. Ibid., 244.
30. Ibid.
31. Ibid., 245.
32. Ibid., 247.
33. Murnane, William, *Ancient Egyptian Coregencies* (Chicago: The Oriental Institute of the University of Chicago, 1977), pp. 37.
34. Ibid., 39.
35. Ibid.
36. West, John Anthony, *The Traveler's Key to Ancient Egypt: A Guide to the Sacred Places of Ancient Egypt* (New York: Alfred A. Knopf, 1985), p. 443.
37. "Egyptian Vandalism 3400 Years Ago: How Posthumous Fame was Denied to a Female Upsurper of the Throne of Egypt," *Scientific American* (1929): 523.
38. Wells, Evelyn, *Hatshepsut* (Garden City: Doubleday & Company, Incorporated, 1969), p. 253.
39. Wimby, Diedre, "The Female Horuses and Great Wives of Kemet," *Black Women in Antiquity: Journal of African Civilizations* Vol 6, No. I (1984): 46.
40. Murnane, William, *Ancient Egyptian Coregencies* (Chicago: The Oriental Institute of the University of Chicago: 1977), pp. 37-38.
41. Wells, Evelyn, *Hatshepsut* (Garden City: Doubleday & Company, Incorporated, 1969), p. 253.

Bibliography

Bratton, Fred Gladstone. *A History of Egyptian Archaeology.* New York: Thomas Y. Crowell Company, 1968.
Breasted, James H. *A History of Egypt.* New York: Charles Scribner's Sons, 1937.

Buttles, Janet R. *The Queens of Egypt*. 1908.

Cottrell, Leonard. *The Lost Pharaohs*. New York: The Universal Library, 1961.

Diop, Cheikh Anta. *The African Origin of Civilization: Myth or Reality*. Westport: Lawrence Hill & Company, 1974.

Fagan, Brian M. *The Rape of the Nile*. New York: Charles Scribner's Sons, 1975.

Groom, Nigel. *Frankincense and Myrrh: A Study of the Arabian Incense Trade*. Great Britain: Butler & Tanner Ltd., 1981.

Kees, Hermann. *Ancient Egypt: A Cultural Topography*. Chicago: The University of Chicago Press, 1961.

Montet, Pierre. *Eternal Egypt*. New York: The New American Library, 1964.

Murnane, William J. *Ancient Egyptian Coregencies*. Chicago: The Oriental Institute of the University of Chicago, 1977.

Murray, Margret A. *The Splendor that was Egypt*. New York: Hawthorne Books, Incorporated, 1963.

Redford, Donald B. *History and Chronology of the Eighteenth Dynasty of Egypt*. Toronto: University of Toronto Press, 1967.

Rogers, J. A. *Worlds Great Men of Color*. New York: Collier Books, 1946.

Romer, John. *People of the Nile: Everyday Life in Ancient Egypt*. New York: Crown Publishers, Incorporated, 1982.

Romer, John. *Valley of the Kings*. New York: William Morrow & Company, Incorporated, 1981.

Sewell, Barbara. *Egypt Under the Pharaohs*. New York: G.P. Putnam's Sons, 1968.

Steindorff, George, and Keith C. Seele. *When Egypt Ruled the East*. Chicago: The University of Chicago Press, 1942.

Watterson, Barbara. *The Gods of Ancient Egypt*. New York: Facts on File, 1984.

Wells, Evelyn. *Hatshepsut*. Garden City: Doubleday & Company, Incorporated, 1969.

West, John Anthony. *The Traveler's Key to Ancient Egypt: A Guide to the Sacred Places of Ancient Egypt*. New York: Alfred A. Knopf, 1985.

Journal Articles

"Adventurous Archeology." *Scientific American*. (1929): 36-37.

"An Archeologist Detective at Work: With Only a Vague Clue as a Starting Point, Queen Meryet-Amun's Tomb was Unearthed." *Scientific American*. (1930): 206-208.

Casperson, Lee W. "The Lunar Dates of Thutmose III." Journal of Near Eastern Studies. 45 139-150.

Clegg, Legrand H. II. "Black Rulers of the Golden Age." *Journal of African Civilizations*. 4 (1982): 81-100.

"Egyptian Vandalism 3400 Years Ago: How Posthumous Fame was Denied to a Female Usurper of the Throne of Egypt." *Scientific American*. (1929): 522-524.

Freed, Rita. "The Art of Living in New Kingdom Egypt." *Archaeology*. 35 (1982): 60-63.

Giveon, Raphael. "Egyptian Objects From Sinai in the Australia Australian Museum." *Australian Journal of Biblical Archaeology*. 2(1974): 29-47.

Kitchen, K. A. "Rev. of *Ancient Egyptian Coregencies*, by William J. Murnane." *Journal of Near Eastern Studies*. 39 (1980): 168-172.

Lang, G.H. "An Ancient Egyptian Queen." *Evangelical Quarterly*. 29 (1957): 207-217.

Lello, Glenn. "Thutmose III's First Lunar Date." *Journal of Near Eastern Studies*. 37 327.

Read, John G. "Early Eighteenth Dynasty Chronology." *Journal of Near Eastern Studies*. 29 (1970): 1-11.

Redford, Donald B. "On the Chronology of the Egyptian Eighteenth Dynasty." *Journal of Near Eastern Studies*. 25 (1966): 113-124.

Redford, Donald B. "Rev. of *La reine Hatchepsout: Sources et Problemes*, by Suzanne Ratie." *Journal of the American Oriental Society*. 104 (1984): 357-359.

Robins, G., and C.C.D. Shute. "The Physical Proportions and Living Stature of New Kingdom Pharaohs." *Journal of Human Evolution* 12 (1983): 455-465.

Shanks, Hershel. "The Exodus and the Crossing of the Red Sea, According to Hans Goedicke." *Biblical Archaeology Review.* 7 (1981): 42-50.

"Solving A 3400 Year Old Egyptian Enigma." *Scientific American.* 144 (1931): 116-117.

Wente, Edward F. "Some Graffiti From the Reign of Hatshepsut." *Journal of Near Eastern Studies.* 43 (1984): 47-54.

Wimby, Diedre. "The Female Horuses and Great Wives of Kemet." *Black Women In Antiquity: Journal of African Civilizations.* Vol. 6, No. I (1984): 36-48.

Winlock, H. E. "On Queen Tetisheri, Grandmother of Ahmose I." *Ancient Egypt* (1921): 14-16.

TIYE: NUBIAN QUEEN OF EGYPT

By Virginia Spottswood Simon

Recent excavations in Egypt and the Sudan have shed more light on the role of a powerful African queen who ruled before Cleopatra and Nefertiti. Queen Tiye (ca. 1415-1340 B.C.), Great Royal spouse of Amenhotep III, reigned as queen consort and queen mother of Egypt for half a century, enjoying an unusual position as confidante to her husband and as publicly cherished wife.

Was it merely power politics that propelled a woman of Nubia-Kush to the position of pharaoh's Great Royal Spouse? Or was it her beauty and charm, a dazzling quality of personality, that set Tiye apart?

Mother of pharaohs Tutankhamen and Akhenaten and mother-in-law of the beauteous Nefertiti, this woman of the South also became a strong national influence in Egypt's domestic and foreign policy.

Ancient Eygptians called Tiye's ancestral homeland Nubia (land of gold). This was the northern portion of the Nubian-Kushite stronghold on the Nile. Today, situated two-thirds in the Sudan and one-third in Egypt, the area is on a geographical parallel with Ethiopia, Chad, Niger, Mali and Senegal. Passengers sailing upstream on Egypt's broad, majestic stretch of the Nile would approach the perilous cataracts of Nubia-Kush after about 500 miles. Nubia-Kush was a slender land, hemmed in by desert and mountains and dependent on the Nile for life. Although handicapped by hostile natural conditions and invaded and exploited for gold, labor and cattle by Egypt over the centuries, these black people maintained cultural and political vitality for the best part of 5000 years, not surrendering it finally until the time of Columbus when they were overrun by Muslim invaders.

Tiye's era, the 14the century B.C., was one of Nubia's rare periods of dependence. Egypt's armies, with their system of more than a dozen incredibly massive forts, had finally reduced these people to colonial status. But rebellion was rife and Kushites never acquiesced to second-class status. To lessen the frequency of revolt and to attempt to solidify relations, Egypt had a well thought out program of pacification.

Pharaohs erected superb temples in Nubia-Kush honoring her gods. Captured Nubian princes were educated in pharaoh's palace schools in Thebes, and then, thoroughly Egyptianized, they were appointed as deputy viceroys to their own country. Gradually Nubia's upper classes, avid for imported novelties and status symbols, were won over to Egypt's material culture and life-style, dressing themselves in her fashions, speaking her language and even burying themselves in pyramids, rather than in the tumulus graves of their forefathers. Nubians who migrated voluntarily into Egypt were often advanced without prejudice to posts of influence. Even those who had come originally as low-status laborers found social and economic mobility possible.

Yuya and Thuya, the parents of Tiye, were such assertive and ambitious Nubians. High priests in the service of the ram god Amun and of the fertility god Min, they presided over the care of sleek Nubian oxen which, with their decorated horns, were essential to every royal festival and jubilee. A son, Aanen, was a priest of Heliopolis, attaining the status of Second Prophet of Amun.

Their daughter, Tiye, was born about 1415 B.C. In Tiye, dark brown skin graced wide-arched brows, high cheekbones and a nose with delicately flared nostrils. Full lips curved above a slightly jutting jaw. And, if she met Nubia's physical ideal of feminine beauty, she was broadhipped as well.

It was customary for a pharaoh assuming the throne to marry a daughter of pharaoh. Such a "daughter" might be a full sister, a half sister—even one's own daughter. By this device the dynasty continuously reinfused itself with its own royal blood, a line which the priests declared was directly descended from the god Amun. But the young ruler, Amenhotep III, defied the priests and arrogantly proclaimed his highly irregular marriage. Thus a Nubian commoner became Great Royal Spouse, and her children, heirs to Egypt's throne with fully royal and fully divine inheritances.

Certainly the young pharaoh saw in marriage to a Nubian woman a powerful instrument by which to pacify the independent-minded nation on his southern border. For 2000 years Nubia had resisted, sturdily and implacably, Egypt's attempts to exploit her own wealth and her access to Central Africa's riches in big game products and fine woods. Like his father and grandfather, Amenhotep III could expect to have to quell many well-organized revolts and to take defeated Kushites captive. But if this had been a purely diplomatic marriage, the king's treatment of Tiye denied it. The records reveal a transcendent love affair. In an unusually personal expression, he proclaimed his Nubian bride:

> . . . the Princess, the most praised, the lady of grace, sweet in her love, who fills the palace with her beauty, the Regent of the North and South, the Great Wife of the King who loves her, the lady of both lands, Tiye . . .

In the earliest days of the marriage he conceded to custom and appeared on state occasions in Thebes with his mother, a princess of the blood. But he soon tired of the formality, relegating his mother to a quiet old age, and Tiye became his constant public companion. From this moment on, he and Tiye became loving husband-wife role models for their children and especially for their son, Akhenaten, and his wife, Nefertiti, who, in an even franker display of affection, would kiss and embrace publicly.

Wedded to her pharaoh when barely 13, Tiye bore him at least four daughters and three sons, the last of whom, Tutankhamen, was born to the healthy Nubian queen when she was almost 50. Three of her sons reigned as pharaohs of Egypt. She passed her full dark Africoid looks down to her children, notably to Tutankhamen, her youngest. The very fleshy lips and jutting jaw of her elder son, Akhenaten, have elicited every explanation except the obvious. Granddaughter Ankhesenamun, child of Akhenaten and Nefertiti, who became Tutankhamen's wife, has an even more Central African look than either.

Constantly and in many ways, Pharaoh Amenhotep III expressed love for his black queen. The gifts he lavished on her made Tiye wealthy in her own right. An ornamental lake, a mile long and a fifth of a mile wide, designed for pleasure excursions in the royal barge, was dug and named Lake of Tiye. Her palaces rose everywhere, elegant with frescoed walls depicting the Nile valley world of plants, birds and animals. Fish pools brought Nile waters into the pillared courtyards of her estates. The King ordered one such massive-gated palace built for her in her hometown of Akhmim even after the arrival, for his harem, of a lovely young princess from an Asian colony.

A most significant gesture was the erection in Nubia, land of her ancestors, of a fine white sandstone temple in Tiye's honor. Pharaoh had already built his own magnificent temple there, honoring Amun, the ram god whose worship originated in Nubia and spread to Egypt. Under Tiye's spell he caused a separate sanctuary to be built in the city of Sedeinga, 10 miles from his own. It was the first time a queen consort had been so honored. This unique action—half love, half politics—could only have had a positive effect on Nubian loyalty.

As she was his equal in life, so would she be in death. In the thirty-first year of his reign, Amenhotep decreed her burial beside him within his own royal tomb. The colossal group sculpture ordered for their joint funerary temple portrays the pair as co-equal monarchs. Although artistic canons of the priests required that a queen be depicted as an adoring possession only knee-high to the king, the great ruler brushed aside the stricture and ordered that Tiye be portrayed as equal. Broad, blunt faces rise from massive granite bodies radiating serenity and majesty. Possessively, affectionately Tiye embraces her spouse with her right arm.

More than a lover though, Tiye was a capable, educated woman. Her library of papyrus scrolls contained religious, historical and scientific texts, poetry and stories. She must have mastered much of their contents. For her opinions commanded respect, and she exerted informed political influence throughout her half-century as queen consort and queen mother of the most powerful nation of her day.

During three critical periods of the 18th dynasty the black queen was the intelligent, stabilizing force in the nation: the years when her husband's health was declining; the years when Amenhotep IV (Akhenaten), her religiously innovative son, neglected Egypt's foreign affairs and defense; and the years when her two youngest sons, Smenkhare and the young Tutankhamen, reigned.

Figure 1. Queen Tiye and Amenhotep III are co-equal monarchs in this joint funerary sculpture.

At 50, Tiye was full of vigor as her husband lapsed into sickness and debility. By this time Prince Akhenaten was co-regent with his father and had established, and taken residence in, the new city and religious capital, Akhetaton, 160 miles north of Thebes. Traveling between the widely separated palaces of her husband and son, Tiye coordinated state policies. When Amenhotep's final illness came, the Asian outposts of Egypt's empire were under frequent attack by Hapiru and Hittites; Egypt's client states in the North now feared for their very survival. But they pleaded in vain for help from the dying pharaoh. Court officials, knowing the queen's influence with her husband, and confident about her judgment, relied on Tiye to persuade the old man to turn over the direction of foreign affairs to his co-regent, Prince Akhenaten.

After his father's death, Akhenaten was crowned pharaoh. But as a pharaoh he was a disappointment to the politically-minded queen mother. Egypt's military might deteriorated to such a point of danger under him that her Asian allies became more fearful than ever. And even though Akhenaten and Nefertiti entertained Tiye at extravagant banquets and built a temple to Aton in her honor, Tiye assessed her son's conduct of foreign affairs realistically. She moved into the vacuum created by his concentration on religious reform and acted for him as Secretary of State. Kings of the Asian client states bypassed him to correspond directly with Tiye to plead for protection. Kings like Tushratta of Mitanni, who had sent his own beautiful daughter to Amenhotep in token of submission, now sent gifts to the queen mother to reaffirm their wish to continue under Egypt's military protectorate.

Tiye also influenced Egyptian arts and fashion. Large, elaborate wigs worn over natural hair, cut close to the scalp, had previously been the style. But for a time, the vogue was short, round wigs based on those favored by Tiye and her daughters. A style of earring worn by Nubian young people before and during puberty became current in the court as well. From a thick gold ear-stud dangled a large, intricately crafted medallion of gold which carried three to six swinging tassels. Each long tassel was a string on which gold beads alternated with beads of semi-precious stones. Tutankhamen and other royal youths of this era wore such Nubian fashions proudly.

The Nubian queen's influence made itself most powerfully felt, however, in a radical new attitude toward royal women. Amenhotep III and, later, his son who married Nefertiti broke tradition by marrying women who were not ''daughters of pharaoh.'' However, even though such a marriage was essential in order to legitimize the pharaoh's claim to the throne and to the property of the dynasty, the women who transmitted that royal Egyptian inheritance were never exalted as the key persons they were. With Tiye's accession to the queenship of Egypt, matters changed. Not only was a commoner proclaimed of equal status with the king, her name and lineage being always published in conjunction with his, but the male heirs of this dynasty were almost totally eclipsed in the light of publicity

Figure 3. Ankhesenamun, Tiye's granddaughter, wearing tasseled Nubian-style earrings.

Figure 2. Nubian queen Tiye, great royal spouse of Amenhotep III, wears short Nubian-style wig.

and honor dispensed to the princesses. Had there been no princes, this would have been understandable. But there were *three* princes, all of whom succeeded their father as pharaohs.

Why, then, were they kept in the background? An explanation of this innovation as well as that of the equal rank accorded Queen Tiye must lie in the Central African tradition of matrilineal succession. A Nubian-Kushite king generally yielded power to a son of his *sister*—not to his own son. Throughout Tiye's long tenure as queen consort and queen mother the Nubian-Kushite theory of royal genealogy permeated palace thinking and practice, giving the princesses a specially venerated status. This concept of the importance of the female in the royal family, so characteristic of the reigns of Tiye's spouse, Amenhotep III, and of her son, Akhenaten, can only have represented a Nubian influence.

Tiye upset, disturbed and even angered those who guarded Egypt's royal and religious traditions. On the other hand, her half-century queenship was a most important factor guaranteeing to Egypt a peaceful colonial association with Nubia. Egypt needed this peace. Egypt's "glorious" 18th dynasty period would have been poor but for the military and domestic manpower; the gold, ivory and fine woods; and the cattle and rich harvests she took annually from Nubia-Kush. Toward the end of that era when Egypt's influence in Asia was diminishing and was challenged by aggressive Assyrian armies, the loyalty of Nubians to Egypt, assured and warranted by Tiye's ethnicity and statesmanship, was an asset beyond compare.

Tiye, as a new bride, barely aware politically, had reluctantly seen her husband depart for Nubia-Kush to fight against rebels of her own race. Perhaps it was she who had later encouraged Amenhotep III to embark on his ambitious program of Nubian pacification as a way of saving her people from a gradual decimation. Whatever the truth of the matter, pharaoh had found this woman of the South compatible and healthy, intelligent and strong-minded, as well as beautiful. And because he had found her so, Egypt's history and that of Nubia-Kush would be changed forever.

REFERENCES

Barocas, Claudio. *Monuments of Civilization: Egypt*. New York: Madison Square Press, 1972.
Breasted, James. *Ancient Records of Egypt*, vol. II. Chicago: University of Chicago Press, 1906.
Collier, Joy. *The Heretic Pharaoh*. New York: John Day Co., 1972.
Cottrell, Leonard. *Life Under the Pharaohs*. New York: Holt, Rinehart and Winston, 1960.
Cottrell, Leonard. *Lady of the Two Lands*. Indianapolis: Bobbs-Merrill Co., 1967.
Desroches-Noblecourt, Christiane. *Tutankhamen*. Boston: New Graphic Society, 1976.
Egyptian Museum, Cairo. Cairo: General Organization for Government Printing Offices, 1961.
Emery, Walter B. *Lost Land Emerging*. New York: Scribner, 1967.
Keating, Rex. *Nubian Twilight*. London: R. Hart-Davis, 1962.

Keating, Rex. *Nubian Rescue*. New York: Hawthorne Books, 1975.

Leclant, Jean. "Egypt in Nubia during the Old, Middle, and New Kingdoms." In *Africa in Antiquity: The Arts of Ancient Nubia and the Sudan*, vol. I, 62-73. Brooklyn: Brooklyn Museum, 1978.

Mertz, Barbara. *Temples, Tombs and Hieroglyphs*. New York: Dodd, Mead and Co., 1978.

Shinnie, Margaret. "Civilizations of the Nile." In *The Horizon History of Africa*, edited by A. Adu Boahan and others, 48-65. New York: American Heritage Publishing Co., 1971.

Snowdon, Jr., Frank M. *Blacks in Antiquity*. Cambridge: Belknap Press of Harvard University Press, 1970.

UNESCO Courier (Entire edition), February-March 1980.

Wenig, Steffen. *Africa in Antiquity: The Arts of Ancient Nubia and the Sudan*, vol. II. Brooklyn: Brooklyn Museum, 1978.

Wilkinson, Charles K. *Egyptian Wall Paintings*. New York: The Metropolitan Museum of Art, 1979.

Williams, Bruce. "The Lost Pharaohs of Nubia." *Archeology*, September-October 1980 (Reprinted in *Journal of African Civilizations*, November 1982).

IMHOTEP THE PHYSICIAN: ARCHETYPE OF THE GREAT MAN

By Charles S. Finch

The beginnings of the healing profession are lost in the dim mists of pre-historic antiquity. Healing as a vocation can be said to have begun at the time when a remote, nameless human ancestor—taking cues from the habits of animals—brought leaves, grasses, or roots to an ill relative in an attempt to relieve his distress. The origin and evolution of healing as a special skill long antedates other important human inventions such as agriculture and animal domestication and might well deserve consideration as "the oldest profession." The accumulated observations and trials of thousands of years brought a wealth of healing knowledge to mankind and by the historical era, medicine as a systematic discipline, as a vertable science, had emerged. As with so many other human achievements, this occurred first in the Nile Valley, reaching its highest level of development—until modern times—in Egypt, land of the pharoahs. When Egyptian dynastic history begins, medicine is already an established, fully-formed science. This we know from the most important medical textbooks of ancient Egypt, now known as the Ebers Papyrus and the Edwin Smith Papyrus, which are in fact copies of medical papyri which date back to pre-pyramid times, to the very earliest historical dynasties. In point of fact, one of the pharoahs of the 1st dynasty was famous as a physician.[1] From the beginning of her history, Egypt possesses a mature, well-validated system of medicine containing a systematic pathology, a completely-formulated pharmacopeia, a formal knowledge of anatomy and physiology, a large medi-cal literature, a well-defined medical teaching curriculum, and a skill in sur-gery and trauma that is hardly matched outside Africa until our own time. It is unthinkable that such knowledge, which is so sophisticated on a scientific level, could have emerged without a long period of anterior development. There is a 2400 year span from Hipppocrates to modern medicine and the mature medical science that exists at the start of the dynastic period in Egypt would have had a pedigree at least as long. If we date the onset of Egyptian dynastic history around the first *known* calendar date of 4236 B.C., which the author believes is closer to the actual beginnings of Egyptian dynastic history rather than the conventional 3200 B.C., our best educated guess would push the origins of Egyptian medicine back close to 7000 B.C. In most writings about Egyptian medicine, there is a persistent emphasis on its "static" quality,

Imhotep: Physician, Sage and Scribe

which is to say the priest-physicians of ancient Egypt followed ancient, pre-established authority so rigidly that they were incapable of any scientific innovation in this domain. On the face of it, such a conclusion is tenuous at best and in any case does not account for how the Egyptians got to such an advanced stage in the first place. If Egyptian medicine was of a calibre beyond that of all later medicine up to our own time, we have to presume that not only was the scientific spirit alive and well in ancient Egypt, but that it actually originated there.

Imhotep, "Father of Medicine"

No individual more fully embodies the highest and finest of Egyptian medicine than the figure of Imhotep. Sir William Osler called him "the first figure of a physician to stand out clearly from the mists of antiquity." In truth, he is the world's first universal genius of whom we have any knowledge. As vizier to the pharoah Djoser, he was a statesman of the first rank; as designer and builder of the world's first great edifice in stone, the step-pyramid of Saqqara, he was an architect of transcendent genius; as the renowned purveyor of wise sayings and parables he was the epitome of the sage; and finally, as the divinely-gifted physician he was accorded that rarest of honors in ancient Egypt, deification as the god of healing. In spite of this, there are those who question whether Imhotep actually was a physician. Jonckeere, when compiling his list of 103 Egyptian physicians mentioned by name in the inscriptions, omitted Imhotep because of the dearth of contemporary witnesses to the fact.[2] Yet within a century after his death, he was venerated by Men-kau-ra (Mycerinus), a third pharoah of the fourth dynasty, as a healer[3] and his powers as a physician made such an impression on succeeding generations both in and out of Egypt that he was eventually deified in his own country and identified with the healing god Asclepios by the Greeks from the sixth century B.C. on. If we use Jonckeere's yardstick, we would have to eliminate Hippocrates from the ranks of physicians because next to nothing is known about his actual life or healing accomplishments. The books attributed to him are almost all written by later followers and even the famous Hippocratic Oath was not written by him but by professional disciples at a time long after his death.[4] Yet no one doubts that Hippocrates existed, that he practiced the healing art, or that he was a clinician of unusual gifts. Hippocrates is, if anything, a more shadowy figure than Imhotep but his life and healing work are not open to question. Neither is that of Imhotep. Hippocrates, who is customarily accorded the title "Father of Medicine," i.e., the practitioner in antiquity most responsible for introducing "clinical" or "scientific" medicine to the world, was himself said to be descended from a long line of "Asclepiads," that is devotees of the Greek healing god Asclepios. In the famous oath ascribed to him—but which he did not compose—he is made to swear by the important healing gods of Greece, including Asclepios[5] and it is clear that neither Hippocrates nor later members of his school forswore "priestly medicine," since they were in the habit of referring patients to the healing temples of Asclepios for special cures.[6] Moreover, by swearing by Asclepios in the Oath, the members of the Hippocratic school were in fact swearing by Imhotep since the two were synonymous in the Greek mind. The reputed clinical or scientific primacy of the Hippocratic school was finally laid to rest in 1930 when J.H. Breasted translated the Edwin Smith Papyrus, a document whose original antedates Hippocrates by over 2500 years. The diagnostic, prognostic, and therapeutic methodology revealed in this document demonstrated that even in our own day, our physicians have not surpassed the clinical acumen of the priest-physicians of the Nile Valley, of whom Imhotep was the epitome. The Egyptian priests told Solon, the great Greek lawgiver, that the Greeks were "as children" compared to the Egyptians,[7] and it is clear from what has just been said that Hippocrates in no way merits the title "Father of Medicine," either by virtue of his antiquity or the level of his scientific thought. If such a title belongs to anyone, it belongs to Imhotep. In spite of their propaganda in favor of Hippocrates, the Greeks themselves knew this. Galen is merely the most eminent and most famous of Greek physicians who continued to travel to the temple of Imhotep in the early centuries A.D. in search of medical knowledge.[8]

Imhotep The Man

As will be seen later on, there was a substantial corpus of myth, legend, and symbol that grew up around the figure of Imhotep, as with other extraordinary men in history, and there are only a few fragments of true biographical detail that can be extracted from the welter of legendary tradition that surrounds his name. His father was Kanofer who preceded Imhotep as a distinguished architect in the service of pharoah and his mother was Khreduonkh who was from a high-born family that originated in Mendes. He was born on the 31st of May in a suburb of Memphis called Ankhtaui ("Life of the Two Lands") and served as prime minister, chief scribe, ritualist, and architect under the pharoah Djoser of the third dynasty. Mastery of any one of these would have marked him as a great man but he seems to have excelled in all. But even these extraordinary talents appeared to have been overshadowed by his gifts as a physician. Hurry, who has written the best English-language monograph on Imhotep, described the stages by which Imhotep was elevated to the status of healing deity. Within a hundred years after his death he was venerated, though not worshipped, as the Great Physician.[9] He held this status for more than 2000 years just before the Persian conquest when he was elevated to the status of full-fledged deity, possibly under Greek or other non-Egyptian influence. Herodotus asserts that at no time during the proper history of Egypt was a mortal man ever deified. Even the divinity of the pharoah

Khreduonkh, mother of Imhotep

was a mythical construct designed to cement the ties between earth and heaven, human and divine. However, if Herodotus is to be relied on, no non-pharoah was ever paid divine honors, whereas the Greeks were very much in the habit of deifying mortal men of heroic stature. The profound veneration that surrounded the name and figure of Imhotep in Egypt in the 6th century when the Greeks made their first significant penetration into Egypt must have made a marked impression on them, as did all things Egyptian, for they forthwith declared their own healing god Asclepios to be a form of Imhotep. It is during Ptolemaic times—332-30 B.C.—that Imhotep, now fully deified, advances to the front rank of the gods in Egypto-Helenic pantheon.

The existence of Imhotep and his relation to the pharoah Djoser is attested to by a statue of Djoser, found near the step-pyramid of Saqqara in 1926, on which Imhotep's name is inscribed. In addition, the Egyptian architect Khnum-ib-re ("opening to the heart of Khnum"), living around 495 B.C., left an inscription which records the names of 25 of his remote ancestors, all of whom were fathers and sons and all of whom were master-builders.[10] The pedigree, according to Hurry, covers a span of 800 years, beginning with Ka-nofer, the father of Imhotep, and with Imhotep in second place. Imhotep, in this record, is described as "the chief of works, both of the South—and of the North-land, governor of the capital and vizier, chief ritual priest of Zozer, the King of Upper and Lower Egypt, the son of Kanofer, chief of works of the South—and of the North-land."[11]

Gerald Massey called Imhotep "the Egyptian Solomon,"[12] and with good reason, for Imhotep was without peer as an architect and builder. Architecture was a sacred science in Egypt embodying the highest in Egyptian scientific and religious thought. Thus, the parallel between Imhotep, builder of the temple, and Solomon, builder of the temple, is quite pertinent. Solomon is "Selmeh" in Hebrew. Looking at this work—"Selmeh"—through the Egyptian language, it can be analyzed in the following manner: "sel"="ser" (for "l" and "r" are linguistically interchangeable) in the Egyptian and "meh" gives "meh" in Egyptian unchanged. The Egyptian word "ser(l)" means "chief, noble, princely, royal;" the Egyptian word "meh" means "cubit," which brought together as "Selmeh" gives, in Egyptian, "the royal cubit."[13] Now the royal cubit was *the* unit of measure used in the construction of all important buildings and temples and therefore was the sign—par excel-lence—of the builder. Moreover, Imhotep's divine father Ptah was the "god of the cubit" because he too was the Divine Mason. From this point of view, then, Massey's linking Imhotep and Solomon is entirely accurate. Modern Freemasons, therefore, do not seem to go back far enough when they desig-nate Solomon as the (legendary) founder of their order.

Imhotep's relationship with the pharoah Djoser is made more revealing by a tradition which curiously echoes the Biblical story of Joseph. This is the so-called Legend of the Seven Years Famine which was found inscribed on a granite rock on the island of Sehel just south of Aswan during the Ptolemaic period. Hurry thinks that the legend itself dates from as early as the third dynasty. The Legend describes a period during Djoser's reign in which the Nile seven times failed to reach its normal flood height, precipitating and prolonging a terrible famine in Egypt. The Nile flood was thought to be controlled by the ram-god Khnum, a Nubian deity whose shrine was situated at Elephantine in Egyptian Nubia. In this time of peril, Djoser turned to Imhotep who thereupon consulted the sacred books locked away in the deepest, most inaccessible regions of the temple. From this Imhotep was able to reveal to the king how he might approach and propitiate Khnum. After paying a personal visit to the temple of Khnum and performing prayers and sacrifices, the god appeared to the king in a dream and promised to release the flood once again so that Egypt might be spared by any further famine. With the return of the Nile flood, the overjoyed king endowed the temple of Khnum with seventy miles of the richest land bordering the Nile and heaped munificent gifts and benefices upon the temple. It is hard indeed to determine how much of this reflects an actual occurrence. There was a tendency in Ptolemaic times to extol and romanticize old Egypt, which is one reason for Imhotep's rise to prominence during the period. However, the Ptolemies had access to all the archives of ancient Egypt and it is from these that many of the traditions that crop up around Imhotep are derived. Whether, as is often the case in such matters, they were embellished in such a way as to add lustre to Imhotep's name in order to justify his deification, is impossible to say. It is difficult, however, not to presume that there was at least a hard kernel of truth in such traditions which give us fleeting glimpses of Imhotep the man.

Sage of Sages

One thing that comes through clearly in pre-Hellenic traditions concerning Imhotep is that he was a sage and adept of the first magnitude. His name is linked very closely with other legendary Egyptian sages such as Hardedef who lived in the fourth dynasty, Kegemni who lived at the end of the third dynasty, Ptah-hotep who lived during the fifth dynasty, and finally and most of all, Amenhotep, son of Hapu, who lived during the 18th dynasty. This latter, like Imhotep, was deified during Ptolemaic times and was considered, in effect, a reincarnation of Imhotep.[14] Imhotep, as the purveyor of ageless oral wisdom, comes through in the "Song of the Harper" where he is linked with the sage Hardedef:

> I have heard the discourses of Imhotep and Hardedef, with whose words
> men speak everywhere . . .[15]

In these simple phrases Imhotep as philosopher and teacher shows himself

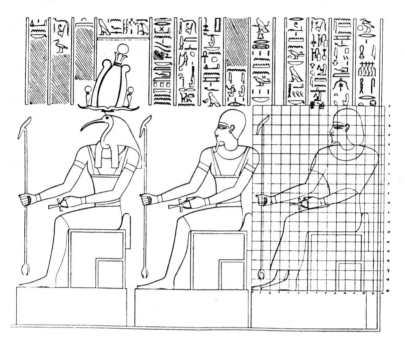

The God Imhotep seated between Thoth and the deified Amenhotep, son of Hapu (rear)

unmistakably. In addition, particularly since we know him as a priest and ritualist, Imhotep's reputation would to a great extent rest on his command over the forces of nature, i.e., as a "magician." Whatever the modern prejudice about such things, the ability to control the forces of nature was a universally accepted idea in antiquity and all the great sages and adepts were acknowledged to have possessed such abilities. Indeed, it is difficult to understand the extraordinary reverence paid to men such as Imhotep and Amenhotep, son of Hapu, in the absence of such abilities. The wonderworks of Moses and the miracles of Jesus are in this vein and it is such powers that cast an aura of divinity around such persons. It is not too much to say that Imhotep is the recognizably first in a line that leads directly to the later "prophets," "avatars," and "great souls" which would include Moses, Zoroaster, Gautama, and Jesus. In the Egypto-Hellenic world he was plainly seen as such.

Imhotep's name in Egyptian was "Iu-em-hetep" which means "he who comes in peace." This name became Hellenized as "Imouthes" and conventionalized in modern times to "Imhotep." Gerald Massey was of the opinion that Imhotep was a pre-existing deity and that the historical man of the third dynasty was merely his namesake. This is rather obscure when it is considered that in the Old Kindgom, the trinity of Memphis consisted of Ptah, Sekhmet, and Nefer-Tum; only in the late period does Iu-em-hetep or Imhotep supplant Nefer-Tum as the third member of the Memphis triad. There is, perhaps, another way of looking at the matter. Osiris, Buddha, and Christ each was a deified man but it is clear that each was the namesake of a divine being that existed before the historical individual. We have remarked elsewhere that a vast corpus of pre-extant saviour and resurrection mythology coalesced around the man Joshua ben Pandera ("Joshua son of the Panther") early in the Piscean Age to create the figure of Jesus the Christ, Son of God.[16] According to Massey, the Christhood had already existed in Egypt for 10,000 years as the "krst" ("kristos" in Greek) the anointed mummy who in different phases was Seker and then Osiris, the sign and symbol of resurrection.[17] Something similar seems to have occurred with respect to Osiris and Buddha. In 1897 Abbe Amelineau discovered the tomb of Osiris, who subsequently was shown to be the Pharoah Zer ("Osiris" = "A*sar*" or "U*ser*"), one of the kings of the first dynasty who was considered to have been a human avatar of Osiris by the Egyptians themselves.[18] Though Osiris was a deity who long pre-existed the historical Zer, it appears that Zer came to personify in human terms the god Osiris on earth. Thus the legend of Osiris being once a pharoah of Egypt, as represented by Plutarch, might actually have had some basis in historical fact. With Buddha, a similar process can be seen. There were seven divine Buddhas prior to the historical Gautama and the worship of Buddha reaches back into Indian proto-history when he was the god of the Black Dravidians of the Indus Valley city-states.[19] The historical Gautama by his life, deeds, and teachings became the incarnation of the eighth Buddha which is to say that the pre-extent Buddha mythology descended upon the figure of the historical Buddha who was Gautama. It should be mentioned also that there are parallels elsewhere in Africa. Among the Yoruba, the worship of Shango revolves around a figure who—as the first king of the kingdom of Oyo and the orisha of lightning and thunder—is both man and god. Thus the process by which an extraordinary individual becomes the human avatar of a pre-existing deity is well-attested throughout history. In the case of Imhotep we see one of the earliest examples in which there is a merging of an historical man and a pre-extant deity.

Imhotep The God

As he came to be regarded as a deity, Imhotep was considered the "son of Ptah," in the process superseding the earliest form of the son of Ptah, Nefer-Tem, whose name, which means "the child Atum," shows a clear connection between the mythos of Ptah and that of Atum-Ra of Heliopolis. Massey maintains that Atum is first a son of Ptah prior to becoming a supreme deity in his own right:

> That son of Ptah was Tum or Atum ... and one of Atum's names or titles
> is Iu the coming son, of Iu-em-hetep, he who comes with peace.[20]

The word "ptah" means "to open" which in this sense really means to "carve out, excavate, sculpt," etc.

He is sometimes represented as a pygmy with a scarab, the symbol of the god Khepera, on his crown. Kheper, the scarab was a form of the creator as "the molder" because the scarab—also known as the Nile beetle—molds a ball of dung into which is deposited its eggs and which is rolled along the banks of the Nile to be buried in a small hole until the Nile flood has subsided. After the period of incubation, the winged scarabs fly up out of the mud, providing a ready image of that which creates itself or resurrects itself out of the "primal ooze." Ptah as the "opener" and as the "molder" in his Khepera-form becomes one of the earliest images of the force of creation and he is represented in Egyptian iconography as a potterer shaping and molding the World Egg on the potter's wheel. He is related to the Nubian ram-god Khnum who is represented as molding human beings out of clay on the potter's wheel. Under these circumstances, Imhotep's connection to Khnum in the Legend of the Seven Years' Famine becomes more intelligible. Ptah is pre-eminently the divine metallurgist, blacksmith, mason, and architect, attributes that he shares with Imhotep. Ptah was often represented as a pygmy or a dwarf because these were thought to know all the secrets of mining and metals.

E.A. Wallis Budge describes the godhood of Imhotep as follows:

> I-em-hetep was the god who sent sleep to those who were suffering and in pain, and those who were afflicted with any kind of disease formed his special charge; he was the good physician of both gods and men, and he healed the bodies of mortals during life, and superintended the arrangements for the preservation of the same after death.[21]

In this aspect, Imhotep is the bringer of peace and plenty, food and water, rest and succour:

> Iu-em-hetep, as is indicated by the name, comes to bring peace and good-will to earth as conqueror of drought, dearth, and darkness.[22]

As we have seen, he is the wise and compassionate teacher, whose highest teachings were communicated orally, making him a personification of the Word or Logos:

> The expounder of the mysteries ... was the Egyptian Jesus ... as Iu-em-hetep, the prince of peace, and prototype of the Hebrew Solomon ... The Egyptian Jesus was equally the Egyptian Solomon, the youthful sage, as sayer and teacher of the oral wisdom.[23]

Various manifestations of Ptah, father of Imhotep

In a sense then, Imhotep, famous for his wise sayings and proverbial wisdom, is recapitulated in the later figures of Solomon and Jesus, both revered for their oral wisdom and teachings.

There were several temples dedicated to Imhotep that were built after the sixth century. The most famous of these was the temple of Imhotep in Memphis which in classical times was called "the Asclepeion." As we have noted earlier, it was so famous as a center of healing and medical knowledge that many important post-Hippocratic Greek physicians, including Galen, Theophrastus, and Dioscorides studied there.[24] It was located close to another famous healing temple, the Serapeum, dedicated to the god Serapis. Imhotep and Serapis were closely associated and this latter represented a late syncretization of Osiris and the divine Apis bull of Memphis who was a form of Ptah. This form of Osiris became paramount in the Hellenic and post-Hellenic period and was part of a trinity that included Isis and the Child Horus. The Romans identified Serapis worship with that of Christianity because the rituals and ceremonials were exactly the same.[25] Another Asclepeion dedicated to Imhotep existed on the "Holy Island" of Philae in Egyptian Nubia and rivalled the one in Memphis as a place of healing pilgrimage. Other temples dedicated to Imhotep-Asclepios were situated at Ptolemais Hermiu, and also, it seems in the Fayum, west of the Nile.[26] Hurry gives a good description of the phenomenon of "incubation" or "temple sleep" utilized by afflicted persons in these healing temples to obtain cures. When all other measures had failed, the sick person would be sent to the temple of the healing god, in this case Imhotep, to offer sacrifices and perform certain rituals to induce the god to send a cure. If these appeals were successful, the god would appear to the suppliant at night in a dream and give specific instructions on how a cure might be obtained. There are at least two surviving stories which illustrate the phenomenon of cure by incubation: both revolve around infertility. In the first story, the wife of a prince of the blood, who had produced no male children, repaired to the temple of Imhotep in her extremity where the god appeared to her in a dream telling her how she might conceive a son. The outcome was successful and the son went on to become a famous wise man. In this instance, the lady's infertility seemed only related to her capacity to bear a male child whereas in the second story, also involving a high-born woman, the sterility was absolute. Nonetheless, during the night in Imhotep's temple, the god appeared to her and provided her instructions that would result in the birth of the son. In this case, the husband, a high-priest, was required to carry out extensive works of renovation at a neglected sanctuary of Imhotep. This being done, a son was duly born and was named after Imhotep. It was commonplace in these cases for the child—born through the benign intervention of the god—to be dedicated to his service and we might presume that this is in fact what happened in the two stories related here. The Greeks too were well-acquainted with incubation and, as expected, it was the temple of Asclepios—Imhotep in his Greek form—that the suppliant visited to obtain cures. Robert Graves describes

> ... numerous oracles of Asclepius, where the sick flock for consultation and for cure, and are told the remedy in their dreams after a fast.[27]

If traditional healing in modern Africa offers any parallel, incubation served an additional function, for African traditional healers today insist that many of their remedies come to them in dreams, usually from a tutelary deity. There is no reason not to believe that the priest-physicians attached to the House of Imhotep experienced something similar.

By mid-classical times, the worship of Imhotep had attained wide prominence. Temples, inscriptions, and bas-reliefs dedicated to him could be found throughout Egypt; moreover he had acquired membership in the important pantheons in Memphis, Philae, and Thebes.[28] In Nubia, his worship was as widespread as it was in Egypt, if the reliefs and inscriptions in that country are any indication. He is found in Meroe associated with the kings and rulers of that important city-state. Moreover, his worship is not unknown among the Romans: at least two Romans emperors, Tiberius and Augustus, are represented in Egyptian temple reliefs doing him homage.

Imhotep And Asclepios

We have had cause to refer repeatedly to the identity of Imhotep and Asclepios and for this reason it is worth examining more closely the figure of

Asclepios himself as the pre-eminent Greek god of healing. According to classical sources.[29] Asclepios was the son of Apollo and a mortal princess Coronis, i.e., "the crow." Among the Greeks, the crow was an oracular bird and it had a similar connotation among the Egyptians though it was associated with the god Set. His mother died while carrying him and on her funeral pyre, Asclepios was cut from her womb by the god Hermes—Thoth in Greek form—at the command of Apollo. Asclepios was placed in the tutelage of Cheiron, the centaur, and became extraordinarily proficient in surgery and the healing powers of drugs and plants. For this reason he was revered as the founder of medicine. He became so skilled in the healing art that he divined the secret of raising the dead to life. After restoring four dead heroes to life, he incurred the wrath of Hades who complained to Zeus that Asclepius was robbing him of his rightful subjects. For this impious presumption, Zeus struck Asclepios dead with a thunderbolt. His father Apollo where-upon killed the cyclopes, renowned as masons and metalworkers, for having forged the thunderbolts of Zeus. Later, Zeus repented of his rash action and restored Asclepios to life as a deity of medicine. The symbol of Asclepios was the serpent and the staff—derived from the caduceus of Hermes—and when the early Romans wished to establish the worship of Asclepios in their own lands, Epidauros, the site of an important Asclepeion, sent them an avatar of the god in the form of a snake.[30]

The mythic history of Asclepios, with his theogamy, commends several things to our attention. Though ostensibly the son of Apollo, Ascelpios is in fact removed from his mother's womb by Hermes, establishing a connection that echoes the fact that Imhotep was considered to be "the image of Thoth,"[31] whom the Greeks called Hermes. The mother of Asclepios, Coronis "the Crow," by virtue of her name would have been an oracle priestess and we know that the temples of Asclepios were, in effect, healing oracles. Asclepios is considered, like Imhotep, a mortal son of a divine father who becomes translated into a deity of healing. The somewhat tangential part that the cyclopes play in the myth still echoes the fact that they, like Imhotep and his divine father Ptah, are masons, metalworkers, and builders. Finally, the snake twined around the staff is a motif originally associated with Thoth, the first healing god of the Egyptian pantheon, and the original Greek god of healing, Hermes, takes it directly from him.

The snake was a potent symbol of renewal and resurrection because of its ability to slough old skin for new. This made it one of the earliest healing types. All things considered, it is no wonder that the Greeks made Asclepios their Imhotep: there was a pronounced reverence among them for things Egyptian and all of their important healing symbols were prefigured in Egypt. Their names were used interchangeably so ubiquitously that in the Greek mind they were one and the same.

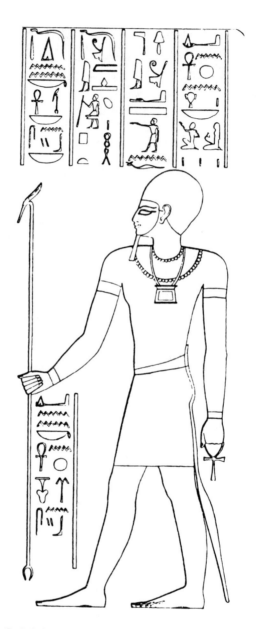

Imhotep, the God, bringer of Peace and Plenty.

Thoth, Divine Messenger and God of Medicine (note the Caduceus in his left hand)

The Hermetic Imhotep

Some mention must be made of Imhotep in the Hermetic or "Trismegistic" literature. The Hermetic corpus represented a fusion of ancient Egyptian thought and Greek philosophy, with the Egyptian elements clearly predominating. It was an esoteric school—allied to and interacting with similar such schools such as Gnosticism—that exerted a powerful if sub-rosa influence on early Christianity and later Medieval thought. Alchemy and Astrology were considered branches of the Hermetic science and later Freemasonry and Rosicrucianism drew deeply from Hermetic currents. Though anathemized by orthodox Christianity, it is a remarkable fact that the great scientists, philosophers, statesmen, and artists of the Western world were devotees of the various branches of the Hermetic art.

Roger Bacon and Paracelcus were alchemists, Copernicus and Newton were astrologers, Washington, Mozart, Napoleon, and Kipling were Freemasons. The paragon of the Hermetic work was Hermes Trismegistus, Hermes the "Thrice-Greatest," who was considered the quintessential Master of all knowledge and wisdom. His three important disciples are Asclepius, Tat, and Ammon. All of these figures represent anthropomorphized Egyptian deities: Asclepius is of course Imouthes/Imhotep, Tat is Thoth, and Ammon is the Theban Amen. Other Egyptian deities figure prominently in the Hermetic mythos and these are Anubis, Khnum, here called Chnum, and Lady Isis. In its surviving fragments, Hermetic philosophy unfolds in a series of Socratic-like discourses between the Master Hermes and his disciples. In this framework, Asclepius-Imhotep carries the titles of "king" and "divine saviour"[32] and he comes forward in the Hermetic opus as the one disciple who is already well-schooled in philosophy. G.R.S. Mead says

> Tat and Asclepius share a common instruction, Asclepius appearing as the older and riper scholar.[33]

Tat, however, is the "St. John" of the three disciples, the one who has Hermes' highest favor and the one who will carry on the authentic teaching. It must be remembered that Tat—being the personification of Thoth—is but an aspect of Hermes himself which would account for his favored position. We have noted earlier how Imhotep was called "the image of Thoth," and we see how—as one of the three disciples of Trismegistus—this is reflected in Hermetic tradition. Hermetic tradition further characterizes him as a "master mason, inventor of poetry, healer, and master astrologer,"[34] in effect, carrying him and his attributes forward from his place in the pantheons of old Egypt.

Troth-Hermes, master of all learning, in his form as cynocephalic ape, seen here dictating to a scribe.

Epilogue

Greek thought and philosophy, both esoteric and exoteric, was lifted almost bodily out of the Egyptian world system and no one figured more prominently in this process than Imhotep as man, god, sage, and symbol. Though we possess mere fragments of his true personal history, he still comes through as a man of extraordinary capacity. he seems to have achieved a perfect synthesis of mind, intellect, and soul, so much so that men thought they saw in him the spark of divinity. The centuries, rather than dimming this spark in men's minds, seemed to have fanned it to a bright flame and, as a consequence, Imhotep the man became Imhotep the god. Massey considered him the prototype of the Saviour and this is corroborated in Hermetic tradition. As physician, builder, and sage, he was the archetype of the Great Man.

Notes

1. According to Manetho, the second pharoah of the first dynasty, Athothis son of Menes, was a great physician who wrote treatises on anatomy. It is therefore just possible that this personage had a hand in writing the treatise that in a much later redaction became the Edwin Smith Papyrus. By the "short chronology" this would put the original of the Edwin Smith Papyrus back to 3000 B.C.; by the "long chronology" back to 4000 B.C. All this furnishes additional evidence showing that Egyptian medicine was already a mature science at the very beginning of Egyptian dynastic history.

2. See Majno, G., *The Healing Hand: Man and Wound in the Ancient World,* Cambridge: Harvard University Press, 1982, p. 480, n. 52.

3. Hurry, J.C., *Imhotep,* New York: AMS Press, Inc., 1978, pp. 45-6.

4. Bogdonoff, M.D., et al, editors, *The Aphorisms of Hippocrates,* "Introduction," Birmingham: Classics of Medicine Library, 1982, pp. 3-7.

5. The Hippocratic Oath opens as follows: "I swear by Apollo, the physician, by *Aesculapius,* by Hygeia, and by Panacea."

6. Majno, op. cit., p. 201. In one of the Hippocratic books, the physician says, "The gods are the real physicians . . ."

7. Plato, *Timaeus,* translated by Desmond Lee, New York: Penguin Books, 1979, p. 35.

8. Hurry, op. cit., p. 115. Hurry also states that "many Egyptian drugs and prescriptions were copied by the Greeks and in due course were incorporated into the Pharmacopeias of other nations."

9. See note 3.

10. Hurry, op. cit., pp. 193-5.

11. ibid.

12. Massey, G., *Ancient Egypt: Light of the World,* New York: Samuel Weiser, 1970, p. 365.

13. Budge, E.A.W., *Egyptian Hieroglyphic Dictionary,* New York: Dover Publications, 1978.

14. Hurry, op. cit., pp. 73, 103.

15. ibid., pp. 24-5.

16. See Finch, C., "Studies in Kamite Origins: The Works of Gerald Massey," *Journal of African Civilizations,* I. Van Sertima, editor, 1982, 4 (2): 63.

17. Massey, op. cit., passim.

18. Budge, E.A.W., *A History of Egypt,* Oosterhout N.B.: Anthropological Publications, vol. 1, 1968, pp. 20, 181.

19. See Higgins, G., *Anacalypsis,* New Hyde Park: University Press, vol. 1, 1965, p. 53.

20. Massey, op. cit., p. 434.

21. Budge, E.A.W., *Gods of the Egyptians,* New York: Dover Publications, vol. 1, 1969, p. 523.

22. Massey, op. cit., p. 418.

23. ibid., p. 500.

24. see note 8.

25. Massey, op. cit., p. 756. In a famous letter to Servianus, the Emperor Hadrian aasserted, "those who worship Serapis are likewise Christians; even those who style themselves the Bishops of Christ are devoted to Serapis." Diodorus relates that all worshippers were given the name Serapis in their death and resurrection showing that Serapis, as a form of Osiris, was a holotype of Christ.

26. See Wilkinson, J.G., *The Manners and Customs of the Ancient Egyptians*, London: John Murray, vol. 3, 1878, p. 205.

27. Graves, R., *The Greek Myths,* New York: Penguin Books, vol. 1, 1977, p. 179.

28. See Hurry, op. cit., pp. 62-144.

29. For a complete survey of all of the classical references to Asclepios, see Graves, op. cit., pp. 173-8.

30. Majno, op. cit., p. 339.

31. See Hurry, op. cit., pp. 60, 66.

32. Mead, G.R.S., *Thrice Greatest Hermes,* London: John M. Watkins, vol. 1, 1949, p. 469.

33. ibid., p. 471.

34. ibid., pp. 464-76; see also Hurry, op. cit., pp. 27, 30, 36, 41.

RAMSES THE GREAT:
THE LIFE & TIMES OF A BOLD BLACK EGYPTIAN KING

By Runoko Rashidi

Although it was the African Sudan, the "Ethiopia" (Land of the Blacks) of ancient times, that gave birth to the oldest civilization, it is in Egypt, child of Ethiopia and greatest nation of antiquity, that the bulk of historical research has been done. For the moment, at least, Egypt continues to be the focal point of our Afrocentric researches, and will probably be the object of much of our studies for some time to come.

Not only were ancient Egypt's origins African, but through the entire Dynastic Age and during all the periods of real splendor from the initial unification of Upper and Lower Egypt by Menes and Hor-Aha in the fourth millennium B.C. to the Assyrian devastation of West (Thebes) in 663 B.C. (a span of time encompassing almost three thousand years), men and women with black skins and wooly hair reigned almost supreme. In the intense and unrelenting struggle to establish and prove scientifically the African foundations of Egyptian civilization, the late Senegalese scholar Cheikh Anta Diop remains a most fierce and ardent champion. Diop, 1923-1986, was among the world's leading Egyptologists, and held the position of Director of the Radiocarbon Laboratory of the Fundamental Institute of Black Africa in Dakar, Senegal. The range of methodologies employed by Dr. Diop in the course of his extensive Afro-Egyptian labors include: examinations of the epidermis of Egyptian royal mummies recovered during the Auguste Ferdinand Mariette Expedition for verification of melanin content; precise osteological measurements and meticulous studies in the relevant areas of anatomy and physical anthropology; careful examinations and comparisons of modern Upper Egyptian and West African blood-groups; detailed Afro-Egyptian linguistic studies; analysis of the ethnic designations employed by the Egyptians themselves; corroborations of distinct Afro-Egyptian cultural traits; documentations of Biblical testimonies and references regarding ethnicity, race and culture; and the writings of early Greek and Roman scholars for descriptions of the physical appearances of the ancient Egyptian people.

Diop firmly believed that "The highest point of Egyptian history was the

This essay is dedicated to the members of the Pyramid Circle of Memphis, Tenn.

Painted limestone relief of Ramses the Great from Abydos.

Nineteenth Dynasty of Ramses II." The Nineteenth Dynasty was indeed an extraordinarily pivotal phase in African history. Akhenaten's determined efforts towards social/religious revolution decades earlier had effectively polarized the Egyptian state. A tremendous power struggle ensued with the Monarchy on one side and the well-organized Amen Priesthood on the other; the conflict of interest resulting ultimately in a prolonged period of political instability. Many districts within the vast dominions seized during the military campaigns of the Eighteenth Dynasty warrior-kings were lost. The nation's military readiness and prestige had sharply declined; a situation that the enemies of Egypt observed with keen interest and growing anticipation. These hostile forces, including numerous Semitic and Indo-European speaking clans, tribes and kingdoms, rose in defiance of their African overlords and instituted a series of steady assaults that if unchecked could rapidly threaten Egypt's very existence.

The Ramesside Founding Father: Menpehtyre Ramses I
"Enduring of Might is Re"
(1295-1294 B.C.)

The founder of the illustrious Nineteenth Egyptian Dynasty and the exalted grandfather of Ramses the Great was from the northeastern corner of the Egyptian Delta near the city of Tanis. The initiator of the Ramessides was called Pramesse until he dropped the definite article at the beginning of his name to become the king known as Ramses I. He was a man of fairly modest background, his father having been a relatively obscure officer in the Egyptian military. Nevertheless, under the guidance of the Horus Horemhab, a former army companion, fervent restorer of the Amen cult, and final sovereign of the glorious Eighteenth Egyptian Dynasty, Pramesse rapidly rose in rank and position, amassing seven different priestly titles. In addition, several statues portray Pramesse as a royal scribe. Before his eventual appointment as Vizier, his other functions at one time or another included: Superintendent of Horses, Superintendent of the River-Mouths, Fortress Commander, Commander of the Army of the Lord of the Two Lands, and Deputy of the King on Upper and Lower Egypt.

The Father of Ramses
Menmare Seti I
"The Man of Set"
(1294-1279 B.C.)

Ramses I was surely an elderly man when he became the first king of Egypt's Nineteenth Dynasty. After a short rule of little more than a year the Ramesside founder was ably succeeded by his son and designated heir—

Statue of Queen Tuya, Mother of Ramses the Great (Vatican).

Menmare Seti I. The "Man of Set" was a man of action, and immediately declared himself the "Bringer of the Renaissance." The new Horus, the father of Ramses the Great, quickly and resolutely set out to regain the empire. Personally leading his troops into battle with Ramses, the Crown Prince and Coregent, under his protective wing, Seti, clashed first with the Hittites of southern Turkey and northern Syria, inflicting upon them heavy losses. Seti's aggressive policy convinced the Hittites to sue for peace, and at the cessation of hostilities a treaty was signed between the two nations that lasted for fifteen years. The peace was at least partially ensured, however, by a line of fortresses constructed along Egypt's eastern frontier. In the west the Egyptians fought and subdued the unruly bands of Libyan nomads.

The rich spoils of military success allowed the Egyptians to build on a scale of colossal magnitude. In the sacred Egyptian city of Abydos Seti had constructed a temple complex that became a national shrine. Seti's temple, with its brilliantly decorated wall-reliefs, was designed in an L-shape and contained seven separate sanctuaries or chapels respectively dedicated to Osiris, Isis, Horus, Ptah, Re, Amen, and Seti himself. Inside the temple was carefully inscribed a chronological list of the Egyptian kings that had been Seti's predecessors. This kinglist has been of tremendous value in establishing Egypt's historical chronology.

Attached to the main temple at Abydos was another sanctuary called the "Osireion." Named after the Egyptian lord of the dead and god of fertility, Osiris, this distinct underground structure which at the time of its discovery was thought by some to have been the very tomb of the god himself, possessed in its center an island surrounded by a moat. This island, upon which stood ten red granite pillars nine feet thick, seems to have represented the site of creation from whence it was believed that Osiris and all life had emerged.

Seti took an active interest in his family and personally supervised his son's upbringing. Queen Tuya appears as the only wife of Seti I and she is always called the Royal Mother of Ramses II. Unfortunately, very little information has surfaced concerning Queen Tuya's life and character. The surviving statues reveal her to have been both strikingly beautiful and extremely dignified. She was lovingly cherished by her husband and genuinely adored by her son. Queen Tuya is believed to have departed the earth around 1256 B.C.

The Man Himself!
Usemare Ramses II
"Strong in Right is Re; Beloved of Amen"
(1279-1213 B.C.)

The sixty-seven year reign of Ramses the Great was for Egypt an era of general prosperity, stable government and extensive building projects. Ancient gods like Ptah, Re and Set were elevated to high status. The worship of

Youthful Ramses II.

Amen was restored and his priests reinstated. Major wars were fought with the Libyans, Hittites and their allies. Wondrous temples from Nubia to the Egyptian Delta were carved out of the naked cliffs. Splendid tombs in the hills of western Waset and Abydos were constructed, renovated and beautified. The new Egyptian city of Pi-Ramses made its impressive debut.

Ramses was deified in his own lifetime, and through the unrelenting projection of his own incomparable personality made the name Ramses, the Son of Amen-Re, synonymous with kingship for centuries. Ramses II was truly great. He was the towering figure of his age and established the models and set the standards that others used to rule by.

In regards to the ethnicity of the great Ramses, Cheikh Anta Diop unhesitatingly threw down the gauntlet, and spoke of him in a language of unmistakable firmness and certitude:

> Ramses II was not leucoderm and could have been even less red-haired, because he reigned over a people who instantly massacred red-haired people as soon as they met them, even in the street; these people were considered as strange beings, unhealthy, bearers of bad luck and unfit for life . . . Ramses II is black. Let's let him sleep in his black skin, for eternity.[1]

Sadly, the mummy of Ramses II has been more than disturbed. In Dynasty XXI the mummies of Ramses II and Set I, along with other royal mummies, were removed from their tombs and reburied in the cliffs at Deir el-Bahari. There the mummies were "discovered" by the Department of Antiquities in 1881 and removed to Cairo.

Nor, as Diop wished, was the great king allowed to "sleep in his black skin." He was subjected to many recent observations and experiments. Speaking of the latter, Ivan Van Sertima makes a number of enormously fascinating observations:

> One of the things that struck me most about Diop as a person was his absolute honesty. He was never afraid to criticize something African or black once it merited criticism. I have never found him out in any equivocation or exaggeration. He told me twice, both in London and in Atlanta, that there was no question whatsoever of the blackness or Africanness of Ramses II. He told me that he had actually seen the mummy, and that the skin of the mummy was as black as his skin. He said, however, that after it was subjected to gamma rays the skin looked grayish. It had lost its original dark color. Yet he felt that it would still have been possible to establish its ethnicity through his method, the melanin dosage test. A similar method is now in use in the United States. He said that the scientists involved had used far more gamma rays than was necessary for their experiment. He asked for permission to examine a specimen of the mummy's skin and hair but he was refused permission. The authorities

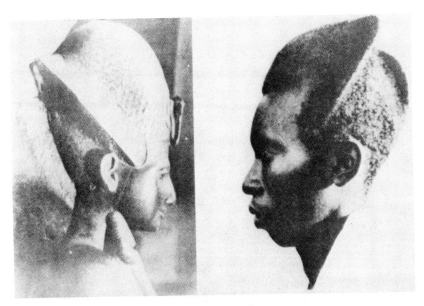

Tutsi warrior from Central Africa and Ramses the Great.

said that it would damage the mummy. Later on, after a certain discovery which was covered up, the scientists abandoned the mummy, suppressed all their reports, and circulated a rumor that this was not really the mummy of Ramses II.[2]

Ramses & The Great Gods Of The Realm
Amen/Amun/Ammon

Amen and his principal city of Waset achieved their greatest importance in Dynasties Eighteen and Nineteen. In Dynasty Eighteen the First Prophet of Amen included in his titles "high priest of Ptah" and "high priest of Re," and maintained jurisdiction over all the priesthoods of Egypt. The formidable militarist Thutmose III attributed his very kingship to Amen, and donated much of the wealth from his many foreign conquests to the temple of Amen. In Dynasty Eighteen Amen became the state god of Egypt. Around 1410 B.C. the priests added the name of the age-old sun-god Re to that of Amen, elevating Amen-Re to "King of the Gods," with Waset declared the birthplace of the universe itself. The power of Amen spread eventually beyond the Nile Valley into Libya and as far as the Atlantic shores of West Africa.

In Ramses II's Egypt the dead as well as the living came under the jurisdic-

Black granite bust of Ramses as Horus.

tion of Amen's priesthood. It governed both the temples on the east bank of Waset and the necropolis on the west bank. It assumed charge of the tombs of Egypt's kings, queens and nobles, and administered the more than four miles of magnificent mortuary temples on the Nile's west bank.

Ptah

This popular god was known as the Master Craftsman, and served along with Hathor as Patron deity of the Egyptian city known as Memphis or the White Walls. Under the Ramsesside rulers the worship of Ptah increased in intensity. Ptah was one of Egypt's oldest gods, and was usually depicted as an upright man encased in mummy wrappings and a tight fitting blue cap. Ptah was equated by the Greeks with their own god Hephaestus. The Romans identified Ptah with the probably better known Vulcan.

Re/Ra

The sun-god of Heliopolis, Re was head of the great ennead, supreme judge, and often linked with other gods aspiring to universality, such as Amen-Re and Re-Harakhty. Although Ramses II regarded himself as a Son of Re (Son of the Sun), the supreme period of prominence of this deity probably occurred during the kingships of Egyptian Dynasty Five.

Set/Sut/Seth/Sutekh

Under Ramses II, Set became the tutelary deity of Egyptian rule over Asia. Anat, who some identify with Astarte, was the consort of Set. It should be remembered that Ramses I himself came from a family which seems to have been particularly devoted to Seth of Avaris. His son and heir, Seti I, was named after the god; and on a stela found at Tanis, Ramses II records that when his father was still Crown Prince and a commander in the army, he came to Avaris to celebrate the 400th anniversary of the foundation of the city and its dedication to Set. Ramses II himself used the site of Avaris as the foundation for his new city of Pi-Ramses (The House of Ramses).

Although the state god of Egypt at that time was Amen of Waset, in the Delta Set was of great importance. Ramses II emphasized his allegiance to him by naming his favorite daughter Bint-Anath "Daughter of Anath" (Set's consort), and by building a temple for Anath at Pi-Ramses. In the Ramesside period, Set was not regarded as merely the deity of the harmful elements in the desert but as the patron of the life-sustaining oases.

Some of the most interesting and original investigations to date concerning the god Set, who was certainly one of Africa's most ancient gods, has been done by my brilliant friend and colleague Charles S. Finch III, M.D. In a recent letter to the author, Dr. Finch beautifully sums up the origins and career of this fascinating yet little understood African deity. In the words of Dr. Finch: Set was the first Kamite male deity—the Son of the Mother before Fatherhood—and an African god par excellence. One of his commonest epithets was "Nehsi" which means Cushite, or Nubian, or Ethiopian (though usually translated as "Negro") and he is known as the "god of the South." At one time he was a god of resurrection, a role taken over by Osiris. He was also a friend of the deceased in many passages of the "Book of the Dead." He "lost out" as it were to Osiris and to a lesser extent Amen-Ra and thus became anathema to the worshippers of those gods who turned him into a figure of evil and death. But they were never able to stamp out his worship—as much as they tried—and on occasion certain of his followers were able to regain political power as shown by the Set names of pharaohs in the 1st and 2nd dynasties—and more interestingly—in the Nineteenth dynasty: Ramses the Great was the son of Seti whom he revered and honored mightily. We know for a fact that the Hyksos, whoever they were, elevated Set to supremacy and the subsequent victory by the followers of Amen-Ra at Waset brought on massive retaliation so that there are virtually no monumental inscriptions extant that tell about the Hyksos period.

The kingdom of Ta-Seti again shows the relation of Set to the land south of Egypt (indeed "south" might be a derivative of "set" or "sut"). So by embracing Set, the early Ramessids were returning to the ancestral, archaic religion both because of their own dispositions and out of a need to counter-balance Amen-Ra.[3]

Ramses II as Militarist: The Kadesh Battle

Ramses II never tired of reporting about the battle of Kadesh. The official account of the Kadesh Battle is found inscribed on temples in Abydos, Abu Simbel, the Ramesseum, Karnak, Luxor, and two hieratic papyri. It occurred in his fifth regnal year near the Orontes River in the Bekaa valley. At this time the Egyptian army was organized into four divisions, each named after one of the chief gods of the realm: Ra, Ptah, Set, and Amen. Included in the Egyptian contingent were the King's pet lion and two of the Monarch's sons.

With the division of Amen under the personal command of Ramses himself, the national army, variously composed of Egyptians, Nubians, and European mercenaries, journeyed deep into Syria to meet a hostile coalition of enemy forces. The opposition, under the charge of the Hittite king Mutawallis, was the most enormous Egypt had ever faced.

Misled by false intelligence reports, Ramses, with only a small personal bodyguard, soon found himself far ahead of the main body of his troops, and it was precisely at this moment that the enemies of Egypt attacked. Near the Syrian city of Kadesh the battle was joined, and it was only Ramses' personal valor and courage that saved the Egyptian army from total disaster. Gathering a small band around him, Pharaoh charged into the Hittite lines no less than four times and held his tiny force together until the Ptah division of his army arrived on the scene to rescue the situation. The Monarch thought enough of this battle to have it commemorated on monuments throughout the Black Land. Withdrawing towards the west, the Egyptians finally signed a treaty with the Hittites which prevailed for the rest of the King's lengthy reign.

Khaemwaset: Ramses' Favored Son

Prince Khaemwaset was the fourth son of Ramses II and stands out as the most energetic, pious and talented of the monarch's many offspring. Khaemwaset was venerated as a sage by later generations, living on in Egyptian popular literature and emerging as a potent magician-hero in a series of Graeco-Roman stories.

On the southern face of the Pyramid of Unas, an inscription states that Khaemwaset undertook works to identify and reconstruct the Unas complex. The Unas Pyramid of the Fifth Dynasty is of particular importance because it contains the first known example of the funerary inscriptions now known as the Pyramid Texts. They occur in the vestibule and burial chamber of the pyramid and were thought to possess magical powers designed to help the king in the afterlife. Khaemwaset's name has also been found on several of the pyramids at Sakkara and Abu Sir, and he was apparently keenly interested in restoring all of the important monuments of the ancient Egyptian kings.

Another great task for Khaemwaset consisted of the preparation and administration of a significant number of the jubilees or sed-festivals which were celebrated from the thirtieth year of his father's reign onwards, usually at intervals of three years. To the temple of Ptah, Ramses II and Khaemwaset added a splendid new Jubilee Hall with many columns on basalt footings.

Ramses II sent this favorite son Khaemwaset to Memphis of the White Walls with the title of High Priest of Ptah, in whose service he spent forty years. He devoted particular attention to the cult of the sacred Apis bulls and to the enlargement of their necropolis that is known as the Serapeum. Several Apis bulls died during the long reign of Ramses II and were buried in separate tombs under the direction of Khaemwaset. As the Governor of Memphis of the White Walls and the High Priest of Ptah, Khaemwaset was actually buried in a tomb amongst the sacred bulls. His mummy was found with a gold mask over the face and ornaments of gold and precious stones on his breast. Khaemwaset died in the 55th years of Ramses II's reign.

The Queens of Ramses The Great
Nefertari

To Ramses II Queen Nefertari was "The Beautiful Companion." Nefertari's two main titles were "King's Great Wife" and "Mistress of the Two Lands."

The temple of Hathor, the northern temple of Abu Simbel, was built by Ramses II to honor this favorite wife, Queen Nefertari. Between the statues of Ramses II are those of Nefertari, and the size of her statues signifies that she will be honored to nearly the same degree as her husband in her relationship to the gods. Both temples at Abu Simbel were used as storehouses for treasures and tribute exacted from Nubia, thus combining the temples' essentially religious function with an eminently practical one.

Two building inscriptions are found, one in the main hall, and the other on the facade. The first reads:

> Ramses, he made it as his monument for the Great King's wife Nefertari, beloved of Mut—a house hewn in the pure mountain of Nubia, of fine white enduring sandstone, as an eternal work.[4]

The second inscription reads:

> Ramses-Meriamon, beloved of Amen, like Re, forever, made a house of very great monuments, for the Great King's wife Nefertari, fair of face. . . . His Majesty commanded to make a house in Nubia hewn in the mountain. Never was the like done before.[5]

After her death Queen Nefertari was worshipped as a divine Osirian, or a soul which had become deified, and under the attributes of Osiris (Asr), Lord of the dead, was adored as a god. Nefertari was housed in a 5,200 square foot tomb, the most splendid in the Valley of the Queens.

Queen Istnofret was a contemporary of Nefertari and the mother of Khaemwaset, Merneptah and Bint-Anath, whose name means in Kanaanite "Daughter of the goddess Anath." Queen Bint-Anath, as the first daughter of Istnofret, became associate chief queen in her mother's place. Ramses II housed his Hittite wife in the Fayum region of Middle Egypt. Among Ramses' other queens were Nebttawy and Hentmire, about whom almost nothing is known beyond their names.

Ramses The Great Builder

Ramses II commissioned more buildings and had more colossal statues than any other Egyptian king, also having his name carved or reliefs cut on many older monuments. Even when Ramses II did not originally construct a monument, he often usurped it for himself by erecting his own statuary and redecorating the walls with his cartouches and stories of his exploits.

We have to acknowledge the tireless architects of Ramses II for the fact that nothing is left of the absolutely enormous buildings of Egypt's Middle Kingdom. They plundered the temples of the Fayum, particularly the Pyramid temples at El-Lahun and Hawara, just as they had plundered those in Memphis of the White Walls and Heliopolis. The remarkable Labyrinth of

Colossi of Ramses the Great at Abu Simbel.

Amenemhet III at Hawara, perhaps the largest single building in antiquity according to eyewitness accounts, suffered severely during Ramses' reign.

Abu Simbel

> Herodotus never saw the huge temple which Ramses II chose to build here at Abu Simbel further south into inner Africa than any other great monument built by the pharoahs to celebrate their power. A few years ago, with immense ingenuity the entire structure was lifted to a new site above the artificial lake which has drowned all the sites of the most ancient kingdoms that flourished here in Nubia even before the first of the pharoahs. But why should he have built this great temple so far to the south? Perhaps because his queen, Nefertari, was herself a Nubian. And also because these were the people, the people of the south, whom he wanted to impress.[6]

Ramses initiated enormous building activities in Nubia. He commissioned temples at Beit-el-Wali, Gerf Hussein, Wadi-es-Sebua, Derr, Abu Simbel and Aksha in Lower Nubia, and at Amara and Barkal in Upper Nubia. The temple of Abu Simbel, one of the largest rock-cut structures in the world, is no doubt a unique piece of architectural work. It is hewn into a mountain of sandstone rock on the left bank of the Nile that was held sacred long before Ramses' temple was cut there. It was dedicated to Re-Harakhte, the god of the rising sun, who is represented as a man with the head of a falcon wearing the solar disc. It is a masterpiece of architectural design and engineering. The whole purpose and position of the temple was devoted to the adoration of the sun at dawn, and it was only at sunrise at certain times of the year that the vast interior was illuminated, when the light penetrated the sanctuary. It must have been for the ancients an unforgettable experience to stand in the main hall at dawn and watch the life-giving light of the sun gradually penetrate into the inner sanctum, the Holy of Holies, of an ancient faith.

On the facade of the temple of Abu Simbel are four colossal seated statues cut out of the living rock. The seated statues, two on each side of the entrance, represent Ramses II wearing the double crown of Egypt. The entrance opens directly into the great hall where two rows of four-square pillars are seen. On the front of these pillars are four gigantic standing statues of the king, again wearing the double crown. Each of the seated colossi are 65 feet high, taller than the Colossi of Memnon. On the walls of the great hall, which are thirty feet high, there are scenes and inscriptions concerning religious ceremonies and the Monarch's military activities against the Hittites.

The Small Temple of Abu Simbel, contemporary with the Great Temple, was dedicated to the ancient and illustrious goddess Hathor and Queen Nefertari. Between 1964 and 1968 both temples were removed to their new location, about 210 miles further away from the river and 65 miles higher, at the cost of some 90 million dollars.

Pi-Ramses

For the international concerns of Egypt and for the regaining of the empire, a capital near Asia and the Mediterranean was needed. To Memphis of the White Walls and Waset, Ramses had the ambition and energy to add a dazzling new urban center. The centerpiece of Pi-Ramses was the former summer palace of Seti I which was added to and enriched by Ramses II. Pi-Ramses was also a place where Egypt's soldiers and chariots could be housed for military readiness.

> Ramses took a strong personal interest in the adornment of the city and was constantly in pursuit of new resources for this purpose. He praised himself for his concern for the labor corps working there. He rewarded the overseer with gold as a mark of honor for finding out a block and preparing it for its purpose; he also assured the workmen that he had filled up the storehouse in advance so that 'each one of you will be cared for monthly. I have filled the storehouse with everything, with bread, meat, cakes, for your food, sandals, linen and much oil, for anointing your heads every ten days and clothing you each year.'[7]

Lid of Ramses the Great's coffin.

Imperial Waset
The Karnak Temple Complex

Begun well before the time of Ramses II, the Karnak temple complex grew to become one of the largest sacred sites in the world, encompassing more than 250 acres. The most celebrated and spectacular part of the Karnak temple complex is the grand hypostyle hall. Ramses II completed this hall in a marvellous manner, and it appears as a stupendous forest of columns—exactly 122 of them. The tallest of these columns are about 75 feet high, and many of them are decorated with the deeply incised hieroglyphics that became a veritable signature of Ramses II.

The Luxor Temple Complex

The magnificent Luxor temple lies just over a mile from the south of the main temple at Karnak. At Luxor, Amen was worshipped in the ithyphallic form of the timeless fertility-god known as Min. The temple is called Luxor, from the Arabic el-Qusur, meaning The Castles, the name given to the village that grew up on the site. The temple is largely the work of Amenhotep III and Ramses II, who added a colonnade court and two obelisks in front of the temple. One remains, the other is in Paris, a gift to France in honor of Jean Francois Champollion's decipherment of Egyptian hieroglyphics. Ramses also had erected at Luxor six colossal statues in his own likeness. Today only four of the statues remain, two seated and two standing.

The Ramesseum

The Ramesseum is the funerary temple of Ramses II located on the West Bank of Waset. It was called "The House of Millions of Years of Ramses II in the Estate of Amen." In the first court of the Ramesseum he set up a statue of granite 56 feet high, only slightly smaller than the colossi of Memnon. The gigantic monolith was quarried at Aswan and then ferried down-river to Waset, offloaded, transported several miles to the temple, and erected on the site. Its original weight has been estimated at about 1,000 tons, about three times the weight of one of Hatshepsut's obelisks at Karnak. It was from the Ramesseum that the English poet Percy Blythe Shelley drew the inspiration to write "My name is Ozymandias [Ramses II], king of kings; Look on my works, ye Mighty, and despair!"

The Immortal Ramses

Having lived vigorously for more than nine decades, Ramses II died in the second month of his 67th regnal year. There was no final death, however, in the African way of thinking; only gradual decay and periodic renewal. Egypt was perhaps the earliest nation to clearly articulate the purely African notions of resurrection and immortality. As one writer succinctly stated, within the context of Egypt, "If Osiris, the Nile, and all vegetation, might rise again, so might man." Man could rise, but only if he made God's words, which were truth, justice and righteousness, manifest on earth. This was fundamental to the African (in this case, Egyptian) metaphysic.

Reclaiming for the African world the ancient Egyptian heritage (which of course includes the knowledge of heroic sovereigns such as Ramses the Great), must be seen as an integral part of the Black liberation movement. It will inspire and direct us. Egypt was the heart and soul of Africa, and we need only glance at her noble traditions, her dignity, humanity and royal splendor to measure our true fall from power. When we examine the Egyptian civilization we note what is perhaps the proudest achievement in all the annals of human history. We must see in Egypt the knowledge that what Black people did, Black people can do. In this way the great deeds of our illustrious ancestors, including the imcomparable Ramses, are resurrected, and ancient history becomes merged both with what is and what we have the power to be. It lays the basis for the forward movement of the African people.

Egyptian Kinglist
Egypt's Late Eighteenth Dynasty Kings/c. 1356-1295 B.C.

Amenhotep IV/Akhenaten, 1356-1340 B.C.
Smenkhkare, 1342-1340 B.C.
Tutankhamen, 1340-1331 B.C.
Ay, 1331-1327 B.C.
Horemhab, 1327-1295 B.C.

Egypt's Nineteenth Dynasty Kings/c. 1295-1187 B.C.

Menpehtyre Ramses I, 1295-1294 B.C.
Menmare Seti I, 1294-1279 B.C.
Usermare Ramses II, 1279-1213 B.C.
Baenre Merneptah, 1213-1204 B.C.
Menmire Amenmesses, 1204-1200 B.C.
Userkheprure Seti II, 1200-1194 B.C.
Siptah, 1194-1188 B.C.
Queen Tewosret, 1188-1187 B.C.

Egypt's Twentieth Dynasty Kings/c. 1187-1069 B.C.

Userkhaure Sethnakhte, 1187-1185 B.C.
Usermare-Meryamen Ramses III, 1185-1154 B.C.
Neferkare Ramses IV, 1154-1148 B.C.
Menmare Ramses V to XI, 1148-1069 B.C.

Notes

1. Cheikh Anta Diop, *Great African Thinkers, Vol. 1. Cheikh Anta Diop*, Eds. Ivan Van Sertima and Larry Williams (New Brunswick: Transaction Books, 1986), p. 219.
2. Ivan Van Sertima, *Personal Communications With The Author*, September 1, 1987.
3. Charles S. Finch III, *Letter To The Author*, November 23, 1982.
4. Walter B. Emery, *Egypt In Nubia*. (London: Hutchinson of London, 1965), p. 199.
5. Emery, p. 199.
6. Basil Davidson, *Africa*. Arts and Entertainment Television Network, 1986.
7. Hermann Kees, *Ancient Egypt: A Cultural Topography* (Chicago: University of Chicago, 1961), p. 169.

Bibliography

Breasted, James H. *History of Egypt*. New York: Charles Scribner's Sons, 1959.

Budge, Ernest Wallis. *Egyptian Obelisks*. Chicago: Aries Publishers, Inc., 1982.

Brigham Young University. *Ramses II: The Pharoah and His Time*. Provo, Utah: Brigham Young University, 1985.

British Museum. *Introductory Guide To The Egyptian Collections*. London: Trustees of the British Museum, 1971.

Davidson, Basil. *Africa*. Arts and Entertainment Television Network, 1986.

Dawson, Warren R. *Who Was Who In Egyptology*. London: Egyptian Exploration Society, 1951.

Diop, Cheikh Anta. *African Origin Of Civilization*, Trans. Mercer Cook. New York: Lawrence Hill, 1974.

Diop, Cheikh Anta. *Great African Thinkers, Vol. 1.*, Eds. Ivan Van Sertima and Larry Williams. New Brunswick: Transaction Books, 1986.

Emery, Walter B. *Egypt In Nubia*. London: Hutchinson of London, 1965.

Finch III, Charles S. *Letter To The Author*, November 23, 1982.

Freed, Rita E. *Ramesses The Great: An Exhibition In The City of Memphis*, 1987.

Gardiner, Alan. *Egypt Of The Pharaohs*. London: Oxford University Press, 1961.

Kamil, Jill. *Sakkara: A Guide to the Necropolis and the Site of Memphis*. London and New York: Longman, n.d.

Kitchen, K.A. *Pharoah Triumphant: The Life And Times Of Ramses The Great*. Warminster, England: Aris & Phillips Ltd., 1982.

Kees, Hermann. *Ancient Egypt: A Cultural Topography*. Chicago: University of Chicago, 1961.

Lichtheim, Miriam. *Ancient Egyptian Literature, Vol. 2*. Berkeley: UC Press, 1974.

Moldenke, Charles E. *The Tale of The Two Brothers: An Egyptian Fairy Tale*. New York, 1892.

Montet, Pierre. *Everyday Life In Egypt In The Days Of Ramesses The Great*. 1958; rpt. Westport, Connecticut: Greenwood Press, 1974.

Rashidi, Runoko. *Kushite Case-Studies*. Los Angeles: Know Thyself!, 1987.

Romer, John. *Valley Of The Kings*. New York: William Morrow and Company, 1981.

Sandars, N.K. *The Sea Peoples: Warriors Of The Ancient Mediterranean*. London: Thames & Hudson, 1985.

Te Veld, H. *Seth, God Of Confusion*. Leiden: E.J. Brill, 1967.

Van Sertima, Ivan. *Personal Communications*, September 1, 1987.

Wainwright, G.A. "The Egyptian Origin Of A Ram-Headed Breastplate From Lagos," *MAN: A Monthly Record of Anthropological Science*; October, 1951, pp. 132-135.

Watterson, Barbara. *The Gods Of Ancient Egypt*. New York: Facts On File Publications, 1984.

West, John Anthony. *The Traveler's Key To Ancient Egypt*. New York: Alfred A. Knopf, 1985.

Williams, Chancellor. *Destruction of Black Civilization*. Chicago: Third World Press, 1976.

SHAKA THE GREAT: WARRIOR-KING AND FOUNDER OF THE ZULU NATION

By Mazisi Kunene

Few African rulers have been highlighted and made into legend as much as Shaka of the Zulus. This is not only because of his own qualities as a warrior king but his genius as a military strategist of consumate quality. Shaka transformed the society and thinking of the whole of central and southern Africa. In little more than ten years he had imprinted his political and military ideas in the vast region of southern Africa and prepared the regions for later confrontations with the invading whites. Shaka is perhaps the last of the heroic figures of past African history. Consequently his legend is not only alive as a political force but also as the mythic material of which histories are made. His role in recent history reinforces the validity of the continuation of African initiative, thought and institutions. In other words, Shaka incorporates the ideas of a united Africa. He avoided the idea of arbitrary integration of states but rather opted for the idea of mutual cooperation among African States. For, contrary to general belief, Shaka did not conquer and incorporate without a political plan. Some of the states (like the Nduande State and Buthelezi States) he incorporated totally but with some, like the Ngwane (now called Swaziland) Lesotho State and Mpondo State, he maintained warm diplomatic relations.

Critical comment on the sources of the Shaka Period

Access to information about the period of Shaka's rule comes from two major sources, namely white traders and adventurers who visited Shaka at his court; and African historical and oral sources. Any image of Shaka veers between praise and condemnation according to these sources. On the one hand, the white traders and later political and historical commentaries of colonial origin depicted Shaka as a master-killer and a ruthless ruler. On the other hand, all African sources from Dube to Dloma to Vilakabi have referred to this period only in terms of admiration and praise. The reasons why the views of the white traders and other white commentators are so divergent from those expressed by African historians are not far to seek. The colonial strategy was not only to conquer but also to dismantle heroic images and heroic personages of the African people. Thus the British Foreign Office was deeply disturbed at the positive and enlogistic comments on Shaka's rule by white visitors, and issued instructions accordingly that: you should make them look evil, make them kill their women and children. Later the same Office was to comment "Strange people these Zulus, they defeat our armies and convert our Bishops". (A reference to Bishop Colenso).

The strategy of eliminating African religious images and beliefs went hand in hand with the strategy of eliminating and/or distorting the images of the heroic figures of African history and African thought. Having done so, the colonial policy was to quickly exchange these African heroic images with their own. Thus, in the end some of the conquered people praised and elevated, not their own heroes, but the heroes of the colonial power. By extension, the settlers and missionaries were heroes and heroines descended from a long line of heroic traditions. The colonising power was able to justify its conquest and to claim a benevolent intent to "rescue the downtrodden and persecuted peoples from tyranny." The indoctrination has gone deep into the ethos of the colonised people. Thus Shaka has been said by some Africans to have been a monster-killer, a homosexual, a psychological case.

It is interesting to notice that the same historical criteria never applies to European kings, popes and heroes, whose history is constantly projected as without blemish. If there are negative qualities in such a hero they are deliberately avoided and/or suppressed. Thus King Henry VIII is depicted as a hero and a lover of the arts who restored the religious authority to England. As for his criminal excesses (the murder of his wives) they are mentioned only in passing as though it had nothing to do with his character or evil nature.

It would be a mistake to think that our intentions here is to claim that African history is dominated by blameless heroes. Like any history that involves military discipline and military conquest, there are occasions when there are excesses. But it does not mean that these excesses characterise the individual or era. Such excesses would by characteristic of such great heroes as Asoka, Alexander the Great, Charlemagne, Napoleon, Peter the Great (who personally chopped off the heads of thousands of rivals and enemies publicly and before his son—"to teach him how to rule"), Gupta, Chin, etc. However their actions are counterbalanced by the historical achievements that made them heroes, not villians.

It should be mentioned that there is a crop of new historians, many of them white, who have set out to put the record straight on the Shakan period and its great achievements. They should not be lumped together with the unenlightened bunch that persist in perpetuating a sense of historical inferiority in the African community.

The image of Shaka drastically changes in the hands of the African writer and African historian. First of all the African historian from South Africa speaks the language and therefore has access to the thoughts and ideas from people themselves. For instance, none of the so called on-the-spot recorders of the Shaka era understood and spoke the Zulu language well. It is as though one were to go to the Kremlin and after a few weeks she/he was to claim to be an expert on the inner politics of the Soviet Union without as much as the knowledge of the Russian language! Besides, these so called on-the-spot recorders, lacked the language of the culture and therefore the reasons behind certain actions. At times these traders got third hand reports from Shaka's enemies planted by some of his ambitious brothers. The second factor that puts the African historian in good standing is his deep knowledge of custom and institutions that govern the life of the Zulu society.

It is natural, therefore, that he would better understand the executions, for instance, of those who had violated the Zulu law and acted in so outrageous a fashion that they *deserved* to be executed. For example, the company that failed to protect its commander Nongalaza Kanondela was executed. This is normal in war. Neglect and cowardice are punishable offences. However, without an understanding as to why the company was executed the observer/recorder merely states that "a group of young braves was executed".

The African historian also has a deeper political sympathy with his history than a foreigner. For, after all, history is part fact, part myth and part propaganda and glorification. In the hands of the African writer like Senghor, Shaka emerges as an appropriate African heroic figure. The same is true of numerous other African writers and commentators. Only very few African writers, such as Ali Mazrui, depict Shaka in negative terms, probably because Mazrui would rather have a Muslim hero or heroes from his family rather than the authentic African hero. Here again the motive is deeply suspect. Instead of Shaka the military genius and political democratiser we see a Shaka of the author's own prejudice and distortion.

Some of the comments on Shaka by Africans and/or African-Americans are based on pure ignorance or distorted secondary white sources. Into this category would unfortunately fall also Mofolo's "Chaka", who, under pressure from missionaries, created a Faustian Shaka of fiction who has little or nothing to do with the Shaka of history. Shaka in this fictitious novel is depicted as a leader of darkness whose power is pitted against the leader of light (i.e. missionaries). Shaka is also depicted not as an intelligent person, but influenced by an evil force in the person of a diviner or a witch. This force, according to the book, totally controls Shaka's mind. Needless to say this is a typically European middle-ages attitude to intellectual and/or physical deviation. Innovation is depicted as the work of the devil, the devil totally controls the minds of those who have surrendered their lives to him in order to attain some ambitious goal.

Alas, it is not part of the Zulu world view and never was. Besides, Shaka detested anything that suggested metaphysical or diabolic manipulation. His attitude to social action was practical and based entirely on the principle of causality. Thus on being told by visiting whites what the stars were, according to their thinking, he asked them specifically if any of their race had been there. The answer was a puzzled silence. These simple traders had taken scientific speculation for divine truth. Any prophecy according to Shaka and according to Zulu thought in general must not be a mere reconstruciton of apparent reality but must be a summary and a prediction based on a perception of divergent forces of reality.

Standing opposite to the fictional Shaka of Mofolo is a work by the great African historical novelist R.R.R. Dlomo. His depiction of Shaka is based on on-the-spot research from many Zulu traditional sources. Dlomo spoke Zulu, wrote in Zulu and was Zulu. It is not surprising therefore that the Shaka we encounter is more realistic and closely approximates the Shaka every Zulu family talks about. Shaka is brave, hates cowardice, he is an innovator; he is a revolutionary who reorganises the whole society; he is as concerned about a boy competitor for his kingship as the rest of the Kings of his period and earlier. He loves his brothers but does not realise they would rather be at home enjoying princely life than a life of service to the empire. In short, the Shaka we see in Dlomo's work is a human being of extraordinary qualities but all the same a normal human being who is neither a god nor a devil.

It would be too narcissistic to analyse my own work—*Emperor Shaka the Great*. Suffice it to say here that I was deeply influenced by the narration of my own families (Ntuli, Ngcobo, Kunene) and R.R.R. Dlomo. From other books such as "Olden Times in Zululand and Natal", "Shaka Zulu", "Cetsh-wayo", I learned some facts about the period but made my own interpretation based on my own educational upbringing. The Shaka that emerged from this research was a man of extraordinary qualities and courage, a true genius in all senses of the word, both positive and negative. It would be correct to say, in my opinion, that Shaka was possessed, not by external forces but by his own genius. In the context of the times, let us therefore analyze and study, not Shaka the individual, but the events that he encountered, reshaped, and re-directed, and which in turn influenced him. This way we can better under-stand Shaka the man or, should we more accurately say, Shaka and his men and women. For indeed Shaka's great ability was as an organiser who not only invented efficient weapons but made heroism an ideal for a whole generation of the next one hundred and fifty years. To achieve these ends he roused in many of his comrades and followers a sense of fraternity, equality, and a sense of a wider political mission.

Southern Africa from the late 16th centuries to early 19th century. A history of rising nationalisms and white invasions.

The tip of the African continent is characterised by the narrowing of the massive land mass into a round tubular protuberance. This is the end of the African continent and the final point of many immigrations from eastern,

central and western parts of the continent. Initially this process was characterised by a flotsam and jetsam of small populations ranging from the Bantu
speaking peoples to the Afro-Asiatic looking Khuikhoi and San peoples. Because of the large landmass to the north of this region, the process of its
peopling was slow and without any land pressure. The major pursuit of the
people in the region is pastoralisation and small garden farming (izife), hunt-
ing and collection of fruits and similar foodstuffs. This picture completes the
image of this paradise.

The San people do not cultivate but are skilled marksmen and therefore
have plenty of meat from game. In addition, they are artists par excellence. To
this day the traveller is amazed at their masterpieces that have lasted hundreds
of years. Far from being primitive they have a highly organised society, similar
and corresponding in many ways to the rest of the African continent. They
share everything and they are peaceful people. Why should they fight? There
is plenty of game, there is enough land for everyone. Theirs is a life in pursuit
of philosophy and reflection on the cosmic order as illustrated in their poetry
and their numerous stories.

This tranquility and peace was only regional and would soon be disturbed
by massive invasions and massive movements of population. The sedimenta-
tion of the African population in Southern Africa had become inevitable not
only because this is the end of the African land mass but also because of the
disturbances to the north. On the western part, throughout the coast and
interior, the Portugese were busy capturing Africans and sending them to
slavery in the Americas. Each year there was a large number of peoples being
shipped into slavery. The same Portugese had started a similar slave trade in
the Eastern part of Africa and established posts all along the coast. Because
they were few in number they had to depend on intrigue, pitting brother
against brother, father against son, nation against nation. Consequently in the
end the whole region was fraught with civil and international wars. The significance of this activity was that it not only destabilized the whole region but
brought about a stampede of peoples to the southern end of the continent. As
stated earlier, this part of the continent *was* populated, although only by a
relatively small community of villages and homesteads. These events created
a restlessness in population movements that in a matter of a few hundred
years had bottled up the whole region. It was not as though whole populations
from the north came to the south but rather that those who were further north
moved to the logical boundaries of the south. Of course the Portuguese were
not the only factor but combined with other factors, such as a search for
pastures, and a natural higher population growth of settled populations, the
region experienced dramatic population growth. This was to be further com-
plicated by the advent of the Dutch settlers (known later as the Boers) in the
south-west tip of the African continent. As this invading group moved north-
wards raiding both cattle and peoples the area experienced from this pincer

movement, extreme destabilisation. These, however, were complicating factors. The biggest challenge came from within.

History of the Rise of African States and African nationalism in the 18th Century

It is important to examine, if only cursorily, the social and political organisation of the African societies in the early and mid 17th/18th century in what is now called South Africa. The most prevalent form of political organisation is characterised by a clan whose territorial boundaries are either defined by a larger conglomerate of clans or, if the clan is powerful enough, by itself. The territorial boundaries were naturally flexible defined less by groups than by natural phenomena such as rivers, valleys, or mountains. The larger the clan the more powerful since it could mobilize a large body of totally loyal and committed individuals.

Some clans, because of their size, drew to themselves affiliate clans or satellite clans whom the central clan protected, thus forming a kind of confederacy of clan states. Such was the case with the powerful Dlamini clan, the Nxumalo clan, the Ngcobo clan (this clan had so many related subclans that it created what amounted to a nation-state of its main clan and subclans), Mthethwa clan, Mtaung clan (this clan was so large that like the Dlamini clan, it split into various linguistic groups). Such clans would either solicit an alliance with other clans either through marriage or war. Smaller clans if they formed an alliance with a larger clan naturally paid tribute to the larger or dominant clan. This meant that dominant clans became extremely wealthy and, as polygamous marriages became the norm to such aristocratic clans the size of these clans increased at an enormous rate.

Needless to say this population explosion, coupled with other factors, led to territorial crisis. The scenario therefore at the end of the 17th century is of a vast population (relatively speaking) becoming more and more conscious of the growing scarcity of land. This signified the end of an era both in military terms and in the style of living. As long as the "north" was open, this population felt no pressure; it could move to and fro following trails to rich lands for its agricultural activities and wide pastures for its animal husbandry or mining regions for its iron and copper products.

However, now that the north was partially occupied and threatened by hostile foreign elements the pressure became almost unbearable. We can evaluate this pressure on the basis of the development of two factors: (a) the reorganisation of society into aggressive semi-militarised clan groups whose objective was to incorporate others and/or seize their territory, and (b) the growing value and importance of iron mining and iron smelting for weaponry. Many families who specialised in iron products attained special status in society. Such was the case for instance with the Mbonambi clan.

The region of relative calm (as opposed to the highly centralised states of the north such as the empire of Monomotapa, Kingdom of Balongongo etc.) suddenly erupted into numerous wars and conflicts of smaller and larger dimensions. Bigger clan-states displaced and swallowed smaller states. Moreover, the more powerful states began to realize that the pursuit of war and summer (harvest time) raids was more profitable than the hard task of stock raising and agriculture. Having attained the habit, they roamed everywhere in the country contemptuous of the very idea of a fixed permanent territory. Some of the smaller clans like the Ntulis were forced to live in the forests or mountain fortresses. The semi nomadic lifestyle was pursued with particular fervor by such powerful clans as the Matiwanes and to a certain extent the Ndwandwes.

All this meant a drastic change in the ethic that had characterised society before. No community was safe from these raiding clans unless it allied itself with more powerful clans. In which case it would either follow their life style, of earning a living through raids or settling down to defend the lands of the adopted clan and its own. Both lifestyles vied with each other to gain access to the resources. In all this it is clear that the weak were at a particular disadvantage, as the code of morality demanding the protection and defence of the weak was thrown to the wind. Not even travellers were safe (hitherto regarded as sacred personages who should be feted and entertained even with the last available morsel of food).

It was in this context that the Dingiswayo empire or "commonwealth" emerged. It was characterized by an extensive network of alliances of smaller and larger clans. Among these clans was the Zulu clan under whom were a few network clans. The clans so grouped together paid tribute to the central Mthethwa authority and, if it waged war, all clans would participate under central Mthethwa general command. In addition these clans paid tribute to neighbouring powerful potentates such as (in the case of the Zulus) Phungashe, Zwide, Matiwane. It meant that smaller clan-states were under great pressure to give away their resources and in some cases young women to placate these powerful robber Kings. At their own level the robber kings waged constant wars against each other to establish full hegemonic claims. The situation was indeed chaotic.

A reference to the Mthethwa empire is relevant here since it played a crucial role in the political and military development of Shaka and many of his comrades in arms. The role of the Mthethwa empire as a stabilizing force cannot be overstated. However, by its every position, it posed a constant challenge to neighbouring rulers such as Zwide who felt that the conquest of the Mthethwa empire would leave him master in the whole of Nguniland. As these great changes were taking place, Dingiswayo was at the helm at the Mthethwa capital of Luyengweni. Shaka's father Senzangakhona was a ruler of the small, constantly harassed Zulu state. It is necessary to mention this since all the early Shaka wars were either because he refused to continue paying tribute or were waged as an act of revenge against patron King Dingiswayo. They were not, as has sometimes been claimed, wars of aggression to fulfill Shaka's ambitions. to understand the role that Shaka played in creating a national entity out of this mounting chaos it is necessary to go back to the circumstances of his birth.

The evolution of Shaka as a Political and Military Leader

Shaka was born of a stormy relationship between his father, King Senzangakhona, and his mother, Princess Nandi. Contrary to general belief Shaka was not illegitimate, a term that never applied to the aristocracy. Moreover, although Shaka was conceived before marriage the young lovers did get married. The customary "cleansing" feast was paid for, which made the marriage legitimate and acceptable to both families. The crucial problem in this relationship lay in the totally different personalities of the parents. Whereas King Senzangakhona was an easy going ruler who cared more for his charm than for the strains of political power, Nandi was a serious introspective, imaginative and strong-willed woman. For her, power lay in her sharp mind and her sharp tongue. Of her the court poet says: "The Assembly, the one whose torrent of angry words frightened".

By all accounts she was a woman of exceptional qualities and power. She was beautiful in the sense of the beauty that radiates from within. Her skin was "as smooth as a grinding stone and as black as the water berries". She was defiant even when Senzangakhona tried to admonish her against challenging the Assembly. It was inevitable, therefore, that Senzangakhona and Nandi should separate. But before the separation a series of devastating experiences occured that deeply affected Shaka. The first and most important was the attempt by Senzangakhona, his father, to kill him. In this he was instigated by his chief wife, Queen Mkhabi.

It should be understood that in African society, because the way the society is organised, i.e. communal, the individual deeply depends on others. A simple rejection by the community is the most traumatic and most severe punishment an individual can suffer. This rejection however pales compared to the rejection that a boy-child can suffer from his father. The father represents not only a boy's model but also serves as an intermediator with the world of the Ancestors. Only through him can a boy such as Shaka organise a feast of the Ancestors. This act of trying to kill him (Shaka) was inexplicable to the young boy.

Shaka's father's act should not, however, be taken in isolation. There were many kings in this period who either killed their heirs because they themselves tried to kill them, or, as in the case of Shaka, decided not to have children. Nevertheless, the constant conflict between mother and father left the young

Shaka confused as to where his loyalties must lie. This is clearly illustrated by his frantic attempts later to get his father to give him the initiation goat and yet, still later, to give him the ceremonial spear. A word of warning must be sounded, however. This is not a Freudian world. Shaka would have had many social parents who would have loved him just as well and consequently softened the blow of his rejection. In other words, Shaka's later development is to attributed to his strength of character and/or his mother's training rather than to the imagined wounds of his childhood.

Nandi and her children face exile

Nandi and her two children, Shaka and his young sister, Nomchoba, now set out into "exile". Their first destination was to Nandi's home of the Langeni clan. It was not long before it became clear that the jibes against her children had become unbearable. We can surmise that Shaka's temper and Nandi's own strong character were contributing factors. However, it is fair to say the Langeni were a small clan compared to the Zulus and therefore Nandi's return to her home would be enough to serve as a causus belli. The Mhlongos (Nandi's people) were justifiably nervous about her presence though it did not justify the amount of cruelty and harrassment meted out to her children. She was soon on her way with her children, this time to the Qwabes, who are related to the Zulus and were in fact the Senior House of the Malandela clan to which both of them belonged.

It is rightly said that exile teaches many things and by the variety of experiences it quickly matures the mind. This was as true of Shaka as it was of Sundiata and of many great rulers. At the Qwabes Shaka quickly grew to a man. Hated by the heir of the Qwabe throne, Prince Phakathwayo, for his resourcefulness and bravado, Shaka soon proved himself to be as witty as he was brave, wherever there were fights with other boys. The constant humiliation of Prince Phakathwayo led him to gang up against Shaka and whenever possible distort the sequence of events that led to a fight.

On the other hand Nandi for the first time was happy. She married the kindly Prince Gendeyana and bore him a son, Ngwadi, who later died in battle fighting against Shaka's murderers. Nandi herself was mellowing and Shaka was growing up normally, despite the boyish confrontations with his cousin, the Qwabe heir. Life at the Qwabes gave Shaka a strong sense of family, unlike the life at the Langeni which made him so bitter that he came back to revenge his family soon after he became King.

Shaka at the Mthethwa Capital

It was not long before Shaka decided to join the Mthethwa army at the age of eighteen years as a recruit. He soon distinguished himself as a fierce and a fearless warrior. His regiment, the Izichwe, gained great reputation for its strong sense of fraternal solidarity and courage in battle. Initially it was commanded by General Buga and it included such great warriors as Nqoboka, and Mgobhozi of the Msane clan who later became Shaka's lifelong fighting partners.

It is necessary at this stage to give a general picture of the methods of fighting and their advantages and disadvantages, prior to Shaka's military innovations in Nguniland. Supplied with such information we can better assess the scale of changes Shaka brought about in the Southern African region. These involved both a change in the code of warfare and actual physical transformation in the methods of warfare. Generally speaking, warfare in Nguniland was, at this time, a ritual activity and, if the ritual stages failed to stop the war, then and only then a reluctant physical encounter. Guided by a strict moral code that limited the scale of physical destruction against the enemy the war code developed many interim stages of ritual confrontation before actual physical fighting. These included (a) the exchange of ambassadors of good will whose task was to persuade the enemy camp against the folly of declaring a war, (b) a ritual dance in which the best dancers of the opposing camps competed; (Whichever party won the dance competition won the war), and (c) a selection of the best fighters from both sides; (the winner won the war for his side).

The final stage of confrontation involved the use of the long throwing spear. Should this bundle of spears be exhausted before the enemy gave up then the army would simply flee. The enemy would then declare itself the victor. The enemy made no attempt to pursue the "defeated" army as this would be considered thoroughly immoral. If necessary the elders on both sides would intervene and stop the war. All they had to do was to stand in between the fighting armies and tell everybody enough was enough. So harmless and civilized were these wars that women and children and old men and women watched them not too far from the arena of battle.

All these approaches were fine as long as everybody adhered strictly to the codes of war. However there were more ambitious rulers such as Phungashe, Matiwane, and Zwide. Zwide was the most ambitious of them all. Spurred by his mother, Queen Ntombazi, he not only attacked without reserve but also captured and killed many rulers in the region. Their skulls were hung in a special house as war trophies!

This was anathema to the whole region of Nguniland. One of the most revered codes of war was that you must allow your enemy to bury and mourn its dead. It was said, those who did not respect the dead could not respect the living. Zuide's practice therefore constituted the most repulsive and immoral act in the whole of Nguniland. This violation of custom did make him feared. In addition he was able to amass a powerful army. He nevertheless still used the throwing spear technique and had no standing army and reluctantly pursued his enemy in flight. In other words his organisation and war machine was still loosely held together by some aspects of customary law or was it limited initiative? What distinguished it from others was the viciousness with which his soldiers fought and the unswerving objective of seizing the head of a ruler.

Matiwane, on the other hand, though as vicious and restless as Zwide nevertheless lacked the persistence and territorial ambition of Zwide. He seems to have had no territorial ambitions but preferred to raid and rob weaker nations from region to region.

It is necessary to mention these facts as they were the key factors in Shaka's strategy to counter the violence and rapaciousness that was rampant in the area. Shaka approached and discussed with Dingiswayo the need to evolve new and more effective methods of countering these rulers and others who after each war went home to prepare for yet another war. This inevitably led to numerous small but troublesome wars. Shaka put several proposals to Dingiswayo, the key being the need to integrate the defeated into one common citizenship. That meant that the defeated must be made to surrender and their region integrated as a district of the kingdom. Secondly, he proposed the aggressive rulers such as Zwide and Matiwane should be executed on being captured as their policies were responsible for wide and continuing disturbances in Nguniland. This proposal was turned down by Dingiswayo who had often captured Zwide and Matiwane and, after a little speech of admonishment, sent them back to their families. This had deeply incensed Shaka who identified not with the privileged aristocracy but with the fate of the soldiers and their families. Dingiswayo still believed naively that he could still persuade these rulers to enjoy the wealth in their territories, only to hear that they were on the war-path against him once more with new allies.

Shaka further proposed a change of war tactics involving not a throwing spear but a more effective short stabbing spear used in hand to hand combat. Dingiswayo could not comprehend the significance of such changes in military tactics and only conceded to a limited use of the short spear technique by the Izichwe regiment of which Shaka was now the new commander. Dingiswayo felt that widescale use of this technique might lead to bloodier wars. But Shaka argued that the slow drainage caused by current wars totalled greater distraction than a short decisive war in which the defeated enemy became part of a common nation.

With this limited mandate Shaka proceeded to the Mbonambi clan who were the skilled smelters of iron. He personally supervised the making of the new weapon. This was to be a short spear with a firm handle that would hold on after many battles. The blade was to be medium sized, not too broad and not too small. This was to be the new weapon which, combined with a skillful use of the shield both as a protective cover and as a way of unbalancing the enemy, was far more effective and economical than the spear-throwing technique. It involved an assault by a determined and a fearless force. This meant special training and an infusion of the idea of discipline: never to turn one's back on the enemy and to retreat only in a disciplined fashion as directed by the commander. Above all the commander must himself be at the frontline. In other words he must only ask of his followers what he himself is prepared to do.

An opportunity was provided for the display of Shaka's military tactics in the inevitable war against Zwide. Although they were highly successful in this war, Dingiswayo still forbade their widescale usage. Shaka was not dismayed. He began to insist on one of his doctrines, namely that war must be fought to protect the populace and therefore the seized cattle and goats of the invaders must be shared by the citizenry as a whole, including the soldiers. Hitherto the practice had been to appropriate the loot only for the aristocracy. Hence many wars were actually for the material and political advantage of the ruling clan. The idea astounded Dingiswayo though his respect and affection for Shaka made him adopt the policy of wait and see.

In the neighbouring forest there lived one of those wildmen who constantly raided the fields of the villages. He, like many others, of his kind, lived a life of banditry. Shaka, whose deep belief in social order and discipline was revolted by this story. His friends and relatives tried to persuade him not to challenge "the fierce giant of the forest", who wheeled his battle axe against all comers like the wind. Shaka was bent on showing the effectiveness of his new fighting tactics but also on demonstrating that society must be protected against all bandits and bullies. Shaka's battle with the forest giant is one of the most celebrated events in Zulu history and poetry. Not only did it establish Shaka as a great war hero but also as a community hero since his act saved the community from continuous harassment. No longer would the shepherds have to be protected as they passed near the forest of the "giant". Stock was now safe and the fields in the valley were free for cultivation by men, women and children.

Nowhere is the tragedy of Shaka's youth better illustrated than in the fact that his father, Senzangakhona, did not know him on seeing a dance at the Mthethwas. Instead he marvelled at this tall handsome young man who danced in perfect movements. The extent of this "tragedy" can only be fully understood in the context of the strong bonds that distinguish the African family. It is as though the deep hostility that Senzangakhona felt towards his wife Nandi was transferred to her children. His attitude to them can only be described as unnatural. However contrary to those who would see these bitter experiences as turning Shaka into an aggressive ruler we believe it gave him the maturity and cynical calculation of events that made him the great political and military genius he was. Far from condemning his ambitions for the expansion of the Zulu State, we believe this to be a normal quality of rulers, if not a responsibility, under the conditions of harassment his small state was in. Moreover, to believe that Shaka's youth distorted his vision one would have to believe that this vision *was* distorted. That claim we consider inaccurate and a

The creation of the women regiments was the high point of Shaka's military organization. These regiments acted as supplementary units in case of a need for the evacuation of population to safer areas. Women regiments were well trained in the use of the long stabbing-knife (isijula) and were as fierce in executing their duties as the male regiments. One is reminded of the Japanese women who during the second world war were trained along similar lines.

The army was to attack in a crescent formation; that is, it would move in a pincer-like movement and aim at encircling the enemy. At the end of each part of the "horns" there were to be the bravest warriors. Similarly the centre was held by the best fighters in the country. Later, after Shaka had observed the movement of the waves, he decided that the Zulu army should attack in wave-formation enabling the frontline constantly to take relief from the next wave of fighters.

The intention of fighting any of the wars was to cripple the enemy so that he does not have to think of waging another war. This did not include killing women and children and the infirm, as some colonial historians have claimed (perhaps judging Shaka's strategy on the basis of their own conduct in colonial wars). Instead there was to be a dual approach, namely to defeat the enemy totally and secondly, to integrate the population of the defeated country into a common Zulu nationhood.

Although Shaka was cynical and skeptical about any interventions of supernatural forces in war he was not unaware of the mental impact such a belief had on the army and/or the enemy. He therefore used dramatic pauses before battle, the singing of special war songs, the use of powerful phrases to launch the army with a devastating attack. In more than one occasion enemies fled from merely hearing the war songs of a particular regiment.

There was to be no distinction between daytime and nightime fighting. To identify themselves the Zulu fighters were to use special watchwords created on the spot before battle.

All of these new codes for the Zulu army meant total reorganisation not only in a physical sense but also in its mental frame. The greatest test for the newly reorganised came at the great battle of Qokli against the large army of Zwide. King Zwide, in his ambitions to be master of Nguniland and all surrounding regions, cold bloodedly murdered King Dingiswayo who had come to negotiate a peace settlement. Besides, Zwide was now keen to teach a lesson to the young Zulu "upstart" whom he considered arrogant and irrelevant to the existing Kingly authority. Shaka chose a hill because of its strategic importance and its relevance to the execution of his military ideas. He could afford to do so since his army now carried its own supplies and was not obliged to fight in areas where there was food available in the neighbourhood. Zwide's army was commanded by his son Nozinhlanga a factor which deeply affected the fighting efficiency of the army. Nozinhlanga was royal but scarcely qualified as a commander. Shaka's army, on the other hand, had the best trained commanders who were to lead the army on the forefront. These commanders included General Ndela, son of Sompisi, Nqoboka, a veteran fighter of the Mtethwa Wars, Mgobhozi of the mountain, also a veteran fighter of the Mtethwa Wars, and Shaka himself. Zwide on the other hand stayed at home.

In vain, the Zwide army attempted to cross the Mhlathuze fords. They were met and repulsed by the small but effectively organised Zulu army which as it turned out, was served by the physical advantage of the river and the hill just as Shaka had intended. The huge Zwide army failed in three days of battle to defeat the small Zulu army. Although there was no decisive victory for either side, the Zulus had won the psychological war. Reinforced by their success and having gained regionwide reputation for standing up to and repulsing the fiercest army in the area, they set out to prepare for the training and integration of numerous recruits. Many smaller clans like the Mbathas, the Mzimelas, now sought the protection of the reputed Zulu army. Meanwhile Kings like Phungasha who had traditionally received tribute from the Zulus were keen to humiliate this "upstart". Phungashe demanded his traditional tribute, only to be answered with a barrage of swear words from Shaka. War between them became inevitable, and in a decisive battle between the Zulu army and Phungashe's army he was thoroughly defeated, to the great shock of Zwide. In any case Zwide, urged by his mother, decided to kill Phungasha who had now sought asylum in his residence.

All this meant that there was now only one large disciplined army of Zwide in the region beside the disarranged and demoralised Mthethwa army. It was to Shaka's political advantage (although he himself did nothing to manipulate these events) that the succession to the Mthethwa's throne was fraught with endless quarrels. The Commander-in-Chief, who was also a relative of the former King Dingiswayo, approached Shaka to take command. Shaka was now in a position to integrate the Mthethwas into the Zulu nation. This he did gradually and cautiously. Even when challenged by Zwide the second time he wisely left the Mthethwa army out of the fray. This meant that if he won the war, he would reinforce his position and become the undisputed master of the region.

Meantime Shaka sought out those who had ill-treated him and his mother in his youth. Contrary to the colonial propaganda Shaka did not wipe out the Langeni clan. Instead he chose men like Hubu and others for special punishment. In fact, the revenge against childhood enemies only involved members of this clan. Although he had defeated his relatives of the Qwabe clan he did not seek out his childhood persecutors. Gross exaggeration has always accompanied the name and reputation of Shaka and one of these exaggerations was that he wiped out whole villages in revenge for their ill-treatment of his mother and himself. Nothing could be further from the truth. In fact for a practical man like Shaka we would have to ask what was his *political* motive in avenging himself and his mother against those of the Langeni clan?

The second confrontation between Shaka's reconstituted army and Zwide's army is a classic case in military histories because of the tactics Shaka used in this war. Instead of organising a frontal attack against Zwide's army, he ordered all grains and foodstuffs to be burnt and destroyed all along the direction leading from the battlefield to the regions of Zululand. After Zwide had mobilised his entire army for a decisive battle with Shaka's relatively small army, he appointed the able General Soshangane as his commander-in-chief. Thus for the first time Shaka's tactics were making an impact on the enemy camp. General Soshangane was a seasoned fighter and not a relative of the King. Zwide was therefore certain he would win the war.

No sooner had the armies met than Shaka ordered his army to retreat in the direction of Zululand. Astounded and certain that the Zulus were panicked by the overwhelming numbers of the Zwide army, they followed them in hot pursuit. The Zulus always ahead, because of their fitness and speed, ran for many days passing through territories of chained corn and millet fields. Occasionally they would stop to eat from their own supplies. Zwides army was not only tiring but also hungry and in disarray. This was the famous moment when Shaka issued his war command "Sigide" and the Zulu army turned in perfect crescent formation and attacked the Zwide army. Defeat became inevitable as some of Zwide's men fled in opposing directions. Shaka had, through his tactic of *strategic retreat* (never used before), decisively defeated the Zwide army. The discipline and efficiency of the Zulu army, combined with Shaka's espionage network, had defeated a greatly superior force. Zwide fled to the northern regions. To forestall any regrouping of the Zwide army, Shaka sent a section of his army to the Zwide capital. Singing Zwide's war songs it lured Zwide's army to its humiliating defeat and destruction of the capital. Worse still, a section of the army deserted Zwide to join the evergrowing Zulu army.

Shaka was now the supreme master of Nguniland. His policy of integrating the defeated armies meant that his army now comprised the original Zulu army, numerous recruits, the remnants of Zwide's army, the Mthethwa army, the Phungashe army and many smaller local armies that voluntarily integrated into this now powerful Zulu army. Only the Chunus resisted being integrated until they were finally defeated after many encounters.

Shaka was now the most powerful ruler in Southern Africa. He had one of two alternatives. He either had to continue the wars of integration that would incorporate the Swazis, the Sothos, the Mpondos, the Xhosas or decide on a powerful Nguni state that maintained good relations with stable neighbouring states. Shaka, and there is simple evidence to support this claim, opted for the latter approach. Although he was intent on fighting many of the roaming armies, like that of Matiwane, he saw his campaign as a mopping up operation to establish law and order in the region. The Zulu armies were in this sense to observe a *Pax Zuluana* but would not be averse to attacking those like Zwide or Soshangane, who, having fled, had established powerful kingdoms in the North (South Mozambique).

Such attacks should be attributed to the normal requirement to secure the safety of the Zulu empire. They were not motivated by the sheer desire for an irrational revenge against Shaka's enemies or love of wars. Such claims are based on a wrong perception of the Zulu state as that of a state ruled and governed by Shaka as an absolute ruler. Shaka, in fact, could only wage war after convincing the High National Council of the validity of such an act. Several informants report numerous occasions in which such debates took place. Although Shaka, for instance, was reluctant to eliminate Mzilikazi (one of his generals who deserted with a regiment) the High Council prevailed on Shaka to launch a decisive punitive attack—"lest such bad examples be followed by others". It is obvious from many sources, that Shaka did not always personally suggest a campaign, but western thinking, having assumed that an African ruler makes all decision, takes it for granted that Shaka decided on all the wars. Having made this false assumption then it must find reason why one man should sanction so many wars. The conclusion is then that he was personally ambitious, revengeful, war-hungry and megalomaniacal. There is never an attempt by these colonial historians to go into the real causes of a particular war or conflict as dictated by violations of African law and custom.

When Shaka had established himself as a powerful ruler, he set out to establish normal and friendly relations with established and stable neighbouring States. Such was the case with the Ngwane State of King Sobhuza I of the Swazis whom he invited to his capital. King Moshoeshoe of the Sothos was also greatly admired by Shaka. When Moshoeshoe was attacked and harrassed by the restless Matiwane, Shaka sent Mdlaka, the great Zulu General, to rout Matiwane's armies. Relations between Shaka and Moshoeshoe were so warm that to this day the Zulu royal family and the Sotho royal families constantly exchange gifts. The relations with the Mpondo state were only soured when King Faku refused to mourn the death of Nandi, Shaka's mother. What we want to illustrate here is that Shaka was not an irrational war-mongering tyrant, as colonial historians have depicted him, but a rational and mature leader of original military and political initiative.

Domestic Policies and Practices

Under this heading we shall include all the events that took place within the Zulu state that reflect on Shaka's character. We begin our survey when Shaka is fully established and is in command of approximately 70,000 standing army. There are smaller and larger royal residencies. In some of these it is said there could be as many as 20-30,000 people engaged in different activities. Not all royal residencies were occupied by the King, some were occupied by the aunts of the King, some, as in the case of Nandi, by the mother of the King.

Shaka had decided not to marry in conformity with his own military law that the army should not marry until at a much later period. Shaka being the leader he was, who believed that the leader must do as he expects the followers to do, stayed unmarried. However he had 120 women who were his "wives" or concubines whom he called his "sisters". Incidentally any young man could have affairs but not necessarily marry. Shaka, like many Kings in this period, earlier loathed the idea of conflicts between father and son for the throne. His solution was in fact not to marry and of one of his "sisters" bore a child, as it happened many times he "gave" the pregnant woman to one of his brothers to look after and integrate the child into his brother's family. This was quite a common practice at the time, aimed mainly at giving a home to an infant. It is rumoured very loudly that Prince Mbulazi, one of the rivals for the Zulu throne at the time of King Mpande (Shaka's brother), was in fact Shaka's son. However there were occasions, it is said, when Shaka killed a boy infant. This was not unique to Shaka, nor does it characterise him as an evil killer. Shaka himself was a survivor from such an attempt by his father, as stated earlier. The stigma has only have attached to Shaka because we know more about him than other contemporary rulers. Father-killing, for that matter, was not unnusual among the ambitious sons of Kings. Dingiswayo was himself involved in such an attempt against his father Jobe.

The absence of an heir was a source of great concern to Nandi, his mother. She made several attempts to hide a newly born boy infant without success. Probably had she succeeded Shaka would not have been assassinated since Princess Mkhabayi's only great concern was that he had no children and therefore would leave chaos should he die in battle. It was too late when Shaka thought of settling down to a normal family life.

Was Shaka a homosexual?

Bizarre as it might sound to a Zulu, who had never heard of homosexuality until the advent of the whites and their city life, Shaka is reputed to have been homosexual. This, claims these falsifiers of history, accounts for his cruelty. First, without proving that Shaka was abnormally cruel, they go on to make the assumption that homosexuality is the passkey to sadism, a prejudice in itself. According to this logic, all the whites who massacred Africans and native Americans should be classified likewise as homosexuals. This kind of logic is difficult to grasp. The only explanation lies in the psychology of those who make these claims. Recently on Channel One in Germany, some German showed drawings supposedly of Shaka (recently made and smoothed over to show his idea of Shaka's girlish appearance and his supposedly smooth skin) Without ever knowing what Shaka really looked like, but rather to illustrate what, in his opinion, a homosexual looks like. This king of thinking is typical of Nazi or crypto-Nazi thinking, which makes it easy to typecast and then eliminate, ideologically or physically. Such claims have also been made in writing, by pseudo-historians who have no idea how Zulu law and custom operated. If Shaka had been a homosexual or had a behaviour pattern that was peculiar, he would never have been King.

If he had succeeded in becoming King he would have been killed or eliminated at an early stage by his relatives. For such behaviour would discredit the authority of the whole Royal Family and jeopoardize its own continued power. In any case any member of the family would have had the *right* to kill Shaka, including his own mother! In African law the behaviour of a ruler reflects on the whole nation. He ideally can only be King because people approve of him, as stated in the highest Zulu political law. But then we are reading statements written by those who know little about how an African aristocracy operates or else who hope to gain fame through notoriety. If all their intentions are to dismantle and disgrace African leaders and African heroes, then there is nothing really new in their statements, and such distortions of African history will eventually be exposed. Of course it is hard sometimes for the westerners or western-indoctrinated African to understand close and intimate friendships in African society without imputing homosexul implications. In any case such claims will die out as the African people begin to write their own authentic history, a process which has already started. This will eliminate obviously effeminate pseudo-Africans who claim to speak from within but are actually themselves closet homosexuals, eager to justify their own tendencies and practices.

Shaka and the Whites —

The encounter between Shaka and the Whites indicates that Shaka saw in the white lifestyle a different system not superior and not inferior but simply different. He was eager to learn from them and to teach them. He thought the practice of imprisoning a wrongdoer was extremely cruel. Why not let a person die with dignity if his crime so deserves it? There were indeed (according to the Zulu law at the time) many such crimes. The question is not why they were so many, but what was the social and political implication of their observance or violation? The reports we often hear from white travellers who visited the Zulu court, were that there were a number of executions but they often omit to state the reasons. Consequently we are given the impression that Shaka was a sadistic, blood thirsty killer, even though he himself never killed anyone except in battle. It would seem as though these whites were unaware of the massive executions, imprisonments and enslavement of women and children in the very Cape where they were coming from. We have no diary listing in detail the violence meted out to the African population in the British occupied Cape regions. It is hard, therefore, to take this lopsided morality or moralisation seriously. One can only express astonishment at the capacity of the western mind to shut off ugly facts about its own society and wax lyrical about the evils and brutalities of a Genghis Khan or an Attila the Hun.

The intention of the whites in approaching Shaka was to obtain land. Here they would settle and study the situation before launching an out and out war. The intention was therefore primarily to search for wealth in the form of minerals, ivory, or whatever was available. These were lower middle-class footmen, and therefore desperate and ruthless, lacking in the kind of morality that is found in more settled families. It is clear from all accounts that Shaka was aware of this. Besides, his vast network of informers had thoroughly briefed him about the Whites of the Cape and Delagoa Bay (eDalagubhe). Small wonder that Shaka's last words were a comment on this impending menace.

It would have been interesting to follow the relations between Shaka and the Whiteman, since Shaka was alert to their intentions, their strengths, and their weaknesses. Unfortunately he was succeeded by the impulsive and uncertain Dingane who acted more on instinct than by planning and strategy.

Shaka and his Mother

The close relation between Shaka and his mother is not suprising. The role of the mother in African society is that of a teacher. It is said that the greatest rulers are those who had the greatest mothers (to teach them). The status of motherhood as a counterbalance to malehood is amply illustrated in the Queen Mother system. In many cases the Queen Mother is appointed to such a position and therefore not necessarily the biological mother of the king. The appointment is a political one. Nevertheless, the position of the biological mother of a king is an important one. It can graduate to an even more important political position of Queen Mother, a position no doubt Nandi occupied, even though in the Zulu system it is not formalized.

In any case the Zulu court was replete with powerful women leaders in Shaka's time. These included his aunt, Princess Mkhabayi (who at first supported him and later conspired to have him assassinated to preserve the Zulu dynasty), Princess Mawa, twin sister of Princess Mkhabayi, and governor of an important military camp, and many others. Indeed it was the first wife of Senzangakhona, Queen Mkhabi, who had put great pressure on him to have Shaka killed. It is to Shaka's credit and is also descriptive of the limitations of his power that he did not have her killed in revenge when he became king.

Nandi played an important role in providing the raison d'etre for the expansion of the political bounderies of the Zulu State. Whereas at first she had acted as a crucial social and political teacher for the young precarious Shaka, now that he was king she served as his alter ego. So important was her position to Shaka that her death later deeply affected him and in some ways disoriented him. In meeting with the whitemen one of his major concerns was to obtain medicines that would prolong her life and ensure her good health. This, of course, is normal in Zulu society since it is thought some of the best medicines are obtained from outsiders, be they African or non-African. This strong bond between Shaka and his mother was made even more important by the fact that Shaka never married. Consequently the women who constituted his court did not have the status of wife and therefore, according to Zulu practice, could not serve as advisers and political analysts and commentators. On the whole the family of Shaka shared very close bonds. The importance of this bond cannot be overemphasised since it was the same bond that led to disastrous consequences. It was the same intense loyalty that, extended, led to Shaka's total blindness to the plots that were being hatched for his assassination by his half-brother Dingane and Mhlangana.

Shaka's relationship with his mother, far from being a Freudian dependency as some have suggested, was born of a shared political ideal and vision. For it was after all his mother's vision that had nurtured his dreams in the darkest days in exile. This twinness in the political structure was quite common in the region. Had not Queen Ntombazi driven her son to a vision of total power and sovereignty over Nguniland and in the process made him the *infant terrible*? Had not Zikodze, King of the Ngwanes (Swazi) been constantly restrained by his mother until in gratitude the Ngwanes had revived the ancient customs of dual kingship? Had not Mantantisi, Queen mother of the young Tlokwa ruler, led her own armies and defeated powerful rulers?

The logic of Shaka's relationship to his mother is thus cast on a wider political canvas. However, one thing was unique to this relationship. The exile, the suffering and humiliation had added to it a special stamp of emotional protectivity and inter-dependence. It is not suprising that Shaka was always deeply concerned about his mother's health. Indeed it was this ruse that his mother used to hide for seven months the pregnancy of one of his "sisters" (concubine). On hearing of his mother's illness Shaka immediately broke the hunt and hurried to his mother's residence. Her death totally destroyed one of Shaka's special worlds. The idea that Shaka killed his mother (as colonial historians have sometimes claimed) is as bizarre as it is vulgar.

This cataclysmic event totally disoriented Shaka. He became uncommunicative, reflective, introspective and above all, temporarily without the energy to control and conduct the affairs of State. The result was a political dislocation on two levels:

- Since the Assembly and the National Courts had so long depended on his quick intellect a general malaise quickly set in. Decisions were then made on the basis of how far they would accommodate the King's state of sadness.

- The period and form of mourning assumed a bizarre initiative by those desiring to show in the most exaggerated manner, their grief. Outer premises and districts began to take the law into their own hands, policing whoever they thought was not mourning hard enough.

Normally the period of mourning is an extremely important one among most peoples in this region. The bereaved family expects to be emotionally nourished and supported by the whole society, precisely because such a death violates the strong social bonds that are idealized by the society. There are numerous rituals that are performed on this occasion. Some of these include, restraint from any pleasurable activity be it participating in a festival, dancing, having physical relations, dressing in a manner to attract attention, singing, talking too loud, planting and harvesting etc. These actions vary in length according to the importance of the deceased. It was to be expected that the mourning period for Nandi's death had to be long. However its length and manner was made more abnormal by Shaka's own personal grief. Far from Shaka making political hay out of his mothers death, as has been suggested, Shaka was genuinely in a state of extreme grief. It was indeed the end of a crucial political and personal cycle for him.

No wonder that these ensured a period of general suffering in the Zulu State unparalleled in the history of the region. This was not only because of the lawlessness of the bands that chose to monitor the style and manner of mourning but also because of the scale and power of the Zulu empire itself. Neighbouring rulers sent large delegations of mourners who, as was the custom, mourned loudly and openly, spreading endless waves of gloom. After this long suffering voices of plotters against Shaka began to speak louder and louder. Even Princess Mkhabayi, his aunt, now began to express concern about Shaka's state of mind and began to support his half-brothers against him. Moreover they held deep grudges against him because of the numerous narrow escapes they had had to face in the wars. They had no great urge to fight in the wars which they, as an aristocracy, felt should be relegated to the common man. It is interesting to note for instance that those brothers who were outstanding warriors, played no role in plotting the assassination of Shaka.

The downdrift towards a growing lawlessness and chaos was stopped by one brave Gala, the son of Nodada of the Bujela clan, who scolded Shaka out of his grief. He stated how the country had been devastated by this mourning which, as he said, surpassed the mourning of all former kings. Snapping out of his gloom, Shaka scolded his councillors for not having alerted him to the state of chaos that had enveloped the country. Is it too much to ask that a man of genius such as Shaka should have areas of mind that are inexplicable even to himself? Nandi's death certainly had an unusual impact on a man who was otherwise of great stoic character and courage.

The Last Campaigns and Shaka's assassination

At this stage of Shaka's rule it can rightly be said that he regretted that there were no more territories to conquer. In every direction he looked, there were either friendly rulers such as Moshoeshoe and Sobhuza I, or those who were too remote to concern himself about. These last campaigns were therefore of a primitive kind either because of a violation of custom or to settle old scores.

It is customary to send mourners to whoever has lost a relative if he be known to you. Among rulers this custom is carried out as a matter of courtesy even if the rulers have never met. The King of the Mpondos had flatly refused to send such a delegation of mourners. It was "logical" that after the period of mourning Shaka should declare a punitive war against the Mpondos. This was by all accounts a reluctant war. The Mpondos fought a guerilla warfare from the thickets of the forest. The Zulus on the other hand felt no deep grudges against the Mpondos. Indeed the war seemed to have been intended to fulfill the age old custom of "cleansing" the nation of a great national tragedy. The highlights of this war were the capture of the Mpondo King's wives (whom Shaka ordered to be released); the death of the great Zulu warrior and commander, Nongala, son of Nondela, through the carelessness of an accompanying unit, and the crossing of the Mzimkhulu river, in which Shaka rescued and carried several young boys.

Additional expeditions were dispatched against small warring factions on the borders of the empire. The most important war in this period was the war against Soshangane, the former General of Zwide, against whom the Zulus had a special grudge. Moreover, Soshangane had built a powerful kingdom in what is now called South Mozambique. A showdown with him had become inevitable if not necessary. This took place in the war of Balule in which the Zulu army fought fiercely but also suffered heavy losses. This campaign took nine years to complete. By the time these regiments returned to Zululand, Dingane was in power. For, as the army advanced toward the north, Dingane and Mhlangane stayed behind on a flimsy excuse that they were suffering from a stomachache. Actually they had plotted with the Princess Mkhabayi and Mbopha, son of Sithayi (Shaka's major domo) to assassinate Shaka. Finding him sitting down with a few of his Councillors and having dispensed with a bodyguard, they suddenly rushed on him with spears. It is said that Shaka at this stage tried to take a spear from Mbopha, who was sitting beside him. But to Shaka's surprise Mbopha himself was part of the plot and it was he who first stabbed Shaka. Shaka's last words were to haunt his killers and many generations thereafter. These words also tell us Shaka's deepest concern about the political situation at the time.

"So you kill me, my brothers", he said, "you think you will rule this land after I am dead? You will never rule. It will be ruled by the swallows (whites) who hover over your heads, and you Mbopha, you whom I trusted so much?"

It was these words that made Dingane rush into action against the Boers without thinking. He was constantly haunted by the fear of white invasion, so that, instead of planning and plotting carefully as Shaka was doing, he ran into precipitous actions. Soon after, he killed not only his brother and co-plotter Mhlangana, but also many of his half-brothers, forcing the survivor Mpande to join the enemy camp of Boers. Needless to say, the outsider and co-plotter Mbopha was killed immediately. Dingane stated that—"Whoever can kill as powerful and fearsome a man as Shaka, can kill us all."

Shaka died at a young age of thirty six. Shaka's death led to a civil war, which was stopped by better counsel, but not before many heroes including his brother, were killed.

Evaluation of Shaka's Era

It is not possible in so short an essay, to go into detail about all the various wars in which Shaka displayed his great military genius. It was sometimes merely to prove a military point that he attacked a particularly defiant group, as was the case when he devised ways to dislodge the Phephethas from their mountain fortresses. His campaign against the Chunus show a man of steel nerves as he talked calmly with an enemy soldier who had not been able to identify him. That is, not until a messenger came to summon him to shore up a weakening section of the battle line. Shaka's main strategy was to consolidate the Nguni State and, having done so, to establish practical relations with established neighbouring states. His distaste for disorder among small states led him constantly to intervene either as a judge on succession issues (as in the case of the Ngcobo clan) or to effect a swift punitive action against a troublesome local ruler, as was the case against Rakosi. This created a busy court in which national and inter-national disputes were constantly being reviewed. The primitive expedition against Rakosi is constantly referred to in the annals of Zulu history since it led to the only breakaway by a Zulu general, namely Mzilikazi, who eventually established himself among the Shonas, in what is now called Zimbabwe. Shaka seems to have been reluctant to chase after Mzilikazi whom he loved and respected for his courage.

The question that often comes up about Shaka is: was Shaka a mindless, sadistic killer? Shaka had two roles, In building the Zulu nation, he had to build a powerful and an efficient military machine. Secondly, he had to establish a political and a social ethic that must bind together disparate and powerful clans and nations. This he had to do within a period of ten years which was the length of his reign. To achieve a powerful military machine he had to effect a fundamental revolution in the thinking of the peoples who formerly considered war as a preoccupation of powerful robber kings, but not as defensive occupation of the weak. He had to create a sense of a single nationhood where none existed before. His inventiveness and spectacular military strategies meant a swift orientation from a slow cumbersome land-based traditional society to a well organized and well disciplined modern society.

We can assess the success of Shaka's unique military strategies from the fact that by the time he died in 1828 virtually all armies in Southern Africa were using his tactics. His successes in battle had become legendary. While the intention of Shaka's armies was to avoid alienating and destroying non-combatants, death of civilians cannot be ruled out. Shaka's military campaigns, as is the case in all wars, meant discipline, and any violation of that discipline meant death, and as in all wars, whether waged by Alexander, or Napoleon, or Attila, killing became the means to an end i.e. to acquiring territory or wealth as the case may be. Shaka's iron discipline and the killing in a war cannot be naively referred to as an act of sadism. Surely the objective of a war, if it is reasonable, absolves the military leadership.

We do not have a single case in which Shaka wiped out whole nations or massacred innocent peoples as in the case of Hitler or the invaders of native pre-European America. Instead evidence exists to this day of absorption and integration of the conquered. Indeed, Isaac's correspondence indicates that he deliberately exaggerated events to keep the sponsorship from trading companies. Internally Shaka's rule was aimed at moulding a nation of heroes. There was nothing Shaka detested more than a coward. To this day many Zulu people feel morally justified to attempt to kill anyone who calls them a coward.

It is also not understood that Shaka, in keeping with tradition and Zulu law, presided over both civilian and criminal cases. The King's Court was the highest court of appeal. The passing of the death sentence was the sole prerogative of the King. Whereas, therefore, in a modern state the various states and provinces can pass a death sentence, in the case of the Zulu State this was entirely in the hand of the King and his counsellors. Many death sentences were witnessed by foreigners that had actually originated from regional or village courts i.e. in addition to serious cases that had been tried and judged by the King's Court. It must be borne in mind that in Zulu society it was considered more dignified to die a quiet death than to suffer the humiliation of imprisonment and the consequent degradation of mind and body. This was Shaka's view and that of the then society. Cases involving compensation of the victim or settlement of boundary disputes received less attention than the spectacular death sentences.

Shaka as chief military commander was also responsible for the sentencing of military personnel for violations of discipline. There was therefore enormous traffic of both civilian and military cases to and fro from the King's High Court. It was impossible for the foreigners to judge the validity or the justice of those courts unless they knew Zulu law, the Zulu language and the Zulu lifestyle and culture.

There is simply no evidence that Shaka was a sadistic killer. If any, it is usually the unreliable claims that came from Shaka's enemies, converts to Christianity (or European lifestyle) and those like Lamula and Mofolo who had been indoctrinated to believe in the validity of the whiteman's civilising mission. In the context of the times, Shaka was no more savage than those who killed thousands upon thousands of Vietnamese in the name of "democracy" or "civilisation". All propaganda efforts to make Shaka evil have failed. Several books, papers and public commentaries point to a new and fresher assessment of Shaka's leadership and genius. The recent television film series entitled "Shaka Zulu" should be denounced, precisely because it is trying to update a discarded myth. Shaka was not an angel, he was a warrior. He was not the devil as he is painted out to be, but, to African people, one of the greatest nation-builders and military geniuses the world has ever seen.

HANNIBAL: NEMESIS OF ROME

By Wayne B. Chandler

"Over the glimmering embers a mighty head was bowed. The red glow from the fire lighted a dark-skinned face, whose features blended something of the savagery and grandeur of a lion's head."[1] For fifteen long years Hannibal had been the scourge of Rome. He had inspired consternation among the noble senators and stark terror among the Roman populace. In battle after battle he had dealt the Roman army decisive defeats, until he had succeeded in shaking the very foundations of mighty Empire. Yet despite this long and arduous campaign, Hannibal faced another challenge, for the greatest contest of them all lay ahead of him. The renowned and courageous Roman general Scipio awaited him on the plains of Zama. As Hannibal reflected on the events of the previous fifteen years, he saw that he had come full circle. The last of the lion's brood, each bound by the pledge to annihilate Rome, was now back where he had begun, in Carthage.

Hannibal's tactical feats have awed the military strategists of many different lands and centuries; his identity has fascinated as many historians. He single handedly put his nation on the world's historical map, for without his existence, Carthage would be unknown save to a few erudite historians. Yet our own knowledge of him is remarkably scanty. The bulk of it rests upon the writings of Livy and Polybius. In fact, without the relatively recent discovery of the site of the battle of Lake Trasimene and the finding of a Latin inscription from Brundisium, or present day Brindisi, Hannibal himself would be no more than a legend, for no biographies of Carthage's greatest hero have survivied. The tragic irony which confronts us is that all the written information about Hannibal comes to us through the scribes of the very people, with whom he warred so bitterly; for Livy was a Roman historian, and Polybius was a Greek.

As one historian notes, "The story of Hannibal is a tragedy, the inevitable outcome of conflict between different races during the previous thousand years into a situation where rivalry and lust for riches, land and power, between the two great Mediterranean nations of the day, could only burst into violent explosion."[2] The two competing nations, were, of course, the Roman Empire and Carthage, the Phoenician Metropolis of North Africa.

Historically, the achievements of the Roman Empire have been well recognized. The richness of its legacy has been taught to many generations of

Hannibal as portrayed by artist Charles Lilly. Lilly is to be commended for painting such a realistic representation of Hannibal, even down to his armor and sword, both of which were found in a Carthagenian grave of a solider believed to have marched with Hannibal.

students of Western Civilization; litanies of its accomplishments saturate every textbook on the subject. But what of her opponent, Carthage? Carthage, the urban progeny of the Phoenicians, has remained at the center of considerable controversy. Were the Carthagenians Negroid, Caucasian, Semitic, or all of the above? Such troublesome inquiries can be more profitably applied to the Phoenicians, founders of Carthage. Thus, we must begin at the very genesis of these people and in doing so remove some of the veils of ambiguity which enshroud Carthage and its inhabitants. In taking this path, we may also begin to enlighten our reader as to the identity of our main character Hannibal and his significance to the black race.

A relationship exists between the Phoenicians and Ham, the progenitor of the black race. Renowned Carthagenian authority Sir Gavin de Beer notes that the Bible refers to the Phoenicians as being "descendants of Ham"[3] who was of course the father of the black race. Mr de Beer goes on to say that he disagrees, for, in his opinion "they [the Phoenicians] were Canaanite descendants from the lineage of Canaan."[4] Although de Beer's statement is in part correct, a gross oversight exists in his reasoning, for Canaan was also a descendant of Ham! In reviewing the biblical passages we find that "Ham is the father of Ca'naan . . . and Ham, the father of Ca'naan, saw the nakedness of his father . . . and the sons of Ham; Cus, and Migraim, and Phut and Ca'naan . . . and Ca'naan begat Sidon [the biblical name for Phoenicia] his firstborn . . ."[5] Thus it is easy to see the family tree. Ham, father of the black race, fathered Canaan, who in turn fathered the Phoenicians.[6] In view of de Beer's previous statements, it is ironic that he goes on to say that "The name Phoenician, given to them by the Greeks, means dark-skinned."[7] This definition is substantiated by Donald Harden, an authority on the ancient Phoenicians, who states: "the word is first found in Homer (singular Phoenix, plural Phoenikes) and appears to denote originally a dark red or brown colour, whence it was transferred . . . to the brown skinned Canaanites."[8]

Furthermore, a strong connection appears to exist between Egypt and Phoenicia, for in ancient times Phoenicia was apparently an outpost and loyal ally of Egypt. Dr Harden brings several interesting points to support this connection between Egypt and Phoenicia. For example, he notes that "St. Augustine in the early fifth century AD says that if you ask the country people in Africa who they are, they will reply in the Punic tongue 'Chanani' [pronounced Canan-e]. The Phoenicians as a people cannot be differentiated from the general mass of [the] Canaanites."[9] Through linguistics we are presented another key of a different nature to unlock ethnological affinities between the Canaanites and the black race. Once more quoting Dr Harden: "What is certain is that by the fourteenth century BC in the Amarna letters [the 18th Dynasty of Akhenaton] the inhabitants of Canaan were calling themselves . . . Kin-Anu."[10] "Kin" meaning "consanguineous, related by blood, in Greek, to kind-genous race."[11] In the ancient Egyptian language "Ken-Belong," Anu is the term utilized by the first blacks, the oldest blacks to describe themselves as a race. Amelineau, a respected Egyptologist, designates the first Black race to occupy Egypt by the name Anu. He shows that "it came slowly down the Nile and founded the cities of Esneh, Erment, . . . and Heliopolis,"[12] for, as he says, "All those cities have the characteristic symbol which serves to denote the name Anu . . . According to Amelineau, this Black race, the Anu, probably created in prehistoric times all the elements of Egyptian civilization."[13] To further quote Amelineau "These Anu . . . were an agricultural people . . . shutting themselves up in walled cities for defensive purposes. To this people we can attribute, without fear or error, the most ancient Egyptian books, the Book of the Dead and the Text of the Pyramids, . . . all the philosophical systems then known and still called Egyptian."[14] Cheikh Anta Diop reiterates the connection between the Anu and the inhabitants of old Arabia: "the Anu were the first Blacks to inhabit Egypt. A number of them remained in Arabia Petraea throughout Egyptian history."[15] Earlier, Drusilla Houston had noted "The ancient inhabitants of Arabia Petrae were of the 'Anu' of the 'Old Race' of Egypt."[16]

What we may infer from this evidence is that the Canaanites were members of the pre-dynastic race which gave birth to the civilization of Egypt. With such an array of new information one may begin to understand better the unique relationship between the two nations. As Marguerite Rutton states in her book *Les Arts du Moyen-Orient Ancien*, "during the course of history the Egyptians were the protectors of Phoenicia. They considered them part of their domain."[17] Chiekh Anta Diop states "Even throughout the most troubled periods of great misfortune, Egypt could count on the Phoenicians as one can more or less count on a brother."[18] Quoting Lenormant, an Egyptologist, Diop goes on to say, "Among the monumental narratives engraved on the walls of Egyptian temples and referring to the great insurrections in Syria against Egyptian hegemony, never do we see on the list of rebels and the vanquished, the names of [the] Sidonians, of the capital, or any of their cities."[19]

Lastly, to cast aside any remaining doubt as to the validity of the aforementioned arguments, we will examine skeletal evidence, which also indicated a strong Negroid presence in Carthage. Eugene Pittard is an invaluable source on this subject. In his text, *Les races et L'histoire*, he quickly dispenses with the theory that the Phoenicians were solely and purely Semitic in type. He declares "The Phoenicians had nothing in common with the official Jewish type: brachycephal, aquiline or Hittite nose, and so on . . . skulls presumably Phoenicians, have been found west of Syracuse; but these skulls are dolichocephalic and prognathous, with Negroid affinities."[20]

Pittard goes on to analyze the work of Bertholon, an archaeologist who has worked with the Carthagenian skeletal evidence. Pittard shows that Bertholon's evidence supports the case for a Negroid presence at Carthage.

This black basalt sarcophagus, made in Egypt was discovered in the ancient Phoenician capitol of Sidon. 'Three such sarcophagi were sent to Phoenicia as gifts during the reign of King Eshmunazar. Dated 6th century B.C. they reflect the powerful Egyptian influences in Phoenician culture. Strong connections between the Phoenicians and Old Kingdom Egypt are manifest in cylinder seals of Egyptian style. Old Kingdom monarchs such as Sneferu of the 3rd dynasty, Sahure of the 5th dynasty and Pepi I of the 6th dynasty all record constant and friendly exchanges with the Phoenicians.

"Bertholon has painted the following portrait of the men he deemed the surviving descendants of the ancient Carthagenians; 'these people had very brown skin. This reflects the Phoenicians' habit of coloring [their] statues reddish brown in order to reproduce the tint of the skin ... The nose is straight, sometimes slightly concave. More often it is fleshy, occasionally flat at the end. The mouth is average, sometimes quite wide. The lips most often are thick, the cheekbones not very prominent.'"[21]

These examples are not intended to suggest a mono-racial society. I believe, as other black historians do, that Carthage was a conglomerate of different racial groups, with a strong but by no means exclusive "Negroid" element. Both Diop and Van Sertima address the racially mixed nature of Carthage.

Chiekh Anta Diop states that "The hinterland of Carthage was inhabited by indigenous Blacks who had been there throughout Antiquity, and by white Libyan tribes. [These tribes, as reported by Herodotus, arrived circa 1450 BC from the North African coast.] Crossbreeding occurred gradually, as [it had] in Spain ..."[22]

Ivan Van Sertima substantiates this in "The African Presence in Early Europe: The Definitional Problem." To quote Van Sertima, "They [the Phoenicians] are not a race but a nation, a conglomerate of peoples who became distinctive through nationhood as a separate entity."[23] Although Van Sertima acknowledges this fact, he also emphasizes the strength of the substantial African element by quoting S. Gsell, an authority on Carthage. Gsell believes that the Negroid representation was in fact dominant. In Gsell's own words: "The anthropological examination of skeletons found in tombs in Carthage proves that there is no racial unity ... The so called Semitic type, characterized by the long, perfectly oval face, the thin aquiline nose and the lengthened cranium, enlarged over the nape of the neck has not been found at Carthage. On the other hand, another cranial form, with a fairly short face, prominent parietal bumps, farther forward and lower down than is usual is common ..."[24] Gsell states that perhaps these traits were characteristic of the real Phoenicians, and goes on to say, "but *most* of the Punic population in Carthage had African and even Negro ancestors."[25]

Although varying somewhat between locations, the amalgamation of races in North Africa seems to have begun rather early in what is commonly considered recorded history. The campaigns of Egypt's first monarch Narmer-Menes was to conquer the White Libyans who resided in Egypt's northern territories. This aggressive act had the effect of actually cementing the two cultures and creating what later came to be known as Upper and Lower Egypt. This gave rise to a series of dynasties unrivalled in the Old World. Although cultural harmony was the outcome, the absorption of the Libyans into Egyptian civilization created a slow but consistent bleaching of the blacks therin. Chiekh Anta Diop also points out that a similar process consumed the black Canaanites. "The Canaanites were surely more rapidly mixed than the Egyptians, for they were less numerous and more directly located on the escape routes of the Whites who finally invaded the territory from all sides. The Jewish people, that is, the first brand called Semitic, descendants of Isaac, seem to have been the product of that crossbreeding. That is why a Latin historian wrote that the Jews are of Negro origin."[26]

Such was the case with the Phoenicians and more properly Carthage. Though Carthage was a mixture of different peoples, the black African constituency seems to have played a dominant role during her seminal cultural phase.

The previous passages show conclusively through skeletal remains and the physiognomy of the descendants of the ancient Phoenicians that an African type exhibiting strong "Negroid" features existed at Carthage. But were these individuals members only of a slave or servant class, as some have claimed? Or did these same blacks comprise a substantial percentage of the Carthagenian aristocracy? Let us examine the available evidence. To further quote Pittard, "Other bones discovered in Punic Carthage and housed in the Lavigerie Museum, come from personages found in special sarcophagi and probably belonging to the Carthagenian elite. Almost all the skulls are dolichocephalic [Negroid] with a rather short face."[27]

"Those who have recently visited the Lavigerie Museum in Carthage" Pittard continues "will recall that magnificent sarcophagus of the Priestess of Tanit, discovered by Father Delattre. That sarcophagus, the most ornate, most artistic yet found, whose eternal image probably represents the goddess herself, must have been the sepulchre of a very high religious personage. Well, the woman buried there had Negro features. She belonged to the African race!"[28] Diop supports this opinion, and declares: ". . . the Carthagenians, both common people and elite, were evidently Negroid."[29]

So it comes as no surprise that the military was also dominated by Africans. "The best troops of the Carthagenian army were the [black] Numidians, from the north coast of African west of the Carthagenian domains, Algeria and Morocco."[30] Of particular interest to us is the fact that an African family known as the Barca's had set a standard of military excellence in Carthage. From this family was born a legend, the black star of the Carthagenians, and the nemesis of Rome—Hannibal.

He was born in 247 BC and named Chenu Bechola, which in the Punic language means "Grace of Baal," Baal being the chief Carthagenian god. Hannibal's family name, Barca, comes from the Punic word for "thunderbolt." Hannibal was one of three sons born to Hamilcar Barca, who also fathered a stepbrother to these three. The Barca family was firmly aristocratic, claiming direct descent from Princess Dido-Elissar, founder of Carthage. Dido-Elissar was sister to King Pygmalion of Tyre as well as being a grandniece of Queen Jezebel. To be descended of such a lineage was an honor, and a responsibility, upheld for many generations by the Barca clan. Hamilcar

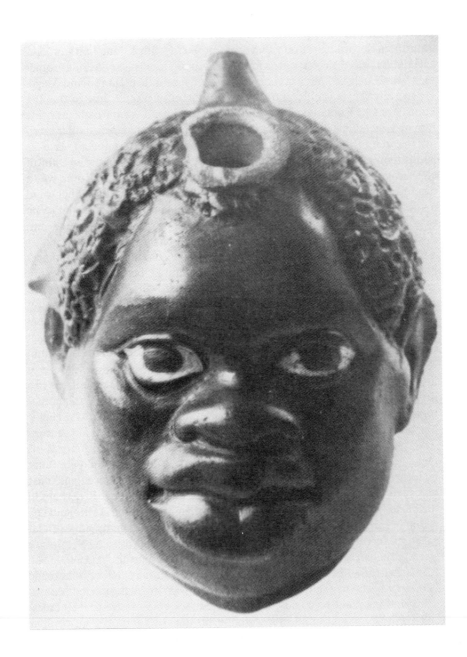

A small jug in the shape of a head exhibiting strong negroid features. Possibly representative of the Phoenicians, it was found at the Phoenician city of Lilybaeum (Marsala) in Sicily, west of Syracuse, and is dated 4th century B.C.

sensed strength and leadership ability in all three of his sons and began to train them accordingly. Soon they were popularly titled, "the lion's brood."

Hannibal was the eldest of the four boys. Apart from Hasdrubal, his brother there was a half-brother also named Hasdrubal and then Hanno and Mago. When Hannibal was nine years of age, his father engaged Rome in the first Punic War (the Romans called the Phoenicians "Poeni" from which has come Punic). Legend has it that during this time, Hamilcar prepared to offer sacrifice in order to assure the success of the venture. Asking Hannibal to place his hand upon the sacrificed animal, he made his young son swear an oath of eternal enmity with Rome. Hamilcar had taught his son that Rome was a deadly enemy and he extracted from young Hannibal the oath that he would do everything in his power to bring an end to her supremacy. And so it came to pass that Hannibal, the Grace of Baal, with sword in hand matured into one of the most awesome figures in the annals of recorded history.

As fate would have it, Hannibal was soon to take command of the Carthagenian legions. In the course of peacetime operations between the first and second Punic Wars, Hamilcar died apparently by drowning as he attempted to cross a river. This occurred in 228 BC. Leadership responsibilities then fell on Hasdrubal the Handsome, Hamilcar's son-in-law, but in 221 BC Hasdrubal was murdered, apparently the victim of a man enraged. Hannibal, now well seasoned at the age of twenty-five, was then capable of assuming command.

Hannibal was by all reports an unusual man. His life was simple. In spite of his position and wealth, he ate sparingly and preferred harsher conditions to a luxurious life. "Shade" he said, "is for women." Which brings us to another topic: Hannibal is connected with but one woman, his wife. Never was Hannibal known to be promiscuous or show signs of infidelity. The second century historian Justin says almost reluctantly that Hannibal's behavior towards his female captives was exemplary, so much so, in fact, that "one would not think he was born in Africa."[31] During the military campaigns which occupied most of his life, he appears to have preferred the solitude of his thoughts, perhaps in the belief that a thinking man is least alone when he is with his own thoughts. From an early age, Hannibal had exhibited great ability in many subjects and a genius in others. To all accounts, he excelled in all aspects of military science, including tactics, troop management, and leadership in general. The Roman historian Livy describes some of the extraordinary talents that made Hannibal peculiarly suited to military life: he was "Indefatigable both physically and mentally, he could endure with equal ease excessive heat or excessive cold; he ate and drank not to flatter his appetites but only so much as would sustain his bodily strength. His time for waking, like his time for sleeping, was never determined by daylight or darkness: when his work was done, then and only then, he rested, without need, moreover, of silence or a soft bed ... Often he was seen lying in his cloak on the bare ground amongst the common soldiers ... His accoutrement, like the horses he rode, was always conspicuous, but not his clothes, which were like those of any other officer of his rank and standing. Mounted or unmounted he was unequalled as a fighting man."[32] A man of many talents, Hannibal was a scholar as well as a soldier. Much as the Carthagenians disliked the Greeks, Hannibal was fluent in the Greek language and is reported to have written books in Greek. The family of Barca appreciated fully the Greek contribution to thought. For at this time in history it had been Greece who maintained the fountainhead of the arts and sciences in the Mediterranean. Another characteristic peculiar to the Barca family was its worship of a special pantheon of gods which appear to be unrelated in any way to those of Carthage. Thus in many respects, Hannibal was both an educated and original thinker. With such a varied array of traits, talents and influence, one can begin to understand the composite power of the man who was destined to become Rome's worst nightmare.

So at twenty five years of age, Hannibal Barca amassed an army to put to an end the arrogance of the Roman Empire. Hannibal's army was composed of professional soldiers who in this day and age would be termed mercenaries. He inspired them all with his confidence and audacity. To all accounts, his men would do the impossible for him and as the saying goes, "the proof is in the pudding," for they did just that. The dedication of Hannibal's men must be remembered, for without it the feats he accomplished seem to stretch the boundaries of credibility. Their loyalty and faith in him is all the more impressive when one recalls that Hannibal's army consisted of a rather motley crew of professional warriors from Carthage, Numidia, Spain, the Balearic Island, and Gaul. Unbound by any sense of patriotism or common cause, their personal admiration and devotion to their commander, Hannibal, turned them into powerful army.

The army which Hannibal commanded was a conglomeration of men from several countries. "The troops under his command were mainly African: 11,850 African foot, 300 Ligurians, and 500 from the Balearics. To these were added 450 Libyo-phoenicians horse-men of mixed blood, half-Punic half-African—about 1,800 Numidians and Moors from the Atlantic coast, a small force of 200 horse from the Ilergetes in Spain. Finally, there were twenty one elephants, to make the land forces complete."[33]

Though Hannibal's main objective was Rome he knew it would be much too rash a decision to charge Rome directly with an act of war. So he strategically forced an attack on Saguntum, an ally of Rome, knowing all too well what Rome's reaction would be. Hannibal's maneuver evoked the inevitable: Rome was infuriated. (The irony in this was that Rome had done virtually the same thing to Carthage when Roman legions invaded Sicily and laid waste an ally of the Carthagenians, thereby breaking the peace alliance and ushering in the first Punic War.)

Rome hastily sent a delegation to Carthage to confront the Carthagenian senate. It appears that their instructions were to try to intimidate the Senate

Map illustrating Hannibals route from Carthagena to Cannae.

into betraying Hannibal by declaring that he had operated without their consent. The delegation hoped to force the Carthagenian senate to give Hannibal
up, whereupon he would be extradited to Rome for what would presumably
be a brief trial and a fatal sentence. Unfortunately for Rome, the Carthagenian senate refused to be intimidated. The Roman delegation issued the ultimatum: "we bring you peace and war. Take which you will." To which the
senators of Carthage replied, "Whichever you please—we do not care." The
Roman senators cried out, "Then, we give you war." The Carthagenian senators replied "We accept it."[34] Thus in the great hall of the Carthagenian
senate the Second Punic War officially begun, but by then Hannibal and his
legions of doom were already like a great serpent winding their way through
Spain. And though no mention was officially made of their destination everyone knew that the invasion of Italy lay on the horizon.

As Hannibal made his way toward the Alps, he was at times assaulted and
ambushed by hostile tribes. Although his troops did not sustain serious injury,
the sporadic onslaughts of these Roman allies were irritating. In May 218 BC,
Hannibal made his way towards the river Ebro which he crossed in July. Once
again he was confronted with a bombardment of tribal hostility. The Carthagenian army quickly repelled the attack. However, in this case, their losses
were more severe. Hannibal moved with relentless expediency and soon he

was crossing the Pyrenees. During this time many of his soldiers (about three thousand of them) voiced reluctance at attempting what they thought was an impossible task. Though he could not afford to lose more men, Hannibal reluctantly dismissed more than seven thousand soldiers who wished to return to their countries and families. Having crossed the Pyrenees, Hannibal now made his way towards the river Rhone. If Rome entertained any doubts as to Hannibal's final destination, this step must have eliminated those doubts. To traverse the Rhone river was Hannibal's first major obstacle, for all were convinced that his elephants would perish in the crossing. The majority of his elephants were of the small African forest variety, about seven feet nine inches at the shoulder, and the deepest portion of the river is estimated at approximately nine feet. Hannibal, seeing only one alternative, had his men begin the immediate construction of huge rafts to ferry the animals across. Loading piers and rafts of about sixty meters in length were built and secured against the current by a network of ropes attached to trees along the embankment. To the piers and rafts were added earth, to make the elephants believe that they were still on dry land. His idea was ingenious and mechanically sound and for the most part it worked. A few elephants stampeded and flung themselves into the river only to find to their and everyone else's surprise that they could actually wade across, keeping their trunks up the water's surface in order to breathe. Not a single elephant was lost! Upon crossing the Rhone Hannibal was informed by his scouts that Scipio, with his Consular army, were encamped near the eastern mouth of the river. Ironically, Scipio received a similar message warning him of Hannibal's arrival from his own scouts, but found it hard to believe. He knew Hannibal had crossed the Ebro but was unaware that he had overcome the Pyrenees.

Surprised, Scipio hastily gathered his army and marched three days to where the Carthagenians had made camp, but when he arrived all he found were footprints in the earth. Hannibal's troops had rested only briefly after the crossing and had moved on three days prior to Scipio's arrival. "On finding the Carthagenian camp deserted and the army gone, he was greatly surprised, for he could scarcely bring himself to believe that Hannibal would try to cross the Alps and reach Italy through barren regions occupied by powerful and treacherous tribes. But that was clearly what Hannibal had set out to do."[35]

Hannibal journeyed onward for four days until he reached what was known as the Island. There he found a civil war being waged between two brothers fighting for kingship. Both sides appealed to him to arbitrate and resolve the conflict. Hannibal did so, and gave dominance to Brancus, the elder, while the younger brother was exiled. Brancus, filled with delight and gratitude, supplied the entire Carthagenian army with food, clothing, and other essential provisions for scaling the Alps. He also provided men to act as a rear guard to protect the soldiers from the savage tribes which were strewn throughout the mountainous peaks.

Hannibal began the ascent towards the Alps. Unfortunately, menacing

Terracota of a African warrior mounted and ready for battle upon a war elephant. Found near Rome and dated late 1st century B.C. to early 1st century A.D.

tribes lurked in the shadows observing his every movement. The Alloborges, a barbaric put powerful local tribe, contemplated an all-out assault on the Carthagenian Army. Meanwhile, the men loaned by Brancus to fortify the rear guard departed and returned home.

The Carthagenian army at this time was experiencing great difficulty in crossing the terrain. Narrow mountainous roads and steep cliffs created extremely harsh conditions, hazardous to both men and animals. The Alloborges, observing their difficulty, chose this time to attack.

Meanwhile, Hannibal had strategically positioned troops at the heights overlooking the passes. These troops were able to descend swiftly on the barbarians and repulse them. Although they suffered no less themselves, the Alloborges succeeded in inflicting heavy losses upon the Carthagenian army. This was the first battle in the Alps. Hannibal moved onward and reached the Alpine river known as the Durance. With much difficulty, he was able to ford this river and continue on one of the most arduous journeys known to man.

For six long days Hannibal and his legions snaked their way through the hazardous and convoluted mountain passes. On the seventh day, Hannibal's army again fell afoul of the treacherous natives. Several of the highland tribes conspired together to attempt to foil the Carthagenians' ascent. They came to Hannibal bearing olive branches, wreaths and other symbols of friendship. Suspicious of their intentions, Hannibal did not share the enthusiasm of his men and remained unconvinced as to the delegation's sincerity. The highlanders said that they had heard of Hannibal's military prowess and of the ruin that had befallen all those who tried to oppose him. They professed a desire to cooperate fully with Hannibal, and offered hostages to guide the army and fight in the Carthagenian ranks.

Having had no wish to aggravate the highlanders by rejecting their gifts out of hand, Hannibal accepted their assistance. However, it is clear that he remained skeptical about their good faith. As Hannibal feared, the highlanders led his army into a trap, a narrow place where an inaccessible cliff lined one side and a precipitous drop formed the other. Due to his mistrust, Hannibal had stationed the elephants, cavalry and pack animals at the head of the column, and the heavy infantry in the rear. This strategic positioning allowed him to fight his way through the highlanders who sought to squeeze him between a rock and a hard place. The battle was bloody, however, and many men, horses and pack-animals perished before the seige was checked. Because the highlanders also occupied the heights, they were able to roll ponderous boulders down upon the Carthagenian Army, thus causing considerable damage. They fought into the night and at day break the gorge was littered with mangled bodies. The enemy finally withdrew, leaving Hannibal's army victorious but exhausted. On this, the eighth day of the alpine ascent, low morale spread through the ranks like a plague.

From this point on Hannibal was no longer troubled by full scale attacks,

Painting of Hannibal crossing the Alps. Artist—Charles Lilly

although he was obliged to suffer small raiding parties of highlanders here and there.

The legions marched on. Hannibal, seeing that his men were becoming discouraged by the hardships that they had suffered, sought an opportunity to rally them together. At the point of elevation where they could first view Italy, Hannibal took the occasion to address his troops. In order to raise their morale, he showed his men the Plain of the Po, the direction in which Rome lay, and he reminded them of the friendly sentiments harbored towards them by the Gauls, enemies of Rome from whom they could expect reinforcements.

On the twelfth day, Hannibal and his men began the descent. Although they endured no attack from the highlanders, the difficulty of the terrain and the severity of the snowy conditions inflicted losses comparable in number to those suffered earlier by enemy attack. Paths were narrow and at some points virtually non-existent. Any man who stumbled on the tenuous path would plummet over the cliffs, lost forever. In one place they found the road blocked and completely impassable. An avalanche had piled a small mountain of snow as well as a stone of monolithic proportions across the path. The men at the forefront of the column, unable to circumnavigate the blockage, began to panic. Hannibal had his men fell many trees, which they piled up and then set ablaze. In this manner, they were able to melt the snow. The heat also penetrated the enormous boulder Hannibal instructed his men to bathe the boulder in vinegar, thus causing it to crack. The men then took pick axes and attacked the rock until they succeeded in pulverizing it. Thus they were able to remove the natural blockade and continue their descent.

On the fifteenth day after they had begun their journey through the Alps, Hannibal's army finally reached the plain. His men rejoiced at the completion of the perilous journey. Tired and hungry, they rested for three days, while their leader took stock of their situation. Since the crossing of the Rhone, Hannibal had lost a total of twenty thousand men. In spite of reinforcements along the way, there remained now under his command twelve thousand African infantry, eight thousand Spaniards, six thousand cavalry, and all of his elephants.

With only twenty six thousand of his orignal men remaining, Hannibal gladly accepted reinforcements from the Gauls and other enemies of Rome, before facing another "impossible" challenge—the Roman army. The size and discipline of the Roman army was awesome. "Rome, at a pinch, could put three quarters of a million men in the field."[36] Such was the magnitude of the foe against which Hannibal had set himself.

In the Po Valley, Scipio awaited Hannibal with eager confidence. Scipio knew tht Hannibal's men must have been tired, battered, and possibly broken in spirit by their ordeal in the Alps. His cocksure attitude is reflected in the speech he gave before the battle. "My men, let me tell you of the sort of warfare you must expect: it will be against an enemy you defeated in the last war both on land at at sea; an enemy from whom you exacted tribute for twenty years; an enemy from whom you took Sicily and Sardinia as prizes of war. You therefore, will enter upon [the battlefield] with the high hearts of victors, they with the despondency of beaten men. Nay more, their readiness to fight at all is due not to courage but necessity—unless you imagine that an enemy who declined combat when his army was still intact has better hopes of success now that he has lost two thirds of his troops during the passage of the Alps. Perhaps you will answer that, though they are few they are nevertheless brave and strong—that they are irresistible fighters. Nonsense! They are ghosts and shadows of men; already half dead with hunger, cold, dirt and neglect; all their strength has been crushed and beaten out of them by the Alpine crags. Cold has dried them up, snowstorms have frozen their sinews stiff, their hands and feet are frostbitten, their horses lame and enfeebled; and they have not a weapon amongst them which is not damaged or broken. What an army! Why, you will not be facing an enemy at all, but only the dregs of what once were men. My chief fear is that we shall have to admit that it was the Alps, not you, who conquered Hannibal."[37] The pathetic picture which Scipio painted for his troops must have inspired laughter among them. Scipio had logically estimated the condition of Hannibal's men, drawing upon his own experience as a fighting man, and his prognosis was certain victory. Consequently, the Roman troops were encouraged to feel the utmost confidence in the outcome of the imminent battle.

Unlike Scipio, Hannibal thought that deeds would constitute better inspiration than mere words. Gathering his men together, he instructed them to form a circle. He then brought to its center prisoners captured in the earlier battles in the Alps. He put to them an offer which they could not refuse: he asked them if they were willing to fight each other to the death, with the victor of each contest gaining his freedom, a horse, and weapons to fight in the Carthagenian ranks. The prisoners accepted, and many died in these impromptu gladiatorial contests. He then stood before his men and addressed them: "My friends, just now, as you were watching other men's fate, you were not unmoved; only think with similar feelings of what is in store for yourselves, and victory is already in our hands. What you have seen was more than a spectacle for your entertainment: it was a sort of image, or allegory, of your own condition. It may indeed be that fate has laid upon you heavier chains and harsher necessities than upon those prisoners of ours. North and south the sea hems you in; you have not a single ship even to escape in with your lives; facing you is the Po, a greater and more turbulent river than the Rhone. Behind you is the Alpine barrier, which even in the freshness and flower of your strength you almost failed to cross. Here then, where you have first come face to face with the enemy, you most conquer or die. But have courage! Circumstances compel you to fight; but those circumstances offer you in the event of victory nobler

Roman Consul Scipio being saved by his son at the battle of Trebia. A tapestry done in 1688 by French artist Gobelins.

rewards than a man might pray for, even from the immortal gods ... The Romans are a proud and merciless people; they claim to make the world their own and subject to their will. They demand the right to dictate to us who our friends should be and who our enemies ... I repeat—success is already yours. God has given to man no sharper spur to victory than contempt of death."[38] Clearly, Hannibal's men were fighting for their freedom and independence as well as for their immediate survival. The determination of both sides indicated that the war would be long and bitter.

Scipio and Hannibal's first encounter was more of a skirmish than a true battle. Even so, the Carthagenians beat the Romans heartily. The Roman general Scipio fell wounded and would have been killed if not for his young son, also named Scipio, who cut the Carthagenian ranks and dragged his father to safety. The Romans scurried from the field beaten and humiliated. So the first blood went to Hannibal.

Wounded and greatly fatigued, Scipio the elder was unable to continue to lead the army. Therefore he relinquished command to his colleague Sempronius. Hannibal, on receiving this information, found it fitted his needs perfectly, for he knew Sempronius to be rash, impetuous, and overly aggressive when giving battle. Thus Hannibal chose to use Sempronius' very own weaknesses against him. The two armies met at the river Trebia. Hannibal ordered his light cavalry to use the stratagem of feigning defeat and to withdraw when attacked by the Romans, all as a ploy to draw Sempronius out into the open for a full scale battle, for Hannibal knew him to be hasty and quick tempered. The Roman elections were soon to come and victory over Hannibal would stand well in Sempronius' favor in the senate. This added even more to Sempronius' over zealousness. Hannibal reconnoitered the ground carefully, and selected a spot for his brother Mago to hide with two thousand men, both mounted and foot. He then ordered his Numidian horsemen to cross the Trebia at dawn, to attack the Roman outpost, and then to withdraw as planned so as to lure the Romans on, and to recross the river. As Hannibal envisioned the trap so it came to be, for Sempronius fell right into it: "The Romans were sent out before they had eaten anything, cold and wet, and when they had crossed the Trebia they were chilled and numbed by the icy cold water. It was winter, bitterly cold, and the most unsuitable weather imaginable for Hannibal's main body of troops, who were accustomed to the hot climate of Africa, southern Spain, and the Balearic Islands. But he made his men eat an early morning meal, warm themselves at fires, and rub their bodies with oil, and so the southerners from the lands of the sun were able to make use of the rigors of winter to their advantage."[39]

The time of reckoning was at hand. Hannibal's light infantry, known as "slingers" because of the rock-like missiles they threw, advanced. Slinging thousands of projectiles at both the Roman soldiers and also their horses, they created much havoc. The Carthagenian cavalry outmaneuvered the Roman horses and the slaughter began in earnest. The Roman Gallic auxiliaries were charged by Hannibal's elephants, which must have appeared as beasts straight from hell to the unsuspecting Europeans. Fearing for their lives, the Gallic Roman contingent broke ranks and frantically retreated. Then Mago and his warriors made their unexpected appearance and delivered a devastating blow to the Roman rear. Encircled, the Roman legions had but one alternative, and that was to attempt to break through Hannibal's men and recross the icy river which came between them and the safety of their camp. But the infantry posed a stalward barrier and the few who succeeded in surmounting it perished in the icy river. And so it was recorded that at the river Trebia the first massacre of the Roman legions took place.

The defeat of the mighty Roman army created an overwhelming response among the empire's people. Gauls in large numbers flocked to Hannibal; more than sixty thousand soldiers, many of them cavalry, joined the Carthagenian army.

The poet Florus compared Hannibal and his army to a thunderbolt launched from the sky, which had pierced through the Alps to strike Italy. What metaphor could be more appropriate for Hannibal Barca, the ebony "thunderbolt" of the Carthagenians?

The Carthagenians moved slowly but steadily across the Italian countryside. At times they were obliged to subdue aggressive Roman allies, but these skirmishes were little more than a nuisance to them. The year was 217 BC and Rome had held its election. The Consuls elected were Caius Flaminius Nepos and Cnaeus Servilius Geminus. Flaminius had a sound reputation as a soldier and a correspondingly high opinion of his own prowess, in matters military as well as political. He took over his command at Arretium, while his colleague Servilius took over the army at Ariminum.

At Arretium, Flaminius intended to deny Hannibal the easy passage over the Apennines into Etruria, but that was not the route Hannibal chose. Hannibal held an exhibition of his prisoners, "making slaves of the Romans and sending the other Italians home without demanding ransom, for them to disseminate his promise to liberate all the communities from the yoke of Rome and to emphasize that he was making war only on Rome and not on Italy":[40] Soon after, Hannibal approached the Apennines through the Po Valley. Much to his dismay he found that melted mountain caps had flooded the flatland. These streams, coupled with early Spring rains, had turned the area into a veritable swampland. For four days Hannibal's men marched through waters waist high and more. Many men and animals drowned. Although Hannibal was carried well above the water by his sole surviving elephant, he himself contracted a severe eye infection. This infection caused him great suffering and eventually cost him the sight of one eye. The Carthagenians emerged from the swamps upon the lush and fertile plains of Etruria. They then proceeded to raid and plunder the entire countryside. Hannibal, knowing word would quickly reach Flaminius of his exploits, prepared a new trap for his arrival. Once more he knew his enemy to be arrogant and impetuous and planned to use these weaknesses against him.

Marching past the Roman front on a more southerly route, Hannibal incited Flaminius into an irrational act. The Roman advisors of Flaminius recommended extreme caution and advised Flaminius to rest and wait for the second consular army to join them before taking on Hannibal's forces. As Hannibal had predicted, the Roman general would hear nothing of it, and proceeded to prepare for battle. In giving the command to march in pursuit of Hannibal, Flaminius had unknowingly sealed his own doom.

Hannibal passed through the valley of Malpasso and stationed his army partly hidden in a range of U-shaped hills. He spread his troops around this basin. The Gauls and the Carthagenian cavalry hid in the west wing, and the Balearic slingers the east, while the encampment of the African and Spanish troops remained in plain view in the center to invite Roman attack. As predicted, Flaminius followed Hannibal and early the next day ordered his men to advance on Hannibal's center wing. With feline swiftness, Hannibal sprung his trap; his men left their hiding places and descended on the Roman army. The Roman army was surrounded, pressed between the three wings of Hannibal's force. The path for their retreat at Malpasso was cut off, and the ground on which they fought was circumscribed perfectly: they could neither flee nor maneuver. Within a mere three hours, fifteen thousand men were slaughtered where they stood! Hannibal's losses were eighteen hundred men, mostly Gauls. The battle fought that day was so fierce that neither army noticed an earthquake, which shook nearby towns and deflected some rivers from their habitual course.

Flaminius paid dearly for his hastiness, as he did not survive the battle. He was stabbed by an Insubrian Gaul named Duccarius. On hearing this report, Hannibal had his men search the battlefield for his body, as it was his custom to locate the corpses of his adversaries; but the body was never found. This example brings to light another admirable quality of Hannibal Barca. Throughout his many battles, he always respected the rank of Rome's commanders. In death he sought out their bodies and ensured their proper burial. Neither this custom nor the sentiment behind it was shared by the Romans.

Hannibal had annihilated organized Roman resistance in the north of Italy. No troops remained along the path to Rome. Therefore, he headed south.

At the prospect of Hannibal marching on Rome, the Senate knew its citizens must be informed. Rome made no effort to minimize the military disaster which had befallen her. "We have been beaten in a great battle," the Praetor, Marcus Pomponius, frankly admitted to the multitudes which crowded around the senate house, awaiting news. The situation was becoming severe, and an air of panic began to engulf the city. A dictator, Quintus Fabius Maximus, was appointed to defend the city, repair the walls, and destroy all bridges over the Tiber River. Hannibal was en route and riding with him was an air of impending doom.

Fabius Maximus had been nurtured in the religious principles of the Roman Empire. He therefore saw as the major problem in Rome a neglect of the basic religious traditions which had always brought the Empire good fortune. A sacrifice to Mars was ordered, vows taken to hold games in honor of Jupiter, a shrine dedicated to Venus, public prayer instituted, and a grand banquet offered to the Roman gods Jupiter, Juno, Neptune, Minerva, and Mercury. Last but not least, an offering was made to the gods of the Sacred Spring, asking for the fortunes of war to favor Rome. Needless to say, all of these efforts were inspired by fear of one man—Hannibal! Fabius felt that if Rome was to survive the terrible experience ahead, they would surely need help from all the gods.

Upon seeing Rome's religious obligations fulfilled, Fabius turned his attention to military matters. In preparation for Hannibal's arrival, orders were given to burn the crops, destroy the bridges, and withdraw all rural populations behind the fortifications of strongly held towns.

Hannibal had no desire to attack Rome at this time and Fabius had no desire to confront Hannibal. Even though they confronted each other, Hannibal could not get Fabius to attack his army in the open countryside. Weary of waiting, Hannibal directed his army to march on Campania, whose capital Capua constituted the most important of Rome's allies. Campania had good seaports, such as Cumae and Neapolis, which he needed for communication with Carthage. In addition, Hannibal hoped to draw Fabius out of Rome and into a contest on the open fields of Capua. As fate would have it, with a little ingenuity from Hannibal, three factors added to what the Carthagenian needed in order to implement a sound strategy. In the ruling circles in Rome, Fabius' policy of delay was meeting growing opposition. Hannibal, knowing this would be the case, sacked and pillaged the surrounding countryside in order to further aggravate Fabius' impatient critics. Furthermore, he deliberately avoided damaging Fabius' own property. This led many in Rome to suspect Fabius of collusion with Hannibal, and accuse him of the high crime of treason. Another incident which fanned this fire was the exchange of prisoners, when two hundred and forty seven more Romans were traded than Carthagenians. In compensation for this difference, Fabius asked that the Senate pay ransom. Upon their refusal, Fabius paid it himself, financing the deal with the sale of his unscathed estates. In this case Fabius in effect helped finance the Carthagenian campaign, and his reputation suffered accordingly.

Luckily Fabius was still Dictator and he conducted his campaign as he thought best. Soon after Fabius followed Hannibal to Campania but he still refused to initiate a confrontation. So Hannibal continued unhindered in his plunder of the area's towns, which were theoretically entitled to the protection of Rome's finest. But Fabius refused to fight, and Rome's allies lacked the protection promised to them in return for the tribute they paid her. Finally unable to withstand any further humiliation, Fabius laid a trap for Hannibal.

Fabius brought in scores of soldiers to surround the perimeter on the plain which Hannibal occupied. Roman garrisons held the only bridge, the sea was at Hannibal's back, to the North was Fabius and his army, and the pass by which Hannibal had entered Capua was blocked by six thousand Roman troops. Hannibal knew he had to regain the pass in order to escape, so he began formulating a plan which was truly ingenious.

From the herds that he had collected to feed his army, Hannibal ordered the selection of two thousand vigorous head of cattle. His men then proceeded to gather dry twigs and small branches which he bound together in bunches. These bunches, known as faggots, were then attached to the horns of the cattle. Upon completion of this cast, four thousand torches adorned these beasts. In the dead of the night, his men lit these torches, and the cattle, terrified by the flames which tormented them, stampeded aimlessly up the hills and into the woodlands. This led the Romans to believe that the Carthagenians were escaping via the heights themselves, instead of trying to transverse the pass. Thus, upon hearing the commotion in the hills, the Romans abandoned the pass in order to pursue what they thought was the enemy. Of course, Hannibal and his men swiftly waltzed through the unguarded pass, taking with them their full baggage train, his stores and booty. They travelled to Allifae, where they set up camp.

Fabius was understandably enraged by Hannibal's brilliant escape, and after regaining what composure he could he followed him cautiously, and encamped at the foot of Mons Calonus. After a brief and indecisive skirmish, Hannibal and his men elected to retire into Winter Quarters and wait out the frigid northern Italian winter.

The year was 216 BC, and Rome's Senate had carried the name of two new consuls. The next military leader was to be Consul-elect Caius Terentius Varro, known as "the people's champion," enemy of the Senate and the aristocrats. He was an unrefined man, with few talents other than demagogy. His Commander-at-Arms was Consul Lucius Aimilius Paullius, a good soldier who had conducted several successful battles and acquired many commendations for his valor. The personalities of the two Consuls could not have been more dramatically opposed. Varro was arrogant and reckless, with little military experience. Fabius was cautious, perhaps overly cautious, but with military skill. The two could never agree on a strategy.

The one thing that they could agree on was that Hannibal must be vanquished. Varro accused the Senate of unnecessarily prolonging the war, for Varro believed that the time was now at hand to take the battle to the Carthagenian. The Consuls amassed their combined legions, eighty thousand men in total, and marched to Cannae to finally engage Hannibal in battle. The battle which ensued was one of the most important in history. Varro boasted of certain victory, and the Roman citizens were gleeful at the prospect. The day of the battle finally arrived. "The Roman army crossed the river to the north bank of the nearby river and drew up in line, facing and parallel to it. Hannibal followed, crossed the river, and drew up his army facing the Romans with his back to the river, his two wings resting on it for his numbers were only about forty thousand men, and the Romans had twice that number, and this disposition prevented Hannibal's flanks from being turned. The Roman infantry was in the center, the Roman cavalry to the right . . ."[41] At this time Gisgo, one of the Carthagenian commanders, was in front of the two armies gazing at the Romans, and their great numerical superiority. Obviously discomforted, he continued along the passage between the two armies until he met Hannibal, who was positioned in the center. Turning to his Commander, he expressed his doubt. Hannibal faced his countryman and friend as he replied: "There is one thing, Gisgo, that you have not yet noticed." "What is that, Sir?" asked Gisgo. "In all that great number of men opposite, there is not a single one whose name is Gisgo." Livy goes on to note that "They both immediately broke into roars of laughter, which acted as a tonic to the rank and file of the Carthagenian army."[42] The battle began with a headlong collision between the cavalry on Hannibal's left and the Roman right. Hannibal's tactical genius allowed his to manipulate the Romans and they were drawn into the center of battle. The Roman army was butchered where it stood; they had no chance of escape. The doubled consular armies, eight legions strong, was utterly annihilated. Hannibal estimated his losses at six thousand men, while the Roman casualties exceeded seventy thousand. Among the Roman casualties were the Consul Aemilius Paullus, two praetors, twenty nine military tribunes, eighty senators, and several ex-consuls and ex-praetors, all of whom had come with the intention of observing the defeat of Hannibal Barca as promised by the optimistic Varro. As for Varro himself, he fled panic-stricken from the field and hastened towards Venusia with a small band of men for his protection. Hannibal claimed the balance of the Roman survivors as prisoners. Hannibal had just eliminated the last of the Roman armies available for her defense, and his name quickly became a legend.

From the Roman knights that had fallen on the battlefield at Cannae, Hannibal's men were able to collect many valuable accoutrements. Hannibal sent to Carthage three bushels of gold rings alone. Aemilius Paullus' body was located and given a ceremonious burial. The three thousand infantry and fifteen hundred cavalry prisoners were paraded before Hannibal, who sent the non-Romans back to their homes, and fixed a ransom figure for the Romans.

Upon hearing the dreadful outcome of the battle of Cannae, Rome and her citizens were horror-struck. Men and women wailed and children screamed, to the point at which the Roman government found it necessary to ban such emotional outbursts. "Weeping and wailing were prohibited, wearing of mourning [garb] was restricted, silence was imposed, and the spreading of rumors was forbidden, and nobody was allowed to leave the city."[43]

The disaster suffered by the Romans at Cannae had other dire ramifications for the Empire. Many of those who were previously allied to Rome now joined Hannibal; one such capricious friend was Capua. Through the seaports now available to him, Hannibal could finally receive aid and support from Carthage. He now sent his brother Mago home with the news of their success. But upon his arrival in Carthage, Mago met with opposition in the Carthagenian senate. The senate finally sent aid, although it was inadequate, and Carthage begrudged him even that! In spite of this meager support, Hannibal roamed and controlled the Italian countryside for fifteen years.

In the years to come, there were small battles and small victories; but Hannibal was never truly challenged again on Italian soil. His only obstacle during this time was a Roman proconsul named Marcus Claudius Marcellus. Hannibal and Marcellus engaged in battle periodically, and in the last twelve years of Hannibal's occupation, Hannibal grew to respect Marcellus' courage and tactical ability. Marcellus became Hannibal's nemesis. Finally, in 208 BC, in a battle near Venusia, Marcellus was killed in an ambush by Hannibal's infamous Numidian horsemen. According to Livy, Hannibal remarked after the first day of what was to be their last battle, "How very curious, we have to deal with an enemy who seems to be incapable of enduring success or failure;

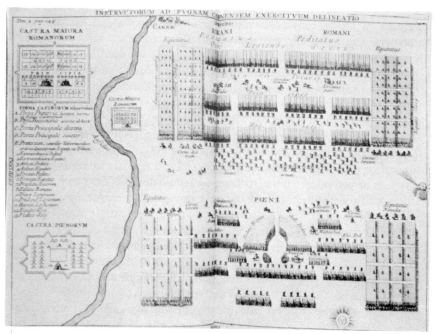

Battle plan of Cannae

if he wins, he cannot leave those whom he has beaten alone; if he loses, he again fights the army that beat him ... he is the only general who, when victorious, allows us no rest, and when we beat him takes none himself."[44] So died Marcus Claudius Marcellus, Hannibal's most dangerous foe. Hannibal had Marcellus' body ceremoniously cremated, and sent the ashes in a silver urn to Marcellus' son.

The tide was slowly beginning to turn towards Rome. Although Hannibal had won several battles, they failed to secure him concessions in his negotiations with Rome. Rome regained valuable ground, including Capua, and the Carthagenian army had also suffered other kinds of losses. As Hannibal's brother Hasdrubal was en route with reinforcements, he was attacked and defeated by Nero. Hasdrubal was killed, his head was severed from his body and pitched into Hannibal's camp. On seeing his brother's head, Hannibal is said to have remarked: "I see there the fate of Carthage."[45]

Meanwhile in Spain, Mago and Hanno Barca had come up against a formidable foe in the shape of the young Scipio, who years earlier had rescued his father from certain death at the battle of Trebia. Scipio had defeated both Hanno and Mago, and gained Spain as Roman territory. Scipio next prepared for what had to be the inevitable: an attack launched at Carthage herself.

Fearing an attack on the undefended city, the Carthagenian Senate agreed to a treaty with Scipio. According to the terms of this treaty, Hannibal and all his troops were to be recalled from Italian soil, and all Roman prisoners were to be returned to her. Among the other provisions of the treaty were the specification that Masinissa, the Numidian ally of the Romans whom the Carthagenians had deposed, was to be reinstated; the cession of Spain to Rome, along with other Mediterranean islands; the surrender of all ships save twenty; the supply of a million gallons of wheat, and six hundred thousand of barley.

Meanwhile, Mago returned to Italy to support Hannibal. En route, he encountered Roman Proconsul Marcus Cornellius. In the ensuing battle, Mago's troops were soundly defeated and Mago himself suffered mortal wounds. Mago died on the way back to Africa. We must assume that Hanno had died in the defense of Spain or soon after, for the loss of this brother is said to be Hannibal's last.

Hannibal prepared to leave Italy, but once again Carthage neglected to send the necessary ships for transportation of his men. Hannibal therefore, in order to make room for the remainder of his legions, had to slaughter his many splendid horses. Their loss was to be crippling to Carthage in the next and last battle.

Hannibal departed from Italy, leaving Rome economically devastated and her people demoralized. "It has been estimated that Hannibal's presence in Italy cost Rome . . . the lives of three hundred thousand men."[46]

Upon Hannibal's return, he found his countrymen to be elated. Having finally grasped the near miraculous achievements of their countryman, the Carthagenians felt secure in the fact that their hero could provide absolute protection for them at home. They therefore broke the treaty with Scipio, and attacked and captured several Roman supply ships. The gloves were off, and the time of war was again at hand.

The sun began to rise over Carthage, and the embers which had lit his dark-skinned face with the red glow of the fire were extinguished. As Hannibal, magnificently aglow, rose to his feet, his eye gazed in the direction of Zama. Needless to say, he and Scipio had never met, but he harbored much respect and admiration for this Roman Consul. Hannibal asked for a personal interview, which Scipio granted. "Exactly half way between the opposing ranks of armed men, . . . the generals met. They were not only the two greatest soldiers of their time, but the equals of any king or commander in the whole history of the world. For a minute mutual admiration struck them dumb and they looked at each other in silence."[47] Hannibal spoke, saying that if fate had decreed that he sue for peace, that he was glad that a great warrior such as Scipio should be the man to whom he had to make his plea. He admitted that he had been the aggressor in this war, but that a sure peace was better and safer than speculation on an uncertain victory. Scipio expressed his reluctance for peace in view of the treaty which Carthage had but recently broken. The fact that Carthage had broken its word caused Scipio to add more rigid stipula-

First meeting of Hannibal and Scipio before the battle of Zama. Though the artist clearly gives Hannibal Euorpean features, he just as clearly depicts his skin as black, which is a strong statement as to his racial make-up. Artist—Gobelins' cloth tapestry dated 1689?

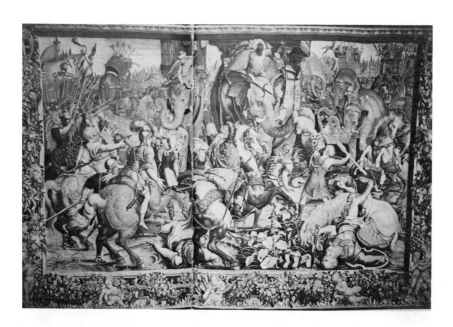

Battle of Zama

tions to the original treaty; these terms were totally unacceptable to Hannibal. The only recourse was war.

Hannibal and Scipio engaged one another at Zama. Although the Carthagenians fought a valiant and strategically sound battle, the victory ultimately fell to Rome. Hannibal left the field with a small party of men, thereby conceding defeat. Scipio marched on Carthage, and question arose as to whether the city should be completely razed or not. Scipio decided against it, and dictated conditions for peace. Of all the terms put to Carthage by Scipio, Rome could not believe that an unconditional surrender of Hannibal's person was not included. Nevertheless, because of this great victory, Scipio was appointed "Scipio Africanus."

Hannibal went on to become a great statesman, and under his leadership as chief magistrate, Carthage quickly recovered its former prosperity. Rome, agitated by Carthage's speedy recovery, was continuously trying to revoke the terms of the treaty. Finally, after the circulation of many rumors regarding Hannibal either trying to raise an army against Rome or allying himself with Rome's enemies, the Carthagenian was forced into exile by his own countrymen, who had come to fear Roman reprisal. The Senate in Carthage ordered his house be burned to the ground, which was immediately done. They then declared him an outlaw and a fugitive. Rome could not have been more pleased; they immediately took the liberty of pursuing him.

Hannibal fled to Tyre, the original mother-city of Carthage, which was

Bronze bust of Scipio Africanus

controlled at that time by Antiochus. There he was greeted warmly, and to Antiochus he divulged a plan to threaten Rome once again. Rome became wary when it was discovered that Hannibal was trying to communicate with some of his veteran commanders. Therefore, Rome decided to send Scipio to uncover the true intentions of Hannibaland Antiochus. This brought about the second famous meeting between Hannibal and Scipio.

This time, on more solacing terms, both men indulged themselves in various topics of conversation. "Then Scipio asked Hannibal who he thought was the greatest general in history. 'Alexander the Great,' replied Hannibal.

'Whom do you put next?' inquired Scipio. 'Phyrrhus,' replied Hannibal. 'Whom do you put next?' continued Scipio. 'Myself,' said Hannibal. Scipio laughed and continued, 'What would you have said if you had beaten me?' 'I should have regarded myself as the greatest general of all' replied Hannibal. Scipio appreciated the compliment."[48]

Sometime later, Hannibal and Antiochus attempted to implement their plans to invade Rome, with no success. This began the Syrian War; the year was 191 BC. Antiochus lost the war and once again Hannibal knew he had to relocate for fear of betrayal of his whereabouts to the Romans. After residing in Armenia and constructing a town which became its capital city, Hannibal, having become virtually a nomad, made his way to Crete. There he acted as a military consultant and aided his allies in securing a victory in battle. Rome discovered Hannibal's role in these battles and ordered him to surrender. Hannibal, tired and weary of the relentless pursuit, managed to elude the Romans once more by consuming poison. His last words were said to be "Let us now put an end to the great anxiety of the Romans, who have thought it too lengthy, and too heavy a task, to wait for the death of a hated old man."[49] So died Hannibal Barca, in the year 183 BC, at the age of sixty four.

Ironically enough, within a year of his death, Scipio Africanus also died. He too had been denounced by his own nation and accused of embezzling money, although he was able to acquit himself of these charges. But he could not exonerate himself from the greater crime of freeing Hannibal after Zama, for which he was apparently never forgiven. Scipio left Rome and it is believed that he too drank of a poisonous solution and met his demise. Still in all, even after Scipio's death, Hannibal's memory and a resurrected and prosperous Carthage kept most members in the senate exasperated. Finally, in 147 BC, Rome was able to provoke Carthage into a serious conflict. The Romans probably expressed abounding joy, for this was what they had wanted for half a century. The Carthagenians, however, refused to lay down and die. So for three years, they were able to hold the Romans at bay behind the massive fortifications of their walled city. Only by starving the inhabitants of Carthage was Rome finally able to take the city. Most of the citizens who had not already taken their lives were slaughtered. The survivors, numbering only fifty thousand, were sold into slavery. Then the city buildings were leveled to the ground, and put to the torch. The fire is said to have burned for seventeen days. Then the land was plowed and sown with salt. Such was the great enmity harbored by Rome towards Carthage, the legendary city of Dido.

Despite the vast number of accomplishments attributed to Hannibal, there is a tendency on the part of most historical academicians to involve themselves with what he did not accomplish and the reasons why. Hannibal's inability to raze Rome, most experts will agree, was due to Carthage's extreme degree of apathy. No aid of any kind was sent to the Carthagenians in the first thirteen years of their sojourn in Italy. Especially crippling was the absence of the proper seige equipment necessary to assault a walled city such as Rome. Consequently, Hannibal was doomed to wander the countryside, laying waste to lesser towns and cities allied to Rome, four hundred in all. On three separate occasions, Hannibal begged for aid from Carthage, but without result. Thus in many ways, Carthage sealed her own doom and destroyed the force that in the next several years could have been her salvation.

Hannibal exemplified many characteristics of several great African leaders who had preceded him. Other great Africans such as Narmer, Sesostris, Tuthmosis, and Taharka shared the combination of military genius and humane qualities one does not expect to find in such consummate fighters. With few exceptions, the great western military commanders seem unrefined and almost barbaric in contrast to this unusual blend. "[Hannibal] never matched the horrors perpetrated by the Romans. What act of Hannibal's can compare with the callousness of the Consul Nero . . . [when] he cut off the head of Hasdrubal . . . ? Julius Caesar later executed four hundred thousand Gauls in a single day to teach them obedience."[50] As common practice, "Roman commanders cut off the hands of their prisoners. Nor have writers ever found anything scandalous to say about Hannibal's private life. Julius Caesar, Octavian Augustus, Tiberius, and almost all other Roman rulers of distinction are commonly accused of drunkenness, adultery, fornication, sodomy, and sadism, as well as, in the case of Tiberius, of almost every aberration that can be found in the textbooks of sexual pathology. In fact, the writers of antiquity who managed to find some more or less scandalous anecdotes about nearly all the great men of their time were nevertheless baffled when it came to Hannibal.[51] As one writer put it "'one would not think he was born in Africa.' This remark is an early example of racial bias."[52]

This last statement brings us to the next issue: that of race. There is little in the way of incontrovertible evidence to direct us on the subject of Hannibal's racial identity. In the book titled *Histoire d'Hannibal*, C. Hennebert says, "There exists no really authentic picture of Hannibal."[53] Hennebert notes that there were several Hannibals in the Carthagenian army and navy over several different periods, just as there were several Magos, Hannos and Hasdrubals. One other Hannibal was Hannibal Monomachous, known for his ferocious cruelty. He once suggested to Hannibal that when food became scarce the men should eat human flesh from the bodies of those they captured. More than one historian has bemoaned the confusion created by frequent recycling of these names; in a note of appreciation, Betty Radice, editor of the Penguin Classics' *The War with Hannibal*, once thanked Jean Maund for "her speed and accuracy, plus her determination not to be defeated by the multiplicity of Hannos, Hasdrubals, and Magos in the Carthagenian forces."[54] Therefore, before we jump to conclusions, let us carefully examine the available information.

Many western historians in our recent past have tried to make a case for a

Coin and bust of accepted representations of Hannibal paired with Alexander the Great to show Greek influences.

Caucasian Hannibal. In their eagerness to claim him, they have generally based their arguments on grossly insufficient evidence. The inability of these authors to assimilate all the available materials has been, and should continue to be, the cause of much embarrassment to them. Yet they persist, apparently confident that sooner or later a suitable image of Hannibal, in the desired

Comparisons of two Buddhas, one done by Gandharan Greeks, the other by indigenous Indians. The Buddha on the left is a realistic iconographic portrayal of this great Indian Sage, while the Buddha on the right is marred with unrealistic Greek influences.

color, will present itself. Two cases exemplifying this treatment come to mind. In his book *Hannibal: An African Hero*, William Jacobs laments "Strangely, for all his importance in history, the figure of Hannibal remains shrouded in mystery. No known coin bears his profile; no statue to him survives. All has vanished . . ."[55] Having admitted that there exists no known record of Hannibal's visage, Jacobs, four lines later, goes on to state "America's blacks . . . like to point out that Hannibal, although white, led an invasion army of thousands of dark-skinned warriors into Italy—a land of whites."[56] To further dramatize my point, a bust found at Capua and dated around the time of Hannibal's invasion of Italy was widely accepted as a valid portrait of the Carthagenian. A noted expert in the field of iconographics was asked to verify the image as a representation of Hannibal Barca. Upon meticulous investigation, he finally released his report which stated: "It was not of him at all, but of the ideal representation of a hero."[57] The Romans acknowledged the fact that the Carthagenians were of a race different from theirs. G. deBeer states "Hannibal is a tragedy . . . the conflict . . . between different races . . ."[58] Frederich Donavuer, a German novelist, writing in the late twenties and early thirties, refers to Hannibal as well as his brothers Hasdrubal and Mago as "dark-skinned." In reference to an episode while Hasdrubal and Mago oc-

cupied Spain, he states "they were both obviously of African extraction. Their complexion was darker than that of the native Iberians. The shape of the nose and the gleaming eyes left no room for doubt as to their racial origin."[59] It appears that prior to recent attempts at whitewashing Hannibal, the world saw him as black.

An examination of the name Hannibal and those who bore it can also provide us with more constructive information. It is known that there have been several Hannibals throughout the course of history. Not one of them has been Caucasian, Semitic, or Asian: they have all belonged to the black race.

The lineage of Hannibal long thought to have ceased, resurfaced in the seventeen hundreds with the arrival into Russia of one Abraham Hannibal. Originally from Ethiopia, he was adopted by Peter the Great, the reigning Czar of Russia. Abraham was visited on one occasion by his real father, who he had not seen since he was eight years old. "While there [in Russia] the father said that the surname of the family was Hannibal, and that Abraham was a descendant of the great Carthagenian General."[60] Abraham Hannibal went on to become a famous mathematician, engineer, and general of the Russian army. Ivan Hannibal, Abraham's son, was also outstanding as a great military leader and strategist. He was victorious over the Turks at the battle of Navarin in 1770, hero of the battle of Chesma, and later became governor of the Ukraine. He died in 1801. Both men claimed descent from Hannibal the Carthagenian, and both men were black, and of African heritage.

At this point, the reader may well ask, why and how did the story arise that Hannibal was white or Semitic. The answer is very simple—the coins. "There are no less than eight supposed portraits of Hannibal, none of which resembles another."[61] Of these eight coins, five are not recognized by European historians, and two were found by iconographers not to be akin to him at all. Therefore, the evidence that Hannibal was either white or Semitic hangs on the strength of a lone coin. This coin, found in Spain at the cite of Carthagena Nova, is dated 220 BC. A bust resembling the visage on the lone coin exists; however, it was found not in Spain, Sicily, Sardinia, or Carthage proper, but in Morocco of all places. The five coins generally discounted by European historians portray dramatically African faces. Acknowledged as Carthagenian, the reader might wonder how the historians account for them. Some historians, both black and white, view them as elephant riders, called mahouts, or perhaps African soldiers of Hannibal's army. Yet another camp holds that the face on these five coins is Hannibal's own. J.A. Rogers one such historian, exclaims: "Hannibal, himself, was a full-blooded Negro with woolly hair, as his coins show."[62] I have examined the coins to which Rogers refers, and one in particular stands out. This coin constitutes a great challenge to the previous representation of Hannibal, and suggests itself as a more sound and logical template for our image of him. Before we examine the coins in question we must delve briefly into the manner of currency minting in ancient times.

A people known as the Lydians, inhabitants of Asia Minor, appear to be the first to use coins as a means of currency. This process began during the seventh century BC. The technique readily spread to the Greeks who employed it so well that they not only set the standard for currency minting in the entire Mediterranean but also monopolized their distribution as well. The Phoenicians began striking coins rather late in history, especially when one considers their proximity to countries which had been minting metal currency for two hundred years. But finally in the fifth century BC they began to strike metal coins.

The symbols embossed upon the coins of the ancient world were much more than arbitrary symbols. Ernle Bradford remarks that "the coins in the ancient world assumed for a mostly illiterate people an importance that is difficult for the modern world to understand—[coins] being both pictures and pronouncements [on them] . . ."[63] This puts to rest the notion, to which historian Frank Snowden, numismatist Ernest Babelon, and others, subscribe, that the ancient Phoenicians chose an elephant rider as a suitable and frequent subject for their coins. There can be no doubt as to the significance of the portraits on the coins in question. In analyzing the more accepted portrait of Hannibal represented by a lone coin from Spain, I find myself confronted with several questions. The evidence presented to support the contention that Hannibal Barca was "white" is inadequate. The connection between this lone Spanish coin and Hannibal is quite tenuous: its only link to him is the fact

This is the coin which the writer feels is the only true and conclusive portraiture of Hannibal Barca. Found in Italy at the battle site of Lake Trasimene, and dated 217 B.C., it coincides with all available data pointing to the obvious conclusion. The fact that the personage on the coin is portrayed in the image of Apollo bears testimony to the fact that he is *not* an elephant rider or African foot soldier, but a person of high acclaim. The Indian elephant on the reverse side of this coin was the last elephant that Hannibal rode, not to mention his most cherised.

that it was minted in Spain a few months after he took command. The nature of the features etched on the face of this coin are extremely ambiguous. First, regardless of what iconographers may infer about its physiognomy, one must take into consideration the tremendous influence of Greek aesthetics and to what degree their notion of the ideal may have changed the features of the subject. The Greeks were masters of the portrayal of gods and goddesses. As Piccard points out, most of their images represent gods rather than men, or else represent men in such a stylized fashion that no precise information can be obtained from them.[64] These images, prevalent in a culture which spread throughout the Mediterranean basin, made their way onto thousands of coins. Francis Pulzky, noted iconographer, once said of such coins proclaimed to represent Hannibal "these are the ideal representation of a hero from the silver coins of Dernes of Phoenicia and Pharnabazus of Phrygia . . ."[65] According to an infamous Greek dichotomy, the people of the world can be divided into two groups, Greeks and Barbarians. Thus, to Greeks it was really the highest compliment for a hero to be given Greek features when his visage was artistically rendered. Other examples of this phenomenon exist: among the illustrations is a picture of a Greek version of the Buddha with the same stylized features making the Buddha look European. The Greeks were in the vanguard of the coin industry and consistently made men and women in their own image. "We know nothing of the organization of Phoenician mints. Their system will have been copied from the Greeks, and it may be that even Greek workmen were employed, just as Greek artists were largely responsibility for the designs on the coins."[66] I must confess that I would not entrust the portrayal of my face to a Greek artist of the second century BC—look at what happened when the Gandharan Greeks went to work on the Buddha!

Secondly, we must look at the period when Hannibal himself took command. The fact that "coins were normally issued by senatorial decree . . ."[67] would make the striking of a coin representing Hannibal Barca in 221 BC rather unlikely, for the young new commander had yet to prove his mettle. The fact that there was a powerful anti-Barca faction residing within the senate itself at that time makes this possibility even more remote. This group actually argued against Hannibal taking leadership of their troops in Spain, wanting instead to require his immediate return to Carthage. Therefore it remains doubtful that the rest of the Senate would add insult to injury by not only allowing Hannibal to remain in Spain but striking a coin in his honor.

Thus it seems more likely that the coin being passed off for Hannibal is a commemorative portrait of Hannibal's brother-in-law, Hasdrubal the Handsome, the recently deceased conqueror of Spain who by all reports was of mixed Spanish blood. Another possibility is that the subject of the portrait was not a man of flesh and blood but instead a portrait of a popular religious subject such as Hercules. Most numismatists and iconographers acknowledge the fact that these coins are a combination of deity and mortal. Such combinations often coupled Melqart, a native Carthagenian hero, or Hercules with the real-life subject. In summary, many obstacles stand between this coin and a clear and direct connection with Hannibal.

Such is not the case for the next coin to be discussed, which, in my opinion, is the only coherent and definitive representation of Hannibal. The coin was found in Italy in the Chiana Valley near Lake Trasimene. This is very significant for two reasons. One is that this is where Hannibal's second major victory over the Romans took place. The second point in its favor is the date of the minting of this coin: 217 BC! But what is perhaps the most compelling argument supporting this coin as the definitive representation of Hannibal is yet to come. An excerpt from deBeer is appropriate: "Hannibal rode the sole remaining elephant, an animal which may have found its way into history, for some years later Cato the Elder recorded that the elephant which fought most bravely in the Second Punic War was called Surus . . . [an] Indian elephant . . . a bronze coin found in the valley of the Clanis (Chgiana), on Hannibal's route to Lake Trasimene, bears on the obverse a Negro's head . . . and on the reverse an equally obvious Indian elephant. It is believed to have been minted at just about this time, 217 BC . . . [and] bears a representation of Hannibal's sole surviving elephant, the Indian Surus."[68] Though deBeer does not acknowledge the negro's head as Hannibal's, several other arguments point to this conclusion. First, given the fact that Hannibal rode this sole surviving elephant which became his trademark, why would he consider putting just anyone's face on the obverse side of this coin. We have already stated that only illustrious or significant personages were chosen to be the subject of these ancient coins. "The Carthagenians rarely used coins or statues or stelae to depict a figure not in the pantheon of gods or in the aristocratic hierarchy."[69] This statement could not be closer to the truth. Another interesting piece of evidence supports an accurate and negroid portrayal of Hannibal. In his book titled *La Monete dell' Italia Antica*, famed numismatist R. Garrucci states that "this most beautiful of coins with an elephant on its reverse has on the obverse a personage in the form of Apollonus [Apollo]."[70] Apollo was a Greek and Roman god, the god of prophecy, medicine and music. According to Garrucci, two other coins of the original five, along with this one from Lake Trasimene, bear the same image of Apollo.

Yet surely neither the Greeks nor Romans would arbitrarily choose to portray Apollo as a Negroid type. Only Hannibal, being Negroid himself, would do such a thing. Hannibal had an inclination toward the god Apollo and may have identified with him. As Picard points out, Hannibal invoked Apollo along with Hercules and some native Carthagenian gods as witnesses to a treaty with Philip V of Macedonia.[71]

In summary, it seems most likely that Hannibal commemorated his victory at Lake Trasimene with the minting of a coin, perhaps even with which to pay his troops. The location of the discovery of this coin, the fact that his cherished elephant graces the reverse, and the dat that the coin was struck all point to this conclusion. I believe that the visage on the coin is the only glimpse of the true Hannibal allowed us. In their determined campaign to obliterate the image of the man who had come so close to annihilating their mighty empire, the avenging Romans also deprived us of a vital piece of the historical record. For the world can never know fully the achievements of Hannibal, general, urban planner, and statesman, near-conqueror of Rome, and a man of the negroid race.

Notes

1. Friedrich Donavuer, Swords Against Carthage (New York: Biblo and Tannen, 1932), p. 244.

2. Sir Gaven de Beer, *Hannibal: Challenging Rome's Supremacy* (New York: The Viking Press, 1969), p. 7

3. Sir Gaven de Beer, ibid., 1969 p. 21

4. idem.

5. Holy Bible: King James Version (New York: American Bible Society, 1816) p. 8

6. Ibid., p. 8

7. Sir Gaven de Beer, ibid., p. 21.

8. Donald Harden, *The Phoenicians* (New York: Praeger Inc., 1962) p. 22

9. Ibid., p. 22

10. Ibid., p. 21

11. Funk and Wagnalls Standard College Dictionary (New York: Harper and Row, 1977), p. 744

12. Abbe Emile Amelineau, *Nouvells Fouilles d'Abydos* (Paris, 1899) p. 248

13. Ibid., p. 248

14. Ibid., p. 248

15. Chiekh Anta Diop, *The African Origins of Civilization* (Westport: Lawrence Hill and Co., 1974) p. 105

16. Drusilla Houston, *Those Wonderful Ethiopians of the Ancient Cushite Empire* (Baltimore: Black Classic Press) p. 112

17. Marguerite Rutton, *Les Arts du Moyen-Orient Ancien* (Paris: University of France Press, 1962) pp. 149-150, as translated by Claire Moore

18. Chiekh Anta Diop, *The African Origin of Civilization: Myth or Reality* (Westport: Lawrence Hill and Co., 1974)

19. Ibid.

20. Eugene Pittard, *Les Races et l'Histoire* (Paris: University of Paris Press, 1924) p. 108

21. Idem.

22. Chiekh Anta Diop, *The African Origin of Civilization: Myth or Reality*, (Westport: Lawrence Hill and Co., 1974), p. 120

23. Ivan Van Sertima, ed, *The African Presence in Early Europe*, (New Brunswick and Oxford: Transaction Books, 1985) p. 137

24. Ibid., p. 137

25. Ibid., p. 137

26. Chiekh Anta Diop, *The African Origin of Civilization: Myth or Reality*, (Westport: Lawrence Hill and Co., 1974) p. 120

27. Eugene Pittard, *Les Races et l'Histoire* (Paris, 1924) p. 310.

28. Ibid., p. 410

29. Diop, p. 118

30. deBeer, p. 98

31. Ernle Bradford, *Hannibal*, (London: Macmillan London Ltd, 1981), p. 38

32. Titus Livius (Livy), *The War with Hannibal*, (New York: Penguin Books, 1965) p. 26

33. Ibid., p. 45

34. Ibid., p. 41

35. de Beer, p. 131

36. Ibid., 172

37. Livy, p. 65

38. Ibid., p. 67

39. Ibid., p. 81

40. de Beer, p. 190

41. Ibid., p. 214

42. Ibid., p. 214

43. Ibid., p. 216

44. Ibid., p. 261

45. Ibid., p. 268

46. Ibid., p. 284

47. Ibid., p. 287

48. Ibid., p. 297

49. Ibid., p. 300

50. William J. Jacobs, *Hannibal: An African Hero*, (McGraw Hill, 1973) p. 87

51. Ibid., p. 87

52. Ernle Bradford, *Hannibal* (London: MacMillan London Ltd., 1981), p. 38

53. J.A. Rogers, Great Men of Color (Collier MacMillan, London, 1972) p. 108

54. Livy, preface to Penguin Classic Edition

55. Jacobs, p. 7

56. Jacobs, p. 8

57. J.A. Rogers, p. 108

58. deBeer, p. 7

59. Donauer, p. 151

60. Van Sertima, ed, *African Presence in Early Europe*, (New Brunswick: Transaction Books, 1985) p. 265

61. J.A. Rogers, p. 107

62. J.A. Rogers, *Sex and Race* (Helga Rogers, New York, NY 1964) p. 88

63. Bradford, p. 38

64. Van Sertima, p. 139

65. J.A. Rogers, *World's Great Men of Color*, p. 108

66. Harden, p. 166

67. *Encyclopedia of Archaeology* (New York, Thomas Y. Crowell & Company, 1977) p. 62

68. deBeer, p. 191

69. Van Sertima, *African Presence in Early Europe* (New Brunswick: Transaction Books, 1985) p. 139

70. R. Garrucci, *La Moneta dell'Italia Antica*, as translated by Dr. Camille Russell (University of Maryland, College Park Campus) p. 88

71. deBeer, p. 96

NKRUMAH: THE MAN AND HIS WORLD

By Selwyn R. Cudjoe[1]

The countries known as underdeveloped have produced the greatest statesmen of the twentieth cen-
tury, men who have substantially altered the shape and direction of world civilisation in the last fifty
years. They are four in number: Lenin, Gandhi, Mao Tse-tung and Nkrumah.
                                    C.L.R. James, *Nkrumah and the Ghana Revolution.*

I can say that from the time I have known you, you have always had as your undeviating aim the
emancipation from a subordinate position of the people of Africa and of African descent and your
struggle for that emancipation of the whole of humanity.
                                    C.L.R. James, Letter to Nkrumah

For anyone who lived in the colonial world in 1957 or thereabouts, the
name Kwame Nkrumah rang out like a bell, clean and clear, symbolic of the
aspirations of all the people who lived under the yoke of colonialism. When
Ghana and its people became independent in 1957, the first African country
to do so in the twentieth century, they struck a mighty blow for the freedom of
colonial peoples against foreign oppression and continued a struggle for colonial liberation that was inaugurated by India in 1947. To all who listened, the
independence of Ghana signaled that the chains of modern African servitude
were broken for all time and Nkrumah joined the caravan of freedom fighters
and colonial liberators such as Ghandi, Bolivar, Marti and others. For most of
us, especially those of us who were not born in Africa, the name of Nkrumah
headed the list, became the beacon that led us to the quest for national
liberation and ignited anew our desire to reclaim our heritage and our national pride.

Kwame Nkrumah, the pride of Africa, was born on September 18, 1909 in
the village of Nkroful in the Western Province of the Gold Coast, a British
colony at the time, into a jeweler's family from the Nzima tribe. On the day
that Kwame (Saturday's child) was born there was great rejoicing not for his
birth but for the funeral rites of his father's mother, who had died a short while
before. His mother, a member of the Anonas clan, was a petty trader (a
market woman) and his father, a member of the Asona clan, was a goldsmith.
On that Saturday in September, Africa gave birth to one of its shining stars.

Kwame grew up under the social and cultural influences of his Akan tribe
but was educated formally at a Catholic primary school in Half Assini where
he came under the influence of a Roman Catholic priest, a German named
George Fischer. He graduated from this school in 1926. Through the influence
of Father Fisher, Nkrumah was baptized into the Roman Catholic faith. Years

Kwame Nkrumah.

later, when he had become the prime minister of Ghana, he would say, "I am a non-demoninational Christian and a Marxist socialist and I have not found any contradiction between the two."[2]

After graduating from primary school, Nkrumah, in the English pedagogical tradition, became a pupil teacher at his primary school before continuing his education, at the age of eighteen, at the Accra Teachers' Training College in Achimota from which he graduated in 1930. It is noteworthy, however, that from this early age, Nkrumah believed in the total independence of his country from the English and argued that "[racial] harmony can only exist when the black race is treated as equal to the white race; that only a free and independent people—a people with a government of their own—can claim equality, racial or otherwise, with another people."[3]

University Training in the United States

After he graduated from Teachers' Training College, Nkrumah taught at various Catholic schools for five years before leaving for the United States where he entered Lincoln University, the first university in the United States to train Afro-Americans for positions of leadership in society. In 1939, he graduated with a Bachelor of Arts in economics and sociology and was accepted as an assistant lecturer in philosophy at Lincoln. By 1942, he had become a full instructor in philosophy and in 1945 was recognized as "the most outstanding professor of the year."[4] In 1942 he received a Bachelor of Theology degree from Lincoln Seminary and a Masters of Science from the University of Pennsylvania. In 1943 he received the Master of Arts in Philosophy from the latter univesity and, although he did all of the course work for his terminal degree, he left the University of Pennsylvania before he finished his thesis.

Much of Nkrumah's political and organizational work began while he was in the United States. At the University of Pennsylvania he organized the African Students' Association of America and Canada believing that "unless territorial freedom was ultimately linked up with the Pan African movement for the liberation of the whole African continent, there would be no hope of freedom and equality for the African and for people of African descent in any part of the world."[5] Apart from meeting C.L.R. James, author of *The Black Jacobins,* from whom he learned "how an underground movement worked," it was the *Philosophy and Opinions of Marcus Garvey* (1923) that left the deepest impression on him and gave him continued encouragement to commit himself to the liberation of Africa.[6]

When Nkrumah ended his sojourn in the United States in 1945, he seems to have had a good understanding of the "colonial question" and the manner in which the "mother countries" exploited and underdeveloped the colonized countries. For him, colonialism was primarily an economic rather than a political phenomenon. Thus he wrote in "Toward Colonial Freedom," a book he drafted at the end of his stay in the United States but did not publish until he got to England:

> Existence for the colonial peoples under imperialist rule means their economic and political exploitation. The imperialist powers need the raw materials and cheap native labour of the colonies for their own capitalist industries. Through their system of monopolist control they eliminate native competition, and use the colonies as dumping grounds for their surplus mass-produced goods. In attempting to legitimise their presence they claim to be improving the welfare of the native population. Such claims are merely a camouflage for their real purpose of exploitation to which they are driven by economic necessity. . . .
>
> Whether the dependent territory is administered as a colony, protectorate or mandate, it is all part of an imperialist plan to perpetuate its economic exploitation. The colonies gain no advantages whatsoever from being dependent; socially and technologically their progress is hindered; they pay for a nominal protection against aggression by providing troops for the mother country in time of war and *their political freedom will never be automatically granted but won by their own endeavours.* Britain may claim that she holds the colonies under trusteeship until they are capable of self-government, but it is not in her interests to relinquish her stranglehold. *The African, however, was perfectly capable of governing himself before the advent of the white man and should be allowed to do so again.* . . .
>
> The African national liberation movement in the African colonies has arisen because of the continuous economic and political exploitation by foreign oppressors. The aim of the movement is to win freedom and independence. This can only be achieved by the political education and organisation of the colonial masses.[7]

This analysis, written in 1945, long before the liberation movement in Africa became popular and the theory of economic underdevelopment gained prominence, demonstrated Nkrumah's grasp of the economic, political, and ideological dimensions of the colonial question and his theoretical brillance. Recognising the need to organize the "colonial masses," he left the United States for London in May 1945 and devoted his next two years, 1945-47, to organizing his countrymen in London for the eventual liberation of his homeland. His stay in the United States not only provided him with a formal education and an opportunity to associate with some of the working class elements, it also opened his eyes to what he called "the true meaning of freedom."[8]

Nkrumah's Preparatory Work in London

While Nkrumah studied in the United States he met C.L.R. James, who gave him a letter of introduction to George Padmore, "the father of African

As a teacher at Axim.

emancipation" and founder of the International African Bureau, an organization that was devoted to "the study of the colonial question and the spread of
propaganda and agitation all over Britain, in Africa and in the territories
inhabited by people of African descent."[9] When Nkrumah arrived in London
in June 1945, he was met by Padmore, who eventually became one of his most
trusted political allies. One month after Nkrumah arrived in London he began to work with Padmore as one of the organizing secretaries to prepare for
the Fifth Pan African Congress that was held in Manchester, England, in
October 1945. This conference, held under the joint chairmanship of W.E.B.

DuBois, a distinguished Afro-American scholar and freedom fighter, and Dr. Peter Milliard, a Black physician from British Guiana, drew over two hundred delegates and listened to reports of conditions in colonial territories from all over the world. According to Nkrumah, the congress endorsed "the principles enunciated in the Declaration of Human Rights and advised Africans and those of African descent wherever they might be to organise themselves into political parties, trade unions, cooperative societies and farmers' organisations in support of their struggle for political freedom and economic advancement."[10] It was into this organizational and theoretical frame that Nkrumah walked when he arrived in Britain in June 1945. By October he was the joint political secretary (together with Padmore) of the conference and made the report on the problems of the West African colonies under European domination.

For the next two years, Nkrumah lived in London "in the very closest association with Padmore."[11] He was the secretary of the Congress's organizational committee and then general secretary of the Working Committee that was elected to implement the program for African liberation. During that period he also assisted in founding the West African National Secretariat (of which he became the general secretary), an organization dedicated to organizing the struggle in West Africa. While organizing in London in 1947, Nkrumah received a letter from Ako Adjei inviting him to return to Ghana to become the general secretary of the United Gold Coast Convention (UGCC); an organization that was committed to using "all legitimate and constitutional means" to ensure that the people of Ghana achieve internal selfgovernment. Realizing that he could best achieve his goal of working for African liberation through confronting the source of the problem, Nkrumah accepted the position and returned to his homeland in December 1947 to continue the struggle for national liberation.

Nkrumah's Return to Ghana

When Nkrumah returned to Ghana, there was turmoil in the colonial world; the colonial liberation movements in China, Burma, India, Ceylon, Indo-China, and Indonesia were enjoying tremendous success. In Africa itself, the embers of sleeping nationalism were gradually coming alive and the struggle for national liberation was but a moment away. In Ghana, Nkrumah realized that his success depended upon the organization of the people and thus five weeks after he set foot on African soil once more he called together the Working Committee of the UGCC and set out the program for the country's ultimate liberation. He organized the work of the party into two phases: the first consisted of the coordination of all the various organizations in the party (women's organizations, farmers' organizations and so on), the consolidation of branches that were formed already and the establishment of new

As a student in America.

branches in every town and hamlet. Further, he established weekend schools to train the masses for the intricacies of self-government. The second aspect of the program consisted of convening "a Constitutional Assembly of the Gold Coast People to draw up the Constitution for Self-Government or National Independence" and the organization of demonstrations, strikes, and boycotts to achieve the end of self-government.[12]

Six months after Nkrumah assumed office, he toured the country and set up more than five hundred branches of the UGCC. He emphasized the need for an educated populace and later founded several newspapers to carry forward his views. Propaganding through his newspapers also became a powerful tool in Ghana's struggle. So successful were these endeavors that it became necessary for the colonial officials to take him out of circulation. Accordingly, he and five other colleagues from UGCC were arrested because of the civil and economic disturbances that began to take place in the colony and Nkrumah was exiled to Lawra in the Northern Territories.

While the six leaders were in prison, there arose a serious rift between Nkrumah and his colleagues and by the time the Watson Committee that was looking into the disturbances concluded its hearings, Nkrumah was considered "a man to be watched." The increasing revolutionary mood of the youths and Nkrumah's growing dissatisfaction with the leadership of the UGCC led to his split with the latter party and the eventual launching of the Convention Peoples' Party (CPP) on June 12, 1949, before an audience of sixty thousand people. Its major demand was self-government of the country within a year.

Rising Nationalism: Nonviolent Positive Action

Having formed the CPP, Nkrumah embarked upon a program of "nonviolent positive action" in which he sought to use "legitimate political agitation, newspaper and educational campaigns and, as a last resort, the constitutional application of strikes, boycotts and non-cooperation based on the principle of absolute non-violence, as used by Ghandi in India."[13] With this decision, the colonial struggles were drawing upon and learning from one another. Meanwhile, the Coussey Committee, appointed by the government, was working on a new constitution for Ghana. When this constitution was published in October 1949, the CPP called together the Ghana People's Representative Assembly on November 20 and denounced the document as "unacceptable to the country as a whole." There ninety thousand Ghanaians came to proclaim their loyalty to a new society and to repudiate colonial rule. As Nkrumah's campaign of positive action began to take hold, a state of emergency was declared throughout the city and Nkrumah was arrested again in January 1950 and imprisoned for three years for fomenting unrest in the country.

In February of the next year, national elections to the Legislative Assembly

On the eve of my departure from London for the Gold Coast in October, 1947.

were held and the CPP, under the leadership of Nkrumah, won the elections while he was still in prison. Nkrumah himself was elected to a seat in the Legislative Assembly. Because a government could not be formed while its leader was in prison, the British goernment was forced to release Nkrumah on February 12, 1951. He became the leader of Government Business in the Legislative Assembly, and on March 5, 1952, he was named the first prime minister of Ghana.

Five years later, on March 5, 1957, Ghana became an independent country within the British Commonwealth. On July 1, 1960, Ghana was declared a republic, and Nkrumah became its first President. In 1961, he was elected general secretary and made life chairman of the Convention People's Party. On February 24, 1966, while Nkrumah was visiting China, he was overthrown by a military coup and removed from all of his posts. Unable to return to the country, he was forced to settle in Conakry, Guinea, where he became an honorable member of the House of Representatives, co-president of Guinea, and general-secretary of the Guinea's Democratic Party.

On April 27, 1972 Kwame Nkrumah died in Bucharest, where he had gone to be treated for an illness. Even though he had been overthrown, his body was returned to Ghana on July 9, 1972, where he was buried in his home village of Nkroful, with all the dignity befitting a great son of the soil, a warrior coming home to rest, having opened the way for independence and having given us the eyes to see that our true vocation lies in the liberation of our people. Kojo Botsio, one of his former colleagues, and Mrs. Nkrumah accompanied the body to Accra, where he was laid in state. *West Africa* in its July 21 issue noted:

> Thouands of Ghanaians, led by Head of State Colonel Acheampong, filed silently past the body as it lay in state in Accra, while flags throughout Ghana flew at half mast and traditional drummers played outside State House, and Radio Ghana re-broadcast some of the ex-President's speeches and devoted special programmes to the former leader. . . .
>
> After lying-in-state the body was returned to the military hospital prior to burial in Dr. Nkrumah's home-town of Nkroful. In Nkroful itself, local townspeople held an all-night vigil outside the home of Madame Nyaniba, mother of the late President.[14]

Colonel Acheampong, Ghana's leader at the time of Nkrumah's death, paid tribute to Nkrumah's contribution to his country and made the following comment:

> In his lifetime he waged a relentless war against colonialism and racism, and even after his death his spirit will, no doubt, continue to inspire the valiant fighters against the twin enemies of Africa. Today we mourn the loss of a great leader whose place in history is well assured. We join world leaders in paying tribute to this worthy son of the soil.[15]

With my mother and Ackah Watson soon after my return to the Gold Coast.

Nkrumah's Accomplishments

During the nine year period (1957-66) that he ruled Ghana Kwame Nkrumah began to make a major mark on the world and gain a reputation as an international statesman. In that period he became totally committed to a united Africa and the end of neocolonialism. It was also a period in which he represented the aspirations of black people throughout the world. As Basil Davidson noted, "Nkrumah's Ghana led the way for black men and women to speak as equals in the councils of the world, and the world began to listen as they spoke, the dignity of Africa began to have a new and modern meaning."[16] In this period Ghana also made rapid strides in the areas of health, education and economic development.[17] These advances, particularly in the area of education, were frowned upon by a small elite, who felt that expanded educational opportunities would abrogate and negate the privileges they enjoyed in the society.

More than most of the other problems, economic development received much attention from Nkrumah's government. Given the colonial-capitalist orientation of the economy that was designed to serve the needs of Britain rather than Ghanaians, Nkrumah's task proved most difficult. As James noted, "Economic relations are the basis of any form of state and the colonialist states of Africa were from start to finish organisations for economic exploitation."[18] Therefore, it was no wonder that "repeatedly . . . it was found that the economic system taken over from the past could not afford a vast expansion of the country's welfare," and this made Nkrumah's task very difficult.[19] As a consequence, by 1960 Nkrumah began to move away from the capitalist-oriented nature of the Ghanaian economy and lay the basis for what he called "scientific socialism." In his book *Neo-Colonialism: The Last Stages of Imperialism* he tried to expose what he described as "the economic stranglehold exercised by foreign monopolistic complexes such as Anglo-American Corporation, and illustrated the ways in which this financial grip perpetuated the paradox of Africa: poverty in the midst of plenty."[20]

As independence proceeded, Nkrumah ran into many problems, perhaps the most notable of which was the manner in which he dismissed his Chief Justice after some persons accused of plotting against his life were acquitted by the courts. Acting within constitutional limits, Nkrumah demanded that the National Assembly bring an amending act that made the acquittals "null and void." Such a move led to criticisms at home and abroad. James sees this incident as one of Nkrumah's major blunders and argues that an unscrupulous head of state, in responding to this crisis, might have found it necessary

> to shoot his Chief Justice while trying to escape, arrange for him to be run over by an errant motor lorry, have a bunch of doctors declare him to be

medically unfit and, Kremlim-fashion, put him out of the way in an asylum, and send him on a long holiday and beg the British government to make him a life peer on resignation, even invite him to dinner and poison him. But what a head of state does not do is to dismiss his Chief Justice after he has given a major decision on a matter in which the whole country is interested. *The very structure, juridicial, political and moral, of the state is at one stroke destroyed, and there is automatically placed on the agenda a violent restoration of some sort of legal connection between government and population.* By this single act, Nkrumah prepared the population of Ghana for the morals of the Mafia.[21]

Another factor that did much to undermine Nkrumah's government was the corruption among the government and party members at the highest levels. Indeed, the achievement of independence seemed to many a means of concentrating all of the state's wealth in their hands. Given the promise of independence, such blatant corruption led to a greater chasm between the rulers and the ruled and the inevitable resentments that it engendered. Certainly, the lifestyles of the elite of the society did much to alienate many Ghanaians from the CPP and introduced a great deal of cynicism into the society.

There were also many problems at the party level (Davidson has argued that the CPP began to govern "from the top down") and there became too close an identification between the ruling party and the state. Soon, this lack of independence on the part of the party led to its degneration. Also, the tendency in some quarters to deify Nkrumah (it is argued that he did nothing to prevent this) led to an unquestioning belief in his ideas (Nkrumahism), and this led to the further breakdown of the party, which should have been the major bulwark of support when the army made its move to depose Nkrumah.[22] If Davidson is to be believed, Nkrumah himself began to become too distant and isolated from the people and could not discern their genuine concerns from superfluous ones. Such isolation necessarily led to growing authoritarianism on Nkrumah's part that further alienated the rank and file. More important, Nkrumah and the CPP, by its actions, lost its democratic base and became a mass party in name only.[23]

Given the divisions in the society (ethnic, political, and otherwise), the difficulty of turning around in nine years an economic system that had served the interest of the colonial powers for a century, the intransigence of an educated elite that was concerned only with its own advancement, and a civil service of colonial bureaucrats whose loyalty was to the "mother country" rather than the local populace made it very difficult for Nkrumah to accomplish all that he had hoped. Therefore, it becomes increasingly difficult to understand why Nkrumah did not concentrate more of his efforts on responding to the legitimate demands and grievances of his people at home and go a little slower on pursuing his international agenda. In retrospect, his commitment to a common continental economic order, military defense sys-

My journey from prison.

tem, and foreign policy initiatives seems idealist, an agenda the continent was not yet prepared to initiate. Given the material basis of those societies (economic, political, social, and otherwise) at that time, it was not possible to achieve the global program that Nkrumah had envisioned.

It would seem, therefore, that as laudable as Nkrumah's attempt to develop an "African personality" was, he might have been moving too quickly for his people. They needed time to understand what he was doing, and the imperialist powers and their stooges at home were not prepared to grant him that time. Indeed, so blind had be become to his political problems at home that in spite of assassination attempts on his life, increasing strikes in the country, and other such disturbances, Nkrumah kept on with his program, almost oblivious to these malfunctionings in his society. Indeed, in 1964, he declared the society a "one-party state," and this alienated him further from his people. It also gave the imperialists more grist for their reactionary mill and rumor-mongering and the charges of his authoritarianism and dictatorial tendencies became even more intense. The promise of independence was beginning to fade and, as one novelist was wont to suggest, that "the beautyful ones" were yet to be born.[24]

Therefore, it was not coincidental that when his ouster occurred, he was undertaking a trip to see what he could have done to bring the Vietnam War to an end. In *Dark Days in Africa* he makes the proud boast that "when the action [of the coup] took place, I was on my way to Hanoi, at the invitation of President Ho Chi Minh, with proposals for ending the war in Vietnam."[25] Such an important undertaking did not prevent the military from taking over the government and gives more credence to the belief that Nkrumah was so concerned wwith his international stature that he forgot a fundamental lesson of politics: one must take care of one's backyard before venturing into the front yard of another, no matter how laudable one's intention might be. In *Dark Days in Africa*, he tries somewhat unsuccessfully to justify his obvious political blindness in this and other political matters. Nkrumah's failure, despite his many successes, was his inability to see and to understand what was going on around him at home.

Nkrumah's Intellectual Achievements

What remains after 1966 is an attempt to reconcile the many intellectual and ideological currents that are to be found in Nkrumah's work. Although it is true that Nkrumah had been writing before he was overthrown, this period of his life (his last) allowed him the necessary leisure to concentrate on his intellectual concerns. As he noted in *Dark Days in Ghana*, "I have been able to read as much as I like, to study the latest books on politics, history, literature, science and philosophy, to step up my writing, to reflect, and to prepare myself physically and mentally for the militant phase of the revolutionary

Part of the Academic Procession at Lincoln University Commencement Day, June 5, 1951, when I received the Honorary Degree of Doctor of Laws. (l. to r.) Kojo Botsio, myself, Dr. W.H. Johnson, and Dr. Horace M. Bond, President of Lincoln.

struggle." He noted further that he was visited by "freedom fighters and members of progressive organisations" and that far from feeling isolated, "I have never felt more in touch with African and world affairs."[26]

Even before he returned to Africa in 1948, Nkrumah was a prolific writer. During his prime ministership he continued to write, and Guinea allowed him the necessary time to reflect upon his experiences. As a result, Nkrumah produced a number of intellectual works for which we can adduce something of his theoretical and philosophical concerns.

From his earliest works, Nkrumah tirelessly explored the evils of imperialism. In 1965, he published *Neo-Colonialism: The Last Stage of Imperialism* in which he analyzed the methods by which the colonial powers controlled the economies of the colonial countries even after they achieved political independence. He contended that through a series of loans and aid, unequal trade, and the penetration of the local economies by the international multinational corporations, the colonial countries were unable to enjoy meaningful (he would say "true") independence. He called this economic control, this new phase of colonialism, necolonialism, and in so doing introduced a new concept into Marxist discourse and opened up a new dimension of understanding into African political thought. He recognized the fundamental importance of the class struggle in Africa despite the narrow base of its industrial proletariat, and perhaps it is in acknowlegment of and tribute to this fact that Amilcar Cabral noted that historically Nkrumah will be known as "the strategist of genius in the struggle against classical colonialism."[27]

A year earlier, Nkrumah had published *Consciencism: Philosophy and Ideology for Decolonization,* the culmination of the "theory of Nkrumahism" that was presented as the official ideology of the Ghanaian government. In this work, Nkrumah examined some of the class contradictions in African society and offered a political and philosophical basis for the African liberation movement. He argued that philosophy is "one of the subtle instruments of ideology and social cohesion. Indeed, it affords a theoretical basis for the cohesion" and "performs this ideological function when it takes shape as political philosophy or as ethics."[28] Such a philosophy, he argued, must take objective account of Africa's situation as it was then and blend into Africa's historical thought patterns. Within that context Nkrumah sought to reconcile what he called traditional African humanist values (which he saw as "socialist" in its social manifestation) with the insights of contemporary Marxism.

In working out his philosophical-ideological position, Nkrumah argued that there exist three broad features of African life: the traditional way of life, the Islamic dimension, and the Western Christian tradition that was introduced by colonialism and continued to use neocolonialism to maintain its presence. With "true independence" a new harmony will be forged among the three features of African life and this new synthesis, *philosophical con-*

The Cabinet, 1954-56.

At work in my study at home.

sciencism, could be developed in such a way that it fit into what he called "the African personality."[29] Because "the social-political ancestor of socialism" is African communalism, one does not have to go very far to recognize that, as Nkrumah believed, this historical unity was dislocated by colonialism and neo-colonialism and could be reconciled only through "scientific socialism," the modern manifestation of African communalism. Thus, he argues:

> whereas in communalism in an untechnical society can be *laissez faire,* in a technical society where sophisticated means of production are at hand, if the underlying principles of communalism are not given centralised and correlated expression, class cleavages arise, which are the result of economic disparities, and accompanying political inequalities. Socialism, therefore, can be and is the defence of the principles of communalism in a modern setting, Socialism is a form of social organisation which, guided by the principles underlying communism, adopts procedures and measures made necessary by demographic and technological developments.[30]

According to Nkrumah, the passage from communalism to socialism "can only lie through revolution: it cannot lie through reform."[31]

What, then, is the final synthesis of this new condition? Nkrumah's ideal state bears a close resemblance to the communist state that Marx outlined in the *Communist Manifesto* whose central principle reads "from each according to his ability; to each according to his need," and in which the freedom of each becomes the necessary precondition for the freedon of all.[32] Thus Nkrumah frames his concept in the following manner:

> Philosophical consciencism seeks to promote individual development, but in such a way that the conditions for the development of all become the conditions for the development of each; that is, in such a way that the individual development does not introduce such diversities as to destroy the egalitarian basis. The social-political practice also seeks to co-ordinate social forces in such a way as to mobilize them logistically for the maximum development of society along true egalitarian lines. For this, planned development is essential.[33]

This, in essence, was Nkrumah's philosophical-ideological position.

In 1969, after spending three years in Guinea, he updated *Consciencism* and argued that the many military coups that had taken place in Africa in the 1960s "have brought into sharp relief the nature and the extent of the class struggle in Africa. Foreign monopoly capitalists are in close association with local reactionaries, and have made use of officers among the armed forces in order to frustrate the purposes of the African Revolution."[34] As a result, the need for Africa to come together became more urgent, and so he argued that "without positive action, a colonial territory cannot be truly liberated. It is doomed to creep in its petty pace from day to day towards the attainment of a sham independece that turns to dust, independence which is shot through and through with the supreme interest of an alien power."[35] The road to "genuine national liberation" lay through the national liberation struggle.

Nkrumah wrote a number of books while he was in exile, the two most important of which are *Handbook of Revolutionary Warfare: A Guide to the Armed Phase of the African Revolution* (1968) and *Class Struggle in Africa* (1970) in which he sought to reemphasize the central points he had made in *Consciencism*. In the former he argued that there is only one true socialism, "scientific socialism; the principles of which are abiding and universal." In the latter he reiterated that although the African Revolution still concentrated its main efforts "on the destruction of imperialism, colonialism and neo-colonialism, [it] is aiming at the same time to bring about a radical transformation of society." This can only be done through the construction of a socialist society.[36] As was noted by one of the authors in *Fighters for National Liberation,* Nkrumah's very generalized argumentation in *Consciencism* gave way, in these latter works, "to a concrete analysis of the structure of African society, based on the position of different social strata in the production process and their division into privileged and oppressed."[37]

Nkrumah also clarified and concretized many of his concepts of socialism and the nature of class struggle in his last books. In his *Handbook of Revolutionary Struggle* he argued that nationalism, Pan-Africanism, and socialism went hand in hand and one could not be realized without the other, a concept that Kwame Toure (Stokely Carmichael) picked up and used most stridently in his advocacy of Nkrumahism. In *Class Struggle in Africa* Nkrumah moved closer to integrating his ideas into a classical socialist framework by arguing that "genuine national independence" can only be achieved on the basis of socialism. Indeed, he seemed to have felt that without revolutionary struggle and an understanding of the class struggle in Africa, no genuine liberation could be achieved.

In essence, this was Nkrumah's understanding of the revolutionary process in his country and in all of Africa, the product of thirty seven years of active struggle and organizing in the United States, England, and Ghana. Whatever the shortcomings of his ideas, they laid the basis for a scientific approach to an examination of the African liberation struggle, a position that had its most important followers in the liberation struggle in southern Africa, where they expanded and enriched Nkrumah's theories. In theoretical terms, few thinkers have added as much to our knowledge of the manner in which colonialism and neo-colonialism function and the irrevocable position that one must take if one is truly to liberate one's country from colonialist and neocolonialist exploitation. In historical terms, he remains "one of the first leaders of the African liberation movement to appeal to his people to be guided by the principles of scientific socialism and to create a vanguard party of working people."[38]

Kwame Nkrumah.

Conclusion

As we look back at Nkrumah's struggle to achieve an independent Ghana, it is very clear that he was continuing a struggle that began with the Fanti Confederation in 1868, when the Fanti Chiefs came together to defend themselves against the political encroachments of the British merchants, a struggle that was carried on at various historical intervals by the Aboriginies Rights Protection Society, the National Congress of British West Africa, and the United Gold Coast Convention of which Nkrumah was a part and from which he launched the decisive struggle for independence. Struggle, he recognized, was a continuous affair, and like Frantz Fanon, he realized that each generation has its own specific contribution to make to the overall liberation of its people. The struggle never stops; it is a continuous process to affirm the sanctity of a people's life. One can only play the part that history has decreed and hope that one plays it well. Only history can judge how successful one has been.

In Nkrumah's case, history has already judged him to be one of the most important figures of the African Revolution. Coming at the moment that he did, he unleashed a force of and for liberation (spiritual, political and otherwise) that changed the face of the African continent forever. More important, Nkrumah may have offered one yardstick by which to measure him when he mused at his alma mater: "It is not the heights to which a man climbs that matter, but the depths from whence he came."[39] Surely, on his trip from the lowly village of Nkroful to the height of African consciousness, in his single-minded pursuit of his aim and in his devotion to his people Kwame Nkrumah reached the highest spiritual plateau that any patriot can reach, an achievement that reminds us all of Marx's famous "Reflections of a Young Man on the Choice of a Profession," when he noted,

> History calls those men the greatest who have ennobled themselves by working for the common good; experience acclaims as happiest the man [or woman] who has made the greatest number of people happy; religion itself teaches us that the ideal being whom all strive to copy sacrificed himself for the sake of mankind, and who would dare to set at nought such judgements?[40]

Notes

1. The biographical note on the author (to which this number refers) may be found in the biographical section.

2. *The Autobiography of Kwame Nkrumah* (Edinburgh: Thomas Nelson, 1957), p. 12.

3. *Ibid.*, p. 14.

4. *Ibid.*, p. 33.

5. *Ibid.*, p. 44

6. See *Ibid.,* p. 45.

7. Quoted in *Ibid.,* pp. 46-47, my emphasis.

8. *Ibid.,* p. 48.

9. C.L.R. James, *Nkrumah and the Ghana Revolution* (Westport, Conn.: Lawrence Hill, 1977), pp. 63-64.

10. *Autobiography of Kwame Nkrumah,* p. 53.

11. *Nkrumah and the Ghana Revolution.,* p. 77.

12. *Autobiography of Kwame Nkrumah,* p. 11.

13. *Ibid.,* p. 112.

14. Quoted in Basil Davidson, *Black Star* (London: Allen Lane, 1973), pp. 205-6.

15. *Quoted in ibid.,* p. 206.

16. *Ibid.,* pp. 158-59.

17. See Kwame Nkrumah, *Dark Days in Africa* (New York: International Publishers, 1968), for Nkrumah's account of the accomplishments of his government in these areas.

18. *Nkrumah and the Ghana Revolution,* p. 14.

19. *Black Star,* p. 132.

20. *Dark Days in Africa,* p. 96.

21. *Nkrumah and the Ghana Revolution,* pp. 10-11.

22. Nkrumah is reputed to have told his followers "to study and learn *Consciencism* [one of Nkrumah's books] and to consolidate their understanding of Nkrumahism." See Kenneth W. Grundy, "The Political Ideology of Nkrumah," in W.A.E. Skurmik, ed. *African Political Thought: Lumumba, Nkrumah, and Toure,* Monograph Series in World Affairs, Vol. 5 (University of Denver, Colorado, 1968), p.. 81. This short article, is one of the most racist and deprecatory analyses of Nkrumah's ideology.

23. See *Black Star,* particularly chapter 4, for a discussion of this point.

24. See, Ayi KweiArmah, *The Beautyful Ones Are Not Yet Born (London: Heinemann,* 1968).

25. *Dark Days in Africa,* p. 9.

26. *Dark Days in Africa,* pp. 147, 148.

27. Quoted in *Black Star,* p. 217. Amilcar Cabral picked up and refined many of Nkrumah's concepts, particularly with regard to culture, history and class struggle.

28. *Consciencism,* p. 66.

29. *Ibid.,* p. 70, 79.

30. *Ibid.,* p. 73.

31. *Ibid.*

32. Marx put it this way in the *Communist Manifesto:* "The old bourgeois society, with its classes and class conflicts, will be replaced by an association in which the free development of each will lead to the free development of all" (R.D. Ryazanoff, ed., *The Communist Manifesto of Karl Marx and Friedrich Engels* [New York: Russell and Russell, 1963]. pp. 53-54).

33. *Ibid.,* p. 98.

34. Author's note.

35. *Consciencism,* p. 104.

36. See Kwame Nkrumah, *Handbook of Revolutionary Warfare: A Guide to the Armed Phase of the African Revolution* (New York: International Publishers, 1968), p. 29, and *Class Struggle in Africa* (New York: International Publishers, 1970), p. 84.

37. R.A. Ulyanovsky, V.G. Khoros, V.V. Vavilov, et. al., *Fighters for National Liberation,* trans. Francis Longman (Moscow: Progress Publishers, 1983), p. 155.

38. *Ibid.,* p. 157.

39. *Autobiography of Kwame Nkrumah,* p. 53.

40. Karl Marx and Frederick Engels, *Collected Works* Vol. 1 (New York: International Publishers, 1975), p. 8.

NELSON MANDELA: "THE SYMBOL OF OUR STRUGGLE"[1]

By R. Hunt Davis, Jr.

August 5, 1987—the evening newscast carries a feature story on Nelson Mandela, noting that it is the twenty-fifth anniversary of his arrest and imprisonment. January 29, 1987—the Secretary of State's Advisory Committee on South Africa issues its report which, among other things, calls for the South African government to release Nelson Mandela. "Release Mandela"— the slogan is printed on the T-shirts worn by African youth throughout South Africa. "Release Mandela"—it is the demand of African political leaders in response to South African President P.W. Botha's call for negotiations between the government and Africans.

Nelson Rolihlahla Mandela, a man now sixty-nine years old, who has been a political prisoner of the government of his country for a quarter of a century, is the embodiment of the African struggle for freedom in South Africa. Indeed, as he stated in a 1961 press release, "The struggle is my life. I will continue fighting for freedom until the end of my days." "How is it," writes his biographer Mary Benson, "that a man imprisoned for more than twenty-three years—who has not been allowed to be quoted by the South African media—has become the embodiment of the struggle for liberation in that country and the vital symbol of a new society?"[2] This biographical essay addresses this question and, in seeking an answer, also attempts to understand better both the man and the struggle that has become his life.

Nelson Mandela was born July 18, 1918, near Umtata, the capital of the Transkei region of South Africa. His father, Henry Gadla Mandela, was chief councillor and a close relative of the paramount chief of the Thembu people. Upon his father's death in 1930, he became the ward of the paramount. Thus Mandela's formative years were spent in the rural areas of the Transkei. Though not a "traditional" setting in the sense that the term is normally applied, nonetheless much of the history and culture of the Xhosa-speaking peoples remained intact and was absorbed by Mandela and his peers. On the other hand, as a member of a leading Transkei family he received a good education at a succession of missionary institutions, and in 1938 he enrolled in Fort Hare University College and thus became one of a relatively small number of African college students in the entire country.

The 1930s were years of increasing African political activity. Though far

Nelson Mandela at the age of nineteen in Umtata, Transkei. Photographer: P. K. A. Gaeshwe (courtesy of Peter Davis). Reprinted from *Nelson Mandela: The Struggle Is My Life* with permission of Pathfinder Press. 410 West St., N.Y., N.Y. 10014.

different in scope and intensity from the upheaval and turmoil that have gripped contemporary South Africa, the political agitation of the time against government legislation to disenfranchise those African males who could still vote on the common rolls stimulated the burgeoning nationalism of young Mandela. His student days at Fort Hare accelerated the process, and in 1940 he was suspended as a result of his participation in a student protest boycott. Confronted with an order from his guardian to accede to the college authorities and also faced with an arranged marriage, Mandela instead turned his back on a rural life as a potential chief and at age twenty-two headed for Johannesburg and a vastly different future.

War-time Johannesburg was a city of ferment and change. Mandela was only one of thousands of rural Africans who were streaming into the cities of South Africa in search of jobs and better opportunities than they could find in the increasingly impoverished rural areas. Along with the other rural migrants, he "learned the facts of life for urban Africans under the color bar: poverty, exclusion from skilled work, overcrowded slums and constant harassment by the police, under the pass laws."[3] Unlike most of the others, however, Mandela already possessed a better education than all but a few of his fellow Africans, and in Johannesburg he was able to complete it. He first earned his B.A. degree through correspondence from the University of South Africa and then studied law at the University of the Witwatersrand. More importantly, in terms of his political education, was that he became a part of a circle of young Africans which was in the formative stage of becoming the new national leadership. Others in the group included Oliver Tambo, former fellow Fort Hare student, future law partner, and future president of the African National Congress (ANC) in exile; Walter Sisulu, who befriended Mandela when he first arrived in Johannesburg, who was secretary-general of the ANC 1949-54, and who was sentenced to life imprisonment at the Rivonia trial in 1963; Anton Lembede, the key intellectual of the group and founding president of the ANC Youth League, who died an early death at the age of thirty-three in 1947; Asby Peter Mda, the seasoned political observer of the new generation who succeeded Lembede as president of the Youth League.

The early 1940s provided a heady intellectual atmosphere for the new generation of political activists of whom Mandela was one. Sensing a potential for fundamental changes in the wartime era, better educated than their elders, and impatient with the cautious approach of the existing African leadership, the new generation in 1944 founded the ANC Youth League. Mandela became its general secretary. The objectives of the Youth League were to revitalize the ANC by serving, as its Manifesto put it, as "the brains-trust and power-station of the spirit of African nationalism" and to rid their people of the sense of inferiority which they had developed over the years of living under oppressive white rule. Through their efforts they were able to transform African politics from a process of polite petition for redress of grievances on the part of the leaders to one of direct action that involved the masses. This culminated with the Youth League's success in getting the ANC to adopt in 1949 the Program of Action:

> The fundamental principles of the programme of action of the African National Congress are inspired by the desire to achieve national freedom. By national freedom we mean freedom from White domination and the attainment of political independence. . . . Like all other people the African people claim the right of self-determination.

Through his involvement with the formulation of Youth League policies and programs, Mandela became increasingly visible in African politics, leading in late 1950 to his election as that organization's president. In this role he played a key part in implementing the Program of Action through a call for civil disobedience which was to take the form of the Defiance Campaign. Working in collaboration with the Indian Congress and other allies, the ANC leadership prepared an ultimatum calling on the government to repeal six "unjust laws," most of which had been enacted since the National Party apartheid election victory of 1948. When the government not surprisingly rejected the ultimatum, the coalition launched the Defiance Campaign on June 26, 1952. It "was to be the most sustained and—in terms of numbers of participants—the most successful organised resistance the ANC was ever to initiate."[4] By the time the Campaign ground to a halt in early 1953, nearly 8,500 protestors went to jail for having consciously and conspicuously broken one or other of the "unjust" laws.

The Defiance Campaign clearly demonstrated the ability of the ANC to mount a massive civil disobedience effort in direct challenge of the government. But, it also marked an even more rigorous effort on the part of the white government to suppress the African political voice. Mandela, who served as the volunteer-in-chief for the Campaign, was one of twenty leaders arrested for their part in it. He received a suspended nine-month sentence, which was the first of many steps the government was to take to silence him. The ANC members, however, recognized the quality of Mandela's leadership and elected him president of the Transvaal Province branch of the ANC, which in turn led to a government banning order prohibiting Mandela from any public appearances. In 1953 the order was extended for two more years, silencing his public voice but not before his 1953 address to the Transvaal ANC was read on his behalf to the delegates. In it, he spoke of the new spirit and pride which gripped the African people, of the insane policies of the government which threatened the peace and stability of the country, and of the internal and external opponents of African freedom. "You can see," he told his audience in conclusion, quoting from Nehru, "that 'there is no easy walk to freedom anywhere and many of us will have to pass through the valley of the shadow of death again and again before we reach the mountain tops of

Winnie and Nelson Mandela celebrate the end of the State of Emergency, December 1960. Reprinted from *Nelson Mandela: The Struggle Is My Life* with permission of Pathfinder Press.

our desires.'" Yet, such dangers and difficulties had not stopped them in the past and would not deter them now. In order to win Africa's freedom, he said, "we must be prepared to face them like men who mean business and who do not waste energy in vain talk and idle action."

During this entire period of political activity, Mandela also had other dimensions to his life. He had married Evelyn Mase while still a student, and they had three children. Unfortunately, their marriage ended in divorce. In the mid-fifties he remarried, taking as his wife a medical social worker named Winnie Nomzamo Madikizela. Winnie Mandela was to become her husband's political co-worker and in recent years has emerged in her own right as one of the most visible and articulate champions of her people's cause. In the process she has herself been hounded and harassed by the authorities and has been subjected to real danger, yet she like her husband did not bow or cave in under the strain and pressure.

Mandela's profession was that of attorney-at-law, and together with Oliver Tambo, he established a practice in Johannesburg. Tambo has written about the clients they served:

> Jails are jam-packed with Africans imprisoned for serious offences—and crimes of violence are ever on the increase in apartheid society—but also for petty infringements of statutory law that no really civilized society would punish with imprisonment. To be unemployed is a crime because no African can for long evade arrest if his passbook does not carry the stamp of authorized and approved employment. To be landless can be a crime. . . . To brew African beer, to drink it or to use the proceeds to supplement the meagre family income is a crime. . . . To cheek a White man can be a crime. To live in the 'wrong' area . . . can be a crime for Africans. South African apartheid laws turn innumerable innocent people into 'criminals.' Apartheid stirs hatred and frustration among people. Young people who should be in school or learning a trade roam the streets, join gangs and wreak their revenge on the society that confronts them with only the dead-end alley of crime or poverty. Our buff office files carried thousands of these stories and if, when we started our law partnership, we had not been rebels against South African apartheid, our experiences in our offices would have remedied the deficiency.[5]

Mandela underscored Tambo's final point with his statement while on trial in 1962 that "the whole life of any thinking African in this country drives him continuously to a conflict between his conscience on the one hand and the law on the other."

The mid-1950s witnessed a further stepping up of the ANC's challenge to the apartheid state and, in turn, intensified efforts on the part of the government to stifle African protests. Nelson Mandela was at the heart of the entire set of events, though many of his activities were behind the scenes since he was subject to government banning orders. Building on the efforts of cooperation with other groups the ANC formalized in 1955 a joint movement with the

Nelson Mandela with Oliver Tambo in Addis Ababa, 1962. Reprinted from *Nelson Mandela: The Struggle Is My Life* with permission of Pathfinder Press.

Indian Congress, the South African Congress of Trade Unions, the Coloured Peoples' Organization, and the Congress of Democrats, which became known as the Congress Alliance. This in turn led to the two-day multiracial Congress of the People, in which 3,000 people gathered at Kliptown in June 1955 to adopt the Freedom Charter. Since that date it has constituted a basic document of the ANC. Its preamble clearly expressed the collective thinking of

Mandela and other banned ANC leaders such as Albert Luthuli:

> We, the people of South Africa, declare for all our country and the world to know:
> That South Africa belongs to all who live in it, black and white, and that no government can justly claim authority unless it is based on the will of the people;
> That our people have been robbed of their birthright to land, liberty and peace by a form of government founded on injustice and inequality;
> That our country will never be prosperous or free until all our people live in brotherhood, enjoying equal rights and opportunities;
> That only a democratic state, based on the will of all the people, can secure to all their birthright without distinction of colour, race, sex or belief;
> And therefore, we, the people of South Africa, black and white together—equals, countrymen and brothers—adopt this FREEDOM CHARTER. And we pledge ourselves to strive together, sparing nothing of our strength and courage, until the democratic changes here set out have been won.

The Charter constituted a revolutionary document, wrote Mandela in 1956, because it envisaged changes that "cannot be won without breaking up the economic and political set-up of present South Africa. To win the demands calls for the organisation, launching, and development of mass struggles on the widest scale." Mandela's statement also articulated the thinking underlying the shift in tactics which he engineered for the ANC. At the beginning of the 1950s, the ANC leadership was able to organize openly, but government banning orders had not only publicly silenced the top strata of that leadership by the mid-50s but the second and third levels as well. Thus emerged the M-Plan, named for Mandela, which envisaged organizing at the grassroots level and developing a mass organization from the bottom up which would enable the ANC to function effectively in the face of government efforts to silence its leaders. In short, under Mandela's direction, the ANC was learning how to cope more effectively with the government's repressive tactics and in the process becoming an organization which truly represented the people and not, as it had done through the 1940s, just the African political elite.

The apartheid state seemed ready, however, to attempt to check each maneuver of the ANC and its allies in its efforts to maintain the exclusive white control of the South African economy and political system. Faced with growing unity and militancy the government arrested 156 people, including Mandela, Luthuli, Tambo, and Sisulu, on December 5, 1956 on the charge of treason. Thus began the infamous Treason Trial, which was to drag on until 1961, when Mandela and the other final thirty defendants were acquitted. Mandela and the other accused, the state charged, were guilty of treason because they were part of an international communist conspiracy to overthrow the state by force (and, it should be remembered, the 1950 Suppression of Communism Act was one of the cornerstone pieces of apartheid legislation). Mandela became one of the key spokespersons for the defendants and in his testimony directly confronted the charge of intent to overthrow the government by force:

> We demand universal adult franchise and we are prepared to exert economic pressure to attain our demands, and we will launch defiance campaigns, stay-at-homes, either singly or together, until the Government should say, 'Gentlemen, we cannot have this state of affairs, laws being defied, and this whole situation created by stay-at-homes. Let's talk.' In my view I would say Yes, let us talk. . . .

Although the court ultimately acquitted all of the defendants, finding that the prosecution had failed to prove either an intention to change the government through violent means or participation in a communist conspiracy, the long trial nonetheless took its toll on the movement. With Mandela and the other leaders caught up with having to defend themselves and the ANC having to raise funds for their defense, organizational efforts lagged and the ANC was unable to initiate campaigns comparable to those at the beginning of the decade. Even the 1957 Alexandria bus boycott, which was a major event in African politics, was as much an undertaking of the local community as of the ANC.

More damaging still was the split in the nationalist movement which occurred in the late 1950s. With Mandela and other key leaders distracted by the Treason Trial, a group of dissidents, known as the Africanist faction and opposed to the alliance approach of the Congress movement, broke away from the ANC in 1959 to form the Pan-Africanist Congress (PAC). Robert Sobukwe was its first president. Among other things, a hitherto united movement now was confronted with organizational rivalry, a rivalry that was to lead to one of the most dramatic and decisive events in South African political history and which changed forever the nature of the African freedom struggle.

The year 1960 saw colonial rule come to an end in much of Africa as numerous countries gained their independence. The "Year of Africa" as it became known had its impact on the course of events in South Africa, as the hopes and expectations of Africans were raised along with the anxieties and fears of the whites. A crisis was rapidly developing in the country. More than two thousand people had been arrested in Natal Province, and a state of emergency had been declared in part of the Transkei, while a protest in South-West Africa ended in a confrontation with the police and eleven killed. Adding to the already tense and expectant atmosphere was British Prime Minister Macmillan's speech to the South African parliament where he advised the government to adjust itself to the "winds of change" which were sweeping the continent.

"We are prepared to exert economic pressure to attain our demands," Mandela had told the court during the Treason Trial. In this spirit ANC president Luthuli called for an economic boycott and demonstrations against the pass laws as part of the African effort to have the winds of change sweep into South Africa. The ANC campaign was to start March 31, but in an effort to promote is own image, the PAC launched its own anti-pass campaign ten days earlier. A large crowd gathered in front of the police station at Sharpeville in the southern Transvaal as PAC volunteers courted arrest for being without their passes. Tragedy ensued:

> The size of the crowd, the insults and threats . . . shouted by individuals in the throng, and the natural anxiety of whites surrounded and outnumbered by people whom they regarded as the enemy, brought police nerves after several hours to a snapping point. No order was given to shoot, and no warning shots were fired to frighten the crowd back from the fence surrounding the station. In a moment of panic, a line of white police opened fire on the crowd and continued to fire (for ten to thirty seconds . . .) as the demonstrators fled. Sixty-seven Africans were shot dead, the great majority being hit in the back as they ran. One hundred eight-six others were wounded, including forty women and eight children. White press reporters recorded the carnage in a series of grisly photographs that were to appear in newspapers all over the world in the days that followed.[6]

The Sharpeville massacre and a related series of events plunged the country into turmoil and crisis. At first the government seemed uncertain in the face of the riots that swept the country, but it soon cracked down hard. It declared a state of emergency, imprisoned Mandela and the others still standing trial for treason along with Luthuli and some two thousand additional activists. It also outlawed the ANC and the PAC, declaring them illegal organizations under the terms of the Suppression of Communism Act. The Sharpeville crisis did accomplish one major thing for Africans—it shifted, if only temporarily, the political initiative to Africans and set the government on the defensive. The cost, though, to African nationalism was overwhelming. The white government clearly showed its determination to remain in power by any means at its disposal, including open violence and stamping out any dissent. The result was to be a hiatus in African politics throughout the sixties, which was in sharp contrast to the ferment and activity of the fifties.

The African nationalist movement undertook one last major non-violent effort to apply pressure on the government to abandon apartheid and enter into discussions with African leaders about building a democratic and just society. One year after Sharpeville, fourteen hundred delegates met in the All-In African Conference to demand "that a National Convention of elected representatives of all adult men and women on an equal basis irrespective of race, colour, creed or other limitations, be called by the Union government not later than 31 May 1961 . . . to determine . . . [by a majority decision] a new non-racial democratic constitution for South Africa." Mandela, now out of jail and having had his bans lapse, made his first public appearance at a political gathering in nine years. His appearance electrified the delegates, and they elected him the head of the National Action Council which was to implement a nation-wide stay-at-home, should the government, as anticipated, fail to heed the call for a National Convention.

On March 29, the judge found Mandela and the other Treason Trial defendants not guilty and discharged them. Mandela left the court room and immediately went underground to organize the stay-at-home for the end of May. The government responded with massive arrests, employers fired strikers, and the leaders called off the proposed three day strike on the second day. Open challenges to the apartheid system, which the Program of Action had initiated, had failed to produce any change. Rather, government repression had intensified. "If the government reaction is to crush by naked force our non-violent struggle," Mandela stated in an interview from the underground with two London journalists, "we will have to reconsider our tactics. In my mind we are closing a chapter on this question of a non-violent policy."[7]

Outlawed and unable to operate openly as a mass political organization on behalf of African rights, the ANC decided to organize an armed wing, *Umkhonto we Sizwe* (Spear of the Nation) with Mandela as commander-in-chief. This, in the words of its manifesto, was created "to carry on the struggle for freedom and democracy by new methods." "The time comes in the life of any nation" the manifesto continues "when there remain only two choices: submit or fight. That time has now come to South Africa. We shall not submit and we have no choice but to hit back by all means within our power in defence of our people, our future and our freedom." Its initial acts of sabotage on December 16, 1961 were undertaken in the hope that "even at this late hour" they would "bring the government and its supporters to their senses before it is too late" and that the necessary changes would take place "before matters reach the desperate stage of civil war."

Mandela was to remain at large and operate underground until April 1962 when an informer tipped off the police on his whereabouts. Brought to trial, he faced two charges—organizing the stay-at-home in 1961 and leaving South Africa without proper travel documents—for which he was found guilty and sentenced to five years in prison. His trial statement of what it was like to be a black man in a white court gave eloquent testimony to the fundamental flaws of the South African political and legal systems when viewed from the African perspective. He challenged the right of the court to hear his case on two grounds. He did not believe that he would receive a fair and proper trial, because as a political trial "which involves a clash of the aspirations of the African people and those of the whites, the country's courts, as presently constituted, cannot be fair and impartial." Secondly, he considered himself "neither legally nor morally bound to obey laws made by a parliament in which I have no representation."

Nelson Mandela and Walter Sisulu, prison yard, Robben Island, 1966. Reprinted from *Nelson Mandela: The Struggle Is My Life* with permission of Pathfinder Press.

Needless to say, the court did not accept Mandela's argument, nor had he believed that it would. Rather, he used his trial to again lay the African case before his country and the world:

> We have warned repeatedly that the government, by resorting continually to violence, will breed in this country counter-violence amongst the people, till ultimately, if there is no dawning of sanity on the part of the government—ultimately, the dispute between the government and my people will finish up by being settled in violence and by force. Already there are indications in this country that people, my people, Africans, are turning to deliberate acts of violence and of force against the government, in order to persuade the government, in the only language which this government shows by its behaviour that it understands.

Indeed, the violence and force which the government employed explained why Mandela found himself on trial:

> But there comes a time, as it came in my life, when a man is denied the right to live a normal life, when he can only live the life of an outlaw because the government has so decreed to use the law to impose a state of

outlawry upon him. I was driven to this situation, and I do not regret having taken the decisions that I did.

Although the court had found him guilty, Mandela knew who the true guilty parties were:

> I have done my duty to my people and to South Africa. I have no doubt that posterity will pronounce that I was innocent and that the criminals that should have been brought before this court are the members of the Verwoerd government.

Mandela had been captured and imprisoned, but others in the resistance underground continued to carry out sabotage through Umkhonto. The ANC, used as it was to operating openly as a lawful organization, was essentially unprepared to operate successfully underground. Some of its leaders, such as Oliver Tambo, fled into exile. The fate of most of the ANC activists who remained inside South Africa was arrest, trial, and imprisonment. In July 1963, Walter Sisulu and the other remaining leaders of Umkhonto were captured at a farm near Rivonia and brought to trial to face a possible death sentence on charges of sabotage. Mandela was brought from prison to face the same charges in what was to become known as the Rivonia Trial.

His statement to the court was the last time the world was to hear directly from him for nearly a decade and a half. He used the opportunity to review once again the long history of efforts by Africans to secure for themselves participation in governing their country and how they were placed in a position by harsh government actions "to accept a permanent state of inferiority, or to defy the government. We chose to defy the law. We first broke the law in a way which avoided any recourse to violence; when this form was legislated against, and then the government resorted to a show of force to crush opposition to its policies, only then did we decide to answer violence with violence. But the violence which we chose to adopt was not terrorism." Of the four forms of violence Mandela said was open to them—sabotage, guerrilla warfare, terrorism, and open revolution—they chose sabotage, for it "did not involve loss of life, and it offered the best hope for future race relations. Bitterness would be kept to a minimum and, if the policy bore fruit, democratic government could become a reality." He also refuted the state's allegations that the ANC had the same aims and objectives as the Communist Party. "The ideological creed of the ANC is, and always has been, the creed of African Nationalism. . . . [which] is the concept of freedom and fulfillment for the African people in their own land." The communist ideology, on the other hand, calls for the establishment of a state based on Marxist principles.

Africans, continued Mandela, were fighting "against two features which are the hallmarks of African life in South Africa . . . poverty and the lack of human dignity, and we do not need communists or so-called 'agitators' to teach us about these things." South Africa was the richest country on the continent, and its white population enjoyed "what may well be the highest standard of living in the world." In sharp contrast stood the poverty and misery of Africans. Forty percent of them lived "in hopelessly overcrowded and, in some cases, drought-striken Reserves"; 30 percent lived on white-owned farms where they worked and lived "under conditions similar to those of the serfs of the Middle Ages"; the remaining 30 percent resided in the urban areas, but most of them were "impoverished by low incomes and high cost of living." "The complaint of Africans, however, is not only that they are poor and the whites are rich, but that the laws which are made by the whites are designed to preserve this situation." Here, Mandela had touched on the heart of the matter. Whites were not going to share the governance of the country with Africans, because they were unwilling to share the wealth of the country with them. This was the essence of white supremacy, and it led directly to the lack of human dignity which Africans experienced. "White supremacy implies black inferiority." The only way Africans could overcome poverty and the lack of human dignity was with equal political rights, "because without them our disabilities will be permanent." This was the ANC cause, and, stated Mandela, "It is a struggle of the African people, inspired by their own suffering and their own experience. It is a struggle for the right to live."

Having put the African case so eloquently before the court, Mandela concluded his statement with a personal testimony:

> During my lifetime I have dedicated myself to this struggle of the African people. I have fought against white domination, and I have fought against black domination. I have cherished the ideal of a democratic and free society in which all persons live together in harmony and with equal opportunities. It is an ideal which I hope to live for and to achieve. But if needs be, it is an ideal for which I am prepared to die.

He did not receive a death sentence, but Nelson Mandela has suffered twenty-five years of imprisonment because he has "cherished the ideal of a democratic and free society" in the land of his birth.

On that June day in 1964 when the South African court sentenced Mandela and seven others—Walter Sisulu, Govan Mbeki, Raymond Mhlaba, Elias Motsoaledi, Andrew Mlangeni, Ahmed Kathrada, and Denis Goldberg—it seemed that the government had triumphed over the African people and that they would have to accept a permanent state of inferiority. Their political organizations were shattered, their leaders in jail or in exile, and the people themselves were seemingly cowed by the force and violence which the government had unleashed against them. A period of quiescence ensued for the remainder of the decade which seemed to bear out the facts of a government victory and an African defeat. Yet there was a resilience among the Africans that white South Africans and external observers alike failed to understand, for they were engaged in "a struggle for the right to live."

The first signs that the hiatus in African politics was ending came in the late

1960s when black students, with Steve Biko as their principal spokesman and driving force, launched the Black Consciousness movement. Its objective was to dispel the mood of hopelessness that had settled upon Africans by emphasizing psychological liberation and self-help. Then, in late 1972 and early 1973, a series of strikes by black workers touched off the first wave of serious black labor unrest in the country since 1946. The black resistance built steadily to culminate in the Soweto rebellion of the summer of 1976. On June 16, some 20,000 Soweto students marched in protest against government education policies, to be met by police bullets in which four students died. Turbulence erupted throughout the country, leading to over seven hundred deaths, mostly at the hands of the police, over the next sixteen months. The government responded as it had after Sharpeville—thousands were arrested, African political organizations were banned, and activists fled the country. And, a new political martyr was added to the African cause when the police beat Steve Biko to death during the course of an extremely brutal interrogation.

The mid-70s, however, were different from the early sixties. The government was unable to suppress the African resistance. No period of African political quiescence returned. Instead, new opposition groups and new leaders emerged to take the place of those which the government had banned. Though the upheaval subsided to some extent by late 1977, school boycotts and other manifestations of protest recurred. More importantly for the future, some 6,000 students left South Africa, most of whom joined the exiled ANC and its guerrilla army. Sabotage also increased, including spectacular bombings of the SASOL coal-to-oil plants and a nuclear reactor facility.

The events of the seventies set the scene for the near state of civil war that was to grip South Africa in the mid-80s. Feeling under pressure, both internally and externally, the government implemented ersatz reform measures that included new constitutional dispensations to Indians and Coloreds in 1983 but excluded Africans. It was, however, a case of no sale. The response was the formation of the United Democratic Front (UDF), composed of over four hundred separate trade union, civic, church, and political organizations, and dedicated to achieving "a single, nonracial unfragmented South Africa." In fact, the spirit of the Freedom Charter pervaded the UDF philosophy, for indeed it was to a large extent the ANC in a new guise. While unable to halt the new constitution, the UDF did succeed in establishing a nearly total black boycott of the political institutions it had set up. No longer was the government able to contain the force of African politics. The ferment and activity of the 1950s had re-emerged with even greater vigor. Thus, when the black townships exploded in September 1984 in protest against increased rents and the police responded with harsh tactics of repression, Africans were able to sustain their open revolt against government authority. Not even 2,200 deaths between September 1984 and January 1987, most of them at the hands of the authorities, and two separate states of emergencies deterred the African resistance. Government authority had for the first time collapsed in much of the African urban areas, and no amount of resort to force seemed able to restore it.

As the protest movement moved from strength to strength, the name of Nelson Mandela was heard more and more and ultimately was to become a key symbol of the spirit of African resistance. Just as the government repression of the 1960s had failed to destroy the African struggle for the right to live, so too it had failed to break Mandela. Former fellow political prisoner, S.R. "Mac" Maharaj, writing in 1978, put the matter succinctly: "By incarcerating Nelson Mandela and other freedom fighters," the government "hoped to wipe their names from the lips of the people of South Africa, to bury them living into oblivion. But the name of Nelson Mandela lives on in the hearts and minds of his people. . . ."[8] Mandela was a born leader in prison as well as outside of it. His morale and political beliefs sustained his fellow prisoners and gave them faith in the future. Also, in the aftermath of Soweto the tide of younger prisoners who flowed through prison where Mandela was held came to know him first-hand and carried word of him back to their people when they were released. Out of this came the "Free Mandela" campaign, started in 1980, which came to stand for the African demand for the government to negotiate with them. This truly represented the essence of Mandela's message to the country from the courtroom of the Rivonia Trial.

During most of his imprisonment, little has been heard from Mandela in his own words. Instead those outside have had to rely on the memoirs and testimony of others—fellow prisoners and occasional visitors—about what his thoughts were on the course of events in South Africa. His own voice has on rare occasion, however, been heard. One such instance was after Soweto in 1976. On June 10, 1980, in honor of the twenty-fifth anniversary of the Freedom Charter, the ANC released a message from Mandela, powerful and uncompromising in its content, noting the significance of June 16, 1976 in the land of apartheid, a land of "the rule of the gun and the hangman":

> The verdict is loud and clear: apartheid has failed. Our people remain unequivocal in its rejection. The young and the old, parent and child, all reject it. . . .
>
> The evils, the cruelty and the inhumanity of apartheid have been there from its inception. And all blacks—Africans, Coloureds and Indians—have opposed it all along the line. What is now unmistakable, what the current wave of unrest has sharply highlighted, is this: that despite all the windowdressing and smooth talk, apartheid has become intolerable. . . .
>
> We face an enemy that is deeprooted, an enemy entrenched and determined not to yield. Our march to freedom is long and difficult. But both within and beyond our borders the prospects of victory grow bright.
>
> The first condition for victory is black unity. . . . Our people—African,

Coloured, Indian and democratic whites—must be united into a single massive and solid wall of resistance, of united mass action. . . .

The world is on our side. . . . At all levels of our struggle, much has been achieved and much remains to be done. But victory is certain!

We who are confined within the grey wall of the Pretoria regime's prisons reach out to our people. . . . We face the future with confidence. For the guns that serve apartheid cannot render it unconquerable. Those who live by the gun shall perish by the gun.

Here, then, in this message is one part of the answer as to why and how Nelson Mandela has become the embodiment of the struggle for liberation and the vital symbol of the new society. He possesses an unquenchable spirit. How else could he, after a dozen years of imprisonment, claim that "victory is certain"? He knows what is needed to triumph—black unity and a willingness to use the gun to overcome an entrenched enemy who is determined not to yield. And, he looks to the future for "our people" who are "African, Coloured, Indian, and democratic whites"; South Africa continues to belong "to all who live in it, black and white."

There is also in Nelson Mandela more than a vision and understanding—there is a deep personal commitment to persevere with the struggle, no matter what the price he has to pay. At the Rivonia Trial, he concluded his statement that the "ideal of a democratic and free society" was one "for which I am prepared to die." And he continues to adhere to his principle. On January 31, 1985, South African President P.W. Botha offered to free Mandela provided that he "unconditionally rejected violence as a political weapon." This was reportedly the sixth occasion that he had been offered his freedom, each time with conditions attached. Despite his long imprisonment, he had rejected each offer as he did this one. His daughter Zinzi read this response to a mass meeting in Soweto on February 10, 1985.

I cherish my own freedom dearly, but I care even more for your freedom. Too many have died since I went to prison. Too many have suffered for the love of freedom. I owe it to their widows, to their orphans, to their mothers and to their fathers who have grieved and wept for them. Not only I have suffered during these long, lonely, wasted years. I am not less life-loving than you are. But I cannot sell my birthright, nor am I prepared to sell the birthright of the people to be free. I am in prison as the representative of the people and of your organisation, the African National Congress, which was banned.

What freedom am I being offered while the organisation of the people remains banned? What freedom am I being offered when I may be arrested on a pass offence? What freedom am I being offered to live my life as a family with my dear wife who remains in banishment in Brandfort? What freedom am I being offered when I must ask for permission to live in an urban area? What freedom am I being offered when I need a stamp in my pass to seek work? What freedom am I being offered when my very South African citizenship is not respected?

Only free men can negotiate. Prisoners cannot enter into contracts. . . .

I cannot and will not give any undertaking at a time when I and you, the people, are not free.

Your freedom and mine cannot be separated. I will return.

To be free is what the struggle has been all about. And Nelson Mandela has the wisdom to know that an individual cannot be free if his people do not share in that freedom. Unlike so many others who lay claim to leadership, Nelson Mandela understands that the objective of true leaders cannot be personal aggrandizement but the welfare of the people whom they lead. For this more than any other reason, he has become "the symbol of our struggle," a struggle which knows no national boundaries.

Notes

1. The quotation comes from Oliver Tambo's introduction to Nelson Mandela, *No Easy Walk to Freedom*, edited by Ruth First (London: Heinemann Educational Books, 1965), p. xiii.

2. Mary Benson, *Nelson Mandela: The Man and the Movement* (New York: W.W. Norton & Co., 1986), p. 13.

3. From the introduction to Nelson Mandela, *The Struggle is My Life: His Speeches and Writings* (New York: Pathfinder Press, 1986), p. 2. Unless otherwise noted, all of the direct quotations from Mandela come from this volume. This is also true for quotations from basic ANC documents.

4. Tom Lodge, *Black Politics in South Africa since 1945* (New York: Longman, 1983), p. 43.

5. Tambo, "Introduction," in Mandela, *No Easy Walk*, pp. ix-x.

6. Gail Gerhart, *Black Power in South Africa: The Evolution of an Ideology* (Berkeley: University of California Press, 1978), p. 238.

7. Quoted in Benson, *Nelson Mandela*, p. 104.

8. From Mandela, *The Struggle is My Life*, p. 200.

For Further Reading

Those interested in becoming better acquainted with Nelson Mandela should begin with a study of what he has had to say about the struggle on behalf of his people to which he committed his life. The recently published Nelson Mandela, *The Struggle Is My Life* (New York: Pathfinder Press, 1986) contains not only his principal speeches and writings but also ANC documents which he helped prepare, memoirs of Robben Island by two fellow political prisoners, and a number of photographs. Mary Benson, *Nelson Mandela: The Man and the Movement* (New York: W.W. Norton & Co., 1986) is an authoritative biography, while Winnie Mandela, *Part of My Soul Went with Him* (New York: W. W. Norton & Co., 1984) provides a more personal view of her husband along with the story of her own life. For a broader understanding of the general course of African politics since the past half century, two books are particularly valuable. Gail Gerhart, *Black Power in South Africa: The Evolution of an Ideology* (Berkeley: University of California Press, 1978) is primarily a study of the intellectual dimension of black politics. Tom Lodge, *Black Politics in South Africa since 1945* (New York: Longman, 1983), on the other hand, focuses on black resistance at the local level. Finally, to learn more about South Africa in the mid-1980s, Joseph Lelyveld, *Move Your Shadow* (New York: Times Books, 1985), makes for compelling reading.

NZINGHA, THE WARRIOR QUEEN

By John Henrik Clarke

Queen Nzingha started the liberation movement in Angola over four hundred years ago in the midst of the slave trade and in spite of it. For most of her life she managed to save her country from some of the worst aspects of this tragic business. She knew that this would require more than just fighting. She was a thinker and her wars against the Portuguese were carefully planned. Her intention was to keep the Portuguese from spreading the slave trade from the coast of Angola to the hinterland, the seat of her people's kingdom. She was a legend in her time and she is a legend in our time.[1]

When she was born in 1583, the Portuguese had lost some of their slave trading posts in West Africa and were being pushed out of the Congo. Their large colony in South America, Brazil, was demanding more slaves. These demands along with the demands of the other markets generally supplied by the Portuguese explains, in part, the pressure the Portuguese put on the country that was going to become known as Angola at the time of Nzingha.[2]

Queen Nzingha, born in 1583, was the daughter of Mani A-Ngola, King of Malambo-Dongo. Her mother was one of his favorite wives.[3] Nzingha grew up with a different temperament than the other children of her day. She was alert, with a quickness of mind not often found in children of her age. Her father gave special attention to her education in political, military and religious matters. She was trained in warfare at an early age and it is said that she killed her first enemy at the age of twelve. Her father, Mani A-Ngola had four children, one son and three daughters. He devoted a lot of time to the development of Nzingha, anticipating the responsibility that she would someday inherit.

This responsibility came early in her life. Angola became more important to the Portuguese after they lost their trading connection with the Congo. They wanted to conquer more territory within Angola. This meant war with Nzingha's father, Mani A-Ngola. The struggle was to last five long years during which Nzingha gave birth to a son. In 1617 her father dies without liberating the Dongo region. His son succeeds him and becomes King under the name of Ngola Mani a-Ngola, with the favorable sanction of his jagas or chiefs. To upgrade his popularity and prestige, Ngola hoped to start his reign with a victory over the Portuguese who, at that time, were solidly established along the coast of Angola, in the Massangano, on the Cuanzo river. Nzingha tries to stop the foolishness of an Angolese attack against Portuguese guns. Enraged,

Ngola retaliates by killing Nzingha's child (who had some right to succession). The bitterness between them was never settled.

The campaign against the Portuguese proved not to be successful. They came so close that they took over the 'quilombo,' (the royal dwelling tent) of Ngola and captured and killed his wife.

In Luanda, Portuguese capital of Angola, Joao Correia de Sousa was replacing the departing governor. Being in a strong position, he decides to send emissaries to negotiate a cease-fire. This tactic had worked in the past in the favor of the Portuguese. The purpose of such a cease-fire was twofold. On the Angola side, Ngola had lost three-fourths of his army and could no longer pursue the war. On the Portuguese side, time was needed to consolidate the victory through reinforcements. It was also decided that Ngola would send an ambassador to Luanda to meet with the Portuguese.

The council of elders decided on the astuteness of the Princess Nzingha to carry out the negotiations and Ngola was forced to recall her from her self-imposed exile. He was also forced to make public apologies for past wrongdoings. The ambassador and her entourage started in great pomp towards Luanda. She was received with the highest of protocol and civility. However, during the negotiations she refused the pillows offered to her (which would have put her on a lower station in relation to the governor's throne) and used instead one of her followers as a chair.

She surprised the Portuguese by her quickness of observation and her bright intelligence. She used great caution in negotiations in the name of her brother and demonstrated such knowledge of the politics of negotiations that it stupefied the governor. They agreed on restitution of prisoners and on a promise of an alliance treaty against Cassange. The Portuguese also agreed to abandon Ambaca, the main cause of the war.

Nzingha remained in Luanda until the treaty was ratified. She used that time to study the organization of the Portuguese and to learn their language. The governor enjoyed her company and they spent hours discussing many subjects, including religion. Nzingha explained that she descended from the jaja sect who believed in ancestors' spirits or occult foreseers and that such spirits had to be dealt with with great care. These beliefs horrified the governor who zealously decided to convert the worthy Nzingha to Catholicism.

Nzingha always saw the practical aspect of religion, the jaga's as well as the missionary's, and from the Catholic church she realized the good sense of a centralized organization with one head—one country—and one religion. She also saw a way to capture the confidence of the Europeans. She was, consequently, baptized in the great cathedral of Luanda with the governor and his lady as godparents.

Back in Casassa, she reports to her brother of the events at Luanda. Secretly, however, she vows to take revenge on her brother and to throw the Portuguese back into the sea. The Portuguese refused to evacuate the town of Ambaca, in

ANN NZINGHA
1582–1663: Leader of Female army
in Matamba in the war against the
Portugese.

Figure 2. Queen Nzingha.

the interior, as promised, and Ngola decides to take arms again. Victory was easy for the Portuguese and Ngola was left alone by his jagas who realized the absurdity of him embarking on such a battle. Ngola, defeated, took refuge on the island of Danji where he was found by Nzingha's secret warriors and was forced to poison himself. Now Nzingha and her people, the Jagas, were fully in power in what was now called Angola. At the age of forty-one, in 1623, she became absolute Monarch of her country.[4]

Nzingha was one of a long line of African women freedom fighters who date back to the reign of Queen Hatshepsut in Egypt, fifteen hundred years before the birth of Christ. She belonged to an ethnic group called the Jagas. The Jagas were an extremely militant group, particularly when they were led by their determined and capable Queen Nzingha. Together they formed a human shield against the Portuguese slave trade. Nzingha never accepted the Portuguese conquest of her country and was always on the military offensive. As part of her excellent strategy against the invaders, she forced an alliance with the Dutch intending to use them to defeat the Portuguese slave trade. At her request, she was given a body of Dutch soldiers. The officer commanding this detachment in 1646 said this of her:

> A cunning and prudent virago, so much addicted to arms that she hardly uses other exercises and withal so generously valiant that she never hurt a Portuguese after quarter was given and commanded all her servants and soldiers alike.

She believed that after defeating the Portuguese, it would be easy to surprise the Dutch and expel them from her country. Consequently, she maintained good relationships with the Dutch and waited for the appropriate time to move against them. Her ambition extended beyond the task of freeing her country from European control. In addition to being Queen of Ndanga, she hoped to extend her domain from Matamba in the east, then to the Atlantic Ocean. To this end she was an astute agitator-propagandist, who could easily summon large groups of her fellow countrymen to hear her. In convincing her people of the evil effects of the Portuguese, she would single out slaves and "slave-soldiers" who were under Portuguese control and direct intensive political and patriotic messages in their direction, appealing to their pride in being African. She offered them land and freedom. This resulted in the desertion of thousands of these "slave-soldiers" who joined her forces and presented a serious security problem for the Portuguese. Politically foresighted, competent, self-sacrificing and devoted to the resistance movement, she attempted to draw many kings and heads of families to her cause in order that they might capture the allegiance of their people and recruit them for the defense of her revolution against the presence of the Portuguese.

Her most enduring weapon was her personality. She was astute and successful in consolidating power. She was particularly good at preserving her position by ruthlessly dealing with her foes and graciously rewarding her friends. She possessed both masculine hardness and personal charm, depending on the need and the occasion. Because of these attributes, her supreme leadership was never seriously challenged. Nzingha's ancestry goes back to the end of the fifteenth century when her great grandfather, the Jaga of Matamba, Zimbo or Gola-Zinga, conquered Mdongo and gave it to his son, Ngola Kiluanju, as an appendage of the other territory held by the Jagas. Nzingha often stated that "she was descended from the Kings who had reigned over the whole state before it was split into two parts." She based her later claim to the right of domination over the entire region on her ancestral connections.

When in 1623, at the age of forty-one, Nzingha became Queen of Ndongo, her right to the throne of Ndongo was being questioned in law. The supporters of her late brother did not waste any time in stirring up dissension against her. She began at once to strengthen her position of power. Two of her immediate acts were the reforming of three laws which had veered from their usual cultural integrity. She forbade her subjects to call her Queen. She preferred to be called King and consequently, mainly when she was leading her army in battle, dressed herself in men's clothing.

The Portuguese began to have second thoughts about her. The priests were disappointed because they had seemingly lost the battle to convert her to Catholicism. In fact, they had not lost this battle. She would later pick her own time and reason for joining their church and use it for her own purposes.

In 1645 and again in 1646 she suffered a series of setbacks in her campaign to drive the Portuguese out of Angola. Her sister, Fungi, was taken as a prisoner of war. The Portuguese beheaded her and threw her body in the river. Nzingha began to weigh the merits of her own God, Tem-Bon-Dumba and the God of the Portuguese. Was it possible, she asked, that the Catholic God was stronger? A number of other questions arose from which there were no satisfactory answers. She had heard the Jesuits say that the Christian God was a just person and an enemy of all suffering. Why then did he assist the invaders of her country? Why were the Portuguese building forts in her country without her consent? With these questions still unresolved, she decided to join this religion and test its strength in her favor. For the remainder of her life she used this religion or put it aside, depending on her needs.

In 1659 she signed a treaty with the Portuguese that brought her no feeling of triumph, though time would later reveal that the treaty was political and military strategy at its best, considering that she was now faced with overwhelming odds and superior weaponry. She had fought the Portuguese for most of her adult life. She was more than seventy-five years old now. Most of her faithful assistants and followers had died or given up the long fight.

On December 17, 1663, this great African woman died. This marked the end of one epoch and the beginning of another. It ended the attempts of an outstanding woman to create an empire. With her passing, the planting of the cross and the Portuguese occupation of the interior of South West African began. The massive expansion of the Portuguese slave trade followed this event.

In the concluding chapter of his book about her life and struggles, Professor Roy A. Glasgow has this to say:

> Queen Nzingha symbolized the quientessence of early Mbunbu resistance. She was, from 1620 until her death in 1663 . . . the most important personality in Angola. Nzingha failed in her mission to expel the Portuguese and become Queen of Ethiopia, embracing Matamba (eastern Ndongo) and Ndongo. However, her historic importance transcend this failure as she awakened and encouraged the first known stirring of nationalism in West Central Africa by organizing the national and international (the Moni-Kongo) assistance in her total opposition to European domination.

In the resistance to the slave trade and the colonial system that followed the death of Queen Nzingha, the African women, with their men, helped to mount offensives all over Africa. Among the most outstanding were: Madame Tinubu of Nigeria, Nandi, the mother of the great Zulu warrior Chaka, Kaipukire of the Herero people of South West Africa and the female army that followed the great Dahomian King, Behanzin Bowelle.

In the country south of Angola-Namibia, that the Europeans called South West Africa, another struggle against the Europeans developed in the nineteenth century and lasted until 1919. During this time the country was plunged into a prolonged struggle against one of the strongest colonial powers of that time. German soldiers were mobilized with all modern armaments against the Herero people of South West Africa. This was one of the most costly colonial wars in history.[5]

Notes

1. The important facts about the early life of Queen Nzingha in the early part of this article were extracted from an unpublished manuscript by Professor Roy A. Glasgow, formerly of Boston University, Boston, Massachusetts.

2. "Anne Zingha of Angola," by Ibrahima Baba Kaka, in the series, *Great African Figures*, ABC Publishers, Paris, France and Dakar, Senegal. pp. 11-45.

3. Some books list her birth year as 1882.

4. "Women in Southern Africa," edited by Christine Qunta, Allison and Busby, London, 1987. 00. 49-51, also see, "World's Great Men of Color," by J.A. Rogers, Edited by John Henrik Clarke, Collier-MacMillan, Co., New York, New York, pp. 246-250.

5. "The Destruction of Black Civilization: Great Issues of a Race From 4500 B.C. to 2000 A.D. by Chancellor Williams, Third World Press, Chicago, 1974. pp. 276-289.

MARCUS MOSIAH GARVEY: MAN OF NOBILITY AND MASS ACTION

By James G. Spady

Each cell within the body's growth
Integral to the round of truth
In my island is my art,
Micrococosm of the whole
Microcontinent apart,
Satisfying miniscule

On this island I will dwell
In its limitation, free
Shored within the outerswell
Rounding its identity

R.L.C. McFarlane, *In Search of Gold*[1]

In an attempt to explore the identity of Marcus Mosiah Garvey, it is necesary to go back to the Parish of St. Ann's Bay on the Island of Jamaica. It is there that his formative years were spent. Each microscopic cell within his body's growth is integral to an understanding of the wholeness of his being.

Marcus Mosiah Garvey was descended from the African race. If we define *nobility* as "the condition of possessing characteristics or properties of a very high kind of order," that is the definition that most appropriately describes Garvey. *Man of Nobility!* Another outstanding characteristic of Garvey's life was his ability to inspire mass action. By mass action we mean both an activity involving a mass of people (popular use of the term), as well as the exertion of energy so that it causes a body or mass to have weight in a gravitational field. Mass when used with length and time constitutes one of the fundamental quantities on which all physical measurements are based. According to the theory of relativity mass increases with increasing velocity.

We watched this principle of mass action in operation both in the distant past of Marcus Garvey and his Universal Negro Improvement Association as well as in the last few weeks of Garvey's centenary. (July of 1987) The way in which I saw masses of people participating in public events honoring Jamaica's National Hero and Africa's revered son, is quite reminiscent of those

Marcus Garvey, 1887-1940
U.N.I.A./Marcus Garvey Archives

mass "monster" conventions and meetings in Harlem's Liberty Hall and downtown New York's Madison Square Garden during the 1920's.

Many of the people we talked to on the streets of Kingston and St. Ann's Bay, Jamaica, said they had not seen the kind of mass activities there since Garvey himself walked the streets and byways of that island. What is it about this black Jamaican that appealed and still appeals to so many people worldwide? How did he manage to develop an organizational structure capable of accommodating a world wide mass movement of African people? Why is it that nearly five decades after his death (47 years ago) masses assemble to pay homage to his work? After witnessing these assemblies, observing, analyzing, and reviewing the growing body of literature on the subject, it is clear that two characteristics stand out:

1. Garvey as a man of nobility
2. Garvey as a man of mass action

Obviously one can point to other significant aspects of Garvey but the nobility of his character and the indomitable will to organize the masses to do something for themselves (to act) dominate our impressions of the man. It was the nobility of his character expressed both formally and informally (in dress, manner and action), added to his unusual ability to organize and inspire millions of Africans to engage in mass action, that endeared him in the hearts, minds and souls of millions.

To paraphrase that great Jamaican poet, McFarlane, one could say of Garvey "on this planet he did dwell free of limitations self-imposed."

Let us begin to examine Garvey's early background through his own "Journey of Self-Discovery." The following account appeared in the *Current History* magazine in September, 1923:

"I was born in the island of Jamaica, British West Indies, on August 17, 1887. My parents were black negroes. My father was a man of brilliant intellect and dashing courage. He was unafraid of consequences. He took human chances in the course of life, as most bold men do, and he failed at the close of his career. He once had a fortune, he died poor. My mother was a sober and conscientous christian, too soft and good for the time in which she lived. She was the direct opposite of my father. He was severe, firm, determined, bold and strong, refusing to yield even to superior forces if he believed he was right. My mother, on the other hand, was always willing to return a smile for a blow, and ever ready to bestow charity upon her enemy. Of this strange combination I was born thirty-six years ago, and ushered into a world of sin, the flesh and the devil.

"I grew up with other black and white boys. I was never whipped by any, but made them all respect the strength of my arms. I got my education from many sources—through private tutors, two public schools, two grammar or high

Birthplace of Marcus Garvey, St. Ann's Bay, Jamaica
Photo by Leandre Jackson ˜ 1987, U.N.I.A./Marcus Garvey Archives

schools and two colleges. My teachers were men and women of varied experiences and abilities; four of them were eminent preachers. They studied me and I studied them. With some I became friendly in after years, others and I drifted apart, because as a boy they wanted to whip me, and I simply refused to be whipped. It annoys me to be defeated; hence to me, to be once defeated is to find cause for an everlasting struggle to reach the top."[2]

It may be helpful to know more about this man of nobility and courage. Marcus Mosiah Garvey was born at 32 Market Street, St. Ann's Bay, Jamaica on August 17, 1887. During a recent visit to the site we learned that there is some dispute as to whether the house presently occupied by the Johnson family is the same house in which Garvey was born. One major informant who denies that it is the home in which Garvey first lived is his boyhood friend, Isaac Rose.

"Garvey *was* born at 32 Market Street but that house pull down and they put up another one there. My granduncle's yard was near it on the other side of the road. The house Garvey was born in was an old board-up house. It was blown down in the 1944 storm."[3]

Unfortunately, little scholarship exists on Garvey's early life in St. Ann's Bay. Aside from Garvey's own accounts that appeared in newspapers and magazines, few intimate recollections of his childhood exist. Fortunately, Isaac Samuel Rose shared his knowledge with the world before his transition. In a 1974 interview with Wenty Bowen, 91-year old Rose made the following observations:

> "I know Garvey from a little boy. Me older than him but him bigger than me. He was a big fella. I was schooled at St. Agnes Church School, Priory, St. Ann. I left Priory because I was a strong boy and other boys always try to fight me and I beat them. Then I come to St. Ann's Bay School and there I met with my friend Marcus Garvey. We also went to Methodist Sunday school together. The church we went to blow down in 1903 and was built back in 1905."[4]

Garvey's father "was a deacon of the Methodist Church and was also regarded as a 'Village lawyer' who settled disputes, wrote letters and gave advice to the peasants. He loved reading, had a small library and subscribed to several local newspapers. He was to bequeath his son not only a persistence of character but also a love of books, and his intellectual abilities."[5] We are indebted to Professor Rupert Lewis, Chairman, Department of Government, University of West Indies in Jamaica for unearthing previously unknown details about Garvey's life. Although some publicists of Garvey materials are better known, Rupert Lewis has done a yeoman job of reconstructing Garvey's Jamaican years.[6] Writing in his most recent book, *Marcus Garvey: Anti-Colonial Champion*, Lewis sheds additional light on the town of St. Ann's Bay around the time of Garvey's birth:

"St. Ann's Bay, a small sea-port town with a population of only two thousand people, did not offer much scope for Marcus. Although a sea-port in shipping contact with other Jamaican ports and the outside world, and therefore, more exposed to change than inland rural towns, it still offered little opportunity to young people. It was for instance, overshadowed by Port Maria, which with four shipping companies operating there, was the hub of the banana trade controlled by the United Fruit Company. Port Maria was therefore, in direct contact with Boston, USA, by sea, and the United Fruit Company maintained its own reliable telephone links with important Jamaican towns. Port Antonio was next in significance on the north coast and was reputed to be even bigger than Kingston."[7]

It was in this small sea port town that Marcus was apprenticed to his godfather, Alfred E. Burrowes, who operated a printery. In addition to acquiring skill in this most valued profession, Marcus found Burrowes to be a very strong influence. This is how Garvey described him:

"My apprentice master was a highly educated and alert man. In the affairs of business and the world he had no peer. He taught me many things before I reached twelve and at fourteen I had enough intelligence and experience to manage men. I was strong and manly, and I made them respect me. I developed a strong and forceful character, and I have maintained it still."[8]

Burrowes appears to have served as Garvey's private tutor as well as the one responsible for providing an excellent training in printing. Note, Garvey describes himself as having a strong and forceful character even as a teenager. His thirst for knowledge was in part fulfilled by reading extensively in his father's personal library. He also had an uncanny ability to get those around him to engage in discussions that would allow him to become better informed.

At the age of fifteen he took on the responsibility of caring for his mother, Sarah, and his sister, Indiana. Rupert Lewis claims that Garvey went to Kingston as early as 1906[9] after working for a short while in Port Maria. He continued to work as a professional printer, first with the Government Printing Office and "later as a compositor in the printing section of P.A. Benjamin Ltd., a firm of manufacturing chemists which at that time had a good export trade with Central America, Cuba and other West Indian islands."[10]

It was not long before Garvey was elected Vice-President of the Kingston Typographical Union. His career was moving upward rapidly. It wasn't long before he became a foreman. It was during this period that he had to make one of his most crucial decisions. Should he join those employees who had only recently organized a trade union or should he remain with management? Garvey opted to join the side of the strikers. This was a turning point. Since early childhood he had been developing strong leadership characteristics. But the biggest test of the strength of his noble character occured on so crucial an issue as the rights of workers. Garvey stood firm in his convictions just as he had seen his father do during his own formative years.

His activities in Kingston during the 5-6 year period (1905 or 1906 to 1911) still require much more examination as does all of his early life in Jamaica. What is known of this period in Garvey's life helps to shed additional light on the development of his political consciousness. The fact that he was elected an Assistant Secretary of the National Club in April, 1910, is an indication of his involvement in this domain.

The National Club was founded a year earlier on March 3, 1909. It was Jamaica's first nationalist political organization. Its founder was Solomon Alexander Gilbert Cox known as "The People's Sandy." Having read law at Middle Temple in London, Cox was deputy clerk of the Court for St. James Parish. The *Gleaner* of 1910 describes Garvey's role at a "tumultous meeting" of the National Club.

Robert A. Hill, Editor of *The Marcus Garvey and Universal Negro Improvement Association Papers* provides a brief account of this important National Club, including its objectives.

"It was created to expose and redress the abuses of crown colony government in Jamaica, focusing on coolie immigration, the judicial system, education, and the autocratic methods of the governor, Sir Sydney Oliver. It proposed to develop a 'more liberal policy' for Jamaica by contesting the seats of members in the Legislative Council who in the general election of 1911 did not pledge to support the policy of the National Club. By this means it hoped

U.N.I.A. Black Cross Nurses Pass the Government Printing Office
Photo by Leandre Jackson ″ 1987 U.N.I.A./Marcus Garvey Archives

to control a political majority in the council. The National Club's manifesto declared that only native born Jamaicans could be members and that each member must pledge himself to Jamaican self-government. The media organ was *Our Own*, a bimonthly that appeared from July 1910 to July 1911. The title of the journal was influenced by the Irish Sinn Fein movement (in Gaelic Sinn Fein means *"Our Own"*).[11]

Amy Jacques Garvey, the wife of Marcus and author of *Garvey and Garveyism*, credits the National Club with providing Garvey his first experience in Newspaper publishing and campaigning for a political candidate. As important an event as this is in his life there is still no definitive essay evaluating the role of the National Club in developing and certainly expanding his political consciousness. Fortunately, Mrs. Garvey asked a former club member, J. Coleman Beecher, just what he was like during this crucial period. Beecher replied, "He was fiercely proud of being black. He carried a pocket dictionary with him and said he studied three or four words daily, and in his room he would write a paragraph or two using these words." Mrs. Garvey gained another account from S.M. DeLeon who recalled that Garvey had "a mature mind from the time he came to Kingston in his teens. He was always busy, planning and doing something for the underprivileged youth. Uplift work we called it, and he had us in the shaft with him."[12]

Both DeLeon (later representative of the UNIA in London) and Beecher (circulation manager of the *Black Man* newspaper in Jamaica), identify characteristics in Garvey that are described by numerous informants describing his later activities in the Universal Negro Improvement Association. Isaac Rose, Garvey's boyhood friend, declared: "Marcus Garvey was a fellow like this; all the time when I meet him he wear jacket and everytime, his two jacket pockets full of papers, reading and telling us things that happen all over the world. Him know I don't know, but him telling us. He was very interested in world affairs."[13]

Another manifestation of Garvey's interest in world affairs is his forays into Central and South America. Prior to leaving Jamaica, Garvey published a short lived journal called *The Watchman*. Both *Our Own* and *The Watchman* have names that reveal Garvey's own remarkable life. It is quite likely that some of Garvey's early contacts in Panama sprang from labourers linked to the National Club in Jamaica. Although the official news organ, *Our Own*, had a circulation of 3,000,[14] it is probable that its distribution went beyond the confines of Jamaica. What is certain is that Garvey's extensive experience in the Government Printing Office provided him not only with technical expertise in the trade but was an invaluable source of information since he was in a position to read the various publications released by that office.

Although the *Jamaica Times Supplement* of May, 1910 reports that "Mr. Marcus Garvey has issued a pamphlet in which he upholds the policy of Mr. Cox and deals with the press which he declares is now the enemy of the people," recent efforts to locate this pamphlet at the National Library of Jamaica and elsewhere proved fruitless. This pamphlet would be useful in determining the extent to which his views on mass-based media had been formulated in 1910. Did Garvey perceive of anti-colonial media as crucial to gaining power in a dominated society? Who were the principal Jamaican pamphleteers in Jamaica who advocated an anticolonial position? To what extent did Dr. Robert Love's *Jamaica Advocate* influence Garvey's own string of newspapers.

In order to trace the genesis of Garvey's philosophy of media, it is necessary to look closely at his early periodicals. How do they reflect an anti-colonial stance? Rupert Lewis sees Dr. Robert Love as a worthy precursor to Garvey who is the highpoint in a continuum beginning in 19th century Jamaica. "Dicussion of Love's work in Jamaica" Lewis argues "is important to show that anti-colonial politics was alive and that black spokesmen such as Love set an example for Garvey. There is a direct line in post-emancipation and black political struggle from George William Gordon and Paul Bogle, to Bedward [Alexander] the evangelical leader, and to the secular spokesman, Dr. Robert Love. This, of course, reflects the progressive movement in Jamaican politics which Garvey's work continued."[15]

Dr. Robert Love, Editor, *Jamaica Advocate*
U.N.I.A./Marcus Garvey Archives

Dr. Robert Love was a native of Nassau, Bahamas, who became a priest in the Anglican church, a physician, and an outstanding political figure and journalist. His newspaper, the *Jamaica Advocate* (1894-1905) inspired Marcus Garvey at an early age. Later in life Garvey was to recall "much of my early education in race consciousness is from Dr. Love. One cannot read his *Jamaica Advocate* without getting race consciousness. If Dr. Love was alive and in robust health, you would not be attacking me, you would be attacking him."

We must now determine to what extent Love's Jamaica Cooperative Association (1897) and People's Convention (1898) influenced Garvey's own Universal Negro Improvement Association and International Conventions. Such a study should assist in gaining a more complete understanding of the philosophical concepts underlying Garvey's institution-building process. The fact that love "could not be bribed" and it was "impossible to intimidate him" must have made an impression on young Marcus Garvey.

Anxious to ameliorate the conditions in Jamaica and elsewhere, Garvey embarked upon a journey that, according to Amy Jacques Garvey, carried him to "Guatemala, Panama, Nicaragua, Bocas-del-Toro, then down to South America, Ecuador, Chile and Peru."[16] Wanting to do something for his people and not having the capital, Garvey went to visit an uncle in Costa Rica who got him a job as a timekeeper on a fruit farm.

This was a period when there was a large West Indian migration to Central and South America. Amy Garvey informs us that "In all of these republics Garvey tried to organize the West Indian immigrants and called on the British Consul to protect them. Invariably he was told that the Consul was there to see after the interest of His Majesty's government and did not intend to disrupt friendly relations with these republics because of West Indian migrants."[17]

J. Charles Zampty, who later became Auditor-General of the U.N.I.A., recalls meeting Garvey during this period. They met in Panama. Zampty recalls that Garvey spent a considerable amount of time preaching to and organizing many interested parties. He already had strong views on colonial exploitation and racist degradation. Because of the blatant expressions of racism in the Canal Zone, Garvey addressed that question directly.[18] This was a few years prior to the establishment of the U.N.I.A.

In the city of Colon, Garvey published the newspaper, *La Prensa* just as he had edited *La Nacionale* in Costa Rica with Simon Aguileria. Amy Garvey said that despite Garvey's efforts "the people did not realize the importance of maintaining a paper and an organization for their own protection and interest. He kept trying and working but the authorities harassed him as an agitator. After two years he felt sick at heart and worn out with malaria and he returned to Jamaica. He related the sufferings of the West Indian workers, who had asked him to see what their home governments would do in their behalf. He headed a delegation that put the workers' problems before the governor of Jamaica; the governor said that the workers should return home if conditions were that bad and not create any incidents for His Majesty's government. When Garvey asked him what the workers could expect at home in the ways of jobs, the governor had no suggestions to offer."[19]

Failing to receive a civil response from His Majesty's representative on the Island of Jamaica, Garvey reasoned that he could be more effective in the Metropolitan Center—England. Both his wife Amy Jacques and his sister's daughter, Ruth Peart Prescott, claim that Garvey went to England with assistance from his sister Indiana. One account claims, "Indiana sent for Marcus to come to England after his return from Central America and so they were together once more."[20] It is generally agreed that upon his arrival Garvey gained employment along the docks of London, Cardiff and Liverpool.

There is evidence that not all of his time was spent at the dock of the bay. Writing from 176, Borough High Street in the southeast section of London, Garvey addressed Sir Frederic George Kenyon, Director of the British Museum in the following manner (6 October 1913):

> "Dear Sir,
> I hereby beg to make application to be admitted as a permanent reader in the Reading Room of the Museum for the purpose of research and reference.
> Enclosed please find testimonial from the Editor of "The African Times and Orient Review."[21]

Garvey concludes "I am a journalist and a student." Duse Mohammed's letter of support for Garvey recommended him "as being a fit and proper person to use the Reading Room of the British Museum."[22]

Interestingly, Garvey asked to see the works of a prominent black author, Dr. Edward Wilmot Blyden of St. Thomas (author of *Christianity, Islam and the Negro Race*). He was the former Liberian Secretary of State and President of Liberian College. It is possible that he either learned of Blyden's writings through the *Jamaica Advocate* where reprints of Blyden's work, that of J.E. Casely-Hayford and others appeared,[23] or from his friend Duse Mohammed Ali. Ali edited and published *The African Times and Orient Review* where Garvey assisted as well as contributed articles for about a year. One article, "The British West Indies In the Mirror of Civilization: History Making by Colonial Negroes," prompted the distinguished Afro-American intellectual William H. Ferris to issue a favourable commentary. "As one who knows the people well," wrote Garvey in this article "I make no apology for prophesying that there will be a turning point in the history of the West Indies; and that the people who inhabit that portion of the Western Hemisphere will be the instruments of uniting a scattered race who, before the close of many centuries, will found an Empire of the North today. This may be regarded as a dream, but I would point my critical friends to history and its lessons. Would Caesar have believed that the country he was invading in 55 B.C. would be the seat of the greatest Empire of the world? Had it been suggested to him would he not have laughed at it as a huge joke? Yet it has come true. England is the seat of the greatest Empire of the world, and its King is above the rest of monarchs in power and dominion. Laugh then you may at what I have been bold enough to prophesy, but as surely as there is an evolution in the natural growth of man and nations, so surely will there be a change in the history of these subjected regions."[24]

This Garvey stated with assurance. His extensive knowledge of revolts throughout the West Indies had already been demonstrated earlier in the article. Why were they revolting in the USA and the Caribbean? "The slaves were inhumanly treated, being beaten, tortured and scourged for the slightest offense. One of the primitive methods of chastisement was 'dance to the treadmill,' an instrument that clipped off the toes when not danced to proper motion."[25] It is the awesome burden of this knowledge that informed Garvey's decision to organize a mass movement.

His extensive contacts with African and West Indian seamen during his two year stay in England and elsewhere on the European continent proved to have been one of the most significant long term relationships he established. Many of these same seamen would show up at ports with *Negro World* in their waistbands, just a few years afterwards.

After reading Booker T. Washington's Autobiography, *Up From Slavery*, Garvey wanted to know where was the Black Man's army and navy. That book had a profound impact on him. Boarding a ship at Southampton, Garvey later recalls that his "young ambitious mind led me into flights of great imagination." No longer was he satisfied to remain in England. "My brain was afire. There was a world of thought to conquer." How could he integrate this world of thought and action?

The genesis of the Universal Negro Improvement Association is graphically described in Garvey's own words: "Where did the name of the organization come from. It was while speaking to a West Indian Negro who was a passenger on the ship with me from Southampton, who was returning home to the West Indies from Basutoland with his Basuto wife, that I further learned of the horrors of native life in Africa. He related to me such horrible and pitiable tales that my heart bled within me. Returning to my cabin, all day and the following night I pondered over the subject matter of that conversation, and at midnight, lying flat on my back, the vision and thought came to me that I should name the organization the Universal Negro Improvement Association and African Communities (Imperial) League. Such a name I thought would embrace the purpose of all black humanity."[26]

Rupert Lewis quite astutely observes "The UNIA at its inception, therefore, was not the consequences of the experiences of only one country. The fact is imperialism since the nineteenth century, had literally been savaging non-white peoples throughout Africa the Caribbean and Asia. Movements against this savagery were developing among the colonial peoples everywhere. The UNIA was a response to this process."[27]

In viewing the UNIA, as a mass based anti-colonial movement, one is able to situate it within the context of a worldwide decolonization process. In this, Garvey is seen as a champion of the anti-colonial cause concerned with race, caste and class issues. Throughout his career Garvey behaves as a man of mass action fully cognizant of the responsibilities and burdens that come with such a leadership role. His movement developed in response to the longings of African masses worldwide.

Wherever Garvey went, he found the black man at the very bottom of the political, social and economic heap. He held extensive dialogues with ex-soldiers who had fought in West India Regiments used by the colonial powers to maintain the suppression of Africans and seize their territories. These treacherous acts of neo-slavocracy greatly incensed him and he worked hard to gain more knowledge about the African conditions.

Not nearly enough attention has been given to the crucial role those men of the high seas played in expanding the activities of the U.N.I.A. They got messages into areas sealed off by the official colonial powers. Scholars of this mass based movement must be far more attentive to the far-flung activities of the 'seamen' element of mass black movements. They were couriers who were courageous and committed. Many a port city was captivated by the message, *"One God, One Aim, One Destiny."*

Although considerable attention has been directed toward the study of Garvey, almost nothing has been done to increase our knowledge of him through those who participated in the formation of the UNIA. They were Garvey's friends from the Government Printing Office, Enos J. Sloly; Richard A. Scarlett, a shopkeeper from Port Maria, who Garvey met during his printing days, V.A. Campbell, printer/civil servant who later became a Postmaster General and Archdeacon Graham of Port Maria; Dawson, a hotelier of Princess Street, Kingston. Informal meetings were held at 49 Princess Street where they had meals. The hotel proprietor was a Mr. Watson.

A July 1914 *Gleaner* article said, "During his stay abroad, Mr. Garvey visited Paris, Madrid, Glasglow and Edinburgh, and met Sir Sydney Oliver, Lord Balfour of Burleigh and Mr. J. Pointer, M.P." More work is yet to be done on his stay outside of England during the period 1912-1914.

On August 1, 1914 the Universal Negro Improvement and Conservation Association and African Communities League was launched. Singificantly, August 1st is traditionally celebrated as Emancipation Day marking freedom from enslavement in the British West Indies. (Blacks in Philadelphia celebrated August 1st in solidarity with West Indians during the 19th century.) The general objects of the UNIA were as follows:

- To establish a Universal confraternity among the race.
- To promote the spirit of race pride and love.
- To reclaim the fallen of the race.
- To administer and assist the needy.
- To assist in civilizing the backward tribes in Africa.
- To strengthen the power of independent African States.
- To establish Commissionaries of Agencies in the principal countries of the world for the protection of all Negroes, irrespective of nationality.
- To establish Universities, College and Secondary Schools for the further education and culture of the boys and girls of the race.
- To conduct a worldwide commercial and industrial intercourse.

Pastor Frank Davis, U.N.I.A. Special Liaison, Kingston, Jamaica, at Heroes Park
Photo by Leandre Jackson ¨ 1987 U.N.I.A./Marcus Garvey Archives

There were, however, local Jamaican objectives.

- To establish educational and industrial colleges for the further education and culture of our boys and girls.
- To reclaim the fallen and degraded (especially the criminal class) and help them to a state of good citizenship.
- To administer to and assist the needy.
- To promote a better taste for commerce and industry.
- To promote a universal confraternity and strengthen the bonds of brotherhood and unity among the races.
- To help generally in the development of the country.[28]

Additional light is shed upon Garvey's plans when one reads a letter to Travers Braxton of the Aborigines Protection Society in London. In this letter he states, "I leave Jamaica on a lecturing tour throughout North, South and

Central America, as also Canada and the West Indies, in the fall of the present year. I may be away from Jamaica for about six months. We publish a fortnightly journal named, "The Negro World." The first appearance will be next week."[29] (His plans to publish a *Negro World* journal did not materialize. However, a *Negro World* newspaper was published four years later.)

Garvey made a strong appeal to Booker T. Washington to assist him, especially in establishing educational facilities. Washington was quite responsive to Garvey's appeal. On one occasion he said, "I have read what you say with reference to the advance being made in educational facilities for the Negroes of that section. I hope that when you come to America you will come to Tuskegee and see for yourself what we are striving to do for the colored young men and women of the South. . . . We shall be very glad to receive copies of *The Negro World*, and shall be glad to send you in exchange the *Tuskegee Student*, published at this institution."[30]

In less than a year, flyers were circulated regarding the establishment of an Industrial Farm and Institute. W.B. Hopkins gave a lecture on the "Economic Value of Native Food." In the midst of all of the activities, Booker T. Washington died. A U.N.I.A. Memorial meeting was held at Collegiate Hall on "The Life and Work of Booker T. Washington."

By early 1916, Garvey was planning earnestly for a trip to the U.S.A. Finally, around March 7, 1916 the S.S. Tallac left the port of Kingston. It arrived in Belize, British Honduras, by the 10th. A 15 March departure places it in New York City on March 24, 1916. Garvey's long awaited trip to the U.S.A. had been completed.

One of the early observers of Garvey was the veteran journalist, Duse Muhammad Ali's associate, John E. Bruce "Grits." Bruce later served on the staff of *The Negro World* and the *Daily Negro Times*. He vividly recalls the experience.

"When Mr. Garvey first came to this country from his island home in Jamaica, B. W. I, I was among the first American Negroes on whom he called. I was then residing in Yonkers on the Hudson, New York. He was a little sawed off and hammered down Black man, with determination written all over his face and an engaging smile that caught you, and compelled you to listen to his story. Like all other Negroes who feel deeply the injustices of the white man, whether they are committed by individuals or by the state, he had a grievance and I listened with interest to its recital (which is much too long to repeat here); but the substance of which was, that the Negroes in the West Indian Island, from which he came, were not receiving fair play at the hands of whites, either in the matter of education or in the industries, and that the school facilities were inadequate, workers under paid, thus preventing them from doing for themselves what they would like to do to improve their educational and economic condition."[31]

In describing Garvey the orator, Bruce said, "Mr. Garvey is a rapid fire talker, and two reporters are necessary to keep up with him at his meetings here in Liberty Hall on Sunday nights when he speaks to audiences of 5,000 or more. I was able to catch enough from his rapidly spoken story, however, to convince me that he had a real mission and I promised him such aid in the furtherance of his plan as I could give him morally and substantially."[32]

Among the early conferees sought by Garvey was W.E.B. DuBois, by this time the editor of *Crisis*, official organ of the National Association for the Advancement of Colored People (NAACP). Garvey's note to DuBois read in part, "I called in order to have asked you if you could be so good as to take the 'chair' at my first public lecture to be delivered at the St. Mark's Hall, 57 W. 138th Street on Tuesday evening 9th May at 8 o'clock."[33] Dr. DuBois regretfully refused the invitation because he was to be out of town.

Armed with a list of contacts provided by John E. Bruce, and others, Marcus Garvey embarked upon an extensive tour that, according to his own account, carried him to 38 states. He stayed in the homes of both prominent and not so prominent black people. As in the case of his visits to Ecuador, Costa Rica, England, Panama Canal Zone and elsewhere, Garvey learned first hand the plight of his people. No black leader had conducted such a survey of this diverse population. These associations established during those first nine (9) months in the U.S.A. were invaluable in the growth and development of his organization.

These lectures were successful by most standards. However, he did not receive unanimous support. In less than four months after he began the lecture tour, a group of Jamaicans issued a letter denouncing Marcus Garvey. They stated, "We have attended his lectures, found them to be pernicious, misleading, and derogatory to the prestige of the Government and the people." Garvey was accused of "drawing a deplorable picture of the prejudice of the Englishman in Jamaica against the blacks, portraying hypocrisy and deceit in his [the Englishman's] attitude towards the blacks, and stated his preference for the prejudice of the American to that of the Englishman."[34] The letter was posted from Philadelphia and appeared in the *Jamaica Times*, Oct. 7, 1916. Among the signees were: Father Raphael of the Greek Orthodox Catholic Church, Dr. Uriah Smith, Ernest P. Duncan, Ernest K. Jones, H.S. Boudin, Philip Hennings, Henry Booth and others.

Interestingly, this denouncement occurred long before the much publicized W.E.B. DuBois attack on Garvey. Dr. Irene Diggs, Professor Emeritus of Sociology and Anthropology at Morgan State University, a former research associate and co-author with DuBois, has contributed to an understanding of DuBois and Garvey.[35] Amy Jacques Garvey provides additional insight into Garvey's experiences in Jamaica prior to coming to the U.S.A.

"Garvey spent many months of hardship and disappointment" she states "unable to get the masses to unite and cooperate for their own good, but still he plodded on. He was up against the plutocracy, the land barons, the white shipping and fruit companies (who made millions yearly out of the island and Africa) and newspapers, whose policy was to make the island safe for big business at any cost, as well as the stockholders."[36]

After eight months of traveling and lecturing among Blacks in the United States Marcus Garvey made a strong contrast between the Afro-American and West Indian positions. Because so little attention is given to what Garvey himself had to say about his early experiences in the U.S.A. and the genesis of the U.N.I.A., it is necessary to quote him directly. In a superb article "West Indies in the Mirror of Truth," that appeared in the *Champion Magazine*, January, 1917, Garvey said:

"I have traveled a good deal through many countries, and from my observations and study, I unhesitantly and unreservably say that the American Negro is the peer of all Negroes, the most progressive and the foremost unit in the expansive chain of scattered Ethiopia. Industrially, financially, educationally and socially, the Negroes of both hemispheres have to defer to the American brothers, the fellow who has revolutionized history in race development inasmuch as to be able within fifty years to produce men and women out of the immediate bond of slavery, the latchets of whose shoes many a 'favored son and daughter' has been unable to loose.

As I travel through the various cities I have been observing with pleasure the active part played by Negro men and women in the commercial and industrial life of the nation. In the cities I have already visited, which include New York, Boston, Philadelphia, Pittsburgh, Baltimore, Washington and Chicago, I have seen commercial enterprises owned and managed by Negro people. I have seen Negro banks in Washington and Chicago, stores, cafés, restaurants, theaters and real estate agencies that fill my heart with joy to realize, in positive truth, and not by sentiment, that at one center of Negrodom, at least, the people of the race have sufficient pride to do things for themselves."[37]

Garvey was balanced in his reporting on the American Negro. Speaking forthright, he added "The acme of American Negro enterprise is not yet reached. You still have a far way to go. You want more stores, more banks and bigger enterprises. I hope that your powerful Negro press and the conscientious element among your leaders will continue to inspire you to achieve; I have detected, during my short stay, that even among you there are leaders who are false, who are mere self-seekers, but on the other hand, I am pleased to find good men and, too, those whose fight for the uplift of the race is one of life and death."[38]

He went further by naming persons whom he felt were capable as conscientious workers/leaders. Garvey did not perceive as leaders those who were not hard workers as well. Clearly he was of the school of thought that felt one led by example. He listed John E. Bruce, Dr. R.R. Wright, Jr., Dr. Parks, Dr. Triley, Rev. J.C. Anderson, and Ida Wells Barnett.

By way of contrast he described the situation in his native region, "The West

Indian Negro who has had seventy-eight years of emancipation has nothing to compare with your progress. Educationally, he has (and this is the exception) made a step forward, but generally he is stagnant. I have discovered a lot of 'vain bluff' as propagated by the irresponsible type of West Indian Negro who has become resident of this country—bluff to the effect that conditions are better in the West Indies than they are in America. Now let me assure you, honestly and truthfully, that they are nothing of the kind. The West Indies in reality could have been the ideal home of the Negro, but the sleeping West Indian has ignored his chance ever since his emancipation, and today he is at the tail end of all that is worth while in the West Indies. The educated men are immigrating to the United States, Canada and Europe; the laboring element are to be found by the thousands in Central and South America. These people are leaving their homes simply because they haven't pride and courage enough to stay at home and combat the forces that make them exiles. If we had the spirit of self-consciousness and reliance, such as you have in America, we would have been ahead of you, and today the standard of Negro development in the West would have been higher. We haven't the pluck in the West Indies to agitate for or demand a square deal and the blame can be attributed to no other source than indolence and lack of pride among themselves."[39]

It is crucial to understand that Marcus Garvey's extensive lecturing, touring and analysis of the black man's domain provided him background to build a mass action movement in the United States. More accurately, his understanding of the national constituency and the potential support base amongst the blacks here encouraged Garvey to establish his international headquarters for a worldwide movement in Harlem, New York.

During 1916 and 1917 Garvey addressed numerous audiences throughout the U.S.A. In doing so he was able to make lasting friendships. One of his main appearances was at Big Bethel A.M.E. Church in Atlanta, Georgia where the Rev. R.H. Singleton, D.D. exhorted his audience: "This is the only chance to hear a great man who has taken his message before the world. Come out early to secure seats. It is worth travelling 11,000 miles to hear." Perhaps the one speech in 1917 that served as a general catalyst for his later organizational activities is one given on July 8, 1917 at Lafayette Hall. Presiding over this meeting was Chandler Owens, Editor of the *Hotel Messenger*, a magazine representing the Headwaiters and Sidewaiters. (Never had waiters/porters been as well represented as by A. Phillip Randolph and Chandler Owens.)

Let us turn to that Sunday afternoon speech by Marcus Mosiah Garvey. It was hotter than July. An outlandish attack had been waged against the Blacks of East St. Louis, Illinois. Among this big audience were police lieutenants, secret-service men, detectives, etc. Here is what they all heard from Garvey's mouth.

"The East St. Louis Riot, or rather massacre, of Monday [July] 2nd, will go down in history as one of the bloodiest outrages against mankind for which any class of people could be held guilty. (Hear! hear.) This is no time for fine words, but a time to lift one's voice against the savagery of a people who claim to be the dispensers of democracy. (cheers) I do not know what special meaning the people of East St. Louis have for democracy of which they are custodians, but I do know that it has no literal meaning for me as used and applied by these same lawless people (hear! hear!) America, that has been ringing the bells of the world, proclaiming to the nations and the people thereof that she has democracy to give to all and sundry, America that has denounced Germany for the deportation of the Belgians into Germany, America that has arraigned Turkey at the bar of public opinion and public justice against the massacre of the Armenians, has herself no satisfaction to give 12,000,000 of her own citizens except the satisfaction of a farcical inquiry that will end where it began, over the brutal murder of men, women and children for no other reason than that they are black people seeking an industrial chance in a country that they have laboured for three hundred years to make great . . . At one time it was slavery, at another time lynching and burning, and up to date it is wholesale butchering. This is a crime against the laws of humanity; it is a crime against the laws of the nation, it is a crime against nature, and a crime against the God of all mankind. (cheers)."[40]

Is it any wonder that on July 2, 1918, exactly one year from that East St. Louis Massacre, a Certificate of Incorporation of the Universal Negro Improvement Association was filed and recorded in New York City. This document has a revered place in Pan African history. Six persons served as directors until its first annual meeting. They were: Isaac B. Allen, Irene M. Blackstone, Walter J. Conway, Carrie B. Mero, Harriet Rogers and Marcus Garvey. Conway was attorney and Counselor at Law for this group. Interestingly, out of six, half were women. This was quite unusual for that time.

Later in themonth, 31 July 1918, yet another important corporate entity was established. It was to be called the African Communities Leagues, Inc. The signers of this document were clearly driven by the need for economic self-reliance:

> "We, the undersigned, all being persons of full age, and at least two-thirds being citizens of the United States, and at least one of us a resident of the state of New York, desiring to form a Stock Corporation, pursuant to the provisions of the Business Corporation Law of the State of New York, do hereby make, sign, acknowledge and file this certificate for that purpose, as follows.[40A] The Commissioner of Deeds was James Watson, a Jamaican.[41]

It was also in 1918 that the constitution and Book of Laws governing the U.N.I.A. began with its Preamble: "The Universal Negro Improvement Association and African Communities League is a social, friendly, humanitarian, charitable, educational, institutional, constructive and expansive society, and is founded by persons, desiring to the utmost, to work for the general uplift of the Negro Peoples of the world. And the members pledge themselves to do all in their power to conserve the rights of their *noble race* and to respect the rights of all mankind, believing always in the Brotherhood of man and the Fatherhood of God. The motto of the organization is 'One God! One Aim! One Destiny!' Therefore let justice be done to all mankind, realizing that if the strong oppresses the weak, confusion and discontent will ever mark the path of man, but with love, faith and charity towards all, the reign of peace and plenty will be heralded into the world and the generations of men shall be called blessed."

This Preamble was learned by its members like citizens of all nations. It is significant to point out that Garvey saw those of African descent in the western hemisphere as part of a nation. A study of the key documents: Papers of incorporation, constitution, national prayer, etc., all connote the oneness of the Negro Peoples of the world.

Significantly many of those persons Garvey met when he first came to the United States played key roles in staffing the rapidly growing institutions. For instance, John E. Bruce not only authored the nation's prayer but also contributed to and assisted in editing the *Negro World* newspaper. Was it not that extraordinary orator and seer Hubert Harrison who became an editor of the *Negro World*? Harrison is also responsible for providing Garvey a platform at the Bethel A.M.E. Church where the founding session of the Liberty League of Negro Americans was held.[42]

What is most interesting is that, although Garvey had been in the U.S.A. for two years, he still had not planned to make it his home. Tony Martin, author of *Marcus Garvey, Hero: A First Biography* states:

> "As 1918 approached, Marcus decided to organize a branch of the U.N.I.A. in New York. He did not hold office in this branch, since he was still planning to return to Jamaica. Socialist and Republican Party organizers tried to form this U.N.I.A. branch into a unit of their respective parties and wrecked it in the process. So Marcus tried again. The same thing happened a second time. This time, thirteen of his followers encouraged him to stay and lead the New York branch himself. He probably did not require too much persuading by this time, and so the U.N.I.A. in New York was off in a big way by 1918. At this point Kingston gave way to Harlem as U.N.I.A. headquarters."[43]

Once Marcus Garvey decided to stay in Harlem and build a mass organization inclusive of Africans from around the world, the organization structure was put in place. A coherent and cohesive ideology of "Africa for the Africans. Those at Home and Those Abroad" became an organizing instrument capable of attracting millions. It was not that Garvey had to walk throughout the land as some "Black Moses." His message of African redemption and self reliance resuscitated the longings of Africans worldwide. There had never

U.N.I.A. Consultants to Liberia, 1921
U.N.I.A./Marcus Garvey Archives

been such a mass movement capable of unifying dispersed Africans into a whole.

Although Booker T. Washington had advocated self-reliance his major institutional effort was Tuskegee Institute, an educational entity located in rural Alabama. Given the fact that the U.N.I.A. was established in the U.S.A. in the midst of World War I, just as a large black population shift occurred from South to North, ex-servicemen returning to assume their rightful places as men/citizens, Caribbean immigration inclining and settling in large metropolises and city dwellers anxious to *make it*, it is not surprising that this movement grew in leaps and bounds. Had Garvey aided in creating an elitist organization like some of those already available for colored persons, it could not have had the appeal.

In interviewing numerous older members of the Universal Negro Improvement Association we asked why did so many people join at that time. Perhaps, it is most simply stated by Thomas W. Harvey, who joined a few years after the U.N.I.A. was incorporated in New York. "Most people can't understand why so many Negroes flocked to the U.N.I.A. It is very simple, the Negro heard in

Salute to the Women's Auxillary of the U.N.I.A.
U.N.I.A./Marcus Garvey Archives

the U.N.I.A. what he wanted to hear. The U.N.I.A. said things to the Negro that he wanted somebody to say long ago."[44]

> A Bureau of Investigation Report on the movement is instructive.
> "Re: Negro Agitators of the 3rd Precinct. Capt. Ward of the 3rd Precinct Police Station today sent me confidential employee of his, who has been attending street meetings of negro agitators in the Harlem negro district (7th Ave. above 125th St.).
> Informant turned over to me a report, which he had made containing an abstract of the remarks of the speakers on various evenings at these street corner meetings. He also gave me a copy of the "Negro World," a newspapers whose editor has been active in speech-making on the street corner. I turned all these papers over to Mr. Stephenson of this office with the request that he examine them carefully and advice me if he deemed the matter of sufficient importance to warrant further action on the part of this office."[45]

The above document represents the high resolution intelligence-gathering operations of the American, British, German, French, Jamaican, and other neo-colonial and colonist nations of that time.

Just as the forces of stabilization were coalescing around the Universal Negro Improvement Association under Garvey's leadership, forces of de-stabilization, espionage, and disunity began to mount a campaign against Garvey and the U.N.I.A. One need only review the mountain of documents now being assembled worldwide to gain some insight into the extent to which Garvey was the concern of white and black leadership during the first quarter of the 20th century.

Operating under the principal doctrine that all African people were members or potential members of the U.N.I.A., Garvey and his leadership cadre did not exercise adequate measures of screening, monitoring and curtailing activities of its constituted body. At the organizational level, a solid structure was in place to accommodate a stratified population. However, the rapid membership growth in some cases exceeded the leadership growth. There simply was neither time nor personnel to exercise rigid controls at the leadership level. In addition, the multi-faceted world African problem was overwhelming. Given the range of problems the U.N.I.A. attempted to address, they did remarkably well.

Operating both domestically and internationally, Garvey and his colleagues had the foresight to elect three delegates to attend the Peace Conference at Versailles in France. Why should the U.N.I.A. participate in this conference? Garvey argued: "Every oppressed group of people will be represented in some way or other at the Peace Conference in France . . . Let there be no compromise. Let us unite to get all that is ours. At the Peace Conference great issues are to be decided, and the Negro must prepare to take his standing without faltering."

The Negro Race was to have Asa Phillip Randolph, Ida Wells Barnett and Eliezer Cadet to represent them at Versailles. Neither Barnett nor Randolph were able to secure a passport. A. Phillip Randolph was active in the militant wing of the socialist movement at the time centered around Eugene Debs. Although Wells-Barnett is less well known, her activities were of equal concern to those charged with the responsibility of issuing passports. Ida Wells Barnett had initially met Garvey during one of his forays into Chicago. Her husband, a prominent attorney, brought him home for dinner.[46] Ida Wells Barnett was a vigorous crusader against injustices, especially lynching. Her book *A Red Record: Tabulated Statistics and Alleged Cause of Lynchings in the United States* is one of the most vivid accounts of lynching ever done. Her scathing articles denouncing the 1892 lynching of 3 young black businessmen in Tennessee resulted in an angry mob wrecking her press. She was physically armed as she went about her job of getting the truth to the people. After the hoodlums destroyed her press, Barnett continued her militant writings in *The New York Age.*

One can not tell the story of Marcus Mosiah Garvey and his efforts to unite Africans worldwide without including the valiant efforts of countless persons of African descent who were driven like Garvey to do something for self. Great leadership is always connected to a strong support network.

The rapid growth of the Universal Negro Improvement Association during the period 1918-22, is a story requiring far more space than allowed in a discussion of a biographical nature, albeit a *collective* biographical history. However, it is safe to state that the single most rapid growth period of this organization occurred during the first four years of its existence in Harlem.

Utilizing his extensive background in printing, Marcus Garvey and his media corps organized a massive membership recruitment campaign in 1919. It netted millions worldwide. What did the instruments of contact say?

"ALL NEGRO COMMUNITIES OF THE WORLD (of America, Africa, The West Indies, Central and South Americas) Are Requested To Form Themselves Into Branches of The Universal Negro Improvement Association and African Communities' League of the World.
For the Consolidation of The Sentiment and Aspirations of the 400,000,000 of The Negro Race Organize For Racial Progress, Industrially, Commercially, Educationally, Politically and Socially. Organize For The Purpose of Founding A Great Nation."

It was during this period that Garvey married an earlier Jamaican associate who had assisted in founding the U.N.I.A.—Amy Ashwood. This public ceremony took place at Liberty Hall (headquarters of the U.N.I.A.) on 25 September 1919. Although this marriage was short lived, Amy Ashwood has recounted her perception of those experiences in her still unpublished manuscript. In addition, Tony Martin should be releasing his *Amy Ashwood Garvey: Pan Africanist, Feminist and Wife No. I.* in 1988 or 1989.

1919 was also the year that the U.N.I.A.'s mammoth Black Star Line Steamship Corporation project was initiated. This project was capitalized by black people and the mere launching of such an ambitious endeavor stimulated considerable interest amongst Africans worldwide. Counter actions were mounted even before the first ship was purchased. Originally known as the *Yarmouth* it was soon christened, the *Frederick Douglass*. Other ships included The *Shadyside*, an excursion boat and the *Kenewha*, renamed *Antonio Maceo* in honor of the Afro Cuban hero of the Cuban Spanish American War. Two of the ships made trips to Jamaica, Cuba and various ports in the U.S.A.

A soundless movie was done of the Blackstar Line Project. Often when Garvey or other speakers visited to address an audience, visuals were used to enhance the appearance. Although most investors never saw the ships, such a major undertaking appealed to the broad masses of people. An investment in the Black Steamline was conceived of as an investment in strenghthening commercial trade between West Indians, Continental Africans and Afro-Americans. There was also a prestige value attached to this enterprise. The assertion that black people invested in the Black Star Line so that they could make a wholesale return to their native land is without evidence. An examination of the stock certificate issued indicated that investors were appropriately apprised of their investments. They knowingly took risks as any investor does. The publicity given to the launching of a black shipping line was converted into increased membership. The U.N.I.A. was very effective in parlaying news accounts (bad and good). They effectively propagated their ideas.

Among the other business enterprises established under the aegis of the African Communities League was the Negro Factories Corporation. Tony Martin has estimated that the varied business agencies of the U.N.I.A. employed over a thousand people around New York in the early 1920's.[47] If this estimate is near accurate, one can say that thousands of blacks were employed in U.N.I.A. businesses worldwide. In many towns, U.N.I.A. run businesses were the only black businesses operated there. In a recent conversation with the daughter of the former President of the Ambler (Pa.) branch of the U.N.I.A., we learned that her father had operated the former U.N.I.A. grocery store for many years after the breakup of a formal body there. Nearly all of the prominent black businessmen in this town were members of the organization.

How were these millions of blacks informed of the other activities? One of the major ways Marcus Garvey and the U.N.I.A. said what blacks "wanted somebody to say long ago," was through their own newspaper, the *Negro World*. What an appropriate name! Carrying news in English, French and Spanish greatly enhanced its appeal to Africans dispersed in several colonized zones. Its contributors and subject matter were of international origin. Many of the articles and poems in the *Negro World* were by members in such

Black Star Line Ship
U.N.I.A./Marcus Garvey Archives

Garvey with Federal Marshals
U.N.I.A./Marcus Garvey Archives

divisions as Louisville, Kentucky, Camaguey, Cuba, Republic of Colombia, Norfolk, Virginia, New Bedford, Mass., Burlington, New Jersey, San Francisco, California, Key West, Florida, and Philadelphia, Pa. There has never been a black periodical before or since *Negro World* that attracted such a diverse range of black writers and subscribers. Bold in its ideas and ideals this newspaper instilled racial pride, engaged in mass education on domestic and international issues (with a large segment being on Africa and the Caribbean), provided a range of literary/artistic materials,[48] propagated, international consciousness, women's issues, and Pan African unity. Moreover, it stands today as the single most important source for serious scholars of this mass movement.

We have addressed the relationship between the U.N.I.A. and organized religion, the pedagogy of the U.N.I.A., the U.N.I.A. and African Nationalism, the Women of the U.N.I.A., the poetry of Marcus Garvey, the U.N.I.A./ACL

Garvey and Colleagues
U.N.I.A./Marcus Garvey Archives

as an economic institution, all these and more in numerous publications over the last 15 years.[49]

The body of materials on Garvey (print and electronic) is growing by leaps and bounds. The centenary of his birth has generated a whole new library.

As we conclude this chapter on Marcus Mosiah Garvey some attention must be drawn to his last years in America. In this essay we concentrated on the shaping of his consciousness in the West Indies, Central and South America and Europe. Those early years remain the least explored area in the growing body of Garvey scholarship.

By 1924 the U.N.I.A. was beset with problems both internally and externally. Garvey has addressed these issues quite cogently in *The Philosophy And Opinions Of Marcus Garvey* edited by his second wife, Amy Jacques Garvey. It is necessary to comment on the role she played not only in parenting his two sons (Marcus, Jr. and Julius), but also in remaining an activist over 50 years. It was she who collected, organized, edited and had published 3 volumes of his philosophy and opinions. In addition she and Thomas W. Harvey sometime individually and often together, provided a large body of primary and secondary sources for many writers. Harvey provided U.C.L.A. issues of the *Negro World* for microfilming. He answered hundreds of letters from black and white students, scholars and lay persons.

One of the most sensitive, perceptive and scholarly essays on Amy Jacques Garvey is co-authored by Rupert Lewis and Maureen Warner-Lewis. They state: "Amy Jacques Garvey was a vigorous upholder of self-respecting nationalism. But this tradition had been shrouded in lies, ridicule and silence, or had been attacked at all levels of the educational system. As such, she was made to feel marginalised. Those who knew her, however, recognized that she was one of the finest embodiments of the black radical tradition in the twentieth century."[50]

From the time Amy Jacques and Marcus were married in July 1922, and even earlier when she was his secretary, they suffered many bizarre experiences. On the other hand, they shared some of the highest peaks of the movement. In our discussions she often discussed the annual international conferences of the U.N.I.A., the undisputed largest Pan African conferences ever held. There were many who attended as invisible men and women. Their identity was concealed because of the ubiquitous presence of hostile forces.

The photograph of Marcus Garvey riding through the streets of Harlem in full regalia, brilliantly accountred in the costume of a noble prince, has almost become an icon of the quite egalitarian annual conventions. It was during the 1920 convention that he was *elected* Provisional President of Africa. There were potentates who at least in title were top persons in the organization. Thousands came from around the world to participate in a democratic forum addressing the issues of primary concern to Africans though not exclusively so. Eamon deValera received very warm support for the Irish struggle against British domination. He in turn gave support to the colonized people in Africa. Garvey's international activities were far more complex than is usually imagined.

At the very height of this mass movement, the court of law became a new battle ground to wage war against the U.N.I.A. and Marcus Garvey. 1922 saw the arrest of Garvey and other Black Star Line officers on charges of using the mails to defraud. It was also the year of his much publicized meeting with Edward M. Clarke, the Imperial Wizard of the Ku Klux Klan. Problems began to mushroom everywhere. Once Garvey returned from a successful tour of Costa Rica, Guatemala, Panama and Jamaica, enemies of the U.N.I.A. intensified their efforts to remove him from the scene. Arrest, trial, courtroom battle!

U.N.I.A. Stalwarts L-R standing—Raymond Kelly, Thomas W. Harvey, Rev. J.C. Tucker
Center—William Sherril, Naomi Taylor
U.N.I.A./Marcus Garvey Archives

"The crux of the prosecution's case was that Garvey and his co-defendants had, knowingly and with criminal intent used the mails to promote the sale of Black Star Stock, after they had become aware that the financial condition of the venture was hopeless. The evidence in support of this was, to say the least, extremely thin."[51]

Although the alleged mail fraud case was the one that resulted in Garvey's jailings, there were many other cases that drew upon the resources, personnel and spirits of Garvey and the U.N.I.A. Writing in *Race First: The Ideological and Organizational Struggles of Marcus Garvey and the Universal Negro Improvement Association*, Tony Martin outlines some of the legal battles:

"The means by which the United States was finally able to remove Garvey from the American scene once and for all was through the mechanism of the courts, and more specifically through the celebrated mail fraud trial in 1923. The conviction handed down at this trial was affirmed by the United States Circuit Court of Appeals in 1925. This case was the most important one but by no means the only one involving Garvey in the United States. From fairly early in his American period, he and his concerns were practically continuously involved in litigation of some sort or another. There were libel suits, some against him, some initiated by him. There were divorce suits and countersuits involving Amy Ashwood Garvey. There were suits brought by Black Star Line and other employees for arrears of pay. There was the income tax case which was not officially declared *nolle prosequi* until 1932. There were cases against former employees for embezzlement or other dishonesty. Garvey had no friend in the courts, as almost all these cases were determined in a manner unfavorable to him."[52]

At the beginning of the mail fraud case, Garvey had as Chief counsel, Cornelius McDougald; Vernal Williams was the back-up counsel. After one day Garvey dismissed McDougald and decided to argue his own case. There is considerable discussion about the wisdom of this decision. However, it does seem likely that the prosecuting state would not have stopped short of immobilizing Garvey.

The activities of a "Marcus Garvey Must Go" group certainly helped to establish a hostile climate in which to hear the case. Martin describes these campaigners as "a temporary alliance of convenience between black socialists, represented principally by A. Philip Randolph and Chandler Owens, some black Urban League officials, the NAACP, and miscellaneous other black integrationists. It represented a formidable coalition of the most influential black integrationist leaders in the land."[53] One cannot ignore the fact that there were employees who had double loyalties, others who refused to segregate the funds received from varied UNIA/ACL enterprises. Although the U.N.I.A.'s auditor general, J. Charles Zampty, capably evaluated accounting procedures, it could not guard against dishonesty.

Finally, Tony Martin's discussion of the indictments is informative: "The ten indictments contained thirteen counts and alleged a scheme to defraud by means of sending certain letters through the mail. Some counts also alleged a conspiracy on the part of the defendants to implement the same scheme. Garvey was convicted on only one count, namely that for the purpose of furthering his scheme, he caused to be sent, on or about December 13, 1920, 'a certain letter or circular enclosed in a post-paid envelope addressed to Benny Dancy, 34 W. 131 Street in New York City. The prosecution produced an empty envelope bearing the Black Star Line stamp and claimed that a particular letter promoting the Black Star Line had been posted in it. Dancy, a Pennsylvania station cleaner, testified that government agents had come to his house and he had handed over the envelope to them there. He could not remember what had been in that particular envelope though he had often received mail from the Black Star Line, the U.N.I.A., and the Negro Factories Corporation. Some of this mail he did not read, but some of what he read, he was sure said "invest more money in The Black Star Line for the case [sic] of purchasing bigger ships and so forth."[54]

An empty envelope! That is the basis of Garvey's conviction. He was sentenced to a maximum of 5 years and fined a thousand dollars. He actually served less than three years, his sentence commuted by President Calvin Coolidge, and he was deported on December 2, 1927.

In a recent conversation with long time U.N.I.A. General Counsel and the President of the Marcus Garvey Memorial Foundation, Atty. Joseph Bailey, it was suggested that this entire case needs to be evaluated. Ideally, Atty. Bailey and a team of legal specialists should undertake this task. Because, even in 1987, that remains one of the least comprehended aspects of Garvey's life.

When he returned to Jamaica he was as enthusiastically welcomed by the masses as his departure from New Orleans had occasioned. Garvey survived the federal sentence still a hero to millions.

His message of "Africa for the Africans" continued to motivate those on the continent. The Nigerian, Nnamdi Azikiwe, a major leader of the West African independence movement noted: "The motto of Garveyism appealed to me— 'One God, One Aim, One Destiny!' And I resolved to formulate my philosophy of life, so far as was practicable towards the evangelization of fatherhood, universal brotherhood and universal happiness." Adam Clayton Powell, a young Harlemite studying at Colgate University when Garvey was deported, was to become the first Black Congressman from that area. "Nobody has influenced me in my philosophy of life, my attitudes, my thinking, my daily expressions more than Marcus Garvey" said Powell "He was and continues to remain, to me and millions of black people in the world, a giant of inspiration."

In Kingston, Jamaica, Garvey entered yet another phase of his life while maintaining his role in the U.N.I.A. Within two years after his return he had

Garvey's London Office, West Kensington, London
U.N.I.A./Marcus Garvey Archives

organized the 6th Annual Convention of the U.N.I.A. Len Nembhard has summarized this convention in a chapter "Great Convention of 1929,"[55] The details of his post 1927 activities in Jamaica can be found in Amy Jacques Garvey's "The Political Activities of Marcus Garvey in Jamaica" (*Jamaica Journal*, June 1972) and Rupert Lewis' recent book, *Marcus Garvey Anti Colonial Champion* (1987). "The Year 1929 was one of the most striking and agonizing 365 days of Garvey's stay in Jamaica" writes Mrs. Garvey. "Subtle, silent, systematic efforts were made to crush him and destroy his movement, when he would not heed the overtures of agents sent to plead with him (for his own good) to give up the fight to change the condition of the black masses."[56] She continues her survey of the period. "Feeling the mighty hand of Imperialism clothed in legal authority, Garvey decided to form a political party, in order to change conditions. He and his colleagues named it "The People's Political Party." (9 years before Norman Manley founded the P.N.P.). "As leader of the party, Garvey spoke at Cross Roads Square on the 10th September 1929, presented the manifesto and elaborated on all proposed reforms. A few days later he was arraigned in court on a second contempt charge, before the same Chief Justice and two other Judges. The basis of the charge was the tenth plank of the manifesto." [A law to impeach and imprison judges who, in disregard of British Justice and constitutional rights, dealt unfairly][57]

This was one of many acts initiated by the Colonial Office and carried out through the good offices of the local judiciary. Of the above charge Garvey was declared guilty and "sentenced to three months' imprisonment, and a fine of one hundred pounds. He served the prison term at the Spanish town prison, as a First Class Misdemeanant."[58]

Garvey was elected to the Kingston and St. Andrew Corporation Council, took his seat after imprisonment, despite efforts to unseat him. "Unable to do anything for the parishes as he was not in the Legislative Council, and being hampered in the Corporation Council in getting his resolutions through, and put into practical use, Garvey, in June 1930 formed the workers and laborers Association, to see what organized effort could do on their behalf."[59]

The People's Political Party, organized by Garvey, was the first political party to enter elective politics in Jamaica. That act alone could have earned him the status of a National Hero. In talking with Garvey's campaign manager, Vivian Durham, one is able to discern the level of sophistication Garvey exercised in his campaign. Clearly more work needs to be done on this most important aspect of Garvey's public career.

Dr. Ken McNeil the distinguished plastic surgeon and son of Garvey's colleague, the Hon. E.A. McNeil of St. Catherine Parish, recently published a most interesting booklet, *Garvey and His Men*. In this he speaks of Garvey's major accomplishments in Jamaica. "To accompany all this" he adds, "he developed a highly sophisticated organization and built in components for financing. There were regular fund raising activities at Edelweis Park which varied from vaudeville with visiting and local dancing girls, theatrical presentations by Harold and Trim, Ranny Williams and other well known artists of the time. There were amateur boxing contests, and a wide variety of party games and other forms of entertainment. These programs were widely advertised in the *Blackman* Newspaper and in pamphlets."[60]

In reconstructing the life of "Marcus Mosiah Garvey: Man of Nobility and Mass Action," one of the most helpful research aides is the voluminous body of printed material he generated. As a master printer he constantly drew upon the early training old man Burrowes provided during his early apprentice. Rupert Lewis points out that Garvey's newspaper *Blackman* occupied the position of "chief representative of Kingston's banana leaders before the May 24th and 27th strike demonstrations occurred. The newspaper was well prepared for this role as it had been waging a systematic onslaught against the bad conditions under which these workers loaded the boats."[61]

Throughout the 1930's Garvey kept the Anti-colonial struggle in the forefront of his own personal and organizational activities. So much is Garvey an organizational man that it is difficult to determine when he is operating outside of that context. In August 1934 Garvey hosted the 7th International

Convention of The Negro Peoples of The World With the U.N.I.A. The "Five Year Plan" was announced at this convention. Delegate Charles L. James of Gary, Indiana (now President General of the U.N.I.A.) and Delegate Johnson of Kingston proposed that the Negro People should capitalize the program at $300,000,000. Such an undertaking did not materialize. With the great depression still impacting on a segment of the black population and some others existing at a "poverty" level, such an ambitious program could not practically have been implemented. Yet, the mere foresight in recognizing the sort of massive recovery Africans needed was commendable.

Just prior to the 1935 elections which McNeil theorizes he would have won, Garvey moved to London, England. Garvey explained the move to England thus: "London is the Metropolitan City of the world. As London goes, so goes the world . . . Being conscious of this mighty power of England, we of the Negro race find it necessary to be as near the source of thought as possible, so that any effort aimed at the Negro for good or ill can be readily dealt with" . . . Garvey saw this "new international campaign under the auspices of the Universal Negro Improvement Association, for Negro solidarity—a solidarity that is supposed to embrace every conscious unit of the black race in every part of the world."[62] In assessing the Last London Years, Rupert Lewis states "To grasp the actual relations, we have to move outside the U.N.I.A. itself to consider the West African Students Union, the Colonial Seamen's Union [African and West Indian Seamen] and West Indian Labor in revolt in the late 1930's. Garvey's contact with the West African Student Union was Ladipo Solanke. Mrs. Amy Jacques Garvey relates that at times her husband financed their publication called WASU and that this contact was an underground one."[63] Just how many more contacts with Africans were underground we may never know. However, in "Africa and the Garvey Movement in the Interim Years," Arnold Hughes states: "While it is no easy task to assess the overall influence of Marcus Garvey on the evolution of Africa's political consciousness, there is sufficient evidence available to suggest that during the years immediately following W.W.I., the U.N.I.A. aroused widespread interest and enjoyed a strong measure of support in black Africa and even after the swift decline in Garvey's political fortunes in the late twenties, many Africans remained true to his ideals."[64]

At the U.N.I.A. Convention in Toronto, 1937, two new orders were inaugurated: the Sisterhood of African Charity and the Brotherhood of African Fellowship. At the conclusion of this event Garvey inaugurated the very first thoroughly organized School of the U.N.I.A., known as the School of African Philosophy. This leadership training program produced all of his successors (1940-87). The 1937 class had 10 graduates, 1937—7 grads. Much more attention has been given to these experiences as well as the last years of Garvey's life and the decade following his death in my book. *Marcus Garvey, Africa and the U.N.I.A.* In January 1940 he had a stroke. On June 10, 1940 Marcus Mosiah

Garvey died. Forty-seven years later his spirit and the great movement of the U.N.I.A. lives on.[65]

George Padmore, a Pan African pioneer from Trinidad, prematurely reported Garvey's death. Notices appeared worldwide including the *Jamaica Gleaner* and the leading Black American papers. Why did Padmore act so irresponsibly given his long term career as a media specialist?

Garvey's secretary, Miss Daisy Whyte, contacted the U.N.I.A. and they assumed the responsibility for burying him.[66] This side of the story is rarely told. Thomas W. Harvey and Ethel Collins *deported* themselves admirably on behalf of the race. As the centenary of Garvey's birth is being celebrated one can only reflect on Garvey's words: "Look for me in the whirlwind of the storm. Look for me all around you; for with God's grace I shall come and bring with me countless millions of Black slaves who have died in America and the West Indies and the millions in Africa to aid you in the fight for Liberty, Freedom and Life."[67]

Acknowledgements

In preparing this chapter, "Marcus Mosiah Garvey: Man of Nobility and Mass Action," many individuals and institutions were helpful. They include Patricia Shakir, Jean Harvey Slappy, Sherry Moore, Marcus Garvey Memorial Foundation, Atty. Joseph A. Bailey, Alma Golden, Louis Jones, Leandre Jackson (Photo Editor), Dr. Ken McNeil, Profs. Rupert Lewis and Maureen Warner Lewis, Drs. Patrick Bryan and Edward Brathwaite; all of the University of the West Indies, Patricia Green, Dr. Derrick Mobley, Richard Aldrich, Leslie Burrs, Marguerite Curtin, Michael "Ibo" Cooper, Michael Henry, Minister of Culture, Government of Jamaica, St. Ann's Parish Library (Jamaica), Jean Blackwell Hutson, Dr. Michael Winston, Curtis Blalock, Isaac and Elaine Foy, Kenny Gamble, Leon Huff, Dr. Claude Offord, Betty J. Curtis, Dr. Charles H. Wesley, Mrs. Dorothy Porter Wesley, Hilbert Keys, Amy Jacques Garvey, The Bailey Sisters. The People of St. Ann's Bay and Kingston, Jamaica, U.N.I.A./A.C.L. Archives, Raymond Trent, Troy Albany, Pamela Petty, Rene Gonzalez, Brian Cirksey, Giles Wright, Reginald Maddox, University of Pennsylvania, Institute of Jamaica, National Library of Jamaica, Free Library of Philadelphia, McFarlane, Jamaica Information Service, Nadine Wilkinson, Maxime McDonough, Ruth Prescott, Dr. Royal Colle, Hon. Thomas W. Harvey, Jamaica Archives, Spanishtown Jamaica, and Estelle James.

Notes

1. R.L.C. McFarlane, "His Island, His Art," *In Search of Gold*, (Poems, 1983-86), Kingston, Jamaica, Classique Press, 1986, p. 9.

2. Marcus Mosiah Garvey, "The Negroes' Greatest Enemy," *Current History*, Vol. 18, September, 1923, pp 951-957.

3. Wenty Brown, "Isaac Rose: Garvey's Boyhood Friend," *Jamaica Journal* (Quarterly of the Institute of Jamaica), Vol. 20, No. 3, August-October 1987, p. 73.

4. Ibid. p. 74.

5. Rupert Lewis, "Marcus Garvey: Anti-Colonial Champion," *The Daily Gleaner* (Kingston, Jamaica), 24 May 1987, Section C. p. 1.

6. Although Rupert Lewis has provided a considerable number of substantive articles on Garvey, almost all of them were published in Jamaica and are not generally known in the United States. They include, "A Political Study of Garveyism in Jamaica and London, 1914-40," Msc Thesis, University of the West Indies, Jamaica, 1971. "Political aspects of Garvey's work in Jamaica 1929-35"; *Jamaica Journal*, March/June, 1973, pp 30-35, "Amy Jacques Garvey—A Political Portrait," *Xaymaca* (Sunday *Jamaica Daily News*) July 29, 1973, "Robert Love—A Democrat in Colonial Jamaica," *Jamaica Journal*, August 1977, pp 59-63, "Garvey's regional influence," *Xaymaca (Sunday Sun)* 19 August 1979, "Garveyism, Communism and the Jamaican Struggle" *Jamaica Daily News*, 18 August 1980, pp 10-11, "El Nacionalismo anticolonial en al pensamiento de Marcus Garvey," Analas del Caribe I, Casa de las Americas, Havana, 1981, 99-113; and *El Caribe Contemporáneo* 7, October, 1983, pp 99-112. Rupert and his wife, Professor Maureen Warner Lewis—co-edited *Garvey, Africa, Europe, the Americas*, Institute of Social and Economic Research, Jamaica, 1986.

7. Rupert Lewis, *Marcus Garvey: Anti-colonial Champion, London, England.* Karis Press, 1987, p. 23.

8. Marcus Garvey, "The Negroes' Greatest Enemy,"

9. Lewis, p. 23, (Robert Hill claims 1905 as the date of Garvey's arrival in Kingston).

10. Ibid.

11. Robert A. Hill, ed. *The Marcus Garvey and Universal Negro Improvement Association Papers*, Vol. 1, (Los Angeles, California) UCLA Press, 1983, p. 21.

12. Amy Jacques Garvey, "The Early Years of Marcus Garvey," *Marcus Garvey and the Vision of Africa*, Ed. John Henrik Clarke with the assistance of Amy Jacques Garvey, NY. Vintage Books, 1974 pp 33-34.

13. Wenty Brown, "Isaac Rose: Garvey's Boyhood Friend," p. 74.

14. Lewis, p. 43.

15. Ibid, p. 25.

16. Amy Jacques Garvey, p. 34.

17. Ibid.

18. James G. Spady, Interview with J. Charles Zampty, 8/71.

19. Amy Jacques Garvey, p. 35.

20. Beverly Hamilton, "Ruth Prescott—Garvey's Neice Remembers," *Flair Magazine*, August 17, 1987, p. 13.

21. Robert Hill, p. 25.

22. Ibid, p. 26.

23. Ibid, p. 31.

24. Ibid, p. 29.

25. Ibid.

26. Amy Jacques Garvey, ed., *Philosophy and Opinion of Marcus Garvey*, Vols. I and II, Atheneum, NY, 1969 pp 126-127.

27. Lewis, p. 49.

28. Hill in Clarke's *Marcus Garvey and the Vision of Africa*, p. 60.

29. Robert A. Hill, *The Marcus Garvey and UNIA Propers*, Vol. I p. 52.

30. Ibid p. 71.

31. John E. Bruce, Manuscript-Typescript on Garvey in Bruce Collection The Schomberg Center for Research in Black Culture, New York Public Library.

32. Ibid.

33. Herbert Aptheker, ed., *The Correspondence of W.E.B. Dubois*, Vol. 1, [Amherst, Mass] University of Mass. Press, 1973. pp 214.

34. Robert Hill, *The Marcus Garvey Papers*, pp 196-197.

35. Irene Diggs, "DuBois and Marcus Garvey," *A Current Bibliography on African Affairs*, Vol. 6. No. 2, Spring, 1973.

36. Amy Jacques Garvey, *Garvey and Garveyism*, N.Y. The Macmillan Co., 1970—pp. 12-13.

37. Marcus M. Garvey, "West Indies in the Mirror of Truth," *Marcus Garvey and the Vision of Africa*, ed. John H. Clarke, p. 89.

38. Ibid.

39. Ibid. p. 90.

40. Robert Hill, *The Marcus Garvey and U.N.I.A. Papers*, Vol. 1, p. 213.

40A. Ibid.

41. James S. Watson was a Jamaican by birth. He became Chief of the corporation tax and contract divisions of the House, Grossman and Vorhares Law Firm. Watson was the first known black judge of New York's Municipal Court. Both James Watson and his daughter, Barbara were associated with the U.N.I.A. (see Robert Hill, the *Marcus Garvey and U.N.I.A. Papers* and James G. Spady's *Marcus Garvey, Africa And The U.N.I.A.: A UMUM Perspective on Concentive Activity In The Pan African World*.

42. See Joel A. Rogers, *World's Great Men of Color*, Vol. II for a more extensive biographical file of Hubert Henry Harrison.

43. Tony Martin, *Marcus Garvey Hero, A First Biography* (Dover, Mass.) The Majority Press, 1983, pp. 46-47.

44. James G. Spady, Interview with Thomas W. Harvey 2/78, Z5929XY, Marcus Garvey Memorial Foundation, U.N.I.A./Marcus Garvey Archives. Thomas W. Harvey became a successor to Garvey and one of the most vital persons in U.N.I.A. history. His involvement as Commissioner of the State of New York, a leader in the Rehabilitating Committee following Garvey's death and President of the organization during the curcial period of the 50's to the 70's make him eligible for a full biography.

45. Robert Hill, *The Marcus Garvey and U.N.I.A. Papers*, pp. 281-282.

46. Alfreda M. Duster, *Crusade For Justice: The Autobiographyy of Ida B. Wells* (Chicago and London), University of Chicago Press, 1970, p. 380.

47. Tony Martin, *Marcus Garvey, Hero; A Biography*, p. 54.

48. Tony Martin, Literary Garveyism, (Dover, Mass.) The Majority Press, 1983.

49. James G. Spady, *Marcus Garvey, Africa and the U.N.I.A.*, "Dr. Nnamdi Azikiwe: Portrait of a Pan African Giant," *Black Collegian*, Dec. 1980/Jan. 1981, *Africa* (London, 1980), *Current Bibliography on African Affairs, Garvey's Voice, Philadelphia Tribune, Presence Africaine, Philadelphia New Observer* and UMUM Publications. For those interested in a complete bibliography of my writings on Garvey and African Nationalism, you may write to: James G. Spady, P.O. Box #15057, Phila., Pa. 19130.

50. Rupert Lewis and Maureen Warren-Lewis, "Amy Jacques Garvey," *Jamaica Journal*, August-October 1987, p. 43.

51. Adolph Edwards, *Marcus Garvey 1887-1940*, London, England, New Beacon Publications, 1967, p. 18.

52. Tony Martin, *Race First* (Westport, Connecticut), Greenwood Press, 1976, p. 191.

53. Ibid pp. 315-316.

54. Ibid pp. 192-193.

55. Len Nembhard, *Trials and Triumphs of Marcus Garvey* (Kingston, Ja.) 1940.

56. Amy Jacques Garvey, "The Political Activities of Marcus Garvey, *Jamaica Journal*, Vol. 6, No. 2, June 1972, p. 2.

57. Ibid p. 3.

58. Ibid.

59. Ibid p. 4.

60. Ken McNeil, O.J. Fr. e.s., *Garvey And His Men: The Leadership Struggle, 1930*, Kingston, Classique, 1987 p. 5.

61. Rupert Lewis *Marcus Garvey: Anti-Colonial Champion*, pp. 258-259.

62. Marcus Garvey "Our New Start, *The Black Man*, Vol. I, No. 7, June, 1935, p. 1.

63. Rupert Lewis, "The Last London Years, 1935-1940," *Marcus Garvey and The Vision of Africa*, ed. John H. Clarke p. 33.

64. Arnold Hughes "Africa and The Garvey Movement In The Interim Years," Lewis and Lewis p. 111.

65. James G. Spady "The Spirit Lives," (an essay saturated in the musical tradition of the composers Kenny Gamble and Leon Huff and the Reggae performers "Third World" (Columbia, 1987) Centennary Journal/Monograph, 1987 (Phila.) U.N.I.A./ACL.

66. Daisy Whyte, Letter to Amy Jacques Garvey, 12 Jyuly 1940. Amy Jacques Garvey/U.N.I.A. Collection, Fisk University.

67. Speech by Marcus Garvey from Atlanta Federal Prison, 1927.

AN OPEN LETTER TO TOUSSAINT L'OUVERTURE OF THE SAN DOMINGO REVOLUTION

By Wilson Harris

Essex, England
AUGUST, 1987

Dear Toussaint,

A brief word about myself. I was born in South America and have voyaged to Europe where I now live. The twentieth century has been, and still is, a turbulent century, more turbulent perhaps than you would have dreamt. And sometimes it seems humanity has lost faith in everything except material goods, material prosperity. Some years ago I read CLR James's richly documented and dramatic study THE BLACK JACOBINS which tells of your rise to power in the last decade of the eighteenth century. You emerge from this as one of the most remarkable and enigmatic characters in history.

I hope you will permit me the liberty of asking certain questions of you.

I trust that in framing and discussing these within my own turbulent century and against the background of yours a mediated response may emerge . . . Such a response I believe is born of the friction of generations each man secretes in himself. It is born equally of the intuitive and the voyaging spirit. It is an inner translation of motivations suspended in history and of misgivings, doubts, paradoxes that are shared by individual persons across the boundaries of time and place.

In essence I am concerned with the psychology, the psyche, of revolution (if I may so put it). Few actors on the stage of politics are better placed than you to unmask a divide between an inner dialect or dialectic of the soul and an outer code or costume that seeks to represent or mimic the soul of revolution. One need only note the peculiar stresses involved in the designing of your letters and communications. So peculiar they lay bare I think something akin to trauma yet hidden potential within the body of a revolutionary age.

It is logical by every count to identify your fate—your rise to power, your seizure by the French, your transportation to France and death in a prison there—with a revolutionary age when one bears in mind that the uprising in Haiti coincided with great turmoil in Europe, with the French Revolution, and with the rise of Napoleon. It coincided as well with the expansion of the British Empire and with the malaise of Southern prosperity and power in America that set in train events that were to culminate in the Civil War in the mid-nineteenth century.

Toussaint Louverture.

Does not revolution imply the eruption of trauma (sometimes severe trauma born of the poisons of a ghetto-fixated world), the eruption as well of hidden potential to break that trauma and to affect the body of a civilisation?

I come back to the matter of your letters of administration, the communications that were addressed to members of the broken plantocracy of the island, to foreign powers, to the Directory in Paris and to various persons. The paradox of these letters, the way in which they were composed, is touched upon by historians but never pursued as a thread into the psychology of revolution. I shall return to this in a moment or two for my concern Toussaint is with the inner drama of your life though let me say at once that I pay full tribute to the collective action of the slaves and their uprising against a system that chained them to the evils of injustice. CLR James characterises this action as "the only successful slave revolt in history."[1]

The very use of the term "slave revolt" may arouse in one an unhappy sensation, a peculiar dread. But on closer reflection should one be more fearful, more in dread, of a revolution by slaves than peasants, priests than intellectuals, gaolers than gaoled? How is one to gauge the extent of the inner brutalisation of the person who rebels against a system he or she may loathe, who raises the sword or the gun or the poisoned chalice or the knife in a cruel and divided world? I find I have no alternative but to pause here and to reflect upon affairs in the Middle East and elsewhere in the world of my century, the Ayatollahs of Iran, the suicide squads of the people who ride the bombs they discharge. Stalin of Russia was reputed to be an ex-priest. There are few revolutionaries with more bloodstained hands than he. You Toussaint, an ex-slave, resorted to severe and harsh measures at times to hold the population in check but you showed equally considerable humanity to your former slave masters within the ferocity of the revolution.

All this must drive us I think to reflect with the greatest care on the paradoxes of psyche and on the difficulties we face in assessing the degree of venom and vengeance that may erupt in theatres of misery and exploitation. Was not the French Revolution an abortive deed in the great hopes and dreams it appeared to entertain, hopes that fell by the wayside because of the so-called incorruptibility of Robespierre and his colleagues as much as within the conquests of Napoleon? How may we approach those hopes and dreams as hidden potential yet blocked design? You did not live to see (though you may have divined it) Napoleon's greed for power when he crowned himself in Notre Dame under the gaze of prelates and philosophers manqué.

Much later—four or five generations after your death in a French dungeon—came the Russian Revolution. You may remember Toussaint the talking drums in Haiti! Well, let me tell you, television in the twentieth century is a kind of talking drum upon which spectres appear. One evening I was looking at television. Harold Macmillan, a distinguished English politician and scholar appeared. As a scholar he may be familiar with your name, who knows? His reply to a question about the Russian Revolution interested me. He said (I am paraphrasing loosely) that the consequences of the Revolution consolidated designs that were closer to the ambitions of Peter the Great than to the dialectics of Karl Marx. Surely he was right? There had been, one knew, potential for profoundest change in Russia but deepseated cultural factors, cultural imperatives and deprivations, re-asserted themselves. And that reassertion was in itself the irony of the dialectics of culture one tends to underestimate or to eclipse when we discuss changes in a people. I won't dwell upon the débâcle of the Haitian Revolution as the nineteenth century progressed. Alas the fabric of our age discloses that the old classifications of so-called order and the habit of restrictive vision are still the address of power politics in the wake of revolutions (whether political, economic, industrial etc. etc.) around the globe.

Despite the failure of mass movements, and the encrustations of fascism that succeed every upheaval to batten upon the modern state, an enigmatic deposit remains in the soil of history that tells us we abandon at our peril the necessity for dialogue with the complex, inner, innovative sensibility of the past. There is, despite accumulative tragedy, a measure of shift in the priorities of the prisonhouse in which so many dreams of true freedom reside, a fissure here and there in every wall, a window of creativity here and there that looms and speaks of subtle translations, subtle transformations, affecting the very grain of passing events. Something is perceived that bears on the innermost, unshackled spirit of humanity despite every political or economic ghetto that entrenches itself again and again.

I wish now Toussaint to return to the way your letters and codes and communications were composed. CLR James points out that you spoke a broken dialect as a slave and "to the end of (your) days could hardly speak French".[2] And yet he makes clear that your letters as a commander and administrator were possessed of the stamp "of masterpiece(s) of diplomatic correspondence."[3]

James makes an eloquent distinction between yourself and other great thinkers who influenced events, an important distinction but one which I tend to see rather differently. Let me quote what he says:

> "Pericles on Democracy, Paine on the Rights of Man, the Declaration of Independence, the Communist Manifesto, these are some of the political documents which, whatsoever the wisdom or weaknesses of their analysis, have moved men and will always move them, for the writers, some of them in spite of themselves, strike chords and awaken aspirations that sleep in the hearts of the majority in every age. But Pericles, Tom Paine, Jefferson, Marx and Engels, were men of a liberal education, formed in the traditions of ethics, philosophy and history. Toussaint was a slave, not six years out of slavery, bearing alone the unaccustomed burden of war and government, dictating his thoughts in the crude words of a broken dialect, *written and rewritten* by secretaries until their devotion and his will had hammered them into adequate shape." (italics mine)[4]

The distinction between yourself and "men of a liberal education" is telling and instructive but I ask you Toussaint, do you entirely subscribe to this? It is a legitimate question to address to you for your secrecy, your aloofness, your labyrinthine mind left their impress upon your colleagues and subordinates. How did you really see yourself as an actor on the stage of history influencing events? Your secretaries were often left in the dark, it seems, about the letters etc. that they helped to compose. One is told of the participation of many agents and secretaries in the composition of communications of state. One learns that "one secretary would write down half of an important letter" and then you, Toussaint, "would send him sixty miles away and conclude it by means of another."[5] And this apparently is but the tip of the iceberg in regard to the many agents who are recruited and dispersed in the composition of some of the dramatic communications you sent abroad.

Perhaps the extremity in which you were placed, the *broken dialect* of the slave revolutionary needs to be closely reconsidered. In it may lie an important clue we tend to overlook that bears on a divide between psyche, as a pregnant but half-eclipsed vessel of universal insight in the world's unconscious, and the vocabulary of politics that is but an inadequate translation of that vessel. It is a paradox I know to reverse the so-called facts in your case. One would say in absolute logic that your "broken dialect" represents inadequacy and the codes in which your letters were framed are the venue of clarity. Yet the question remains: how false is such clarity, the clarity of politics, how susceptible is it to disinformation, to half-truths if not lies, how consistent is it with expediency and propaganda? How remote is it from what it seeks to translate?

These questions are true to your life Toussaint. They mirror the abrupt terrain of your decisions, your secrecy, the contradictions that arise in the texture of your political being.

With a lesser man one would not pursue the matter but with you it is an essential quest for despite every failure or web of cross-purpose in your statecraft you are increasingly regarded as being possessed by, or as possessing, a visionary compass that far outstripped the imagination of your contemporaries. And if this is really so the divide between *broken dialect or inner vision* and *political costume or code* is relevant to the psyche of revolution and to cultural deprivations in yourself, in your agents, and in the masses you led.

It is the blend of all these that may offer a window of illumination into the problematic of the modern state and its desire to break with the divine right of kings and create in its place what is called a democracy. Let me say at this juncture within my own century and just under two centuries since your death that democracy remains the exception rather than the rule in the modern world.

I would assert that in your case *broken dialect may be equated with inner vision to run hand in hand with a potential dialectic of democracy*. I think this is truly so within the specific limitations yet the revolutionary complex of your own time. And I would like to ask: may not the extremities of your situation help to uncover a *neglected divide* between *potential dialectic* and *outer code or frame or dress* with regard to the liberal thinkers to whom CLR James refers in the passage I quoted but a short while ago in this letter? May not those extremities teach us something about the complex philosophies of an Engels or a Hegel or a Marx, the legendary utterances of a Pericles or a Jefferson, the tone of indignation and suppressed passion in the writings of a Tom Paine or the speeches of a Martin Luther King? I think this may be so though in a less extreme, a much less brutal, much less tormenting way than is visible in your political career.

Every crisis of vision in the life of the conditioned mind, the enslaved—as well as the sophisticated, biased—mind is a crisis of language that sets in train a variety of agents and agencies intent on translating an inner momentum or passion, an inner changed perception of passing events that has its seed in the depths of unconscious processes of dialect/dialectic and the psychical gestation of visionary reality. Such a paradox of the *inner fertilisation of ideas* and *their outer reflection in day to day affairs* may be triggered into play by a complication of events in the theatre of history.

It is a play that we tend to identify with sovereign property in the sense that an area of achievement, whether in science or music or painting or sculpture, belongs absolutely to a particular thinker or philosopher or composer. This was clearly true of the Age of Reason, as it was called, in the late eighteenth century when you lived. Now that the mystery of mind has returned as a filter of achievement in the realm of science—and absolute Reason discloses its hubris or bias—a greater emphasis is placed on *intuitive agents or agencies* within the scope or the capacity of tradition. Within the scope or the capacity of psyche to translate and re-translate again and again what appears to be untranslatable. Psyche then breaks the barrier of lies to revisit the organ of truth.

In this context therefore your situation Toussaint is consistent with the pains and the labours and the trials of "men of liberal education" whose crucial intervention in affairs we need to assess and re-assess within a medium of half-whole, half-broken, consciousness . . . Indeed an extremity, such as the extremity that affected your discourse and led you to play a mysterious drama or game with your French secretaries and fellow generals, British diplomats and others, helps us to question complacent assumptions about "liberal education." How liberal is "liberal education" within a ghetto-fixated humanity?

Perhaps such liberality borders upon an illusion and props up or disguises the *status quo* except when an inner/outer tension erupts, a leap, a momentum, the leap or tension we equate with genius, the leap or the revisitation of dismembered truth.

Alas in your case the leap of genius was a bitter pill to contain. It set you apart from others within an illiterate society. It made you conscious of the limitations affecting yourself that you had to transform. It made you, as historians tend to stress, secretive and aloof. It was a bitter pill that tinctured your hopes with fatalism and with a curious submission to a void or a vacancy (if I may so put it) within the Revolution and within civilisation. I am sure I do not exaggerate the dilemma with which you wrestled. Everything that happened, everything you did, seems to bear it out. A void or a vacancy within things was a measure of the incredibly difficult quest for the regeneration of society that you faced. It is not impertinent, I hope, in all the circumstances, to ask the questions I am asking. To what extent one wonders was your statecraft subconsciously—if not wholly consciously—aligned to the concealment from public view of the void or the vacancy of which I have spoken? To what extent nevertheless did you pin your faith to a renovation or profound recycling of the presmises of capital and labour in Haiti in league with a new sensibility in Europe?

It is important, indeed imperative, to press you about such matters in the light of the tangle of letters you wrote to the Directory in Paris in the late seventeen-nineties to justify your expulsion of the liberal Frenchman Sonthonax.

Note the fact that Sonthonax was a liberal (whatever liberal signified at that time), that he was liked and admired by the people of Haiti. I shall return to the expulsion of this man, this liberal Frenchman, in a little while. Let us note however in the meatime that your letters with regard to him betrayed a profound uneasiness, almost one is tempted to say a kind of neurosis, about Independence for Hatit, about the inevitable purges, the inevitable massacres that were the automatic response of the sovereign state to undesired opposition within itself.

So much for the Age of Reason when a matter of this sort, a concern of this sort, a question of this sort about the fate of Independence seems irrational! Perhaps you Toussaint were judged irrational for harbouring such misgivings!

Sonthonax, as I have said, was a liberal Frenchman and, one ventures to say, despite the charges levelled by you against him that I shall outline shortly, a good administrator who favoured Independence for Haiti. It is ironic that Sonthonax in the end, in his absence—and your absence too from Haiti, your imprisonment in France—won the argument. Haiti in 1804 under General Dessalines became independent. It was the first sovereign state in the Caribbean. The consequences of such sovereignty, the links between General (later Emperor) Dessalines and Duvalier of the twentieth century, are there for all to see who are interested in the political tragedies of the modern world.

May I therefore put my question to you in another way. Does the proliferation of sovereign states, and the absolute privileges attendant upon sovereignty, prompt us to visualise a central vacuum that resides at the heart of human culture and world-civilisation? Should one despair of that vacuum or see it as a ceaseless challenge to devise means, guide-lines, checks, balances, upon the entrenched powers of tyrannous regimes?

Should we equate your fate with heartrending insight into the life-blood of generations which serves the purposes of the state not to validate the unique capacity of the human person but to harness the masses to material ends? As I ask this question I glance through your dungeon in France into the miasma of concentration camps in my own twentieth century. And this prompts me to make a further inquiry of this *open* letter to you: is not such harness—the harness to which I referred a moment ago—a symptom of a Stalinesque/ Hitlerite megalomania in which humanity is essentially irrelevant, essentially doomed, and therefore the born fodder of the state, factory fodder, plantation fodder, war fodder etc., etc.?

How easy was it Toussaint for you to perceive a certain absurdity in the political anti-climax of your life? I say easy—perhaps I should have said *hard, difficult*. For this, believe me, is no facile or idle or despairing question. I would argue that in your incarceration, in the imprisonment of a man who believed in the Revolution and in preserving a civilisation link with France, lay a seed—a nebulous but poignant seed—of the theatre of the absurd which was to become one of the main literary movements in the French and European imagination. One may say, I would argue, that the theatre of the absurd has its uncertain roots in the consequences of the débâcle of the French Revolution as much as in the consequences of the débâcle of the Russian Revolution. Napoleon played his absurd, heroic/anti-heroic role that inspired Dostoevsky to create a Raskolnikov. The assassinated Trotsky played his role. So did the Emperor Dessalines who was assassinated in the wake of Haitian Independence. White and black players in the theatre of the absurd! And you, in your letters, in the drama of your correspondence, in a web of contradictions and secrecies, were in league with symptoms of peculiar derangement that were to flower in the literature of France (the French language in which your thoughts were composed). Baudelaire and Rimbaud lay just beneath the horizon, bobbing in time just two or three generation away from your death. *Les Fleurs du mal* preceded the *Drunken Boat* and the voyage of the seer into the abyss. Abyss? Void? Vacancy? All this was consistent with the pleasures and the addictions of prosperous plantation Haiti prior to the Revolution. For prosperity-in-slavery may have bred not only wealth but an addiction to styles of decadence and to the administration of subtle poisons, subtle treacheries of the soul, the treachery of fate that was to loom in your imprisonment Toussaint.

The tide was set as much in Haiti as in Paris, as much in the world of the plantation as in the sophisticated metropolis. And the theatre of the absurd was to come into its own—as if to buttress a history of the absurd—in the twentieth century with the plays of Samuel Beckett, Eugene Ionesco, and others.

It is arguable, you may agree from within the shadows or the lights of history where you reside that the vacuum at the heart of world-civilisation—a vacuum that the United Nations promises to fill in the uncertain future—is consistent with tragedy, with a submission to absurdities of history. And yet—even as I say this—I sense a complex juxtaposition of bodies we need to visualise within the theatre of history that offers a fracture, a hairline fissure, in the mould of the absurd . . .

Take, for instance, another assassination quite different from the killing of the Emperor and tyrant Dessalines. Martin Luther King was a good, perhaps a great man. He like yourself was prone to fatalistic expectation in the speeches he made. But there was a rhythm of hope in his voice even as he foresaw a violent death. From King's death, some would say, grew the resurrection of hope in the ghettos of the South.

I touch upon this juxtaposition (you Toussaint and King) to illumine your submission to fate in 1802. It seems a far cry from King's bullet and yet there is a poetic irony. Dessalines, it is said, was slain by a silver bullet but he was not your true heir or descendant. Perhaps King was in a theatre of hope . . . It is clear from the records that you knew the risks you ran when you met the French in a situation that exposed you to seizure. It was a gamble on behalf of cementing a meaningful accord. You were seized, taken on board a French vessel and transported (if I may use such a word in respect of Europe rather than Australia) to France. That happened, as I said a moment ago, in the year 1802. You died within the following year.

There is no record, as far as I know, of a summation of your life's adventure—if I may use such a colourful term—in those last months and days. Not much of an adventure it was then within the claustrophobic limits of a cell! And yet you were there because of a measure of hope you entertained when you fell into the trap. Hope that resides within an inner, however broken, dialect or dialectic. Hope in the designs of the future, a submission to the agency of the future that links you however gropingly with others you could not name whose lives and deaths bring a fracture or unsettlement into theatres of history. A fracture or complex illumination of hope however overlaid still by absurdity.

I shall pursue this thread within the tangle of letters you wrote to justify your expulsion of Sonthonax from Haiti in 1797. It becomes necessary to qualify CLR James's assertion that your behaviour with regard to Sonthonax was so wholly unpredictable it remains "an unsolved enigma to this day."[6]

Enigma it was perhaps (but not insoluble by any means I would think). It requires of us, in the late twentieth century, to weigh the balance of contradictions rather differently from how appearances may dictate. (I stress the *late twentieth century* because the rigidities of a cult of Reason have collapsed and the alchemy of the mind awakens us to intuitive clues and dimensions we neglect at our peril.) I would use the word "enigma" to imply something historians may find perhaps slightly unpalatable. Enigma, yes, when one begins to wonder whether your abilities as a commander, your great energies in the field, your indomitable will (as the records declare) may count in the final analysis for less than the spectre of the future—the burden of the present-in-the-future-by which you were haunted.

It is here in that spectre, that accompanied you into prison, that one may find, I would venture to say, a clue to the ambivalences that run through the letters you wrote in 1797. James, as a historian and a realist, presents the facts fairly and vividly but misses, I think, this terror or spectre that lives and acts and creates its curious fictions in the letters you wrote, letters that are the substance of a drama in their charges and counter-charges, letters that hint in the lurid veil they throw over events of a vacuum in the Revolution you had begun to dread.

With regard to the plain facts so-called one cannot fail to see Toussaint how attached you were to Sonthonax, how much you prized his friendship. Indeed you wrote expressing "friendship without end."[7] And yet within a matter of weeks or days you had ordered his expulsion from Haiti. A curious state of mind, a bolt from the blue! Not it would seem the behavioue of someone of indomitable or iron will but of a man driven by inner and concealed furies that seek to adorn themselves in flights of fancy and theatrical devotion before they resolve to unveil an abyss. "Friendship without end."

Sonthonax, your greatly admired friend, should have understood something that was brewing within you, something unbearable, beyond the gifts of any secretary or agent to translate, a calamitous foreboding about the death of the Revolution in France, but he did not until the ground between you—that he thought was fixed forever—opened at his feet. He was the shadow of your own projected or fore-thrown departure from Haiti. The crucial importance of the sudden break between yourself and your friend leads James to write that your views had changed "and with (that change) the course of the black revolution (in Haiti)."[8] This helps I am sure to arouse our curiosity about the inner clues that reside in your behaviour towards Sonthonax, clues that bear on the apparent illogicality of decision at the heart of your world, broken ties, broken relationships etc. James says your views had changed but I tend to disagree. Rather it seems to me they had remained virtually untranslated or untranslatable over a long time until you could no longer bear it. You seized your friend (as you were to be seized in the future). You denounced him to the Democracy in Paris.

That denunciation came on the heels of Sonthonax's departure in a letter written to the Directory in Paris in September 1797. You said in that letter that Sonthonax had proposed to you *at the end of 1796* that you should sever the link with France, *massacre the whites on the island,* and declare the colony a sovereign and independent state. Is this not a somewhat outrageous accusation? Would Sonthonax, a white and an apparently liberal Frenchman, (however despairing he too may have felt about the progress of the Revolution in France) have proposed a *massacre* of the whites in Haiti? What a horrendous precedent this would have been in the Caribbean!

Toussaint Louverture, the liberator of Haiti, who was followed by Dessalines who completed the work begun by the liberator.

It is true that a declaration of Independence may have been feasible in 1796 or 1797. The British and the Spanish appeared to be in no position to stop this especially as the French were in process of negotiating with you to grant you the rights you sought. The revolt was in principle successful by late 1796, certainly by the middle to the end of 1797. At least that is how I read the situation! In effect the link with France was a Gordian knot that had been sliced except that culture dies hard and the significance of the Revolution had left its root in the perception of an age. Indeed the French Revolution and the Directory in Paris were still an interfused banner—however tattered in your eyes and in Sonthonax's eyes—under which you fought, still fought, the *ancien régime.*

The tangled accusations against Sonthonax need to be scrutinised closely. For you wrote to the Directory *in February 1797* (bear in mind that Sonthonax is said to have made his treasonable proposals to you at the end of 1796) clearing your close colleague and friend of rumor and innuendo and affirming his integrity and loyalty to his brothers in the Revolution.

You Toussaint were appointed Commander-in-Chief on the island by the French in May 1797 and in the dramatic episodes you relate in your letters to Paris you tell of being approached by Sonthonax at this time, of his entreating you again to execute the proposals he had advanced in December 1796. Your obsession with detail in this context is such that the matter had clearly preyed upon your mind for a long time and in the circumstances makes one wonder how you could have written as you did in February!

A Gordian knot of psyche! Insoluble enigma (as James declares) or the substance of an inner drama, an inner theatre, in which outer absurdity and untranslatable hope (untranslatable in the institutional and brute circumstances of your time) are so blended and interfused that one needs to discern a complex pattern of surrender within yourself as a true message to the future. Sonthonax, it would seem, became an agent of fate upon whom you projected some portion of the burden to which I referred earlier in this letter, some portion of the spectre of the present-in-the-future. Nothing can be forced before its true age, its maturity and innermost alchemy of imagination, has arrived within a juxtaposition of bodies and personalities within community, the living, the dead, the unborn. There is a dialect of the soul in the heart of the world we need to rehearse and approach from different angles again and again in our inadequate codes, formal discourse, realisms, and rhetorics of clarity so-called.

In the closing pages of this letter I would like to raise the issue of voodoo in Haiti of which you were aware Toussaint in your time I am sure. It would have influenced your vision of nature and of the cosmos. How could it be otherwise? Voodoo was an important cultural and religious reality in the lives of the people before the Revolution happened and afterwards when Independence came in 1804. And voodoo or vodun remains bizarre Haitian theatre today.

Alfred Métraux has written an important study and anthropological inquiry into voodoo ritual, its sanctuaries, its origins and history. He writes—

> "Voodoo has preserved one of the fundamental characteristics of the African religions from which it is derived: worship is sustained by groups of adherents who voluntarily place themselves under the authority of a priest or priestess whose sanctuary or *humfo* they frequent. The faithful who have been initiated in the same sanctuary and who congregate to worship the gods to which it is sacred, form a sort of fraternity called the *humfo* society. The importance of this cult-group depends to a great extent on the personality and influence of the priest and priestess who preside.
>
> This complex religion with its ill-defined frontiers may perhaps be more easily approached through a study of its social and material frameworks. It is the priests and their numerous acolytes who have formed . . . a more or less coherent system."[9]

The sanction of voodoo, however "ill-defined," was (and still is) clearly hierarchical. This extraordinary religion appears to touch the lives of all the people, rulers and ruled, though consistent efforts have been made to deny its all-pervasive impact. Métraux mounted a curious apology for the studies he made and for his book.

> "Certain Haitians will no doubt be saddened that a foreigner whom they welcomed so warmly has, like so many others before him, felt the need to write a book on Voodoo which they look upon as one of the most embarrassing aspects of their national culture. Let them understand that I have not given way to a wish to exploit a subject . . ."[10]

May I affirm equally all necessary restraint and care in addressing you about such issues. Yet the basic culture, the basic rituals of a society, may sometimes throw light on traumas of childhood and adolescence, on the craft of leadership, on the omens—so to speak—that figure in various calculations on the way people may react to political and economic events.

Would you not agree that politicians in hierarchical societies which are imbued with the charisma of the gods, as Haiti is, must—whether they actually desire it or not—fulfil a function that raises them up and sets them apart from the people? There is pride in such elevation but it incurs or battens upon a rigidity of ritual consensus.

That consensus implies that the gods must be obeyed and placated and served. They may wear new masks but within the fixed elevation and levels upon which they move they seem themselves unfree and incapable of offering more to an exploited body politic than an amelioration of bitter labour and dreaded functions. Note my emphasis on a hierarchy of functions in which the amelioration of back-breaking, body-breaking performance is all the elevated gods possess as their gift to the masses.

I have no doubt that the broken dialect you spoke was steeped in the pain of such knowledge. In such a society real change therefore comes with profoundest difficulty, cultural formations and habits re-group themselves to preserve a fixed ideal, so to speak, or prepossession.

Without a shadow of doubt, I would think all this added fuel to your conviction that the transforming of a disadvantaged society rests upon agents and agencies beyond the absolute function of the sovereign state. In such a context—in such rapport with agents and agencies within a medium of values and consciousness—the originality of a society, the originality of persons, may find unsuspected channels of expression.

Alas in this regard little has happened to affect society as a whole. Projects in the mid-twentieth century for a regional federation of the West Indies have collapsed. The miniscule sovereign states of the Caribbean remain in pawn to an inbuilt helplessness that affects both rulers and ruled.

Take your birthplace Toussaint. Three out of four persons there cannot read or write. It is true that illiteracy exists on a global scale but when allied to extreme poverty it reinforces the *humfo* (in voodoo terminology) prisonhouse or perverse sanctuary of the state. Nevertheless the equation of function with deprivation in poor societies may tell us something we do not normally reflect upon of the phenomenon of illiteracy in the world at large and in the rich countries of the West.

Recent surveys in the United States that explored a sample (as the saying goes) of persons between the ages of eighteen and twenty-five have shown that a large proportion of those interviewed find great difficulty in reading a newspaper or a magazine, a menu or a bus schedule. Less than nine per cent were equipped to read and paraphrase a four-line poem by Emily Dickinson.

With regard to older people it is significant that the rise in illiteracy amongst these in Europe and America is no rise at all but the disclosure of a hidden deficiency that lay concealed for decades and generations. Unskilled workers earned their living in farms and factories without being called upon to read or write. Indeed they raised their families and appeared to achieve job satisfaction (as the slogan goes). It is only within the past ten or fifteen years that such jobs have tended to vanish or to fall within the compass of machines and computers. And now, as a consequence of technological change, the hidden illiteracy of the unskilled worker has become alarmingly visible.

At the other pole or extreme in the West, pilots, for instance, earn astronomical salaries. They are required, needless to say, to read manuals and to write reports. They function within a new technology that makes them privileged citizens of the computer age. But in the foreseeable future shifts in technology will occur. They will then be exposed to even more advanced computers that may make them irrelevant or highlight deficiencies in their present performance. At a sophisticated level therefore they are potentially the new unskilled, the new illiterates.

To come back to Haiti therefore Toussaint—after our disgression into the

Toussaint Louverture.

faculties of the West—we may see, I think, that the amelioration of function, the amelioration of hardship in the field or in any condition of social work, is not in itself an incentive to break the thraldom of illiteracy. Why delve into concepts that have no immediate bearing on the pay packet? Why should a street-sweeper do more than sweep the streets, a pilot more than drive his ship or plane?

Incentive towards *a literacy of the imagination* that transcends immediate status or function has no measurable price-tag and rather than bringing a quick amelioration of distressing circumstances invokes pressure within and without oneself in concentrating upon the infinite, sometimes alien, detail in the fabric of the modern world. It is born from vital and penetrative rather than profit-making curiosity. It arises from extremity, it is cross-cultural in grain in exploring juxtapositions through which one begins to read a particular situation in the light of another's life and disability.

One begins to read you Toussaint within the paradoxes of the pantheon of the Haitian gods. I can imagine you playing Legba, the god of the crossroads. It is Legba who questions, subtly repudiates, the hierarchy to which he himself belongs. He appears at the crossroads as an unprepossessing, crippled old man dressed in rags. But in the twinkling of an eye he demonstrates the terrifying strength of indomitable youth. He delivers bolts of lightning.

Alfred Métraux refers to Legba as the god who "removes the barrier"[11] but desists, as far as I can see, from expanding on this concept. I think *you* would say that Legba *reads* the gods as sustaining an irony or a paradox of Spirit. The gods are but masks of Spirit. Their consolidation into absolute function breeds an illiteracy of soul in reading the metamorphoses of reality. Legba appears to fail his followers. He shakes the *humfo*, he shakes the perverse sanctuary of the state, but it remains. A vacuum hovers everywhere. And yet within a blend of apparently incompatible appearances, strength and weakness, age and youth, you Toussaint—within the theatre of Legba—wrestle with the *absurdity of despair*. Does not such 'absurdity of despair' resemble yet differ from the conventional language of the absurd to uncover a poignancy, an inimitable texture of hope?

Well there it is. I have asked questions of you across a divide of generations. A veritable flood has passed under the bridge at the crossroads where Legba goes and comes. I perceive your presence there as a momentous personality, half-legend, half-history. Adieu!

Notes

1. CLR James, *The Black Jacobins* (new edition, Allison and Busby, London, 1980), page 1x
2. Ibid., page 104
3. Ibid., page 104
4. Ibid., page 197
5. Ibid., page 249

6. Ibid., page 188
7. Ibid., page 190
8. Ibid., page 190
9. Alfred Métraux, *Voodoo in Haiti*, (Andre Deutsch, London, 1972) pages 61-62
10. Ibid., page 22
11. Ibid., page 101

BIOGRAPHICAL NOTES ON CONTRIBUTORS

BEANE, Wendell Charles

Wendell Charles Beane is an historian of religions who does research using a theological and phenomenological approach to the study of World Religions. A graduate of the University of Chicago (Ph.D.), he has been a Fellow of The American Institute of Indian Studies and teaches Hinduism, mythology, mysteries, and ethics at the University of Wisconsin-Oshkosh. He studied history, French, and pastoral theology at Howard University. He has written scholarly articles for international journals, such as *History of Religions* (Chicago), *Religious Studies* (Cambridge), and *World Faiths Insight* (London). He is the author of *Myth, Cult, and Symbols in Sakta Hinduism: A Study of the Indian Mother Goddess*; (E. J. Brill, 1977) and co-editor of *Myths, Rites, Symbols: A Mircea Eliade Reader* (Harper and Row, 1976). He has delivered papers before the American Academy of Religion, the University of Wisconsin Madison Annual Conference on South Asia, and the National Medical Association. Dr. Beane is an associate professor of Religious Studies at the University of Wisconsin-Oshkosh, Oshkosh, Wisconsin.

CHANDLER, Wayne B.

Wayne B. Chandler is an anthrophotojournalist and vice-president of Clover International. He is a graduate of the University of California at Berkeley, co-producer and writer of *A People's History To Date—4000 B.C. to 1985* and *365 Days of Black History*, parts I and II. He has done extensive research into the origins of race and ancient civilizations. Through Clover International and its photo archives, he has been instrumental in unearthing key photographs and materials relating to the African presence in the Olmec civilization. He presently resides in Washington, D.C.

CHINYELU, Mamadi Moses

Mamadi Moses Chinyelu was for many years a staff writer for daily and twice-weekly publications, as well as a freelance writer. He has published short histories on African-Americans in Philadelphia, on the African-American community in Washington D.C. during World War One, as well as an account of the Buffalo Soldiers. He participated in the Second World African Festival of Arts and Culture in 1977 held in Lagos, Nigeria, and later that year was commissioned by the Capitol News Service to photograph the dedication of the Black Press Archives (in which Frederick Douglass was an inductee). This is housed at Howard University's Moorland Spingarn Research Center, as part of the sesquicentennial celebration of the African-American press. Chinyelu has also been commissioned by Philadelphia's Freedom Theatre to research the history of Africans, ancient and modern. His essay, "The Voice of One Crying in the Wilderness: Constructing an African Mass Communication Pyramid from the Community Level to the International Level," was published in the Fall, 1983 edition of *The Black Law Journal* (UCLA). This has been compared to David Walker's *Appeal* and recognized for presenting with great clarity the way in which African people are manipulated by the mass communication industry.

Chinyelu lives in Marlboro County, South Carolina, where he is the director of the Pee Dee Self-Help Corporation, a cultural and economic development firm. He was recently a consultant to the Robeson County (N.C.) Bicentennial Commission, where he was the founding chairman of the Black History Committee.

CLARKE, John Henrik

Editor, writer, historian. His books include: *William Stryon's Nat Turner: Ten Black Writers Respond* (1968), *Malcolm X, The Man and His Time* (1969), *Harlem U.S.A.* (1971), *Marcus Garvey and the Vision of Africa* (1974). Research Director of the First African Heritage Exposition; Associate Editor, *Freedomways Magazine*, Professor of African History and former Chairman, Black and Puerto Rican Studies Department, Hunter College, New York. On Editorial Board of the *Journal of African Civilizations*.

CLEGG II, Legrand

Legrand Clegg II is a member of the Board of Trustees at Compton Community College in Compton, California. He is also Chief Deputy City Attorney for the City of Compton. He has engaged in research on black history and culture since 1963 and his work has appeared in a number of national journals and magazines since 1969. He has lectured on university campuses across the U.S. and has co-produced a filmstrip entitled "The Black Roots of Civilization."

CUDJOE, Selwyn R.

Selwyn R. Cudjoe, an Associate Professor in the Black Studies Department at Wellesley College, is the author of *Resistance and Caribbean Literature* (Athens, Ohio: Ohio University Press, 1980) and *V. S. Naipaul: A Materialist Reading* (Amherst: University of Massachusetts Press, 1988.)

DAVIS, Hunt

R. Hunt Davis, Jr. is Professor of History and Director, Center for African Studies, at the University of Florida. He is also the editor of *The African Studies Review*, which is the journal of the African Studies Association. His research has dealt primarily with South African history and has resulted in publications dealing with the development of African nationalism, the history of African education, linkages between Afro-Americans and Africans in South Africa, U.S. foreign policy toward South Africa, and other topics.

FINCH, Charles S.

Charles S. Finch, M.D. is a board-certified family physician who is curently Assistant Professor of Community Medicine and Family Practice at the Morehouse School of Medicine. Dr. Finch completed his undergraduate training at Yale College, his medical training at Jefferson Medical College, and his Family Medicine Residency at the University of California, Irvine Medical Center. He has worked as an epidemiologist for the Center for Disease Control and was formerly a clinical preceptor at the Duke-Watts Family Medicine Clinic in Durham, North Carolina. He was the founder and chairman of the Raleigh Afro-American Life Focus Project between 1981 and 1982 and is a co-founder and Co-Convener of Bennu, Inc. of Atlanta. He is currently the Associate Editor of the *Journal of African Civilizations* and the author of "The African Background of Medical Science," "The Works of Gerald Massey: Studies in Kamite Origins," and—with Mr. Larry Williams of Bennu, Inc.—the co-author of "The Great Queens of Ethiopia," all published in the *Journal of African Civilizations*. In addition Dr. Finch has visited Senegal, West Africa where he has begun studies on the empirical basis of traditional West African medicine. On his most recent visit, he interviewed Dr. Cheikh Anta Diop, an interview which was published in the re-issue of "Egypt Revisited" edition of the *Journal of African Civilizations*.

HARRIS, Joseph E.

Received his B.A. and M.A. degrees from Howard University and his Ph.D. in history from Northwestern University. He was formerly chairman of the Department of History and has taught at the University of Nairobi. Prior to coming to Howard, was professor history at Williams College. Author of several works including The African Presence in Asia (Northwestern, 1971).

HARRIS, Wilson

Wilson Harris was born in British Guiana (now Guyana) in 1921. He was educated at Queen's College, Georgetown. He studied land surveying and led many survey parties (mapping and geomorphological research) in the interior. He was Senior Surveyor of Projects for the Government of British Guiana from 1955-1958. He went to live in London in 1959.

Writer in Residence, University of West Indies and University of Toronto, 1970; Commonwealth Fellow, Leeds University, 1971; Visiting Professor, University of Texas at Austin, 1972; Guggenheim Fellow, 1973; Henfield Fellow, UEA, 1974; Southern Arts Writer's Fellowship, 1976; Guest Lecturer, University of Mysore, 1978; Visiting Lecturer, Yale University, 1979; Writer in Residence, University of Newcastle, Australia, 1979; Visiting Professor, University of Texas at Austin, 1981-82; Regents' Lecturer, University of California, 1983; Awarded Hon. D. Litt. by the University of the West Indies, 1984.

His publications include: *Eternity to Season* (poems) 1954; *Palace of the Peacock* (1960) *The Far Journey of Oudin* (1961) *The Whole Armour* (1962) *The Secret Ladder* (1963) *Heartland* (1964) *The Eye of the Scarecrow* (1965) *The Waiting Room* (1967); *Tradition, the Writer and Society: Critical Essays* (1967) *Tumatumari* (1968) *Ascent to Omai* (1970) *The Sleepers of Roraima* (a Carib Trilogy), 1970; *The Age of the Rainmakers* (1971) *Black Marsden* (1972) *Companions of the Day and Night* (1975) *Da Silva da Silva's Cultivated Wilderness* and *Genesis of the Clowns* (1977); *The Tree of the Sun* (1978) *Explorations* (essays) 1981; *The Angel at the Gate* (1982) *The Womb of Space: the cross-cultural imagination* (1983) *Carnival* (1985) *The Intimate Rehearsal* (1987). Of these 24 titles, 19 are novels published by Faber and Faber, London.

KUNENE, Mazizi

Mazisi Kunene was born in South Africa in 1930 and is a member of the Senior House of the Swazi Royal House. He was educated in South Africa where he attained his B.A. Hons and M.A. degree at the University of Natal. From very early childhood he was active in politics and community affairs. He began writing poetry at the age of 9 and was encouraged by his father, Mdabuli, who saw in his talent the "verification of the ancestral law and vision." It was his father who narrated to him many stories of the ancestral heroes and taught him about the love that governs his family. Born of the two largest clans in South Africa i.e. the Dlamini clan and the Ngcobo clan, he absorbed the varied histories of peoples of Southern Africa with whom his families had association.

In 1959 he was one of the two students given a grant to study in England for a Ph.D. degree at the University of London. Concurrently with this responsibility he was directed by his organization, the African National Congress, to initiate a solidarity anti-apartheid campaign overseas. This he executed with his friend Tennyson Makiwane with the help of the committee for African Organizations in London. He served as Director of Education, and later as a representative of the African National Congress in Europe and the Americas. Later he was chosen to serve as a Director of Financial Affairs in which capacity he initiated the Vocational Training Program which was the basis for SOMAFCO and other projects.

He is currently a Professor of Literature at the University of California in Los Angeles and is engaged in writing many literary works in the Zulu language. Some of his published works include his epic poem "Emperor Shaka the Great" (a translation from his original Zulu epic "Nodumehlezi"), "Anthem of the Decade," "Zulu Poems," "Ancestors and the Sacred Mountain," etc.

LEWIS, David Levering

David Levering Lewis, formerly a professor of history at the University of the District of Columbia, is now a professor of history at Rutgers University. He is a distinguished Woodrow Wilson International Fellow and author of *King: A Biography*. Published by the University of Illinois Press in 1970, it is considered to be "the best book on King to date."

MARSH, Clifton E.

Dr. Clifton E. Marsh earned his Ph.D. from Syracuse University. He has published two books, *From Black Muslims to Muslims, The Transition From Separatism to Islam*. 1984, Scarecrow Press. His second book is, *The Danish Virgin Islands: A Socio-historical Analysis of The Emancipation of 1848 and the Labor Revolt of 1878*. Wynham Hall Press, Bristol, Indiana. Dr. Marsh has published articles in Phylon, Western Journal of Black Studies. Dr. Marsh's speciality is collective behavior, race relations and rape and sexual assault. Presently, he is a Lecturer in the Black Studies Department at California State University at Long Beach.

RASHIDI, Runoko

Cultural Historian with a special interest in the Kushite nations of antiquity. Rashidi is actively engaged in researching and reconstructing the Black Presence in Asian antiquity. A regular contributor to the *Journal of African Civilizations*. Guest Editor of *The African Presence in Early Asia*, published by the *Journal of African Civilizations* (1985). Author of *Kushite Case-Studies* (Revised Edition; Los Angeles, 1987). From 1981 to 1984 African History Research Specialist for Compton Community College. From 1986 to 1987 History Editor for the National Black Computer Network, based in Los Angeles.

REDD, Danita R.

An educator and holistic counselor with a special interest in the roles and images of Black Women in antiquity. She authored "The Black Madonnas of Europe: Diffusion of the African Isis" for *The African Presence in Early Europe*, 1985 and prepared the glossary for *The African Presence In Early Asia*, 1985. Has authored and directed several reader theatres including "Young, Gifted and Black: Part II" in 1979. Member of Amenta, a California-based think tank, since 1979. Member of several educational and counseling organizations. Took educational tours of Egypt (1981) and the Yucatan (1984). Received M.A. in Education and B.A. in Speech Communications from CPSU, San Luis Obispo. Currently employed at CSU, Los Angeles as a Learning Skills Specialist with the Special Services Project/Learning Resource Center.

SIMON, Virginia Spottswood

Freelance writer. A.B. Livingstone College; M.A. Wellesley College, Assistant professor of English at Bloomburg (PA) State University (1972-1977). During three years of residence in Egypt (1961-1964) examined Nubian-Kushite ruins before their inundation by Lake Nasser and studied artifacts of this culture in the Cairo Museum. Author of "African King in Confederate Capital" in Negro History Bulletin (Jan-Feb-March, 1983) and of "Christ came to Nubia-Kush" in the A.M.E. Zion Quarterly Review (October, 1983). Currently working on a history of Egypto-Sudanese people from Stone Age times to the present.

SPADY, James

James G. Spady contributed several entries on Philadelphians to the first comprehensive Black biographical dictionary based on scholarly research, *Dictionary of American Negro Biography*, (W.W. Norton, Inc.) edited by Drs. Rayford W. Logan and Michael R. Winston. His essay on the surrealistic aesthetic of "Dr. J." appeared in both French and English publications. Other writings by Spady have appeared and been cited in publications in Europe, Canada, Africa, Asia and the Caribbean. They included, among others, *The Mainline Times, American Literary Scholarship, Philadelphia Inquirer, The Oracle, Washington Post, Philadelphia Independent, Black Scholar, Germantown Courier, Philadelphia Tribune, Journal of National Medical Association*, Africa (London, England), *Presence Africaine* (Paris, France), *Black Images* (Toronto, Canada), *College Language Association Journal, Washington Star, The Garvey Voice, Black Books Bulletin, Indigene: An Anthology of Future*

Black Arts and Blacks in Science: Ancient and Modern (Transaction Books, Rutgers University and London (U.K.). He is an Associate Editor of the *Afro-American Journal of Philosophy* and is currently doing a biography of Philly Joe Jones. A chapter of that biography is being excerpted and published in the California based jazz magazine, *BeBop and Beyond,* as are other articles on jazz by Spady. He recently edited a festschrift, *Cecil B. Moore: A Soldier For Justice,* and wrote the afterword for the 1985 reprint of *Drusilla Dunjee Houston's The Wonderful Ethiopians of the Ancient Cushite Empire.*

His most recently published work is the book, *Marcus Garvey, Africa and the Universal Negro Improvement Association: A UMUM Perspective on Concentric Activity in the Pan African World,* 1985 (Marcus Garvey Memorial Foundation, P.O. Box 42621, Philadelphia, Pa. 19101-2621).

T'SHAKA, Oba

Oba T'Shaka is a professor in the Department of Black Studies at San Francisco State University where he serves as Department chairman. Professor T'Shaka has taught at San Francisco State since 1972 in the areas of Black political theory, Afrikan philosophy with an emphasis on Kemetic and Dogon studies, Ancient Afrikan History and Afrikan-American history. T'Shaka is the author of two books *The Political Legacy of Malcolm X,* and *The Arts of Organizing.* He is also editor and publisher of the Journal of Black Studies published at San Francisco State University. T'Shaka is a movement organizer with 27 years of experience. He served as chair of San Francisco CORE from 1963-65 and led the job campaigns against Luckies Supermarket, the Downtown Department Stores and the Bank of America. He served as national treasurer of CORE, and led the drive to transform CORE into a nationalist organization. In 1974 he served as Chair of the North American Political Committee to the Sixth Pan Afrikan Congress. He presently holds the chair of the Pan Afrikan Peoples Organization and is National Vice Chair of Organization and Training for the Black United Front. His articles have appeared in *Black Scholar, Black Books Bulletin, Black Dialogue, The Journal of Black Poetry,* and the *Journal of Black Studies.*

VAN SERTIMA, Ivan

Ivan Van Sertima was born in Guyana, South America. He was educated at the School of Oriental and African Studies, London University and the Rutgers Graduate School and holds degrees in African Studies, Linguistics and Anthropology.

He is a literary critic, a linguist, and an anthropologist and has made a name in all three fields. As a literary critic, he is the author of *Caribbean Writers,* a collection of critical essays on the Caribbean Novel. He is also the author of several major literary reviews published in Denmark, India, Britain and the United States. He was honored for his work in this field by being asked by the Nobel Committee of the Swedish Academy to nominate candidates for the Nobel Prize in Literature, from 1976-1980. As a linguist, he has published essays on the dialect of the Sea Islands off the Georgia Coast. He is also the compiler of the *Swahili Dictionary of Legal Terms*, based on his fieldwork in Tanzania, East Africa, in 1967. He is the author of *They Came Before Columbus: The African Presence in Ancient America*, which was published by Random House in 1977 and is now in its tenth printing. It was published in French in 1981 and in the same year was awarded the Clarence L. Holte Prize, a prize awarded every two years "for a work of excellence in literature and the humanities relating to the cultural heritage of Africa and the African diaspora."

He has recently been appointed by UNESCO to the *International Commission for a new History of the Scientific and Cultural Development of Mankind.*

Professor Van Sertima is an associate professor of African Studies at Rutgers University in New Jersey and editor of the *Journal of African Civilizations*. He was also visiting professor at Princeton University from 1981 to 1983.

90 minute audio cassette tapes

LEGACIES, INC., the audio arm of the *Journal of African Civilizations*, complements a distinguished series of books which have gained an international reputation over the last eleven years.

The editor of these books has been asked to join UNESCO's International Commission engaged in the rewriting of the scientific and cultural history of mankind.

In lectures, brilliant and wide-ranging in scholarship, yet lucid and passionate in delivery, he presents this new and absorbing history.

It is the story of mankind told in a way in which it has never been told before–a history based on a whole new world of research and discovery. It is the drama of forgotten peoples and civilizations, brought to you through an unusually fresh and liberating vision of the human legacy.

Dr. Van Sertima, editor of the Journal, and the voice that speaks to you from these cassettes is "the most important black cultural thinker in the United States. He leads a school of researchers in anthropology, medicine, human paleontology, linguistics, art, science, and cultural history. He is attempting nothing less than to restructure African Civilization, and to give the African a new conception of himself. As a speaker he is compelling; what he reveals is often startling. He tells the truth about man and his beginnings in a language that makes him a great humanist."

But it is not just the contents of these cassettes that are compelling. The photo inserts are memorable. All book covers and complementary tape inserts are designed and selected by award-winning photographer, Jacqueline Patten-Van Sertima, to complete an outstanding library.

Invest now in a **better** education.